Paradigms of International Human Rights Law

Paradigms of International Human Rights Law

Aaron Xavier Fellmeth

OXFORD
UNIVERSITY PRESS

OXFORD
UNIVERSITY PRESS

Oxford University Press is a department of the University of Oxford. It furthers the University's objective of excellence in research, scholarship, and education by publishing worldwide. Oxford is a registered trademark of Oxford University Press in the UK and certain other countries.

Published in the United States of America by Oxford University Press
198 Madison Avenue, New York, NY 10016, United States of America.

Library of Congress Cataloging-in-Publication Data

Names: Fellmeth, Aaron Xavier, author.
Title: Paradigms of international human rights law / Aaron Xavier Fellmeth.
Description: New York : Oxford University Press, 2016. | Includes bibliographical references and index.
Identifiers: LCCN 2015051058 | ISBN 9780190611279 ((hardback) : alk. paper)
Subjects: LCSH: Human rights. | International law.
Classification: LCC K3240 .F45 2016 | DDC 341.4/8—dc23 LC record available at http://lccn.loc.gov/2015051058

9 8 7 6 5 4 3 2 1

Printed by Edwards Brothers Malloy, United States of America

To the memory of

Dr. Andrew "Sandy" Askland:

adventurer, sage, friend.

CONTENTS

Acknowledgments xi
Table of Abbreviations & Citations xiii

Introduction 1

PART ONE Human Rights and Fundamental Duties

1. The Concept of Fundamental Duties 15
  A. The Universal Duties Movement 15
    1. Individual Duties 15
      a. Individual Duties in the International Bill of Rights and Other Human Rights Instruments 15
      b. Individual Duties in Human Rights-Related Declarations 21
      c. The IAC and UNESCO Declarations of Human Responsibilities 24
      d. General Practice of States 26
      e. Individual Duties in International Criminal Law 27
      f. Why Nonbinding Duties? 28
    2. Corporate Duties 31
  B. Five Classes of Beneficiaries of Moral Duties: A Typology 37
    1. Duties toward Other Individuals 37
      a. Universal Duties 37
      b. Relational Duties 40
    2. Duties toward Groups 41
    3. Duties toward Humankind as a Whole 45
    4. Duties toward Oneself 48
    5. Ecological Duties 51
      a. Duties Directly toward Nonhuman Animals 51
      b. Duties Directly toward Plants 54
      c. Duties Directly toward the Natural Environment 56
      d. Duties toward Individuals Relative to a Safe and Healthy Natural Environment 57
  C. Conclusion 59

2. Duties and Rights as Alternative Paradigms 61
  A. Universal Human Duties as a Legal Concept 62
    1. Why Individual Duties? 62
    2. Objections to Individual Duties under IHRL 67
      a. Individual Duties Would Be Redundant 67
      b. Rights Render Individual Duties Unnecessary 68

c. Individual Duties Would Undermine or Weaken Human Rights 68
d. Duties Are Not as Forceful as Rights 71
e. Moral Duties Are Too Indeterminate and Variable to Sustain Legal Implementation 72
f. Most Universal Legal Duties Are Inappropriate Subjects for Public International Law 73
3. Summary 77
B. Corporate Human Rights Duties as a Legal Concept 77
C. State Fundamental Duties as an Alternative to Individual Human Rights 79
1. Tonal Connotations of Rights and Duties Paradigms 83
2. Identification of the Relevant Duty Holder and Extent of Its Duties 87
3. Ascertainment of Interests of the Right Holder and Right Claiming 90
a. Duties toward Animals 93
b. Duties toward Future Generations 95
c. Ecological Duties 98

PART TWO Nondiscrimination and Substantive Right Claiming Paradigms

3. Nondiscrimination as a Claiming Paradigm 109
A. Two Methods of Value Protection 109
B. The International Legal Definition of Discrimination 112
1. Similar Situations 113
2. Legitimate Aim 116
3. Proportionality 119
C. Contextual Factors in Discrimination Analysis 121
1. Prohibited Grounds 123
a. The Open Approach 125
b. The Closed List Approach 130
2. The Protected Interest 140
Nondiscrimination in Identified Rights 140
3. The Individual and Social Consequences of Discrimination 146
a. Justified Distinctions 148
b. Distinctions to Counter Discrimination: Affirmative Action 151
4. Source of the Threat 155
5. Intention to Discriminate 159
D. Rationalizing Nondiscrimination Doctrine 165
1. Prohibited Grounds 165
2. The Interests Protected 175
3. Public and Private Discriminators 177
4. Intention to Discriminate 178

4. Interchangeability and Complementarity of Substantive and Nondiscrimination Paradigms 179
A. The Extent and Limits of Equivalence 179
1. General Substitutability 180
2. Limits on Substitutability 187
3. The *Ius Cogens* Question 190
4. Group Rights and Discrimination 191

B. Legal Implications and Systemic Consequences of the Choice of Paradigms 197
1. The Substantive Rights Claiming Paradigm 198
2. The Discrimination Claiming Paradigm 201
C. Complementarity of Nondiscrimination and Substantive Rights Claims 208

PART THREE Negative and Positive Human Rights

5. Are Negative and Positive Distinct and Meaningful Categories? 215
A. The Conventional Distinction between Negative and Positive Rights 215
1. Common Definitions 215
2. The Basis for the Negative and Positive Distinction 218
B. What Makes a Right Negative? 221
C. Can There Be Negative Rights? 225
D. The Concept of "Basic" Positive Rights 230
1. A Justification for Devoting More Resources to Some Rights than to Others 230
2. Is Shue's Definition of Basic Rights Overinclusive? 232
3. Does International Human Rights Law Recognize Some Rights as More "Basic" than Others? 236
4. Basic Rights and the Duty of Fulfillment 237
5. The Enforceability of Positive Rights 240
Summary 241

6. The Legal Consequences of Negative and Positive Paradigms 243
A. The Scope of Negative and Positive Rights 243
1. Negative and Positive as Non-opposites 243
2. Nonuniformity in the Strength and Scope of Rights within Categories 244
3. Pseudo-Positive Rights 245
B. Complementary Framing 248
C. Ambiguously Framed Rights 252

7. Structural Implications of Negative and Positive Paradigms 259
A. Positive Rights and Economic Development 260
B. Is There a Negative Duty to Renounce Benefits from Injustice? 265
C. Are Positive Rights Generally Desirable? 268
1. Ethics and Positive Rights 268
2. Positive Rights as a Practical Concept 275

Epilogue 283

Index 287

ACKNOWLEDGMENTS

The author is indebted to Linda Demaine, Andrew Hessick, James Nickel, Steven Ratner, and two anonymous OUP reviewers for comments on parts of early drafts of portions of this work. All opinions expressed herein are the author's own.

TABLE OF ABBREVIATIONS & CITATIONS

Arab Charter	Arab Charter on Human Rights, May 22, 2004, *reprinted in* 12 INT'L HUM. RTS. REP. 893 (2005) *and* 24 BOSTON U. INT'L L.J. 147 (2006)
ACHR	American Convention on Human Rights, Nov. 22, 1969, O.A.S.Treaty Series No. 36, 1144 U.N.T.S. 123
American Declaration	American Declaration of the Rights and Duties of Man, May 2, 1948, O.A.S. Res. XXX, *reprinted in* BASIC DOCUMENTS PERTAINING TO HUMAN RIGHTS IN THE INTER-AMERICAN SYSTEM, OAS/Ser. L/V/I.4 Rev. 9 (2003)
Banjul Charter	African Charter on Human and Peoples' Rights, June 27, 1981, OAU Doc. CAB/LEG/67/3 rev.5, 1520 U.N.T.S. 217
CCPR	International Covenant on Civil and Political Rights, G.A. Res. 2200A (XXI), 21 U.N. GAOR Supp. (No. 16) at 52, U.N. Doc. A/6316 (1966), 999 U.N.T.S. 171
CEDAW	Convention on the Elimination of All Forms of Discrimination against Women, Dec. 18, 1979, G.A. Res. 34/180, 34 U.N. GAOR Supp. (No. 46) at 193, U.N. Doc. A/34/46, 1249 U.N.T.S. 13
CERD	International Convention on the Elimination of All Forms of Racial Discrimination, Dec. 21, 1965, 660 U.N.T.S. 195
CESCR	International Covenant on Economic, Social and Cultural Rights, G.A. Res. 2200A (XXI), 21 U.N. GAOR Supp. (No. 16) at 49, U.N. Doc. A/6316 (1966), 993 U.N.T.S. 3
CJEU	Court of Justice of the European Union
ECHR	European Convention for the Protection of Human Rights and Fundamental Freedoms, Nov. 4, 1950, 213 U.N.T.S. 222
ECOSOC	economic, social, and cultural rights
E.H.R.R.	*European Human Rights Reports*
ESC	European Social Charter (revised), May 3, 1996, CETS No. 163, 2151 U.N.T.S. 277

EU Charter	Charter of Fundamental Rights of the European Union, Dec. 7, 2000, O.J. EC 2000/C 364/01
IHRL	international human rights law
OAS	Organization of American States
UDHR	Universal Declaration of Human Rights, G.A. Res. 217A (III), U.N. Doc. A/810 at 71 (1948)

Introduction

The international system of human rights law is really not one system at all. It is a constellation of systems having different and overlapping geographic scopes and subject matters. International lawyers refer to it as "the" human rights system because, like many fictions, this one serves an analytical function. It allows us to group together distinct but closely related legal regimes sharing the common purpose of protecting and promoting human dignity, primarily on an individual level. Although the fragmentation of treaty regimes and interpretive authorities has attracted periodic attention,[1] the significance of the choices in how human rights regimes structure, frame, and operationalize international human rights has received relatively little attention.

Not because the diversity is subtle. A cursory review of any major human rights instrument reveals rights that are both expansive and narrow; some seemingly framed as individual rights, others as group rights, and still others as state duties; some focusing on disparities in treatment between groups and others on universal substantive guarantees; some as restraints on state behavior and others as requirements for proactive measures for the benefit of the right holders. The mechanics of international human rights law (IHRL) are complex and varied, but there are definite trends in how human rights instruments structure the value system they protect and promote. The reasons for these trends are undertheorized, and the consequences surprisingly neglected, given that human dignity is at once critical as a goal of the world public order and nebulous in its theoretical foundations.

The first purpose of this book, and the one reflected in its organization, is to begin a structural critique of some of these systemic features of IHRL. Most scholarly discussions of IHRL focus on a handful of contentious issues, such as which interests are worthy of inclusion in the human rights pantheon; why states obey IHRL, when they

1. *See, e.g.*, Mehrdad Payandeh, *Fragmentation within International Human Rights Law*, *in* A Farewell to Fragmentation (Mads Adenas & Eirik Bjorge eds., 2015); Harlon Grant Cohen, *From Fragmentation to Constitutionalization*, 25 Pac. McGeorge Global Bus. & Dev. L.J. 381 (2012); Gus Waschefort, *Beyond Fragmentation: An Issues-Based Approach to "Human Rights,"* 2012 S. Afr. Y.B. Int'l L. 61; Lucas Lixinski, *Choice of Forum in International Human Rights Adjudication and the Unity/Fragmentation Debate: Is Plurality the Way Forward?*, 2008 Ital. Y.B. Int'l L. 183; Mónica Pinto, *Fragmentation or Unification among International Institutions: Human Rights Tribunals*, 31 Int'l L. & Pol. 833 (1999).

do; why IHRL is so selectively enforced and how to remedy the deficiency; and how to cope with a purportedly universal body of ethics-based laws in a culturally diverse world. Such questions are obviously worthy of sustained consideration and debate. Recognizing a new human right in a treaty or solemn declaration, for example, ranks among the least reversible of all social acts. A human right, once sanctified as such, is difficult to abandon. Political and legal elites in the world's most influential states show consequent caution in accepting an interest as a universal human right.

Yet, much of the diplomatic debate about the inclusion of new or more specific human rights in public international law revolves not so much around the substance, but around the form and formulation of the right. When a resolution was proposed in the United Nations General Assembly declaring a universal right of access to clean water and sanitation, such human rights leaders as Canada, the United Kingdom, the United States, and Sweden abstained at the vote.[2] Their abstention cannot be explained by the failure to recognize the necessity of clean water to human dignity—specifically, to the life, health, and minimum comfort of all human beings. As long as one accepts that there are such things as human rights, the right to adequate clean water for these purposes is simply beyond dispute. The parameters of the right, however, are not so easily settled. Worthwhile debates over which interests should be chosen for global protection as human rights should not obscure the importance of the structural and mechanical questions—how those interests are molded into the form of enforceable rules to constrain the behavior of powerful actors.

The seemingly prosaic mechanics of structuring, framing, and phrasing rights are indeed at least as consequential as, if less glamorous than, the choice of the right itself. A candidate for a new right may be framed as absolute or variously qualified, as waivable or mandatory, as a right to equal treatment or minimum treatment, as individual or collective or corporate, as primarily a duty or primarily a right, as negative or positive, as enforceable against private parties or the state. Human rights are not all framed in the same manner precisely because of the importance of these structural choices to the functioning of the human rights system.

A second purpose of the book is to make some progress in bridging moral theory with legal theory in the human rights field. The discussion will deal with both the doctrinal aspect of IHRL as well as its moral and political dimensions. It is in my view as fruitless to analyze IHRL without recourse to ethical theory as it would be to analyze international trade law without reference to economic theory. Human rights law is built upon a foundation of moral beliefs about the meaning and value of human life and flourishing, the interests that all human beings share, and the way they should be treated at a minimum. All justifiable universal moral rights need not be universal legal human rights, because not all morally relevant behavior requires or can justify legal regulation. The reverse is not true; by virtue of calling the regime "human rights law" and making it universal, we imply recognition of a moral theory that justifies all rules of IHRL. But not one of the instruments that define IHRL proceeded from a clearly articulated philosophical theory. They begin with human dignity and self-determination (each term being undefined) as a basis for the system, and proceed directly to enumerate the rights that putatively follow from that basis.

2. G.A. Res. 10967 (July 28, 2010), *available at* http://www.un.org/News/Press/docs/2010/ga10967.doc.htm.

To the extent the work of the diplomats who drafted and negotiated these instruments embodies a coherent ethical theory, the result was diluted by the necessity of political compromise. And these were not just compromises over trivial variations in phrasing: they reflect fundamental disagreements over the priorities of different segments of the international community. Modern human rights practice drags around this baggage of early formulations of human rights and duties, and it is left to the authoritative decision-makers such as international tribunals, national courts, and treaty-monitoring bodies, to interpret the inherited language consistent with a coherent moral vision, in service to a complex and diverse modern world public order.

That moral and legal visions of international human rights share much in common may seem to facilitate the task of reconciliation. In both cases, the goal of the system is to guide and constrain the behavior of relevant actors in service to human dignity. Both must balance competing claims of individuals to scarce resources, and both must make difficult choices about the relative priorities of individual and community interests. However, their differences are important for the discussion that will follow. Both legal and moral rights give the right holder a normative advantage and the duty holder a normative disadvantage, but these advantages and disadvantages have a different character in moral and legal theory. First, many philosophers consider moral human rights to correlate to universal duties. In other words, all persons, not just governments, have moral duties to respect universal moral rights.[3] Yet, IHRL primarily governs state behavior and applies to private organizations and individuals only in few and limited cases. It does not follow from this observation that IHRL never imposes individual legal duties, nor that the world community could not develop its doctrines more in that direction. That is a subject Part I of this book will explore.

A second difference is that moral rights entitle the right holder to demand some action or omission on the part of a duty holder, or to be or not to be in a certain state, as a matter of justice or right behavior. Moral rights are therefore enforced mainly by informal social sanctions and the dictates of conscience.[4] Legal rights, in contrast, always entitle the right holder to demand some action or omission on the part of a specific, identified duty holder on pain of enforcement by legal authorities.[5] Specifically, legal human rights are enforced by an authoritative process of decision, whose actors include most prominently:

- the state through its governmental agencies and courts;
- foreign states;
- groups of states united by regional or multilateral treaty arrangements;
- the United Nations Security Council;

3. *See* Thomas Pogge, *Human Rights and Human Responsibilities*, *in* GLOBAL JUSTICE AND TRANSNATIONAL POLITICS 151, 159 (Ciaran Cronin & Pablo de Greiff eds., 2002).

4. *See generally* H.L.A. Hart, *Legal and Moral Obligation*, *in* ESSAYS IN MORAL PHILOSOPHY 82 (A.I. Melden ed., 1958).

5. Philosopher David Lyons has asserted that there can be a legal right without any provision for enforcement. David Lyons, *Utility and Justice*, *in* THEORIES OF RIGHTS 110, 122–23 (Jeremy Waldron ed., 1984). In making this argument, Lyons misapprehends the nature of legal rights and law in general. Legal rights are legal *by definition* because the legislative authority provides

- the United Nations Human Rights Council;
- treaty-monitoring bodies such as the Human Rights Committee; the Committee on Economic, Social and Cultural Rights; the Committee on the Elimination of Racial Discrimination; or the Inter-American Commission on Human Rights; and
- international and regional tribunals, such as the International Criminal Court, the International Court of Justice, or the European Court of Human Rights.

Unless formally adopted as legal rights, moral rights are not enforceable by these institutions. Philosophers frequently propose conceptions of human rights for the achievement of abstract social goals, such as the rectification of inequalities in the absence of a specific violation of a right by an identifiable duty holder.[6] But rights as a political agenda do not always translate well to rights as legal prescriptions. Without enforceable standards to evaluate the duty holder's compliance with its obligations, "rights" serve a mainly rhetorical function. The formal enforceability of IHRL and its structure and content play reciprocally determinative roles. Enforceability critically influences the general structure and content of IHRL, and the structure and content of IHRL affect its enforceability in return.

Third, universal moral rights express ultimate moral concerns that supposedly do not derive from any temporal political authority, whereas legal human rights derive from the treaties and customs adopted by the international community. It is entirely possible—some might say typical—for legal human rights to diverge from moral human rights as a result. Legal rights can be based on economic efficiency or political concerns; they need not be based on moral rights. As Allen Buchanan has noted, this observation applies equally in IHRL.[7] Nonetheless, one of the central goals of IHRL is to ensure that rights and duties adopted into the public order system are consistent with moral human rights based on a concept of human dignity.

for the possibility of enforcement. The fact that some legal rights are inconsistently enforced merely indicates the important role politics play in any legal regime; they do not suggest that the neglect of enforcement is proper or that the rights can be meaningful without it. Moral rights may well be unenforceable, but the very definition of a legal right is that it is accompanied by the threat of coercive sanctions. An unenforceable legal right is merely a rhetorical device and no right in a juridical sense at all. Hence the ancient maxim, *ubi ius ibi remedium. See* Aaron X. Fellmeth & Maurice Horwitz, Guide to Latin in International Law 281 (2009); *cf.* Marbury v. Madison, 5 U.S. 137, 163 (1803) ("The Government of the United States has been emphatically termed a government of laws, and not of men. It will certainly cease to deserve this high appellation if the laws furnish no remedy for the violation of a vested legal right.").

6. *See, e.g.*, Thomas W. Pogge, World Poverty and Human Rights 47 (2d ed. 2008).

7. Allen Buchanan, The Heart of Human Rights 11, 53–56 (2013). Buchanan goes astray in appendix 1 of his book, however, in characterizing many internationally recognized human rights as "nonrights norms" that assert duties on the part of states not correlative to the rights of individuals. Most of the rights he lists—such as the UDHR article 9 right to freedom from arbitrary arrest, detention, or exile; or CESCR article 10(2) right of paid work leave for new mothers—very clearly give rise to individual human rights. What perhaps has confused Buchanan is that such rights are necessarily implemented by, and enforced pursuant to, the municipal legislation of states. But the same is true of nearly all human rights.

The evaluation and proposal of moral justifications for the main structural aspects of IHRL comprises another of this book's main purposes.

The book's structural critique examines three core paradigms of IHRL. The features of the system examined here are not paradigms in Kuhn's sense of a single, fundamental worldview that includes theories and methodology, held by the proponents of a belief system.[8] Even assuming there is a clear dichotomy between paradigmatic and non-paradigmatic belief systems in the realm of natural science, the diversity of fundamental theories about human rights law and ethics would make that dichotomy contested at best when applied to the present subject. Instead, the term is used here in the colloquial sense of a typical pattern, model, or (non-Platonic) archetype. The specific paradigms treated in this book were chosen because each of them undergirds the fundamental assumptions and beliefs of international lawyers and, to a lesser extent, philosophers about how IHRL does, can, and should operate to protect and promote human dignity.

The first paradigm is the decision to frame fundamental human interests in terms of individual rights instead of duties, whether individual, collective, or corporate. The primacy of rights as a paradigm has gone virtually unquestioned in mainstream legal theory for so long that it might not seem worthwhile to examine it anew. Certainly, the sporadic attempts to introduce *individual* duties into the pantheon of IHRL have met with a cold reception. But that frigidity has not yet resulted from well-reasoned objections to the concept of individual legal duties under IHRL. There are many reasons for considering the adoption of individual duties into IHRL. One is that, as noted above, individuals have universal moral duties toward each other. Although it does not follow inexorably that individuals should have universal legal duties toward each other, the fact of moral obligation makes the possibility and consequences of correlative legal duties worth considering. Another reason is that some individuals have the power to affect the human rights of other individuals negatively in a manner, if not comparable to the state's power, at least approaching it. This of course raises the question whether fundamental legal duties should be imposed on powerful multinational business organizations under international law, a subject that has received much attention recently. The very substantial political and economic power of some business organizations, either alone or in collusion with other business organizations or states, has proved to pose a grave threat to human rights in some places and at some times. The possibility of and potential policy bases for international regulation of corporate behavior relating to human rights require examination as well.

If we decide that a broad corpus of legally enforceable individual or corporate human duties would nonetheless make a poor addition to IHRL, it is worth considering whether duties bear greater emphasis than they have so far received, for several reasons. Reorienting IHRL doctrine toward duties might allow us to expand the set of actors responsible for behaving morally in international relations, even if that set excludes individuals in almost all cases. Moreover, we might find that duties can accomplish some objectives, such as protecting important interests not attributable to individual human beings, that the concept of human rights, if it is to remain coherent, cannot effectively achieve.

8. Thomas S. Kuhn, The Structure of Scientific Revolutions (1962).

The second feature to be analyzed is the central role that nondiscrimination rights play in the protection of human dignity. The human right to freedom from discrimination and the related right to equal protection of the laws pertain to a general interest in the legal recognition of the equal dignity of all persons, but in themselves they have no other substantive content. All other major human rights are delimited in scope by specific substantive content, such as a right to specific resources or procedures (for example, adequate nutrition, education, healthcare, a fair trial) or a right to freedom from unwarranted interference in the exercise of a specific freedom (life, speech, movement, property). The decision to include a broad nondiscrimination right alongside the specific substantive rights, and the manner in which the nondiscrimination right is interpreted, have important consequences for the structure and functioning of IHRL. The nondiscrimination right is both necessary and unique in ways that could benefit from further elucidation.

The final set of paradigms examined here is based on the much-debated distinction between positive and negative rights. The term "positive rights" is used by moral theorists in a manner incoherent in the context of the international legal system. Therefore, the first analytical step must be clarification of how positive and negative rights should be defined and distinguished. With the definitions settled, the relationship between the two rights can then be clarified and their social and legal effects can be analyzed.

However defined, the positive and negative rights paradigms engender heated debate over the proper role of the state and its human rights system in human relationships. Much of this debate revolves around the question of how far states are obligated to go in recognizing and enforcing positive rights. This question turns in part on the moral obligations, character, and capabilities of state governments, as well as the character of the societies they govern. The idea that state governments may not pose the only, or even the primary, threat to human rights has become a serious question only recently, and in some countries, the contrary suggestion provokes a perfervid reaction among many political and legal elites and the politically conscious public. To answer this question intelligently, however, calls for a dispassionate analysis of whether all positive rights can and should be treated equally, and the circumstances under which a globally uniform doctrine advances or impedes equal human dignity.

* * *

As a *caveat lector*, it is important to establish what this book is not. It is not a comprehensive analysis of all structural, much less theoretical, features of IHRL. It does not purport to resolve if or how human rights should be hierarchically arranged, how human rights law relates to other areas of international law, or whether implementing a concept of minority group rights is feasible or desirable. Neither does it analyze all the theoretical aspects of human rights, such as whether human dignity is a coherent and justifiable concept; whether IHRL qualifies as *ius cogens*; or how IHRL can be justified on a positivist or metaphysical natural law theory. Least of all does this book enter into questions of substance, such as whether and to what extent there are or should be human rights to intellectual property protection, to benefit from the scientific research of others, or to abortion. An analysis of the three sets of paradigms covered here is in my view sufficient for one extended discussion, and it will largely be confined to them.

PART ONE

Human Rights and Fundamental Duties

> The true source of rights is duty. If we all discharge our duties, rights will not be far to seek. If leaving duties unperformed we run after rights, they will escape us like a will-o'-the-wisp. The more we pursue them, the farther will they fly.
>
> —MOHANDAS GANDHI[1]

> A Declaration of Rights is, by reciprocity, a Declaration of Duties also. Whatever is my right as a man is also the right of another; and it becomes my duty to guarantee as well as to possess.
>
> —THOMAS PAINE[2]

> [A] declaration of rights would be but a lop-sided job, without a declaration of duties to match it on the other side.
>
> —JEREMY BENTHAM[3]

In 1984, Allen Buchanan hypothesized that historians of moral and political philosophy might some day label our period the Age of rights.[4] A few years later, Louis Henkin did exactly that, interpreting the sea change in international law—from preserving the prerogatives of state sovereignty to protecting and promoting

1. MOHANDAS K. GANDHI, INDIA OF MY DREAMS 51 (1947).

2. THOMAS PAINE, THE RIGHTS OF MAN 114 (Heritage Press ed. 1961) (1791).

3. Jeremy Bentham, *Anarchical Fallacies*, *in* 2 THE WORKS OF JEREMY BENTHAM 489, 526 (John Bowring ed., 1843).

4. Allen Buchanan, *What's So Special about Rights?*, 2 SOCIAL PHILOS. & POL'Y 61, 61 (1984).

human dignity—as the inauguration of a new era.[5] Although calling it an "Age" may overstate the case, the international political and academic discourse has certainly shifted toward a reliance on rights to address a panoply of social ills. In recent years, such concepts as a "human right to science," a "human right to intellectual property," and a "human right to the Internet" have been proposed, adopted in human rights treaties, and sometimes characterized as *lex lata*—a statement of existing positive law rather than a recommendation or aspiration for its future development.[6]

The tendency to reframe values as universal human rights rather than interests of varying weight represents a potentially problematic trend. As rights multiply, their value decreases, primarily for several reasons. The first is that more rights mean more potential conflicts with other rights. A human right to a pristine and self-sustaining environment might conflict with a human right to property if the property owner wishes to engage in polluting mineral extraction, to clear-cut a carbon-absorbing forest, or to dam a river for irrigation. A human right to intellectual property might conflict with the human right to the highest attainable standard of health if a drug developer uses its right to recover the maximum profits from its patentable pharmaceutical inventions. When two or more human rights clash, legal authorities are forced to develop ad hoc theories or rely on subjective judgments to resolve the conflict. The resulting human rights decisions push international human rights law (IHRL) about in unpredictable and sometimes inconsistent doctrinal directions.

Moreover, proliferating human rights drain the state's power to achieve important non-right public policy goals. Human rights are not "trumps" in the sense of defeating all non-right policy goals[7]: they must still be factored into a consequentialist calculus in some way. However, human rights do benefit from a presumption that they will triumph over conflicting non-right policy goals absent especially strong reasons. A consequentialist calculus designed to balance competing social priorities is not permitted to allocate to human rights

5. Louis Henkin, The Age of Rights (1990).

6. *See, e.g.*, UDHR art. 27(2); CESCR art. 15(1); U.N. Human Rights Council, Res. L13, 20th Sess., U.N. Doc. A/HRC/20/L.13; Yildirim c. Turquie, Eur. Ct. Hum. Rts. App. No. 3111/10, Dec. 18, 2012; Ronald A. Cass, *Liberty and Property: Human Rights and the Protection of Intellectual Property*, Washington Legal Foundation: Critical Legal Issues Working Paper Series, No. 161, Jan. 2009, at 13–17, *available at* http://www.viacom.com/news/News_Docs/cassintellectualproperty.pdf; Lea Shaver, *The Right to Science and Culture*, 121 Wisc. L. Rev. 121 (2010).

7. Ronald Dworkin, *Rights as Trumps*, *in* Theories of Rights 153 (Jeremy Waldron ed., 1984).

the same weight that other interests are given, whether individual or societal. Rights do benefit, then, from a presumption of superiority in a way that other interests do not. That does not mean rights always prevail over other conflicting interests, but the idea is that they should prevail as a rule. Too many human rights will inevitably impede the state's ability to protect important non-right societal interests, such as preservating endangered species, protecting the oceans or atmosphere from pollution, reducing types of crime not directly implicating human rights (such as money laundering), or promoting economic growth. Relatedly, because the wealth and coercive power of states are finite, allocating more resources for the protection of human rights under international law diverts resources from important non-right priorities. State policies dealing with such problems may not protect or promote any specific human right directly, but they radiate a prosocial glow that positively affects human dignity nonetheless, and neglecting such social interests affects many human rights indirectly. Indeed, if human rights multiply faster than state resources, the rights themselves can be enforced less successfully. The resulting attenuation of enforcement devalues all relatively neglected rights. Without questioning the value of distributing science and access to the Internet, then, one might still doubt that an internationally protected human right is the appropriate paradigm for serving every important human interest.

One way to counterbalance the proliferation of human rights would be to attribute fundamental duties to all persons. Duties are a neglected subject in studies of IHRL, but when philosophers as varied as Gandhi, Paine, and Bentham all agree on one point, it seems worthwhile giving the idea some consideration. As they each insist, duties ride in company with rights. International law does, of course, impose legal duties on states, but discussion of duties is usually relegated to an afterthought. Debates usually center instead about what a right means—the scope and content of the entitlement it confers on the right holder. Meaningful individual duties in particular are almost entirely absent from IHRL.

Considering the history of political and moral theory, this intense modern focus on rights seems like something of an anomaly. The most influential early philosophers, and many of their intellectual progeny of the Enlightenment, were far more concerned with justice and moral duties than with individual rights. Plato and Aristotle based their ethics on analyses of individual and political virtue, and Confucius (551–479 B.C.E.) developed a political and social theory based on filial piety toward the emperor and one's parents. If everyone were to perform his duties to his superiors, everyone would receive his due and society would be justly ordered.[8] Confucius's theory assumed that universal individual rights were unnecessary because superiors could be trusted to act justly. Christian morality, based in part on the Decalogue, is similarly heavily oriented toward duties, and minimizes individual rights. Even influential Enlightenment philosophers such as Kant and Bentham, although far more concerned about safeguarding individual human values such as dignity or utility, built their theories around visions of moral duty or the public good rather than individual rights.

The modern focus on rights in public international law is partly an artifact of the Enlightenment turn toward individualism in European political theory. Despite the long history of philosophical concern with human moral duties, the political theories of John Locke, Jean-Jacques Rousseau, and Thomas Jefferson most influenced the development of political institutions beginning in the late eighteenth century. Their concern with the rights of citizens broadly shaped modern European and American political traditions, most directly through the 1789 French Declaration of the Rights of Man and of the Citizen and the 1791 U.S. Bill of Rights.

The preference for consecrating rights rather than duties followed naturally from the pathologies of the municipal public orders of that era. The laws of the European states in the seventeenth and eighteenth centuries allowed the government to intervene frequently and heavy-handedly in many aspects of life we would consider quintessentially private today, such as sexual behavior, religious observance, and political belief and organization. In many cases, they authorized harsh punishments for trivial crimes, with minimal protections against arbitrary judgments and abuses. There were few powerful business organizations influencing the quotidian lives of ordinary Europeans, and individual wealth and political power tended to follow patronage by the sovereign. From the state appeared to flow all ills, at least to the propertied male bourgeoisie. Individuals, many philosophers thought at the time, did not pose a significant threat to each other in comparison to the Leviathan. There is no reason in principle that they could not have framed the fundamental interests individuals have in liberty, privacy, and just treatment in terms of *state* duties rather than *individual* human rights. Possibly the choice was one of expediency. If the source of individual rights can be framed as originating from God or nature, the state has no power to deny those rights. As states are creations of human political

8. *See* JOHN KING FAIRBANK, CHINA: A NEW HISTORY 67–68 (1992).

activity, what has God or nature to say about their duties? But propagating the myth of natural rights no longer serves any need when states acknowledge their service to their constituencies as the source of their legitimacy, and we are today free to examine whether a primary focus on human rights instead of state duties continues to serve human dignity and other critical community interests. As the discussion in the following chapters will show, there are significant advantages to focusing on state duties rather than individual rights.

As for universal *individual* duties, these seemed much less pressing than human rights, perhaps more a matter for private morals than legal obligation. In theory, universal fundamental duties could assist the state in fulfilling international human rights obligations and fortify the rights themselves by turning members of society into allies for the enforcement of individual rights. For example, in requiring the individual to respect the human rights of others, IHRL could reduce the onus on the state to guarantee individual rights, by spreading responsibility to additional persons who might otherwise play a destructive role in the lives of others. Yet, the interventionist nature of Enlightenment states may have made the idea of private duties seem superfluous and, worse, seem to open the door to additional state intervention in private affairs. If states at the time already imposed numerous and oppressive duties on individuals, a bill of private duties would only compound the perceived faults of the existing political regimes.

There are two answers to this point. First, the objection merely reflects an unproved empirical assumption that the state would do more harm than good in being required by international law to hold individuals to private duties. This is a point that calls for evidence and analysis. Second, it is a practical objection to a normative proposal. The logical starting point for the analysis is to ask whether there are sufficient reasons why individuals *should* have universal legal duties toward each other, before asking whether it is feasible to implement them.

On that normative question, we may begin from the assumption that all individuals do have moral duties toward each other. As the quotations that began this part suggest, there are moral as well as prudential reasons we might consider complementing universal human rights with universal human duties. In this Part, I will explore some of these reasons. On the empirical question, it certainly does not follow from the assumption of universal moral duties that all individuals should have *legal* duties toward each other. There are good reasons to doubt that public international law is the right vehicle for teaching and enforcing universal individual moral duties. These reasons, too, will be explored in this Part.

The idea of emphasizing duties rather than, or in a manner complementary to, rights is not revolutionary. Rights always implicate duties, because rights justify claims by the right holder against the holder of a correlative duty. Notwithstanding some creative arguments that rights can exist without duties, a right that does not authorize the right holder to demand an act or omission by another cannot form the basis of a moral, much less a legal, relationship. By defining a "right" as implicating a duty, theorists emphasize the relational aspect of rights in line with Wesley Hohfeld's frequently invoked definition of "claim-rights," which correlate to a duty to act or not act on demand of the right holder.[9] One theorist has written that rights are "merely the shadows cast by duties" owed by others,[10] but that claim is no more accurate than a claim that duties are merely shadows cast by rights. They are two sides of the same coin, "jural correlates" in Hohfeld's terms. A right, whether legal or moral, necessarily implicates an interest sufficiently compelling that it justifies holding some person or persons subject to a categorical duty to act or not act with respect to the right holder.[11] Moral rights claims are, as Joseph Raz put it, "typically intermediate conclusions in arguments from ultimate values to duties."[12] Legal human rights claims are justified by a normative order that strongly prioritizes these claims in pursuit of a general community policy of protecting and promoting human dignity.

The correlation between legal rights and duties arises from the nature of such rights as tools of social ordering. As noted, the purpose of a right is to elevate an interest above the quotidian utilitarian calculus of needs and desires by giving the right holder a strongly advantaged position when making claims. Rights are not absolute in the sense of an entitlement to unconditional deference; even one person's human right may subserve another's superior human right, and in exceptional cases a social need can justify limiting or even suppressing the right entirely. This is because the holder of the duty correlative to that right could have conflicting duties of equal or higher moral urgency. When the duty holder finds it impossible to fulfill all duties to all right holders, the former is excused from discharging the duty to its full extent and, therefore, observing the right to its full extent; *impossibilium nulla obligatio est.* But again, the default expectation

9. Wesley Newcomb Hohfeld, *Fundamental Legal Conceptions as Applied in Judicial Reasoning*, 23 Yale L.J. 16, 38 (1913).

10. Howard Warrender, The Political Philosophy of Hobbes 19 (1957).

11. *See* Richard B. Brandt, Ethical Theory 438 (1959); Joseph Raz, *On the Nature of Rights*, 93 Mind 194, 195 (1984).

12. Raz, *supra* note 11, at 208.

is that the right will be observed by the duty holder despite very important countervailing concerns and interests.

Joel Feinberg has suggested advantages to advocating free-floating moral "manifesto rights" for the recognition of natural human needs—rights that "need not be correlated with another's duty."[13] However, he seems to recognize that these are not really rights, and his use of the term "rights" is apparently rhetorical. Even such rhetoric is dicey, however. Rights are social; needs are biological and psychological. All human beings naturally need affection, but there is no person, except arguably one's family, who holds a moral duty to give one affection. To speak of a right to affection because it is a human need confuses the vocabulary of ethics precisely because it ignores the moral significance of the social relationship (if any) between the right holder and the duty holder. A person cannot have a *meaningful* right without someone else holding a duty to act on the right.[14] Much less can a person have a legal right without a correlative duty holder, for the reasons explained earlier.

Protecting a value or interest through a rights paradigm or a duties paradigm, then, may seem like six of one and a half dozen of the other. Such a conclusion would be mistaken. The international system of human rights law is, as Allen Buchanan has described it, "subject-centered"[15] for a reason. Efficient legal systems tend to delegate the authority to initiate the enforcement of protected values to those persons with the most direct interest in that enforcement. But more important, as this Part will discuss, duties do not necessarily correlate to another person's right, and there are significant other consequences to protecting an interest through duties rather than rights.

13. Joel Feinberg, *The Nature and Value of Rights*, 4 J. Value Inquiry 243, 255 (1970); Joel Feinberg, Rights, Justice and the Bounds of Liberty 139–40 (1980).

14. *See* Onora O'Neill, *Women's Rights, Whose Obligations?*, *in* Bounds of Justice 97, 103 (2000).

15. Allen Buchanan, *Justice as Reciprocity versus Subject-Centered Justice*, 19 Philos. & Pub. Affairs 227 (1990).

1

The Concept of Fundamental Duties

A. THE UNIVERSAL DUTIES MOVEMENT

1. Individual Duties

International human rights law is a growth industry. Through the gradual and sporadic negotiation of new treaties[1] as well as a steady stream of new jurisprudence and United Nations declarations, the *corpus iuris* of international human rights law (IHRL) keeps becoming more elaborate and detailed, gaining in new rights, and expanding older ones. The European Court of Human Rights alone delivered 3,659 judgments in 2013, more than double the number rendered in 2012, resulting in a wealth of interpretation and a significant expansion of some rights.[2] More persons and groups have more formal, internationally recognized human rights than ever before in history, and the trend shows no sign of abating.

Although human rights advocates tend to view these developments as salutary, some states and academics have perceived a burgeoning imbalance between rights and duties. As its name implies, IHRL concerns itself overwhelmingly with its eponymous subject rather than duties. Misgivings about this perceived imbalance are not new. Since the founding of the United Nations, some members of the international community have pressed for a closer parity between rights and duties in declarations and treaties. They succeeded in introducing the language of duties to parts of several instruments, but no international instrument sets forth definite, legally binding individual duties.

a. Individual Duties in the International Bill of Rights and Other Human Rights Instruments

The international bill of rights mentions or alludes to individual duties in several places. Article 1 of the Universal Declaration of Human Rights (UDHR) states

1. Most recently, for example, the 2003 Maputo Protocol to the African Charter on Human and Peoples' Rights on the Rights of Women in Africa, the 2006 Convention on the Rights of Persons with Disabilities, the 2006 International Convention for the Protection of All Persons from Enforced Disappearance, and several Council of Europe conventions.

2. European Court of Human Rights, Analysis of Statistics 2013, Jan. 2014, at 5, *available at* http://www.echr.coe.int/Documents/Stats_analysis_2013_ENG.pdf.

that all persons "should act towards one another in a spirit of brotherhood."[3] Article 29 adds that "everyone has duties to the community in which alone the free and full development of his personality is possible."[4] The unspecified nature of these duties was evidently intentional, and maintained in opposition to Soviet and other attempts to introduce extensive individual duties to the state as a basis for limiting the exercise of human rights in a manner uncongenial to the state's own "rights."[5] The use of the term "community," as an intermediate between "state" and "other individuals," is telling. The preambles of both the International Covenant on Civil and Political Rights (CCPR) and the International Covenant on Economic, Social, and Cultural Rights (CESCR) echo this language: "the individual, having duties to other individuals and to the community to which he belongs, is under a responsibility to strive for the promotion and observance of" the human rights in the instruments.[6] As their wording and placement in prefatory provisions suggests, these provisions are not intended to establish actual legal duties. Their operational effect is merely to urge those who read the instruments to behave in a socially responsible manner and in accordance with the spirit of the treaties.

In regional human rights instruments, the push for individual duties has taken a slightly more concrete form. The American Declaration of the Rights and Duties of Man includes the concept of individual duties in its very title. Its preamble exhorts "all men" to "conduct themselves as brothers to one another," and counsels that:

> The fulfillment of duty by each individual is a prerequisite to the rights of all. Rights and duties are interrelated in every social and political activity of man. While rights exalt individual liberty, duties express the dignity of that liberty.

The preamble goes on to posit a number of general duties of "man"—not necessarily of individual men—most of which approach the nonsensical in their final formulations. The first two are putative duties to serve "spiritual development . . . with all his strength and resources" and to "preserve, practice and foster culture by every means within his power." The preamble concludes by stipulating a "duty of every man" to hold moral conduct always "in high respect." Chapter II of the Declaration then goes on to posit a long list of duties:

> Article XXIX. It is the duty of the individual so to conduct himself in relation to others that each and every one may fully form and develop his personality.

3. UDHR art. 1.

4. UDHR art. 29(1).

5. *See generally* John H. Knox, *Horizontal Human Rights*, 102 AM. J. INT'L L. 1, 3–15 (2008).

6. CCPR pmbl.; CESCR pmbl.

Article XXX. It is the duty of every person to aid, support, educate and protect his minor children, and it is the duty of children to honor their parents always and to aid, support and protect them when they need it.

Article XXXI. It is the duty of every person to acquire at least an elementary education.

Article XXXII. It is the duty of every person to vote in the popular elections of the country of which he is a national, when he is legally capable of doing so.

Article XXXIII. It is the duty of every person to obey the law and other legitimate commands of the authorities of his country and those of the country in which he may be.

Article XXXIV. It is the duty of every able-bodied person to render whatever civil and military service his country may require for its defense and preservation, and, in case of public disaster, to render such services as may be in his power.

It is likewise his duty to hold any public office to which he may be elected by popular vote in the state of which he is a national.

Article XXXV. It is the duty of every person to cooperate with the state and the community with respect to social security and welfare, in accordance with his ability and with existing circumstances.

Article XXXVI. It is the duty of every person to pay the taxes established by law for the support of public services.

Article XXXVII. It is the duty of every person to work, as far as his capacity and possibilities permit, in order to obtain the means of livelihood or to benefit his community.

Article XXXVIII. It is the duty of every person to refrain from taking part in political activities that, according to law, are reserved exclusively to the citizens of the state in which he is an alien.

The Declaration is of course merely hortatory; the formulation of its provisions is designed to suggest the recognition of a preexisting fact ("it is the duty of every person") rather than to create an enforceable mandate. Most of the duties posited are indeed either evidently unenforceable or so vague as to offer no standards for the evaluation of whether an individual has complied with the duty. Some articles border on obscurantism. Others are explainable by the specific political circumstances and events of the time, such as the article XXXVIII duty to refrain from foreign political activities that are reserved exclusively to citizens of the foreign state—a vestigial "keep out" sign from the Cold War.

The American Convention on Human Rights (ACHR) references individual duties as well, albeit condensed into a single article rather than a list in the style of the Declaration. Its sole provision does not specify the content of such duties at all:

Article 32. Relationship between Duties and Rights

1. Every person has responsibilities to his family, his community, and mankind.
2. The rights of each person are limited by the rights of others, by the security of all, and by the just demands of the general welfare, in a democratic society.

The Banjul Charter is specific in stipulating duties like the American Declaration, with the significant difference that, unlike the latter, the Charter is a binding treaty. Chapter II provides:

> **Article 27**
> 1. Every individual shall have duties towards his family and society, the State and other legally recognised communities and the international community.
> 2. The rights and freedoms of each individual shall be exercised with due regard to the rights of others, collective security, morality and common interest.
>
> **Article 28**
> Every individual shall have the duty to respect and consider his fellow beings without discrimination, and to maintain relations aimed at promoting, safeguarding and reinforcing mutual respect and tolerance.
>
> **Article 29**
> The individual shall also have the duty:
>
> 1. To preserve the harmonious development of the family and to work for the cohesion and respect of the family; to respect his parents at all times, to maintain them in case of need;
> 2. To serve his national community by placing his physical and intellectual abilities at its service;
> 3. Not to compromise the security of the State whose national or resident he is;
> 4. To preserve and strengthen social and national solidarity, particularly when the latter is threatened;
> 5. To preserve and strengthen the national independence and the territorial integrity of his country and to contribute to its defence in accordance with the law;
> 6. To work to the best of his abilities and competence, and to pay taxes imposed by law in the interest of the society;
> 7. To preserve and strengthen positive African cultural values in his relations with other members of the society, in the spirit of tolerance, dialogue and consultation and, in general, to contribute to the promotion of the moral well being of society;
> 8. To contribute to the best of his abilities, at all times and at all levels, to the promotion and achievement of African unity.

Whatever may be one's opinion on the substance of these provisions,[7] the articles indicate no more intention to create legally binding duties than the American Declaration's comparable provisions, which makes anomalous the Charter's mandatory language ("shall") and appearance among the substantive provisions of a

7. For a critique of the substantive duties in the Banjul Charter, *see* Makau W. Mutua, *The African Human Rights System in a Comparative Perspective*, 5 LEGAL F. 31, 33 (1993).

binding treaty. Article 27(1) of the Charter commands an empty set of duties within broad categories of social activity. It is reminiscent of the preamble to the European Union (EU) Charter of Fundamental Rights: "Enjoyment of these rights entails responsibilities and duties with regard to other persons, to the human community and to future generations."[8] The term "responsibilities" has generally been used to denote "duties" in the sense of moral mandates to act or refrain from acting in a certain way.[9] Without including any substantive content or prescribing any specific course of action, such commands have none of the precision necessary to inform the supposed duty holders how to comply with their obligations.

Articles 27(2), 28, and 29 of the Banjul Charter ostensibly require individuals to act within firmer parameters, but these too are illusory. Most of the commands are vague and as devoid of content as article 27(1). How does one place one's physical and intellectual abilities at the service of the national community? How does one preserve and strengthen social and national solidarity? But more telling is the fact that the treaty gives no indication of creating a system by which persons who refuse to serve and preserve and strengthen may be judged internationally deficient and brought into conformity with their duties. The state alone remains the authority on defining the individual's duties toward itself, his or her community, and other individuals, which was exactly the situation before the Banjul Charter was adopted. Chapter II of the Charter, like the duty provisions of the International Bill of Rights, can best be understood as social propaganda intended to moderate and qualify the Charter's enumeration of rights.

Finally, the European Framework Convention on the Protection of National Minorities, aside from recognizing minority rights, also provides in article 20 for individual duties:

> In the exercise of the rights and freedoms flowing from the principles enshrined in the present framework Convention, any person belonging to a national minority shall respect the national legislation and the rights of others, in particular those of persons belonging to the majority or to other national minorities.[10]

Again the word "shall" appears to suggest that the provision was intended to elevate "national legislation and the rights of others" to an international legal obligation. But here, too, it is clear that the provision serves a rhetorical purpose. Like the other

8. Charter of Fundamental Rights of the European Union, Dec. 18, 2000, pmbl., para. 6, 40 I.L.M. 266.

9. A U.N. Human Rights Commission's Special Rapporteur studying the two terms came to the same conclusion. *See* Economic and Social Council, Commission on Human Rights, Report of Mr. Miguel Alfonso Martínez, Special Rapporteur appointed by the Sub-Commission on the Promotion and Protection of Human Rights to Undertake the Study Requested by the Commission in Its Resolution 2000/63, 58th Sess., Mar. 19, 2002, U.N. Doc. E/CN.4/2002/107, at 9, para. 28.

10. Framework Convention for the Protection of National Minorities art. 20, Feb. 1, 1995, ETS No. 157, 2152 U.N.T.S. 243.

provisions discussed here, the article 20 is vague and omits any interpretive guidance or provision for enforcement.

If such language has no direct legal effect, why include it? The explanatory reports do not say, but the most likely reason is to implicitly legitimate state measures limiting the rights. The explanatory report of the National Minorities Convention, for example, does make clear that such limits do not justify the parties in ignoring the Convention, but it goes no further.[11] Taking the European Framework Convention as an example, article 7 provides:

> The Parties shall ensure respect for the right of every person belonging to a national minority to freedom of peaceful assembly, freedom of association, freedom of expression, and freedom of thought, conscience and religion.

If members of a national minority assembled for a peaceful protest on public property without first seeking a permit required by law, the state could invoke article 20 to disperse the assembly. The group members who ignore their duty to respect national legislation, the state could argue, fail to properly exercise their article 7 assembly right.

This interpretation finds some support in the European Convention for the Protection of Human Rights and Fundamental Freedoms (ECHR). Article 10 of the ECHR provides that the right to freedom of expression "carries with it duties and responsibilities" that justify restrictions on its exercise.[12] The Strasbourg Court has extended this point to hold duties to be "inherent in" certain guaranteed rights, such as the right to privacy, family life, or freedom from degrading treatment or punishment.[13] In neither case has this led to the imposition of legal duties on individuals, however. They are, in effect, observations about the nature of rights, which are never unlimited. The court did not interpret "duties and responsibilities" to impose a separate basis in international law for a cause of action against someone who exercises his rights abusively. It has used that provision instead as a justification for adopting interpretive limitations on the right. The provisions would be construed to imply, for example, that a state that denies a person the right to defame another does not violate the defamer's freedom of expression, because the state has the duty to protect the victim's reputation and privacy. To the extent the "duties and responsibilities" seem to allege that a person who violates the rights of another has violated his own duty to respect the victim's reputation and privacy, it is a moral observation rather than a legal prescription. There is no separate, individual duty to respect reputation and privacy under the ECHR, at least as that term has been interpreted so far. The point is that some limitations on rights are justifiable to protect the equally weighty, or weightier, interests of others to whom a duty is owed.

11. *Id.*, Explanatory Report, Feb. 1995, Council of Europe Doc. H(95)10, 34 I.L.M. 351 (1995), *available at* http://conventions.coe.int/Treaty/EN/Reports/Html/157.htm.

12. ECHR art. 10(2).

13. *E.g., M.C. v. Bulgaria*, 40 E.H.R.R. 20, para. 150 (2005); *X & Y v. Netherlands*, 8 E.H.R.R. 235, para. 23 (1986).

If the purpose of article 20 of the European Framework Convention is to justify state limits on the exercise of minority rights, its approach is awkward and ambiguous. A more direct approach to balancing minority rights with other public interests would be to qualify article 7 as granting a right "subject to compliance with reasonable and proportionate regulations prescribed by law and necessary in a democratic state for the public welfare." By instead bringing in a separate duty to respect national legislation, article 20 puts a different spin on the dynamic. It does not clearly provide that the state is authorized to limit the article 7 right. Granted, such a limitation is implicit in all human rights, but a well-drafted provision would give guidance as to the circumstances under which limitations would be acceptable, and to what extent. The larger trouble is that it implies that, by violating national law, the minority group member is also separately violating the treaty. He would not be doing so, of course. International custom does not permit treaties to bind individuals merely by implication: they would have to provide for such duties explicitly. In any case, the Framework Convention provides no means for detecting and punishing individual violations of its provisions apart from state legislation, which (again) requires no treaty in the first place. The "rights of others" qualification is especially problematic for this reason; it may be read to imply that an individual whose right is violated by a minority group member in the exercise of the latter's rights under the Framework Convention may be entitled to claim a remedy pursuant to the Convention. But it is a false promise; the Convention contemplates no procedures for such a remedy.

B. Individual Duties in Human Rights-Related Declarations

Duties make their appearance in other international human rights–related declarations as well. Principle 1 of the Stockholm Declaration on the Human Environment recognizes a "responsibility to protect and improve the environment for present and future generations."[14] More recently, the Association of Southeast Asian Nations (ASEAN) has referenced individual duties in its Human Rights Declaration. Article 1 states that all persons "should act towards one another in a spirit of humanity," and article 6 provides:

> The enjoyment of human rights and fundamental freedoms must be balanced with the performance of corresponding duties as every person has responsibilities to all other individuals, the community and the society where one lives. It is ultimately the primary responsibility of all ASEAN Member States to promote and protect all human rights and fundamental freedoms.[15]

14. Stockholm Declaration of the United Nations Conference on the Human Environment, June 14, 1992, *reprinted in* Basic Documents of International Environmental Law 21 (Harald Hohmann ed., 1992).

15. ASEAN Human Rights Declaration art. 6 (Nov. 19, 2012), *at* http://www.asean.org/news/asean-statement-communiques/item/asean-human-rights-declaration.

Article 8 continues the theme:

> The human rights and fundamental freedoms of every person shall be exercised with due regard to the human rights and fundamental freedoms of others.[16]

Perhaps the least anodyne statement of duties appears in article 35 of the U.N. Declaration on the Rights of Indigenous Peoples, which suggests individual duties to indigenous communities: "Indigenous peoples have the right to determine the responsibilities of individuals to their communities."[17] This provision does not actually specify individual duties; it instead delegates the right to specify such duties to specific groups, which could be very problematic indeed from a human rights standpoint, if an indigenous group decides to impose responsibilities that cut deeply into individual human rights.[18]

Despite the abundance of references to duties in human rights treaties and declarations, the instruments rarely offer a lucid glimpse into the reason for their inclusion. The major exception is the American Declaration, which posits in its preamble an unusually defined basis for individual duties:

> The fulfillment of duty by each individual is a prerequisite to the rights of all. Rights and duties are interrelated in every social and political activity of man. While rights exalt individual liberty, duties express the dignity of that liberty.
>
> Duties of a juridical nature presuppose others of a moral nature which support them in principle and constitute their basis.
>
> Inasmuch as spiritual development is the supreme end of human existence and the highest expression thereof, it is the duty of man to serve that end with all his strength and resources.
>
> Since culture is the highest social and historical expression of that spiritual development, it is the duty of man to preserve, practice and foster culture by every means within his power.
>
> And, since moral conduct constitutes the noblest flowering of culture, it is the duty of every man always to hold it in high respect.[19]

16. *Id.* art. 8.

17. G.A. Res. 61/295, art. 35 (2007).

18. *Cf.* Rebecca Gross, *The "I" in Indigenous: Enforcing Individual Rights Guarantees in an Indigenous Group Context*, 23 N.Y. Int'l L. Rev. 65 (2010).

19. American Declaration of the Rights and Duties of Man, pmbl., OAS Res. XXX, adopted by the Ninth International Conference of American States (1948), *reprinted in* Basic Documents Pertaining to Human Rights in the Inter-American System, OEA/Ser.L.V/II.82 doc.6 rev.1 at 17 (1992). As explicit as the Declaration's philosophy might be, it hardly expresses ideas of indisputable and universal appeal. The assumption that "spiritual development"—whatever that might be—is the "supreme end of human existence and the highest expression thereof" is debatable, and the assertion that every person has a duty (presumably moral rather than legal) to serve that end "with all his strength and resources" seems to devalue every other interest, including quite natural desires for comfort, happiness, and health, as well as other values, such as the preservation of the natural environment. What it means for "culture" to

Again, however, we are not dealing with binding prescriptions. A declaration is not a binding legal instrument in the first place, and preambular language in a declaration conveys additional tentativeness. The American Declaration takes pains to dampen the effect of its exhortations, moreover, by suggesting that they express "duties . . . of a moral nature" that support rather than constitute legal duties.

The invocation of duties in declarations such as these is perhaps less controversial than their inclusion in treaties, because declarations are not in themselves legally binding. The hortatory nature of declarations may explain the international community's willingness to include duties in their substantive provisions rather than relegating them to a preamble. However, declarations of sufficiently broad subscription may ultimately be used as evidence of the development of customary international law, and so their provisions justify consideration and perhaps concern. In treaties a fortiori, the statements may be interpreted as legally binding. The Committee on Economic, Social and Cultural Rights has in fact interpreted CESCR article 11 to impose private duties:

> While only States are parties to the Covenant and are thus ultimately accountable for compliance with it, all members of society—individuals, families, local communities, non-governmental organizations, civil society organizations, as well as the private business sector—have responsibilities in the realization of the right to adequate food.[20]

The Committee has made comparable assertions about individual and corporate responsibilities to realize the individual right to health and other rights.[21] Similarly, that committee as well as the Committee on the Elimination of Racial Discrimination have suggested that business organizations and individuals have human rights "responsibilities" directly under the treaties, such as an "obligation not to disseminate racist ideas."[22]

The committees' tasks are the respective monitoring and interpretation of the CESCR's and CEDR's provisions; they have no authority to declare moral norms, and

be the "highest social and historical expression" of spiritual development is entirely obscure, but moral conduct is most certainly not a consequence of culture unless "moral conduct" tautologically means any conduct accepted by a given culture. Many cultures include practices that cannot be justified on any acceptable moral theory, including hereditary castes, endemic domestic violence, clitoral mutilation, honor killings, and religious intolerance, not to speak of historical cultural practices such as slavery and ritual human sacrifice.

20. Comm. on Econ., Soc. & Cultural Rts., Gen. Comment No. 12, para. 20, *in* Report of the Committee on Economic, Social, and Cultural Rights, U.N. ESCOR, Supp. No. 2, at 102, 106, U.N. Doc. E/2000/22 (2000).

21. U.N. Econ. & Soc. Council, Comm. on Econ., Soc. & Cultural Rts., General Comment No. 14, para. 42, U.N. Doc. E/C.12/2000/4 (Aug. 11, 2000).

22. TBB-Turkish Union in Berlin/Brandenburg v. Germany, Commun. No. 48/2010 (Feb. 26, 2013), para. 12.7 (*citing* CERD Committee, General Recommendation XV on Article 4 of the Convention, para. 4 (Mar. 17, 1993), *in* CERD Committee Annual Report, U.N, GAOR, 48th Sess., Supp. No. 18, at 115, U.N. Doc. A/48/18 (1994)).

no particular expertise in deciphering social norms. Given their function, it might appear that the committees were attempting to suggest that these "responsibilities" are legally binding on individuals and nonstate groups. Even if the committees were merely soapboxing, however, their interpretations may be used to support arguments for limiting human rights in cases where an individual duty could potentially limit some recognized human right. It appears, then, that the committees have adopted an agenda of elevating the hortatory mention of individual and corporate duties in their instruments to binding rules, albeit without practical effect to date.

c. The IAC and UNESCO Declarations of Human Responsibilities

In 1997, a nongovernmental organization (NGO) calling itself the InterAction Council (IAC) drafted a more comprehensive effort to promote individual duties—a Draft Declaration on Human Social Responsibilities—as a "complement" to the UDHR.[23] The IAC is composed of former heads of state and government, but as an NGO it has no formal standing under international law. Nonetheless, its draft was briefly considered at the U.N. Human Rights Commission before that body was disbanded and replaced by the Human Rights Council.[24]

The IAC draft's preamble began with the claim that "the exclusive insistence on rights can result in conflict, division, and endless dispute, and the neglect of human responsibilities can lead to lawlessness and chaos." It posited a universal responsibility of "all people" "to foster a better social order, both at home and globally," and to that end proposed a set of articles purporting to define fundamental human social duties. Like the UDHR, the IAC draft was consciously structured as a set of moral rather than legal injunctions, but it was formulated with even less precision than the UDHR. For example, it provides:

> **Article 1**
> Every person, regardless of gender, ethnic origin, social status, political opinion, language, age, nationality, or religion, has a responsibility to treat all people in a humane way.
>
> **Article 2**
> No person should lend support to any form of inhumane behavior, but all people have a responsibility to strive for the dignity and self-esteem of all others.
>
> **Article 3**
> ... Everyone has a responsibility to promote good and to avoid evil in all things.

23. Inter-Action Council, A Universal Declaration of Human Responsibilities (Sept. 1, 1997), *at* http://asiwide.or.jp/iac/UDHR/EngDecl1.htm.

24. U.N. Commission on Hum. Rts., Promotion and Protection of Human Rights: Human Rights and Human Responsibilities, Annex I, U.N. Doc. E/CN.4/2003/105 (2003). The Human Rights Council has not taken up the draft to date.

Article 8
Every person has a responsibility to behave with integrity, honesty and fairness. No person or group should rob or arbitrarily deprive any other person or group of their property.[25]

Articles 1 and 2 do not define what it means to treat someone humanely or to act inhumanely. Article 3 offers no definition of "good" or "evil." Other articles contain similar, although not always so nebulous, moral injunctions: nobody should lie or steal, abuse their children, treat sex partners callously, and so forth.

The IAC draft was soon referred to the U.N. Economic, Social and Cultural Organization (UNESCO) and, as noted, the U.N. Human Rights Commission for possible eventual consideration by the General Assembly.[26] Meanwhile, UNESCO was considering its own draft declaration along very similar lines.[27] These drafts were not adopted or referred to the General Assembly, and received little official attention.[28] As political statements, they lack specificity and do not advance much on merely saying that all persons should be ethical and considerate, however one might choose to interpret those terms.

The IAC and UNESCO declarations have been subjected to criticism about their effects on the value processes of international law,[29] but seventeen years later, they have had no significant legal consequences. The most cogent criticisms of the declarations impugn their lack of content. Certainly, most provisions of the IAC and UNESCO declarations did little more than promote playground morality. Nobody questions that all persons have an ethical duty to be good rather than evil, so it was never clear what the drafters hoped to accomplish.[30]

At present, there is no significant chance of resurgent enthusiasm for universal declarations of human responsibilities. However, it would be a mistake to consider the demise of the draft declarations to reflect a failure of their underlying ideas. A declaration of universal moral duties articulated with foresight and precision could in theory be as useful as a declaration of universal moral rights. Such a declaration could, moreover, pave the way to an international law of fundamental human duties in the same way that the UDHR broke the ground for the International Bill of Rights, the anti-discrimination treaties, and other foundational instruments of

25. Universal Declaration of Responsibilities, *supra* note 23, arts. 1–3, 8.

26. *See* Economic and Social Council, Commission on Human Rights, Report of Mr. Miguel Alfonso Martínez, Special Rapporteur appointed by the Sub-Commission on the Promotion and Protection of Human Rights to Undertake the Study Requested by the Commission in Its Resolution 2000/63, 58th Sess., Mar. 19, 2002, U.N. Doc. E/CN.4/2002/107, at 5.

27. UNESCO, Universal Declaration of Human Responsibilities (Apr. 5, 1997), *available at* http://globalethic.org/Center/unesco.htm.

28. Ben Saul, *In the Shadow of Human Rights: Human Duties, Obligations, and Responsibilities*, 32 Colum. Hum. Rts. L. Rev. 565, 578–81 (2001).

29. *See generally* Knox, *supra* note 5.

30. One philosopher characterized the draft as reminiscent of "a teenager's first writing attempts." Thomas Pogge, *Human Rights and Human Responsibilities*, *in* Global Justice and Transnational Politics 151, 155–56 (Ciaran Cronin & Pablo de Greiff eds., 2002).

IHRL. The consequences of taking international law in this direction pose a separate question, dealt with in the next chapter.

D. General Practice of States

The municipal constitutions of several countries declare fundamental citizen duties together with rights. Not all municipal constitutional duties reflect universal moral considerations. Some are moral duties applicable only to specific duty holders (mostly involving family relationships, such as a duty of adults to support their parents or children, or to provide for their spouses).[31] Others impose duties that are prudential rather than moral in nature, such as the Bulgarian Constitution's provision making the "study and use of the Bulgarian language" an "obligation of every Bulgarian citizen,"[32] or the Chinese constitutional provision making it a "duty" to pay taxes in accordance with the law.[33]

But some constitutional provisions do incorporate purported universal duties. They may include such duties as not abusing rights to the detriment of national security, public health, "morality," or the rights of others;[34] not inciting racial or religious enmity; not seeking to overthrow the state;[35] attending formal education;[36] protecting the environment;[37] defending the country against attack;[38] or assisting others in case of natural disaster.[39]

Some constitutional duties are extremely abstract, such as those in the Indian constitution:

> It shall be the duty of every citizen of India—
>
> (a) to abide by the Constitution and respect its ideals and institutions, the National Flag and the National Anthem;
> (b) to cherish and follow the noble ideals which inspired our national struggle for freedom;
> (c) to uphold and protect the sovereignty, unity and integrity of India;

31. *See, e.g.*, Const. of the Rep. of Bulgaria art. 47(1) (2007); Const. of the People's Rep. of China art. 49; Grundgesetz für die Bundesrepublik Deutschland art. 6(2) (1949).

32. Const. of the Rep. of Bulgaria art. 36(1).

33. Const. of the People's Rep. of China art. 56 (1982).

34. *See, e.g.*, Const. of the Rep. of Bulgaria arts. 37(2), 39(2), 41(1), 58(1); Const. of the People's Rep. of China arts. 36, 54; Const. of Indonesia art. 28J (1959).

35. *See, e.g.*, Const. of the Rep. of Bulgaria art. 44(2).

36. *See, e.g.*, Const. of the People's Rep. of China art. 46; Const. of Indonesia art. 31(2).

37. *See, e.g.*, Const. of the Rep. of Bulgaria art. 55; Const. of India art. 51A(g).

38. *See, e.g.*, Const. of the Rep. of Bulgaria art. 59(1); Const. of the People's Rep. of China art. 55; Const. of India art. 51A(d) (2007); Const. of Indonesia art. 30.

39. *See, e.g.*, Const. of the Rep. of Bulgaria art. 61. The U.K. government once tentatively explored adding "responsibilities" in the sense of "what we owe to society" to its constitutional framework as well, although it eventually abandoned the effort. Ministry of Justice, Rights and Responsibilities: Developing Our Constitutional Framework, Cm. 7577 (2009) (on file with author).

. . .

(e) to promote harmony and the spirit of common brotherhood amongst all the people of India transcending religious, linguistic and regional or sectional diversities; to renounce practices derogatory to the dignity of women;

(f) to value and preserve the rich heritage of our composite culture;

. . .

(h) to develop the scientific temper, humanism and the spirit of inquiry and reform;

(i) to safeguard public property and to abjure violence;

(j) to strive towards excellence in all spheres of individual and collective activity so that the nation constantly rises to higher levels of endeavour and achievement . . . .[40]

The incorporation of universal moral duties into municipal constitutions is not nearly sufficiently widespread to qualify as a general practice of states. To the extent that duties are incorporated, the variance in their coverage is substantial, and the duties themselves are nearly always too vague to be legally enforceable. Although it may be entertaining to imagine how Indian law would enforce a duty to cherish noble ideals, any answer to that conundrum is bound to be highly subjective and arguable. Such a provision must be rhetorical and not intended as legally binding. Some provisions seem to propose good candidates for universal moral duties, such as those requiring citizens not to infringe the rights of others, to protect the environment, or to assist others during natural disasters. However, even these lack the specificity required to elevate them to enforceable legal duties. Municipal constitutions can do some things better, and some things much worse, than municipal legislation, and ultimately any relevant duties must be adopted in better defined legislation, which would render the constitutional provisions moot.

E. Individual Duties in International Criminal Law

IHRL is not the only field of public international law in which universal duties have been proposed or used. Individual duties in the related fields of international criminal law and the international law of armed conflict, also known as international humanitarian law, are now well established. Some of these duties are relational, in the sense that they apply to combatants in an armed conflict with respect to a limited class of persons (e.g., civilians, prisoners of war, combatants who are hors de combat). It is now well established that individual persons have general duties to respect laws of armed conflict[41] and may be punished or held liable under international law for violating their duties.

But some of these duties may properly be considered universal. The Genocide Convention specifically makes genocidal acts a "crime under international law" for which individuals, whether public officials or private persons, may be

40. Const. of India art. 51A.

41. *See* Steven R. Ratner, *Law Promotion beyond Law Talk: The Red Cross, Persuasion, and the Laws of War*, 22 Eur. J. Int'l L. 459, 486 (2011).

punished.[42] Although the Convention originally envisioned enforcement by states, the Convention may be said to establish an individual duty under international law not to participate or aid in genocide. In 1993, the U.N. Security Council began empowering ad hoc international criminal tribunals to prosecute and punish individuals not just for violations of their duties under the laws of armed conflict, such as grave breaches of the Geneva Conventions of 1949, but also crimes against humanity such as genocide, mass rape, and torture.[43] The possibility of international criminal prosecution for violation of such duties became general in 2002, when the Statute of the International Criminal Court (ICC) entered into force.[44] The ICC Statute permits prosecution for certain war crimes, crimes against humanity, genocide, and the crime of aggression when committed by a national, or on the territory, of a state party.[45]

Such duties are very limited; they mostly prohibit a short list of specific and very serious offenses or participation in large-scale atrocities. In addition, they are not *primarily* duties to other individuals, but rather duties to the international community. International criminal law is not oriented toward vindicating the rights of the victims of atrocities other than their right to retribution, although it does have a compensatory element. Its predominant function is to enforce an individual as well as a state duty to respect certain fundamental human rights as well as important interests protected by the international law of armed conflict. As a body of law codifying universal human duties, it is significant but distinctly limited.

F. Why Nonbinding Duties?

In summary, although IHRL is almost exclusively a system of legal duties imposed on states toward individuals, some—mostly ambivalent—efforts have been made to color IHRL with complementary individual duties. Except for serious violations of international criminal law, most prominently war crimes and crimes against humanity, these ventures have nearly always taken the form of vaguely worded moral exhortations rather than duties binding on individuals. Even when phrased as binding principles in international or constitutional legal instruments, the duties take forms far too vague to guide juridical interpretation, and they omit any mechanism for the detection of violations, or the interpretation and enforcement of the principles.

The terms of the treaties and declarations suggest that the motivations for including these exhortations are varied. One reason is a concern that international law might seem to license selfish and antisocial behavior by recognizing extensive human rights without corresponding duties to use the rights in a socially responsible manner. The drafters apparently hoped to influence the cultural and psychological conception of human rights rather than to create an independent legal basis

42. Convention on the Prevention and Punishment of the Crime of Genocide arts. I, IV, 78 U.N.T.S. 277.

43. S.C. Res. 827 (1993) (former Yugoslavia); Statute of the International Criminal Tribunal for the Former Yugoslavia arts. 1–7; S.C. Res. 955 (1994) (Rwanda); Statute of the International Criminal Tribunal for Rwanda arts. 1–6.

44. G.A. Res. 51/207 (1997); Rome Statute of the International Criminal Court, July 17, 1998.

45. Rome Statute of the ICC, arts. 5, 12.

for constraining individual behavior. If right holders believe in a mutuality of rights and societal interests, they are less likely to abuse their rights or interpret them solipsistically. Nonbinding exhortations are an appropriate vehicle to persuade right holders to act with consideration for the rights of others and in a spirit of human fraternity and social solidarity.

A complementary concern, to which I alluded earlier, is to provide a grounding for state limitations on human rights. No human right is absolute; all rights must yield to conflicting rights and to broader societal concerns at some times and in some ways. To say that right holders have a duty to exercise their rights in a socially responsible manner implies that state measures limiting the exercise of rights, mostly obviously to protect other rights or important societal interests, are not so much infringing or limiting the right as qualifying the right in recognition of the right holder's preexisting duties.

Another, more sinister, motivation for including these provisions might be the preservation of state policies and cultural practices inimical to individual freedom. The ASEAN Human Rights Declaration includes the following statement: "the realisation of human rights must be considered in the regional and national context bearing in mind different political, economic, legal, social, cultural, historical and religious backgrounds."[46] Read together with the Declaration's emphasis on duties, the qualification raises concerns that the ASEAN members are attempting to justify violations of human rights in order to preserve traditional inequities, enhance state authority, protect existing political prerogatives, or accelerate economic development without regard to the human cost. As a result, the U.N. Human Rights Council's Coordination Committee,[47] the U.N. High Commissioner for Human Rights,[48] U.S. State Department,[49] and various NGOs all expressed concerns with or objections to the Declaration. However, as with the other declarations invoking duties, the nonbinding nature of the Declaration mutes its potential influence over IHRL even in the region.

Underlying most references to duties in such instruments is an important philosophical point: arguments for international human rights are necessarily based on ethical considerations. It is possible that some internationally protected human rights have a weak basis in moral theory, but in no case can IHRL disregard the ethical implications of the law as interpreted and applied by the international

46. ASEAN Human Rights Declaration, *supra* note 15, art. 7.

47. Statement by the High Commissioner for Human Rights at the Bali Democracy Forum, Nov. 7, 2012, *available at* http://www.ohchr.org/EN/NewsEvents/Pages/DisplayNews.aspx?NewsID=12752&LangID=E.

48. U.N. Human Rights Council, Coordinating Committee of the Special Procedures, Open Letter: ASEAN Human Rights Declaration Should Maintain International Standards (Nov. 16, 2012) (on file with author).

49. *See* U.S. Department of State, Press Statement, ASEAN Declaration on Human Rights, PRN 2012/1826, Nov. 20, 2012, *at* http://www.state.gov/r/pa/prs/ps/2012/11/200915.htm (describing as "concerning aspects" of the Declaration: "the use of the concept of 'cultural relativism' to suggest that rights in the UDHR do not apply everywhere; . . . introducing novel limits to rights; and language that could be read to suggest that individual rights are subject to group veto.").

community. All moral theories that justify universal human rights equally justify universal duties that persons have toward one another and toward the state as a collective representative of society. But, in recognition that not all moral duties should be legal duties, the instruments leave their references to duties in precatory terms, nonbinding instruments, or precatory terms in nonbinding instruments. The attachment of mandatory terms to the duties—"must" and "shall"—seems to represent a crude lunge at rhetorical force rather than an effort to codify the duties as law.

That no serious attempt has been made to incorporate binding individual duties into the corpus of IHRL is not entirely surprising. The purpose of IHRL is to preserve and promote human dignity, and in many places the state represents an important threat to human dignity through laws and practices designed to maintain a ruling class or clique in power, to promote economic development without regard to equity, or to enforce an official ideology to the detriment of fundamental individual rights and freedoms. To the extent that the state maintains a monopoly over, or greatly disproportionate, political and economic power in a society, individual rights act as a bulwark against state intrusions into the sphere of individual liberties. A code of individual duties might conceivably serve the goal of promoting human dignity, but it cannot protect individuals against oppression by the state, and, as evident from the concerns over the ASEAN Declaration, may be used to undermine human rights. The promotion of individual duties to other individuals represents a less direct threat to human rights, but it still could be used as a derivative basis for limiting rights by a state purporting to act parens patriae, as the guardian of the rights of others.

In addition, some have claimed that individual duties themselves would conflict with individual rights through a "horizontal effect" that would not present such serious problems if even equivalent positive duties were assigned to the state.[50] However, this argument assumes that the only positive obligation imposed on the state by IHRL is to ensure compensation to victims of human rights violations by other individuals. Such is not at all the case. State positive duties under IHRL include the obligation to protect human rights by enacting laws and taking enforcement measures that regulate the behavior of private individuals through deterrence and punishment and, therefore, potentially threaten the exercise of human rights by those individuals. The threat to individual rights posed by individual duties is not necessarily greater or lesser than the threat posed by state duties. The only difference is that the duties are imposed by states rather than international law. The scope and content of the duty, and therefore its potential to conflict with a human right, are unrelated to whether the duty is imposed on the individual directly by international law or through the intermediation of a state government.

Nonetheless, these concerns offer no blanket reason to oppose the international legalization of human duties. They instead raise practical concerns about the way individual duties could, and most probably would in some cases, be used by a state ambivalent about or hostile to IHRL. As to whether the objections to an

50. *E.g.*, Samantha Besson, *Les obligations positives de protection des droits fondamentaux—Un essai en dogmatique comparative*, 1 Rev. de Droit Suisse 49, 66–69 (2003).

international codification of individual duties are valid and cogent in general, that question will be examined in the next chapter.

2. Corporate Duties

The ever-growing wealth, political power, and social influence of multinational enterprises (MNEs) makes them increasingly important actors in the human rights arena. Many MNEs more resemble states than individual persons in their political weight and power over large numbers of human lives. Reports in the 1990s of devastating pollution generated by corporate oil drilling and mineral extraction, and human rights abuses committed by states allegedly with the connivance or at the instigation of MNEs, caused activists and scholars to begin advocating the extension of IHRL duties from states to business firms either directly or through codes of corporate social responsibility (CSR).[51]

The calls for legal regulation of MNEs became especially insistent after some states and human rights authorities began attributing "human rights" to business organizations themselves. Protocol No. 1 to the ECHR establishes a right to the peaceful enjoyment of "possessions" for not just individuals but every "legal person."[52] In its *Anheuser-Busch, Inc. v. Portugal* decision of 2007, the Grand Chamber of the European Court of Human Rights extended this right to trademarks,[53] despite the fact that trademarks are merely commercial rights licensed by the state for utilitarian reasons rather than personal property. In *Citizens United v. Federal Election Commission*,[54] the U.S. Supreme Court decided that these same organizations had a constitutional "civil right" to influence political elections by contributing money to candidates for public office. Two years later, the Court held that business organizations have a right to practice religion.[55]

These tentative steps to recognize business organizations as having human dignity sufficient to sustain fundamental rights are based on a misapprehension of the relationship between the concept of dignity and the nature of organizations. The basis of IHRL in human dignity means that at its core IHRL serves to ensure that human beings—their longevity, comfort, happiness, prosperity, autonomy, and intellectual and moral development—are treated as innately valuable and worthy of

51. *See, e.g.*, Andrew Clapham, Human Rights Duties of Non-state Actors (2006); Steven Ratner, *Corporations and Human Rights: A Theory of Responsibility*, 111 Yale L.J. 443, 502 (2001); Beth Stephens, *The Amorality of Profit: Transnational Corporations and Human Rights*, 20 Berk. J. Int'l L. 45 (2002); David Kinley & Junko Tadaki, *From Talk to Walk: The Emergence of Human Rights Responsibilities for Corporations at International Law*, 44 Va. J. Int'l L. 931 (2004); *see also* Jordan J. Paust, *Human Rights Responsibilities of Private Corporations*, 35 Vand. J. Transnat'l L. 801 (2002); Nils Rosemann, *The UN Norms on Corporate Human Rights Responsibilities*, Friedrich Ebert Stiftung Dialogue on Globalization, No. 20, Aug. 2005, *available at* http://library.fes.de/pdf-files/iez/global/04669.pdf.

52. ECHR, Procotol No. 1, art. 1.

53. 45 E.H.R.R. 36 (2007).

54. 558 U.S. 310 (2010).

55. Burwell v. Hobby Lobby, 134 S. Ct. 2751, 573 U.S. __ (2014).

protection and promotion. A business organization is self-evidently not a human being, it is not innately valuable, it cannot suffer or love, and it feels no pleasure or happiness. A business organization is rather a mere tool whose sole purpose is the promotion of social welfare by facilitating private commercial relationships. Because business organizations exist solely to serve individuals, any moral rights they may have derive from the rights of the individuals they serve—the owners, employees, and public that authorize and tolerate the organization's existence. It follows that any rights attributable to a business organization must be derived from the individuals for whom the organization acts as an agent.[56] Yet, it does not follow that whatever a person has a right to do as an individual, that person may do through a business organization, because as an entity invented by law to serve certain social welfare functions, the organization's powers and rights are properly limited by law. There may be reasons for attributing some derivative rights to organizations, but IHRL is not currently structured to recognize derivative human rights of this kind. If it were to develop such a doctrine, it would have to be carefully tailored to support the fundamental moral and legal interests for which the organization was created and the manner in which the organization serves those interests. Equally important, the rights recognized would have to be limited for those purposes alone. It is logically coherent to accept that business organizations may have derivative "human" rights to own property, to engage in commercial speech, and to due process of law, while denying the organization rights to other kinds of speech (for example, political or religious) or to the privilege against self-incrimination or double jeopardy.

Conversely, it is logically possible to impose human rights *duties* on business organizations without granting them their own human rights. Any organization can be expected, and is morally bound, to respect human rights without itself being human and having human rights, because the organization acts as an agent of individuals who have such moral duties. It is a general maxim of ethics that, what a person cannot morally do himself, he may not commission others to do for him. The reasons for limiting or not recognizing certain corporate human rights do not apply with equal force to duties to respect the human rights of others.

Whether MNEs should have legal duties to respect human rights is another question. Actually, it is two questions.[57] The first is whether business organizations should be directly bound by IHRL, either in general or when operating in a foreign state. Although business organizations are not parties to human rights treaties, states may agree on their behalf to make such organizations directly liable under international law. The other question is whether states should be obligated by international law to impose liability schemes on their business organizations for violations of IHRL, either in general or when operating in a foreign country. Some human rights instruments already either expressly declare, or have been

56. For an extended explanation of this point, *see* MEIR DAN-COHEN, RIGHTS, PERSONS, AND ORGANIZATIONS 57–78 (1986); *see also* JACK DONNELLY, UNIVERSAL HUMAN RIGHTS IN THEORY AND PRACTICE 25 (2d ed. 2003).

57. *See* Carlos M. Vásquez, *Direct vs. Indirect Obligations of Corporations under International Law*, 43 COLUM. J. TRANSNAT'L L. 927 (2005).

authoritatively interpreted to mean, that states must not only refrain from violating the prohibitions of the instrument, but they also must take positive measures to prevent prohibited violations of substantive rights by private actors, which would include MNEs.[58] Of course, this is not the same as holding MNEs directly accountable under IHRL.

In a move toward direct duties, a number of voluntary corporate codes of conduct in international business have been proposed by various international organizations, such as the Organization for Economic Cooperation and Development, the International Labor Organization, and the European Union.[59] In 2003, the U.N. Human Rights Commission proposed to extend international human rights duties to MNEs through the "Norms on the Responsibilities of Transnational Corporations and Other Business Enterprises with Regard to Human Rights." The Commission's approach combined legally binding state duties to regulate MNEs with direct and legally binding MNE duties:

> 1. States have the primary responsibility to promote, secure the fulfilment of, respect, ensure respect of and protect human rights recognized in international as well as national law, including ensuring that transnational corporations and other business enterprises respect human rights. Within their respective spheres of activity and influence, transnational corporations and other business enterprises have the obligation to promote, secure the fulfilment of, respect, ensure respect of and protect human rights recognized in international as well as national law, including the rights and interests of indigenous peoples and other vulnerable groups.[60]

To implement these requirements, the Norms call on states to establish a legal and administrative framework to ensure that MNEs comply with the Norms.[61] The Norms also set forth a list of more specific duties directly attributable to MNEs. The implementation provisions would require MNEs to adopt internal compliance programs to effectuate the Norms, incorporate the Norms into their commercial and other business agreements, and provide reparations to persons harmed by violations of the Norms. The Norms also propose periodic monitoring and verification of compliance by the United Nations, presumably through an agency to be assembled for that purpose.[62]

58. *See* Knox, *supra* note 5, at 22–24; *see, e.g., Siliadin v. France*, ECHR App. No. 73316/01, Judgment of 26 July 2005, 45 I.L.M. 962, paras. 77–89 (finding a positive obligation to protect vulnerable persons against private forced labor).

59. For a brief history of these efforts, *see* Rosemann, *supra* note 51.

60. U.N. Human Rights Comm'n, Subcomm'n on Promotion & Prot. of Hum. Rts., Norms on the Responsibilities of Transnational Corporations and Other Business Entities with Regard to Human Rights, Aug. 26, 2003, U.N. Doc. E/CN.4/Sub.2/2003/12/Rev.2, para. 1, *approved* Aug. 13, 2003, U.N. Doc. E/CN.4/Sub.2/2003/L.11 at 52 (2003).

61. *Id.* para. 17.

62. *Id.* paras. 15, 16, 18.

The Norms were bitterly criticized by business firms and ultimately rejected by states in the form proposed, but they did furnish the basis for a more modest effort. In 2005, the U.N. Secretary-General appointed John Ruggie as its Special Representative for Business and Human Rights. Ruggie drafted Guiding Principles on Business and Human Rights, which were adopted unanimously by the Human Rights Council in 2011.[63] The Guiding Principles contain most of the same duties as the Norms, although they more clearly separate the duties of states from the purported duties of MNEs. The first ten principles would impose state duties to regulate business firms in a manner that protects the human rights of those exposed to MNE activities. The positive duties apply to states that allow business firms to operate within their territory, but not to states whose corporations operate in foreign countries as well.[64] Although the Council's restraint may encourage faster acceptance of the Principles, the limitation of human rights duties to the territory of the state exonerates capital-exporting states from any legal duty to take serious steps for the prevention and punishment of foreign abuses by corporations formed under their laws and sheltered within their jurisdictions. Foreign investors colluding with dictatorial states to repress the state's own citizens for the benefit of the investment face no mandatory sanction under the Principles. The Principles are, moreover, mostly phrased in hortatory terms ("should") rather than as legally binding commands; Ruggie maintained that business organizations were not yet bound by international law to observe human rights duties.[65] But the Principles were a step toward the recognition of at least indirect duties on MNEs to respect human rights.

The CSR project continues today. Moral injunctions have historically proved impotent in restraining business behavior, and so human rights advocates have taken refuge in the hope that "social norms"—stable community expectations of rights behavior—will somehow restrain business organizations from participating in or instigating human rights violations. For example, in 2003, an article in the *American Journal of International Law* announced that "a growing body of evidence is demonstrating that compliance with human rights standards enhances a company's bottom line."[66] Similarly, in 2009, Ruggie announced:

> As a well established and institutionalized social norm, the corporate responsibility to respect [human rights] exists independently of State duties and variations in national law. There may be situations in which companies have

63. Human Rights Council, Report of the Special Representative of the Secretary-General on the Issue of Human Rights and Transnational Corporations and Other Business Enterprises, U.N. Doc. A/HRC/17/31, Annex (Mar. 21, 2011).

64. Human Rights Council, Report of the Special Representative of the Secretary-General on the Issue of Human Rights and Transnational Corporations and Other Business Enterprises, John Ruggie, U.N. Doc. A/HRC/17/31 (Mar. 21, 2011), *adopted by* H.R. Council Res. 17/4, U.N. Doc. A/HRC/RES/17/4 (July 6, 2011).

65. *See* John Ruggie, *Business and Human Rights: The Evolving International Agenda*, 101 Am. J. Int'l L. 819 (2007).

66. David Weissbrodt & Maria Kruger, *Norms on the Responsibilities of Transnational Corporations and Other Business Enterprises with regard to Human Rights*, 97 Am. J. Int'l L. 901, 921 (2003).

> additional responsibilities. But the responsibility to respect is the baseline norm for all companies in all situations.[67]

Presumably, a business organization that acts at variance with these norms is to suffer some kind of social sanction, such as consumer boycott or blacklisting.[68]

In reality, MNEs do not frequently suffer significant consumer or commercial sanctions for complicity in despoliation of the environment or serious violations of human rights. Wishful thinking about a consistent and effective popular response to such behavior would be harmless if it did not deflect attention from the need to take concrete steps to protect human rights from the depredations of corrupt governments and willing corporate colluders. Directly binding international legal duties are not the only way to accomplish meaningful deterrence and restitution, but they are one potential means to that end. Some international human rights authorities have already considered the possibility of such duties. As noted, the CESCR Committee has asserted that corporations as well as individuals have "responsibilities" to help individuals obtain adequate nutrition and realize their right to health.

A few rationales might be advanced for binding business organizations by IHRL. One is that deterrence of business firm complicity in human rights violations will be more effective if international law imposes liability directly on the firms than if the law relies solely on the intermediation of states themselves. Territorial jurisdiction is a central concept of international law, and although the state of the foreign investor may have nationality jurisdiction over the acts of its business organizations abroad, primary jurisdiction vests with the host state. In cases of alleged human rights violations by MNEs, the host state may claim to be powerless to stop an MNE rampaging through its territory, violating human rights and despoiling the natural environment. It is more common, however, that the host state allegedly either instigated the human rights violations with the complicity or cooperation of a foreign investor,[69] or the foreign investor itself is accused of committing violations of labor or environmental standards in collusion with the host state.[70]

States are not currently obligated by international law to regulate the activities of private MNEs in foreign territory, and, if they were so bound, they might not feel obligated to interrupt a highly profitable foreign business operation based on harms to foreign nationals. Even a state willing to hold its business organizations accountable, however, may face domestic jurisdictional and other obstacles to providing remedies for foreign nationals harmed by the activities of a foreign company in a foreign jurisdiction. A notorious case in point is the Union Carbide gas leak disaster in Bhopal, India. In 1984, an accident at Union Carbide's subsidiary in

67. U.N. Secretary General, Special Representative's Report on the Issue of Human Rights and Transnational Corporations and Other Business Enterprises (Apr. 22, 2009), U.N. Doc. A/HRC/11/13, para. 48.

68. *Cf. id.* para. 46.

69. *See, e.g.*, Wiwa v. Royal Dutch Petroleum, 226 F.3d 88 (2d Cir. 2000); Doe I v. Unocal Corp., 395 F.3d 932 (9th Cir. 2002).

70. *See, e.g.*, Aguinda v. Texaco, Inc., 303 F.3d 470 (2d Cir. 2002).

Bhopal caused toxic gas to leak into the surrounding neighborhoods, causing thousands of deaths and hundreds of thousands of serious injuries. The relatively meager resources of Union Carbide's Indian subsidiary corporation could not possibly have covered the necessary compensation. When Indian victims sought to draw on the U.S. parent company's assets, they found the door blocked by the limited liability of Union Carbide India.[71] Without direct liability of MNEs for violations of internationally recognized human rights, there may be no accessible remedy for victims of human rights violations. Usually, MNEs will use subsidiary companies in the host state to limit the liability of the parent and other affiliated companies, as Union Carbide did. The result may well be that a subsidiary company involved in human rights violations has insufficient assets to satisfy the claims of its victims. Rules holding MNE affiliates, or the parent company, to a duty to post bonds or obtain insurance to compensate any victims of human rights violations could go a long way toward ensuring that remedies are available.[72]

These are prudential reasons for imposing human rights duties on MNEs, but they do not themselves threaten anyone's human rights because, as noted, MNEs themselves exist for prudential reasons in the first place. Regulation of the MNE's activities is merely the cost of legal recognition and limited liability. Of course, it would make no sense to impose precisely the same duties on business organizations that bind states. MNEs and states are not in the same situation with respect to the nationals of the countries in which they operate. Most positive duties to which states have committed—duties to provide sustenance and water, to protect against private violence, to provide free primary education, to ensure the availability of healthcare to all, and so on—would not apply to business organizations, at least not in the same way. Others could apply analogously, though. There is no reason a business organization could not be duty-bound under international law to respect negative rights, such as the right to life, freedom from torture, or freedom of movement, or against coerced labor and slavery. They could equally be bound by a duty to respect and not despoil the natural environment. Most important, given the history of human rights litigation, they could be bound not to assist or collaborate with any state government's denial of internationally recognized human rights.

The details of how a system imposing IHRL duties directly on MNEs could be designed is beyond the scope of this discussion. No doubt it would involve some complications with regard to concurrent jurisdiction of states and the mechanics of setting up an international monitoring and enforcement institution. Here, it suffices to observe that there are no moral or conceptual reasons that business organizations could not have some negative legal duties under IHRL, and there are at least some persuasive theoretical and practical arguments for imposing such duties.

71. *In re* Union Carbide Corp. Gas Plant Disaster at Bhopal, India in Dec. 1984, 809 F.2d 195 (2d Cir. 1987).

72. I am not here suggesting that there are no sound arguments against direct corporate liability under IHRL; I am merely pointing out that the absence of such liability opens a door to systemic in justice. Direct corporate liability is not the only means for addressing that injustice, nor is it necessarily the best such means.

B. FIVE CLASSES OF BENEFICIARIES OF MORAL DUTIES: A TYPOLOGY

In examining how duties could be incorporated into the IHRL system, it will be helpful to classify different types of beneficiaries of moral duties so as to better understand what kinds of legal duties could arise. Clarification here is especially useful because some disagreements about the acceptability of universal legal duties seem to turn on stronger objections to some types of beneficiaries than to others. For our purposes, moral duties will be divided into five general categories: duties to other individuals, duties to groups of individuals (including states), duties to humankind as a whole, duties to oneself, and ecological duties.

1. Duties toward Other Individuals

All laws are social tools designed to achieve results deemed desirable by the political elites who adopt them. Policy goals drive the identification of which results are desirable, and policy goals in turn arise in a liberal community from theories about the public good. The public good that underlies IHRL is the protection and promotion of human dignity. Whatever the theory underlying municipal systems of human rights or civil rights, the theory grounding the *international* system of human rights law is that all persons everywhere have an interest in the protection and promotion of the dignity of all other human beings. The universality of this interest justifies an international system of human rights.

However, perhaps it is more than an "interest." Perhaps it is a duty. Much modern philosophy of human rights is based on an assumption something like this: "[E]ach of us has an obligation to help ensure that every individual has the opportunity to have a minimally decent human life."[73] From this assumption of universal moral duties, it does not necessarily follow that IHRL should ascribe legal duties to individuals to promote human rights. Duties under IHRL could in theory be directly owed by individuals to other individuals, or they could be allocated to institutions representative of those individuals, such as states, international agencies, or business organizations. Neither does it follow that individual moral duties are owed to all other individuals equally, or that individuals do not have equally important moral duties respecting subjects other than individual human beings. As noted earlier, several international instruments mention or purport to prescribe individual moral duties, sometimes in the language of legal obligation. Some of these duties appear to be universal in the sense of applying to every individual human being. Other duties are relational; they apply to only to certain persons and arise by nature of a special relationship between the right holder and duty holder. Still others may not apply to individuals at all.

A. Universal Duties

Moral duties of the Kantian variety are sustained by a categorical imperative based on human dignity, which Kant and his adherents believe arise from two uniquely

73. Allen Buchanan, *Equality and Human Rights*, 4 Politics, Philos. & Econ. 69, 73 (2005).

human characteristics: autonomy and rationality. As such, Kantian moral duties apply to all human beings universally, although how Kant would have treated children, psychotics, or mentally disabled individuals requires some extrapolation. In any case, duties based on human dignity may be formulated broadly or narrowly. The categorical imperative itself is an extremely broad formulation of moral duties.[74]

It is also possible to base moral duties on a less abstract and a priori ground than dignity. Ethically justifiable values are based on concern for the interests of others. Because all human beings have interests, one could base a moral theory on the conclusion that all human beings have duties to take those interests into account. Not all such duties give rise to a right for the interested person, but interests of sufficient importance and universality might be used to justify a duty on principles of justice. All, or nearly all, persons share such interests, including the continuation and prolongation of life and the conditions for what I will call "flourishing," which may generally be taken to include such goods as comfort, social intercourse, enlightenment, privacy, and a sphere of liberty. Such interests may justify a set of minimum moral duties of all persons toward all other persons. Many duties can be justified on either ground. Most philosophers believe that human moral rights correlate to universal moral duties, meaning that every human being has duties to every other human being to observe the others' rights.[75] A duty of this kind is invoked in several of the international human rights declarations and national constitutions noted earlier.

There is a correlation, albeit an imperfect one, between universal moral duties and internationally recognized human rights. For example, IHRL recognizes a right to freedom of movement, which in turn reflects every person's interest in autonomy as well as a prohibition on impeding a person's free movement merely for one's own ends. IHRL accordingly imposes on states certain duties not to impede a person's movement.[76] Obviously, a person kidnaped or falsely imprisoned by another suffers the same infringement of his dignity or harm to his important interests, which in turn justifies recognizing a universal moral duty on the part of individuals not to engage in such activities. This may explain why private persons in every civilized state today have a municipal legal duty not to kidnap or falsely imprison another person. Many internationally recognized human rights seem to correlate to moral duties that apply not just to states, but to everyone.

Certain other internationally recognized human rights do not correlate to universal moral duties—most evidently those duties that by their nature only the state may undertake, such as the duty to provide a fair trial. Other, mostly positive, human rights under international law do not reflect universal moral duties because such duties cannot be justified. For example, all children have a right to a primary education,[77] but every individual does not owe to every child a duty of instruction, fortunately for children.

74. For a broadly Kantian theory of international law, with special emphasis on human rights law, *see* Fernando R. Tesón, A Philosophy of International Law (1998).

75. *See, e.g.*, Alan Gewirth, The Community of Rights 6–19 (1996).

76. *See, e.g.*, UDHR arts. 9, 13; CCPR art. 12.

77. *See, e.g.*, UDHR art. 26; CESCR art. 13.

Finally, not all universal moral duties to others necessarily correlate to someone else's right. For example, an argument could be made that all persons have a duty not to reproduce under circumstances where the resulting child will in all probability face malnutrition, neglect, or abuse. But many believe that someone who does not yet exist cannot have vested rights. It would require a fairly abstruse argument to conclude that a child that has not yet been conceived has a right not to be conceived and born under such conditions. In the alternative, one could argue that society has a strong interest in discouraging such reproduction, but it is not clear that society has a moral right to demand that individuals not reproduce under such unfavorable circumstances. I believe that one could formulate an argument supporting such a right, but inevitably some would not find it compelling. We could nonetheless justify a universal, individual moral duty not to reproduce when one cannot support the resulting child and give him or her a decent chance at a healthy and fulfilling life, on various grounds without positing a nonexistent child's right not to be born or even a societal right not to be burdened with unsupported or severely disadvantaged children. For example, we could argue that all individuals have a moral duty to act responsibly in their decisions to bring sentient life into the world based on the nature of persons as potentially rational and moral actors.[78]

To summarize, individuals have some universal moral duties to others that are credible candidates for legal duties. Not all such moral duties correlate to human rights, legal or moral, and not all human rights recognized in international law correlate to universal moral duties. Some duties rest with states alone for conceptual or moral reasons. We could not justify correlating all human rights under international law to universal legal duties even if we thought it were in some ways desirable. But it is possible to justify imposing universal moral duties that do not correlate to any legal or moral right.

The most straightforward argument that individual duties toward other individuals need not enter the realm of international law is that all civilized states already establish and enforce most such rules in their domestic laws. A state's body of private law is designed specifically to enforce certain individual and corporate duties with regard to other individuals. Of course, states sometimes fall short in their legislation and enforcement machinery, leaving some or even many persons without an effective remedy for violations of their unquestioned moral rights. Laws against spousal abuse and rape, for example, are notoriously underenforced in many countries.[79] Whether imposing individual duties under IHRL is an appropriate solution will be examined in the next chapter.

78. This is not the place to make such an argument. Here, I will merely observe its obvious Kantian overtones. The idea seems to implicate capability theory, but capability theorists have mostly focused so far on deriving rights from capabilities. *See, e.g.*, MARTHA NUSSBAUM, FRONTIERS OF JUSTICE: DISABILITY, NATIONALITY, SPECIES MEMBERSHIP 70 (2006). The role of capabilities in generating moral duties strikes me as a promising subject of exploration.

79. *See, e.g.*, Amici Curiae Brief for the Center for Justice and International Law et al., Jessica Ruth Gonzales v. The United States of America, Inter-Am. Comm'n on Hum. Rts., Petition No. P-1490-5, July 6, 2007 (on file with author).

B. Relational Duties

Although moral human rights are universal within the set of human beings by definition, their correlative duties are not necessarily so. Many moral duties correlative to universal rights apply to specific persons rather than to all persons everywhere, because they arise from relationships between the duty holder and right holder. This asymmetry of rights and duties applies a fortiori to IHRL, in which the addressees of duty are primarily states. For example, the right to participate in government is universal without correlating to a universal duty. It would make no sense for one individual to demand of another that the latter facilitate the former's right to participate in government, by driving her to a distant polling place.

Nor do states universally hold moral or legal duties toward all persons who hold the right. A person may claim only that his own state of nationality respect his right to participate in government, because states hold a duty toward its nationals only. A state has no duty to allow a foreign national to exercise this right within its jurisdiction, because the relationship that justifies the duty is between the nationals of a state and the government that represents those nationals. There would be no moral basis for, say, a Pole to demand the right to participate in elections in Mexico. A state does not benefit from a non-national's duties of loyalty, to pay taxes, or to serve in the military, and so it owes no correlative duty of representation and accountability to a non-national.

Individuals have relational moral duties to other individuals as well. Friends have special moral duties of loyalty and honesty to each other because of their relationship. Although all persons may have a moral duty to care for children to some degree, parents and guardians have a special moral duty because of their relationship to the child. Such duties are universal only in the sense that all persons *in such relationships* hold the correlative duties. As Larry Alexander has observed:

> personal commitments, relations, and identifications morally permit and may require particular persons to have greater moral concern for some than for others, even if the preferred individuals merit no greater moral concern from people in general because they possess no greater moral worth than others. My family and my neighbors are morally no more worthy and deserving of concern than others' families or neighbors, but they are certainly more deserving of my concern.[80]

Alexander's claims may be justified on such grounds as explicit assumption of a duty (for example, by marriage or adoption), a duty arising from past actions with moral consequences (for example, by causing the conception of a child), or shared interests and ability to affect another (for example, neighbors or professional colleagues). The logic underlying this observation applies with equal force to other grounds for moral concern, such as common membership in a social group. This is by no means to suggest that such relationships override all other moral considerations. But special relationships can give rise to moral duties of a type weightier than ordinary universal moral duties.

80. Larry Alexander, *What Makes Wrongful Discrimination Wrong? Biases, Preferences, Stereotypes, and Proxies*, 141 U. Pa. L. Rev. 149, 160 (1992).

As implied in the participation-in-government example, in the realm of international human rights law, nationality is a prominent basis for relational duties. This observation does not apply to states alone. An individual person has reasons for treating others of his nationality with greater moral concern compared to his concern for foreigners in some respects. The division of the world public order into states as administrative divisions means that persons of a common nationality are bound more closely to the same political and economic fate as are persons of different nationalities, and they are more capable of affecting the lives of other nationals than those of non-nationals. It is likely, then, that individuals have moral duties to all other individuals of their nationality that do not apply to foreigners.[81]

Public law is of course a blunt instrument for making nice moral distinctions between individual moral rights and duties. It is possible for IHRL to recognize relational moral duties as legal duties, but only for reasonably homogenized relationship types. Thus, article 27 of the Banjul Charter, the U.N. Convention on the Rights of the Child, and several national constitutions mention duties of parents to their children. Different kinds of parent-child relationships (depending, for example, on the age of the child, whether the child lives with the parent, whether the two are related by blood or adoption, the economic resources of the parents, etc.) may give rise to some nuances in moral duty, but these instruments generally set minimum standards of duty that all parents owe to their children, whatever their circumstances. In some cases, the nuances of culture and human relationships suggest that relational moral duties are too variable for any international legal recognition at all. Some moral duties also simply lack sufficient importance to merit consideration as international legal duties. The duty of loyalty between friends just mentioned is not only too subtle to translate to a legal duty, but insufficiently pressing and important to human interests to assume a cloak of legality while informal motives, pressures, and sanctions can enforce it.

2. Duties toward Groups

Relational duties may apply to either individuals or groups, but all duties to discrete groups are relational in the sense that a person's relationship with the group determines any duties that person may have toward the group as such. A person may owe moral duties to his extended family group to behave in a caring and responsible manner because of the affective, genetic, social, and economic ties that bind the family together. He may owe duties to his local community to do his part to keep it safe, cleanly, and orderly, because he benefits from the efforts of others in the community to do the same.[82] These are not the same as duties owed to specific family members or neighbors, which are relational individual duties discussed above. They are instead owed to the family or community as a group with which the individual in question has a morally relevant relationship.

81. An exception may be made for non-nationals resident in one's state, who have an increased capacity to affect and be affected by those with whom they live in proximity, although not sharing the same nationality.

82. *See* Joel Feinberg, Rights, Justice, and the Bounds of Liberty 135 (1980).

What are commonly called group duties can be usefully divided into duties to all members of the group as individuals and duties toward the group itself as a corporate entity. Only the latter qualify as group duties as I am using the term. This is not to deny that group duties are in fact individual duties in a very important sense. All duties to a group ultimately reduce to a collective duty to the individuals who compose it, in the present and perhaps in some cases past and future.

This of course raises the question of why we should treat group duties as something distinct from duties to individuals in a group. There are two primary reasons. The first is based on the potential absence of individual rights to ground the duty. Duties to pay taxes, contribute military service, answer census questions, or vote in elections are all legal duties to the state with a potential moral grounding that, it could be argued, are difficult to justify as an aggregate of moral duties to other nationals of the state. The duty to the state arises from the benefits the individual receives from the state (protection of his person and property, various government-provided services, transportation and communications infrastructure, the rule of law, etc.). No individual provides these benefits to any other individual in his or her private capacity, and we may even assume *arguendo* that no single individual has a moral right to demand these things of any other individual.

That no individual rights grounds the duty to the group does not in itself require a distinction between individual and group duties, however, because individuals can owe other individuals a duty even though the beneficiary of the duty has no right correlative to the duty. The classic example is the person, *A*, who faces two strangers drowning, *X* and *Y*, and can only save one. Neither *X* nor *Y* has a right to demand that he be the one saved, but *A* may have a moral duty to try to save one of them. We might say that *A* owes the moral duty to the "group" of *X* and *Y*. That duty remains derivative of the duties toward *X* and *Y* as individuals, in the sense that he owes it to each of them to try to save that person. We might conclude that, if he tries to save neither, he violates the duty to each individual. However, suppose that *A* had already decided that, if he were going to save one of them, he would save *X*. When he fails even to try to save *X* or *Y*, in what sense has he violated a duty to *Y*? *Y* would not have been saved in either case. By acting to save *X*, *A* is justified in letting *Y* drown, because saving *X* fulfills his moral duty to the group of *X* and *Y*. It makes sense, then, to speak of duties to the group when the individual in question has a definite duty to some or all members of a group, but the identity of those members is indeterminate.

The other case in which it makes sense to speak of group duties is when such a duty would solve a collective action problem.[83] This might occur, for example, when, irrespective of any rights, no individual has a sufficient interest in any other individual's behavior to hold the former to a moral duty. For example, although all persons may have an interest in an accurate census because it determines such benefits as political representation or the allocation of public funds, no individual has a sufficient interest in any other individual's census participation to hold that individual to a duty. However, just as small inefficiencies can aggregate to create massive inefficiencies, so can small interests aggregate over large populations to create weighty group interests. Although no individual may have a powerful interest in

83. *See generally* MANCUR OLSON, THE LOGIC OF COLLECTIVE ACTION (rev. ed. 1971).

the relevant act, and the duty to the group is no greater than the sum of the duties to its individual members, that sum is quite elevated because of the number of members. In a state of any size, the aggregate of even very weak duties owed to all nationals of that state may provide a strong reason to act in the interests of the group members. To the extent individuals owe a powerful moral duty to a group such as the state, transmuting the moral duty into a legal one to the state instead of each individual national may serve administrative efficiency when the individual duties are weak by depriving numerous individuals, each with a very small interest in the observance of the duty, of standing to complain of that duty's violation. Instead, the state assumes the role of beneficiary and enforces the duty itself, solving a collective action problem and also weeding out duplicative or trivial complaints. In such cases, redirecting the duty toward the group can serve important interests that would not justify a duty toward individual group members.

Municipal criminal laws furnish a good example. These impose duties toward the state to act in accordance with the laws; with some exceptions, criminal laws do not directly impose duties toward the victim. A person who criminally harms an individual violates a moral duty toward that individual, but he violates a legal duty toward the state.[84] The victim may have a right to seek to vindicate his interests through a tort action against the criminal, but the (civil) legal duty to every individual not to harm him by criminal acts is conceptually and usually doctrinally distinct from the legal duty to the state not to violate the law. That explains why violations of law that harm no individual, such as intoxicated driving that does not result in an accident, can still be crimes. No individual might be threatened by any other individual intoxicated driver, but members of society as a whole have an interest that each other individual abstain when driving. The reverse is also true: a tortious harm caused to an individual may violate a duty to the victim and create a duty of compensation without also breaching any duty to the state. In most states, a person has a duty of reasonable care to all individuals foreseeably affected by the person's acts. A tortious breach of this duty need not violate any criminal law, especially if it resulted from negligence rather than malice.

This raises the question of why, if individual legal duties to the state are so common, there is any need to elevate them to international legal duties. All states already prohibit treason against themselves by law; elevating the legal duty to an international one would not seem to add anything worthwhile. States are usually able to enforce private duties respecting themselves without the need for international assistance. Only when the machinery of government breaks down—in "failed states"—does it become necessary for international law to assist in the enforcement of individual legal duties to the state. In such cases, the most problematical under-enforced duties are almost always duties to observe individual human rights—as in Somalia, Sudan, and the Democratic Republic of the Congo. So, despite the efforts to incorporate individual duties into, or as a complement to, IHRL, the case for such duties is weak.

For this reason, arguments that individuals should owe international legal duties to the state as such, separate from the aggregate interests of the nationals of the state, offer no advantage for the world public order and instead tend to invite state

84. *See* Henry T. Terry, *The Correspondence of Duties and Rights*, 25 Yale L.J. 171, 174 (1916).

abuse of individual rights. Left on a level of vague moral injunction, such assertions are unexceptionable. For example, one writer has claimed that "all right holders have responsibility to participate in and contribute to society."[85] The coherence of this statement depends on what exactly is meant by "participate in and contribute to." Conceived broadly enough, it merely suggests a duty to cooperate in the development of society as a collectivity. Used as a basis for qualifying internationally recognized human rights, such a formulation easily lends itself to repressive policies that curtail individual liberty for the benefit of those holding the levers of power. It is not a great leap from an individual duty to contribute to society to an individual duty to sacrifice the individual's own interests to the interests of others in society whenever the state or majority deems such sacrifice to be in its own interests, or the interests of its most influential constituencies.

With regard to moral duties toward private groups, individuals may have moral duties toward groups of which they are a member based on the group's role in assisting individuals to develop an identity and relate to others beneficially within the group.[86] International law increasingly recognizes that groups have certain rights precisely because of their importance to individual identity and self-fulfillment. However, the case for internationally recognized individual legal duties toward groups will rarely be persuasive for the same reasons and a few additional ones. Municipal legislation and enforcement generally protect the interests of groups from privately caused harms. Only when the state fails to protect groups against private violations of their interests can a case be made that private duties toward such groups need recognition and enforcement at the international level. Such failures occur often enough, but it does not necessarily follow that the international recognition of a private duty is an appropriate solution. More tellingly, many persons are members of groups that have played some role in identity formation and personal fulfillment without having strong moral duties toward the group. What fundamental duties should international law recognize a person has toward his bowling league, video game guild or clan, or neighborhood homeowner's association?

In contrast, international law now establishes that states owe legal duties to groups as well as individuals. Some international human rights instruments establish or propose positive duties without clear reference to correlative rights of any individual. The most prominent examples are certain duties toward indigenous societies and minority groups. However, state duties toward groups need not correlate to a right. For example, it would be possible for a state to have a legal duty to protect indigenous tribes from cultural dissolution by encouraging the teaching and use of an indigenous language or ceremony without the group, or any individual in it, having a right to force others, or to have others compelled, to learn the language or practice the ceremony.

In a sense, duties to prevent discrimination are group duties, insofar as they pertain to discrimination against members of a specific group qua group members. When an employer refuses to hire employees in a certain class, that person is

85. Audrey R. Chapman, *Reintegrating Rights and Responsibilities*, *in* International Rights and Responsibilities for the Future 3, 15 (Kenneth W. Hunter & Timothy Mack eds., 1996).

86. *See* Kwame A. Appiah, The Ethics of Identity (2005).

violating a moral right not just of the job applicant who is refused, but all members of the class, who suffer disrespect of their identity as group members. The full extent of the nondiscrimination duty, like duties toward individuals, does not necessarily entail a correlative right in members of the group. A nondiscrimination duty is a duty that does not always implicate a correlative right in the group itself. For example, CEDAW provides in article 5(a) that states must take appropriate measures to:

> modify the social and cultural patterns of conduct of men and women, with a view to achieving the elimination of prejudices and customary and all other practices which are based on the idea of the inferiority or the superiority of either of the sexes or on stereotyped roles for men and women.

It does not necessarily follow that individuals have a correlative right that the state infringes by failing to take such measures. It is possible that the *group* of individuals (men or women, respectively) have such a right, and that individual members of the group could have standing to assert a violation of the right on behalf of the group members. However, it is not *necessary* for the group members to have such a right, as long as there is some reliable means of enforcing the state's duty. Standing to challenge the breach of a duty does not necessarily depend on the challenger holding a right correlative to that duty. For reasons of convenience and economy, states may require a showing of a right, but there is no theoretical reason that such a showing should be necessary. In the context of international law, there is in particular no reason states that are parties to a human rights treaty such as CEDAW should not be able to challenge another state party's failure to implement its article 5(a) duties, even though the duty to modify social and cultural patterns does not give rise to a correlative right for the challenging state. Nothing in CEDAW article 29, which provides for dispute settlement relating to the interpretation or application of the convention, accordingly imposes a condition that a state invoking dispute settlement must show that one of its rights has been violated, as opposed to the rights of the nationals of the respondent state.

3. Duties toward Humankind as a Whole

It may seem anomalous to treat as sui generis duties to humankind when they could be classified as a special case of individual duties (specifically, duties to all individuals that do not arise out of a special relationship to those individuals) or group duties (the group here comprising all living human beings). The type of duty under consideration here is not a group duty as I have defined it, however, because groups are by definition a subset of humankind as a whole, and specifically a subset with which the individual has a morally relevant relationship. As for universal duties toward individuals, they differ from the genus of duties I am describing in two respects.

First, like group duties, duties toward humankind are not necessarily directed toward every single individual, but may be fulfilled if some subset of members of humankind benefit from performance of the duties, and they may be violated if some subset of members of humankind suffers due to a breach of the duties. Perhaps the best-known example of such general duties are virtues. Virtues may be conceived as duties to oneself, but they may also (or alternatively) be conceived as duties toward humankind generally. A universal moral duty to act generously toward others or charitably toward those in need, for example, does not mean that any specific individual has the right to demand acts of generosity or charity from a duty holder.[87] However, a duty holder who never acts generously toward *any* individual could be conceived as having breached a duty to humankind.

In public international law, direct individual duties toward humankind have been incorporated into the *corpus iuris* through international criminal law and international humanitarian law through the concept of "crimes against humanity." Such crimes are considered to be directed, not only against the dignity of their individual targets, but against the dignity of human beings in general and perhaps the humanity (in the sense of qualifying as a rational, moral actor) of the perpetrators themselves. In other words, some kinds of acts seem to deny the equal value of human life and flourishing in their victims, and the actor's feelings of fraternity with the human race.

Crimes against humanity were first defined in the Nuremberg Charter to include a limited list of the most serious wrongs:

> murder, extermination, enslavement, deportation, and other inhumane acts committed against any civilian population, before or during the war, or persecutions on political, racial, or religious grounds in execution of or in connection with any crime within the jurisdiction of the Tribunal, whether or not in violation of domestic law of the country where perpetrated.[88]

The meaning of the term has morphed since the Nuremberg trials to become more inclusive and focused. It is more inclusive in that new candidates for crimes against humanity, such as committing aggressive warfare or instituting apartheid, are now included. It is more focused in requiring more explicitly that such acts be "widespread or systematic" to qualify as crimes against humanity.[89]

Although some have impugned the coherence of this idea as adopted in international legal doctrine,[90] it has its committed defenders,[91] and in any case the idea was codified in the Rome Statute of the International Criminal Court after having become well entrenched in customary international law. The necessity of a duty-based definition of crimes against humanity is evident from the kinds of acts

87. *Cf.* FEINBERG, *supra* note 82, at 139.

88. Charter of the International Military Tribunal, Aug. 8, 1945, art. 6(c), 59 Stat. 1544, 1547, 82 U.N.T.S. 279, 288 (1945), *reprinted in* 1 INT'L MILITARY TRIBUNAL, NUREMBERG, TRIAL OF THE MAJOR WAR CRIMINALS BEFORE THE INTERNATIONAL MILITARY TRIBUNAL, NUREMBERG, 14 NOVEMBER 1945–1 OCTOBER 1946, at 10 (1947).

89. Rome Statute of the International Criminal Court art. 7(1), United Nations Diplomatic Conference of Plenipotentiaries on the Establishment of an International Criminal Court, July 17, 1998, art. 7(1) U.N. Doc. A/CONF.183/9.

90. *See generally* Charles Chernor Jalloh, *What Makes a Crime against Humanity a Crime against Humanity*, 28 AM. U. INT'L L. REV. 381 (2013); Larissa van den Herik & Elies van Sliedregt, *Removing or Reincarnating the Policy Requirement of Crimes against Humanity: An Introductory Note*, 23 LEIDEN J. INT'L L. 825 (2010).

91. *E.g.*, Christopher Macleod, *Towards a Philosophical Account of Crimes against Humanity*, 21 EUR. J. INT'L L. 281 (2010); David Luban, *A Theory of Crimes against Humanity*, 29 YALE

prohibited. Suppose a state, group, or political official were to decide to engage in the wholesale slaughter of the state's population, ostensibly based on disagreement with the political ideology of a large part of that population, but in reality the killing is extremely widespread and arbitrary—the Khmer Rouge purges in Cambodia could serve as an example. The killings violate the human right to life of many individuals, and to the extent that the killings are based on political beliefs, they also violate the rights to freedom of conscience and to participation in government, and against discrimination. But in what sense can an individual claim that, apart from and in addition to these rights, he has a right not to be a victim of genocide, or even a right to be a member of a class not targeted for genocide? The rationale for treating crimes against humanity as exceptional is less related to the individual's interest in life and equal treatment, or even to the magnitude of harm caused, but rather to the actor's intentions and the nature of his behavior as a denial of the equal worth of human life and flourishing. Crimes against humanity are more comprehensible, then, as a general duty toward humankind to respect the equal dignity of all persons by not engaging in the prescribed acts. The extreme moral turpitude and large-scale harm caused by the acts justify treating them as criminal offenses under international law on the same reasoning that justifies states in treating certain immoral and harmful acts as crimes against the state under municipal law.

The second difference between duties toward humanity and toward all individuals is conceptual. Duties toward all individuals apply only to living persons. Duties toward humanity could encompass future generations as well. Genocide, enslavement, and segregation and persecution of racial, ethnic, political, and religious minorities impoverish the human race by eliminating some of its diversity, furnishing a deplorable example for the future, and reducing the respect of all persons in the moral status and rationality of the human species. The elimination or reduction of the genetic, cultural, and intellectual diversity that such minorities contribute to humanity constitutes a harm to future generations.

Some philosophers have argued that future generations—persons of indeterminate identity who do not yet exist but will in the future—have "rights" against currently living persons.[92] The basic idea is that future generations will certainly exist, and they will have interests that the present generation can affect. If that is correct, it may be possible to contrive an argument that at least some duties toward humankind, in the sense of future generations of humankind, are not independent, but correlate to rights. As will be discussed in the next chapter, there are reasons to doubt that attributing moral rights to future generations is philosophically coherent or practically feasible. In any case, from both legal and political standpoints,

J. Int'l L. 85 (2004); Beth Van Schaack, *The Definition of Crimes against Humanity: Resolving the Incoherence*, 37 Colum. J. Transnat'l L. 787 (1999).

92. *E.g.*, Joel Feinberg, *The Rights of Animals and Unborn Generations*, *in* Philosophy and Environmental Crisis 43, 64–66 (William T. Blackstone ed., 1974); *see also* Richard P. Hiskes, The Human Right to a Green Future (2009). Others conceive of the issue as one of justice rather than rights. *See, e.g.*, Axel Gosseries & Lukas H. Meyer, Intergenerational Justice (2009); Janna Thompson, Intergenerational Justice (2009); Joerg Chet Tremmel, A Theory of Intergenerational Justice (2009).

relying on a rights paradigm to protect the interests of future generations is highly problematic. The question may be considered irrelevant from a practical standpoint, though, if it is possible for presently living persons to have moral and legal duties toward future generations of humanity.

There are many possible reasons for accepting moral duties toward future generations. Among these reasons, two are especially persuasive. First, as observed by advocates of future generations having rights, such persons will certainly exist and have the same dignity and fundamental interests in life, freedom, comfort, enlightenment, and so forth as do presently existing generations. Insofar as moral duties are based on respect for the dignity and interests of all persons, such duties must be projected into the future to protect those interests. Second, future generations will be direct descendants of presently living persons, and at a minimum all persons bear significant responsibilities toward the human beings that they personally create, as well as the foreseeable (because inevitable) consequences of creating those human beings—the births of grandchildren, great-grandchildren, ad infinitum being not the least of these consequences. Other reasons could be advanced as well, but these furnish an adequate ethical basis for treating the interests of future generations as sufficiently important to ground duties in the present generation.

The moral reasons provide a basis for international legal duties toward future generations, just as the moral reasons for individual rights provide a basis for IHRL. International legal duties toward future generations could include the preservation of human cultural diversity and culturally significant objects, the preservation of the natural environment, and the transmission of an economy not excessively burdened by debt. Indeed, public international law already seems to recognize and protect some such interests, under the rubric of "world cultural heritage," "the common heritage of humankind," and similar terms in a network of international treaties and declarations.[93]

4. Duties toward Oneself

Martin Luther King, Jr. famously said: "We not only have the right to be free, we have a duty to be free."[94] The right to be free is a right against other persons who would control us excessively; the duty to be free is, at a minimum, a duty one has to oneself. Individuals cannot hold moral or legal rights against themselves in any

93. *E.g.*, UNESCO Universal Declaration on Cultural Diversity, Nov. 2, 2001, UNESCO Doc. 31C/Res 25, Annex 1 (2001); UNESCO Convention concerning the Protection of the World Cultural and Natural Heritage, Nov. 16, 1972, UNESCO Records of the General Conference, 17th Sess., vol. 1, at 135, *available at* http://whc.unesco.org/archive/convention-en.pdf; UNESCO Convention for the Safeguarding of the Intangible Cultural Heritage, Oct. 17, 2003, Doc. No. MISC/2003/CLT/CH/14, *available at* http://www.wipo.int/wipolex/en/other_treaties/text.jsp?file_id=217653; Council of Europe Framework Convention on the Value of Cultural Heritage for Society, CETS No. 199, Oct. 27, 2005; European Convention on Offences Relating to Cultural Property, ETS No. 119, June 23, 1985.

94. Martin Luther King, Jr., Address to MIA Mass Meeting at Holt Street Baptist Church, Montgomery, Ala., Nov. 14, 1956, *transcription printed in* 3 The Papers of Martin Luther King, Jr. 424, 428 (1997).

meaningful sense, however. Both kinds of rights are social tools; they are means for demanding that others—the duty holders—respect the right.

In contrast, a person can have a moral duty to himself. Kant and Locke both developed theories incorporating the notion that persons have natural ethical duties to themselves. Locke never developed a comprehensive ethical theory, but his political philosophy denied a person the right to kill himself or submit to arbitrary power unless in service of some "nobler use."[95] Kant's more developed theory suggested a dignity-based argument for duties to oneself. The doctrine of the categorical imperative developed by Kant requires in one of its formulations that all persons act in a manner that would establish a universal rule for others to follow. Kant argued that human practical reason dictates the categorical imperative as a rule of moral behavior, because humans as moral agents have ultimate inherent value (dignity) and so must always be treated as ends unto themselves rather than merely as a means to a person's goals. It follows, Kant argued, that what properly constrains a person to behave morally must not be fear of sanctions or the thirst for benefits, but his own practical reason. Practical reason establishes that all duties proceed from a person's duty (to himself) to cultivate his own moral perfection, and so all duties to others arise from this duty to oneself.[96]

It is unnecessary to subscribe entirely to Kant's theory of intrinsic human dignity to accept the possibility of duties to oneself. In addition, the recognition that human beings are intrinsically valuable implies additional duties to oneself as a self-valuing being, such as a duty to take reasonable steps to maintain one's health.[97] Some human rights authorities have accordingly justified restrictions on certain human rights based on the concept that their exercise can impair the very dignity that human rights law as a whole is designed to protect. Thus, the U.N. Human Rights Committee accepted France's justification of a prohibition on "dwarf-tossing" events as a form of entertainment on the ground inter alia that such

95. 2 John Locke, Two Treatises of Civil Government ch. 2 (1690).

96. Immanuel Kant, The Metaphysics of Morals 543 (Mary J. Gregor trans., 1999) (1797). In his *Rechtslehre* passages explaining duties to oneself, Kant rather overshoots the mark:

> The capacity to set oneself an end—any end whatsoever—is what characterizes humanity (as distinguished from animality). Hence there is also bound up with the end of humanity in our own person the rational will, and so the duty, to make ourselves worthy of humanity by culture in general, by procuring or promoting the *capacity* to realize all sorts of possible ends, so far as this is to be found in the human being himself. In other words, the human being has a duty to cultivate the crude predisposition of his nature, by which the animal is first raised into the human being.

Id. at 522–23; *see id.* at 565. This contradicts Kant's own theory when he argued that what characterizes humanity is specifically the capacity to act rationally as a moral being. *See id.* at 518. If it were as Kant suggests in the quoted passage, then persons would have a duty to cultivate the capacity to murder and pillage, because these are ends one can set for oneself (albeit not by practical reason).

97. If one rejects the concept of human dignity, then the case for duties to oneself can still be made along hedonistic or Epicurean lines, but IHRL is founded on a presupposition of human dignity, so these lines of reasoning will not be explored here.

treatment was degrading to the dignity of the individuals involved.[98] Similarly, the European Commission on Human Rights has held that prostitution could be banned on dignity grounds, and the Strasbourg Court determined that certain voluntary, private sadomasochistic practices could be criminally prohibited on the same basis:

> *L'ingérence aurait également été nécessaire pour la protection de la morale car des actes de torture, infligés dans les circonstances de la cause, ne sauraient pas être tolérés dans une société démocratique, dont le respect que les êtres humains se doivent constituerait une valeur essentielle.*[99]
>
> The interference would have been equally necessary for the protection of public morals because acts of torture inflicted under the circumstances of the case, should not be tolerated in any democratic society, in which respect for human beings must constitute an essential value.

A rationale for such duties that does not rely on a priori reasoning is that, if a belief in human dignity is premised on human rationality and moral capacity, then it follows that all persons have a duty to struggle to overcome their irrationality and immoral impulses in order to justify social recognition of their value. The duty to oneself would be based on the advantages to oneself of cultivating one's capacities to increase one's merit for social reasons. Even apart from practical self-interest, a person may have a duty to himself to cultivate whatever characteristics make him valuable as a moral being—the pursuit of such virtues as charity, caring for others, enlightenment, and courage.

That said, arguments for moral duties to oneself face a difficult transition to legal duties, because dictating to adults what virtues they should cultivate is at odds with most liberal theories of the state. Many consider it to be paternalistic and misguided. The case for legal duties to oneself becomes still weaker in the international arena, where cultural pluralism justifies some flexibility in conceptions of virtues when harm to another person is not at stake. This point will therefore not pursued further.

A related question is whether states can have duties to themselves. Vattel argued that they could at least have a duty to preserve themselves.[100] However, this concept of group duties to themselves suffers from a reification of the state so common in the eighteenth century. In Vattel's conception, the state's duty to preserve itself arises from its "right" to continue in existence as a state. But, just as one cannot have a right against oneself, a state cannot have a right against itself. Any such right to exist derives from the rights of self-determination of its constituent population. Once a population no longer wishes to associate together as a state, there is no longer a "state" to claim a right to exist. If the state's duty to preserve its existence is

98. Wackenheim v. France, Communication No. 854/1999, U.N. Doc. CCPR/C/75/D/754/1999 (2002).

99. F. c. Suisse, App. No. 11680/85, Eur. Hum. Rts. Comm'n, D.R. 55, at 178, Mar. 10, 1988; K.A. & A.D. c. Belgique, App. Nos. 42758/98 & 45558/99, para. 67, Eur. Ct. H.R. (2005).

100. Emerich de Vattel, Le droit des gens § 16 (1758).

derivative, then, it is not a duty to itself at all. The same line of reasoning denies that states can have any other non-derivative duties to themselves.

5. Ecological Duties

An ethical theory may well support duties of either or both of two kinds toward animals, plants, or other living beings: direct duties and derivative duties. If one accepts that any living being that has interests is a legitimate subject of moral concern, then it is possible to have direct duties toward such living beings. An argument has even been made that nonliving natural features have rights, a subject I will address below. However, those who deny the possibility of direct duties toward nonhuman animals may still acknowledge the possibility that persons have moral duties toward animals or the natural environment that are instrumental to, and therefore derivative of, the interests other persons (including future generations) take in them.

A. Duties Directly toward Nonhuman Animals

To determine whether it makes sense to speak of direct duties toward animals or the natural environment, we should begin with the easiest case—sentient animals. A surprising number of theorists deny that any animals can have rights. One of the most often invoked bases for human rights is the concept of intrinsic human dignity.[101] "Dignity" in the human rights context refers to ultimate and persistent, inherent value—an idea that before the foundation of the international human rights system had been developed most fully by Kant. Kant considered dignity as something not just valuable, but above all price. The dignity of human beings meant that they could never be treated merely as means to someone else's end, but must always be considered an end unto themselves.[102] Kant's philosophy rejects the possibility of duties to animals other than human beings, because his ethics is premised on the uniqueness of humans as reasoning beings. A person's duty to any subject, Kant claims, "is moral constraint by that subject's will."[103] Thus, although Kant believes in duties "with regard to" animals or inanimate objects, he characterizes these as duties to oneself to act in a certain way toward these objects.[104]

However, many philosophers and jurists have made strong cases for recognizing the moral rights of nonhuman animals.[105] In most cases, these arguments are

101. *E.g.*, UDHR pmbl., art. 1; CCPR pmbl., art. 1; CESCR pmbl.; Convention on Cluster Munitions, May 30, 2008, pmbl., Doc. CCM/77, 48 I.L.M. 357 (2009). The concept of "dignity" has in some cases even been invoked as a "general principle of law" that justifies derogating from voluntary individual freedoms. *See, e.g.*, *Omega v. Oberbürgermeisterin der Stadt Bonn*, Eur. Ct. Just. Case No. C-36/02, [2004] E.C.R. I-9609.

102. *See* Immanuel Kant, *Groundwork of the Metaphysics of Morals*, *in* Practical Philosophy 37, 84 (Mary J. Gregor trans., 1996) (1785).

103. Kant, *supra* note 96, at 563.

104. *Id.* at 563–64.

105. *E.g.*, Jeremy Bentham, Introduction to the Principles of Morals and Legislation ch. 17 (1789); Peter Singer, Animal Liberation (updated ed. 2009); Paola Cavalieri, The

dignity-based or rights-based in some way. For example, in a 2000 case, the High Court of Kerala in India viewed the concept of dignity as justifying animal rights.[106] Martha Nussbaum, in proposing a "capabilities-based approach" to the moral position of animals, treats their inherent dignity and interests as giving rise to "entitlements" or "rights."[107] Even utilitarian arguments tend frequently invoke the animal's interest in avoiding unnecessary suffering,[108] which, if not an assertion of rights, comes very close to it. Nonetheless, not everyone is persuaded by these arguments.

Some argue against animal rights for purely pragmatic reasons by, for instance, claiming that attributing legal rights to animals "would have serious, detrimental impacts on human rights and freedoms" because of the limitations that animal rights would necessarily put on the human ability to treat animals as property.[109] This is a practical and not a moral argument, however, and at best a speculative one. The same argument could have been used by slave owners against the recognition of the rights of enslaved human beings; inconvenience to a person perpetrating an immoral practice does not excuse, much less justify, the practice.

Many others over the years have made out reasoned moral cases against animal rights. Most opponents of such rights rely on biological or psychological characteristics supposedly unique to humans. The most common traits used to justify an anthropocentric view of rights relies on greater-than-average animal intelligence, exceptional capacity to suffer, "free will" or the ability to make "choices," purposeful behavior, membership in a community, possession of moral sense or ability to fulfill moral duties, language, or some combination of these.[110] Onora O'Neill, for

Animal Question (2001); David DeGrazia, Taking Animals Seriously (1996); Steven Wise, Rattling the Cage (2000); Tom Regan, The Case for Animal Rights (1983); Tom Regan, *The Moral Basis of Vegetarianism*, 5 Can. J. Phil. 181 (1975); Feinberg, *supra* note 92, at 43, 49–50; Christine M. Korsgaard, *Facing the Animal You See in the Mirror*, 16 Harv. Rev. Philo. 2 (2007); Steven M. Wise, *Hardly a Revolution: The Eligibility of Nonhuman Animals for Dignity Rights in a Liberal Democracy*, 22 Vt. L. Rev. 793 (1998). In her short treatise on animals, Mary Midgley deliberately renounces using the word "right." Mary Midgley, Animals and Why They Matter 62–63 (1983). However, her reason—that the word "right" ambiguously embraces both very general and very specific interests—seems to me to misapprehend the semantics at issue. The scope of any concept needs to be defined with reasonable precision to be either morally justifiable or legally enforceable. Any extremely broad use of a term such as "right" (in her example, a "right to life, liberty, and the pursuit of property") is rhetorical, and gives too little guidance to qualify as a statement of moral or legal right. We can agree that rights phrased too broadly will fail a moral or legal justification without rejecting the term "right" when used with adequate precision. The same is true of any other language we choose to employ. We could just as easily posit an "interest in life, liberty and the pursuit of property" or a "duty of equal treatment," or a "concern to avoid suffering," and it would be equally overbroad and unhelpful unless adequately defined.

106. Nair v. Union of India, Kerala High Ct., Case No. 155/1999, Judgment of June 6, 2000, AIR 2000 Ker 340.

107. Nussbaum, *supra* note 78, at 337, 376–77, 392, 398–99.

108. Singer, *supra* note 105, at 7–8.

109. David R. Schmahmann & Lori J. Polacheck, *The Case against Animal Rights*, 22 B.C. Envtl. Affairs L. Rev. 747 (1995).

110. Most notably, Joseph Raz, The Morality of Freedom 177 (1986); W.D. Lamont, Principles of Moral Judgment 83–85 (1946); Carl Wellman, Real Rights 176 (1995);

example, has doubted whether the case for animal rights can be convincing: "It is not clear how very *general* arguments for the unimportance of the differences between human and non-human animals can be used to establish a very *selective* parity of rights and obligations."[111] Although so far no philosopher—O'Neill included[112]—has formulated a compelling case against animal rights, there is widespread opposition among many philosophers to animal rights as a concept.

Advocates for animal interests have a variety of answers, ranging from impugning the rationality of opposing arguments and attacking their a priori reasoning and reliance on morally irrelevant criteria; to pointing out false or unproven assumptions about animal intelligence, emotions, biology, and social behavior on which such arguments are based; to pointing out inconsistencies in their reasoning regarding the rights of animals and the rights of human beings incapable of or impaired in rational thought, such as infants, the mentally disabled, and senile persons. They also point out that many morally relevant considerations arise from our animal nature, such as desires for life, reproduction, social intercourse, and the avoidance of pain, rather than our rational nature. Many of these arguments are well-developed, and after more than four decades of sustained and intense effort, the numerous opponents of animal rights have been able to offer no especially persuasive reason that humans should have all the intrinsic rights and animals should have none.

Nevertheless, even for those who find the case for animal rights unpersuasive, it does not follow that human beings have no duties directly toward them. Animals may not be capable of making conscious and elaborate plans for the future, but any sentient being is capable of suffering and experiencing pleasure, and any social animal seeks and enjoys social relations by definition. Some animals may even contemplate the past, and many of the more intelligent species certainly contemplate

FEINBERG, *supra* note 82, at 159; RAYMOND G. FREY, INTERESTS AND RIGHTS: THE CASE AGAINST ANIMALS (1980); THOMAS SCANLON, WHAT WE OWE TO EACH OTHER 185–86 (1998); H.J. McCloskey, *Rights*, 15 PHIL. Q. 121, 124 (1965); Michael Meyer, *The Simple Dignity of Sentient Life: Speciesism and Human Dignity*, 32 J. SOC. PHIL. 115, 121 (2001); Ruth Cigman, *Death, Misfortune and Species Inequality*, 10 PHIL. & PUB. AFFAIRS 47, 47–60 (1981); Roger Brownsword, *Bioethics Today, Bioethics Tomorrow*, 17 NOTRE DAME J.L. ETHICS & PUB. POLICY 15, 21 (2003); Michael Levin, *Animal Rights Evaluated*, 37 HUMANIST 14 (1977); Michael Fox, *Animal Liberation: A Critique*, 88 ETHICS 134 (1978); Jan Narveson, *Animal Rights*, 7 CAN. J. PHIL. 161 (1977); Gary E. Jones & Clifton Perry, *On Animal Rights*, 1 INT'L J. APPLIED PHIL. 39 (1982); Carl Cohen, *The Case for the Use of Animals in Biomedical Research*, 315 N.E. J. MED. 866 (1986); Michael Wreen, *In Defense of Speciesism*, 5(3) Art. 4 ETHICS & ANIMALS (1984).

111. *See, e.g.*, Onora O'Neill, *Environmental Values, Anthropocentrism and Speciesism*, 6 ENVTL. VALUES 127, 138 (1997).

112. To begin with, O'Neill's argument confuses equal interests with equal consideration. Nobody claims that animals have moral duties or the same rights as human beings. Similar interests justify similar treatment, and morally relevant differences justify different treatment. If animals have an interest in living and being free from torture no different from that of human beings, then a strong case can be made, and has been made by others, for giving them corresponding rights. If animals have no interest in freedom of expression or an education, it follows that we would not attribute those rights to animals. Selectivity in no way suggests that the justification for animal rights is incompatible with the justification for human rights.

the future. At the very least, these capabilities justify some moral concern for such beings. Moral concern, in turn, gives rise to moral duties toward animals. It is for this reason that civilized states prohibit by law gratuitous cruelty to animals. Animals may or may not have rights under such municipal laws, but humans in all civilized societies have legal duties toward them. There is no immediately apparent, principled reason that either states or individuals, or both, could not have duties toward animals under international law as well. There may be practical reasons for limiting such duties, however, and these will be discussed in the next chapter.

B. Duties Directly toward Plants

If we can have duties toward animals, why not plants, and if plants, why not forests, kelp beds, and other ecosystems? Most arguments against plant rights echo those against animal rights, which, as noted, have not proved especially cogent. However, the absence of sentience is a very important distinction between plants and animals. From this, many conclude that plants cannot have interests and, therefore, rights. Joel Feinberg argues:

> Trees are not the sorts of beings who have their "own sakes," despite the fact that they have biological propensities. Having no conscious wants or goals of their own, trees cannot know satisfaction or frustration, pleasure or pain.... The reason is that an interest, however the concept is finally to be analyzed, presupposes at least rudimentary cognitive equipment. Interests are compounded out of *desires* and *aims*, both of which presuppose something like *belief*, or cognitive awareness.[113]

Feinberg denies that plants have interests arising from real needs by comparing plant needs to the "needs" of mechanical objects such as an automobile. Just as a plant needs water, minerals, and sunlight, a car "needs gas and oil to function," but we would not say a car has interests.[114]

Whatever the merits of the argument in favor of plant rights, Feinberg's refutation is unconvincing. In comparing inanimate objects to plants, he has confused semantics with reality. Cars have no needs because they are created by human beings and exist purely to serve as their instrumental tools. The "need" we impute to the car to function is rhetorical. Cars do not need to function; human beings desire that cars function. The automobile does not need gasoline, the human driver needs the automobile to have gasoline so he can use it. If a human being intends to disassemble the automobile to salvage its parts, he would not say it needs gasoline. He would say it needs to be drained of gasoline.

A plant, in contrast, needs sunlight, water, and minerals independent of human subjectivity, because it requires these things in order to fulfill its teleology, which is to say its genetic demands. This point is reminiscent of Butler's devil's advocate:

> What is it to be intelligent if to know how to do what one wants to do, and to do it repeatedly, is not to be intelligent? Some say that the rose-seed does not want

113. Feinberg, *supra* note 105, at 52.

114. *Id.* at 54.

> to grow into a rosebush. Why, then, in the name of all that is reasonable, does it grow? Likely enough it is unaware of the want that is spurring it on to action. We have no reason to suppose that a human embryo knows that it wants to grow into a baby, or a baby into a man.[115]

As Butler suggests, even the most rudimentary understanding of biology shows that all living beings, plants included, have "aims." If they have aims, there is no reason to deny they have interests in pursuing those aims. It is unclear why either consciousness or feelings such as pleasure and frustration should be necessary to having interests, except by way of tautology. Any living being with an innate teleology can have an "interest" in a broad sense if we define interests to mean striving after some end.[116] As noted, the teleology of plants, like that of other living beings, is defined by their genetic code. The genetic aim in every case is to live, thrive, and reproduce. Per Butler, a plant may not consciously want these things, but it strives to do them nevertheless. Biologically, it needs to thrive and reproduce just as much as human beings do. Inert matter such as stones, mountains, and watercourses have no such teleology and so are excluded from the argument.

One way that many moral theorists go wrong in considering these matters is in making consciousness a precondition to having interests. Such a viewpoint would deny moral relevance to most human interests. An interest need not be conscious—much or most human cognition occurs on an unconscious level in any case[117]—but their interests exist and deserve moral consideration nonetheless. Assuming *arguendo* that consciousness of an interest makes the interest more morally compelling, if we base rights *entirely* on hedonic considerations, we will have transitioned from a deontological theory to a consequentialist theory, and "rights" become a figure of speech rather than a weighty moral mandate. If rights are to be based on dignity—that is, intrinsic value—then a coherent argument can be made that all living things have dignity. They have dignity because, by nature of being alive, they have aims and interests.

This argument will not persuade everyone, and in any case, it does not follow from the argument that the moral interests of individual plants, if any, give rise to moral rights for plants ("floral rights?"). It may argue for a universal human duty toward plants of some kind, but it would be a very narrow duty given that plants have narrower interests than animals by virtue of their inability to experience fear, suffering, hope, or pleasure of the same kind that animals feel. It seems very unlikely that the duty would be of sufficient moral weight to justify even a minimal legal duty against gratuitously killing specific plants or disabling their reproductive

115. Samuel Butler, Erewhon 238 (Penguin Classics ed. 1987) (1872).

116. On this point, *see generally* Paul W. Taylor, Respect for Nature: A Theory of Environmental Ethics (1986); Nicholas Agar, Life's Intrinsic Value (2001).

117. *See generally* John A. Bargh, Social Psychology and the Unconscious: The Automaticity of Mental Processes (2014); Daniel M. Wegner, The Illusion of Conscious Will (2002); Unintended Thought (James S. Uleman & John A. Bargh eds., 1989); Fritz Strack & Roland Deutsch, *Reflective and Impulsive Determinants of Social Behavior*, 8 J. Pers. & Soc. Psych. 220 (2004).

ability. To show excessive moral concern for plants would underprotect human and animal interests, because all humans and animals rely directly or indirectly on killing plants for sustenance.[118] If the plant's genetic code gives it crude interests, then so do the genetic codes of all living beings, including those whose codes dictate that they feed on plants. Given the genetic basis for my argument, the most we could accept by way of moral duties to plants themselves, as opposed to instrumental duties regarding plants, might be a duty not to exterminate an entire species of plant. Even this duty, though, could arguably be overridden with sufficiently strong moral arguments.

The weakness of the argument for duties toward plants explains why municipal legal duties toward plants are all derivative. They relate to either the state's or some other (direct or indirect) human or ecological interest in the plant. The argument for a duty to respect the human interests in the safety, health, and reproduction of plants is much stronger, and will be taken up below.

c. Duties Directly toward the Natural Environment

Most philosophers believe the natural environment—ecosystems such as rivers, forests, and oceans—cannot have rights, either because they are an abstraction or because they lack interests. However, Christopher Stone has argued that such natural features should benefit from human-like rights on their own merits.[119] Stone claims that such rights are based on the needs of such features. That a forest needs clean air, water, insects, or animals to help it propagate, and so forth, become evident when deprived of such things. Trees wither and die. That a stream needs freedom from chemical pollution is evident when its waters become cloudy and putrid or choked off, fish die, and so forth. To prevent such catastrophes, Stone recommends that human guardians be appointed, presumably by the United Nations, to represent either the environment as a whole or specific ecosystems or parts of ecosystems.[120]

Stone's claim is unconvincing because it relies on anthropomorphizing natural features. All it amounts to is that a natural feature's right has been violated when it deviates from its natural state due to human intervention. But Stone seems to define a feature's natural state as freedom from human alteration, whereas it is unclear why the "rights" of natural features are not violated by the animals or impersonal forces that constantly act on them. If a stream "needs" to maintain its water flow, why does it violate the stream's rights if a human being dams the stream, but not if a beaver or landslide blocks its flow? The needs Stone imputes to natural features are similar to those that Feinberg attributes to an automobile; the "needs" are perceived rather than objective. They merely reflect the observer's own subjective notions about how the features should look and function, which

118. This is not the same as arguing that the mere convenience of humans or animals justifies overriding other important moral considerations.

119. *E.g.*, Christopher D. Stone, Should Trees Have Standing? Law, Morality, and the Environment 8 (3d ed. 2010); Christopher D. Stone, *Should Trees Have Standing? Towards Legal Rights for Natural Objects*, 45 S. Cal. L. Rev. 450 (1972).

120. Stone, *supra* note 119, at 104.

in turn reflect his subjective preference that human beings not alter the natural features. Real interests are grounded on aims and desires, and neither abstractions nor inert matter have either. Without interests, there is no basis for claiming rights; what claim can a rock or lake make on you? Natural features have uses and value, but their value is instrumental to living organisms. It makes no more sense to speak of ecological rights per se than to assert the planet Mercury or a regular hexagon has rights.

If the case for the natural environment having rights is flawed, is it nonetheless possible to have moral duties toward the natural environment? Even the case for weak duties made out for plants does not apply to the natural environment. Natural features such as mountains and lakes do not have an innate teleology—these are continuously determined by climactic, geological, and other exogenous forces, and there is no final state in which they have achieved their ends. Forests and coral reefs may rely on many living organisms and natural features to thrive and reproduce, but they do not have a single genetic code and, therefore, a single interest. The interests of such organisms are complementary, because ecosystems rely on a cycle of reproduction and destruction of living beings to maintain themselves. But the interests of living organisms in the ecosystem is instrumental to their own interests, and so our moral concern for an ecosystem depends on the sum of our concerns for the living beings that rely on it. The case for duties directly toward an ecosystem as such, then, seems to me very weak.

D. Duties toward Individuals Relative to a Safe and Healthy Natural Environment

An international human right to a safe and healthy environment is more easily morally supportable and legally feasible than an international plant right. Indeed, the recognition of a human ecological right is inevitable, because, outside of post-apocalyptic science fiction, a healthy natural environment is necessary for human and animal survival and prosperity, and insofar as we consider human and animal interests worthy of moral consideration, our duties to humans and animals must encompass duties not to harm the natural environment excessively. Moreover, a safe environment is critical to the exercise of many other human rights, most prominently the rights to life and health, as well as cultural rights for societies living in a manner directly reliant on or closely tied to the natural environment.

In trying to encode environmental values in the world public order, the international community has deployed human rights concepts freely. The 1972 Stockholm Declaration on the Human Environment asserts in Principle 1 that "Man has the fundamental right to . . . adequate conditions of life, in an environment of a quality that permits a life of dignity and wellbeing, and he bears a solemn responsibility to protect and improve the environment for present and future generations."[121] Similarly, former U.S. Supreme Court Justice William Douglas argued for a "wilderness bill of rights" to protect, not the natural environment itself, but the putative rights of those individuals whose "spiritual values" include environmental

121. Declaration of the United Nations Conference on the Human Environment, U.N. Doc. A/CONF.48/14 & Corr.1, ch. I (June 16, 1972).

sanctity.[122] The movement for the recognition of human rights to a safe and healthy environment began to gather official recognition in the late 1980s when the Organization of American States incorporated the right into the Protocol of San Salvador.[123] Soon afterward, the U.N. Human Rights Commission adopted a resolution recognizing an individual right "to live in an environment adequate for their health and well-being,"[124] and the Rio Declaration on Environment and Development proclaimed that human beings "are entitled to a healthy and productive life in harmony with nature."[125]

The instrumental importance of the natural environment to human beings and other animals is beyond debate, and the case for an individual human right to a safe and healthy environment is a strong one insofar as it protects individuals from isolated threats to their fundamental interests such as life and health.[126] Arguing that individuals have a right, for their own economic, health, mental, or other benefit, to a clean environment does not require any real conceptual expansion of human rights law. It merely means expanding the catalog of existing rights. As a human right, a safe and healthy environment entails state duties to protect and preserve the environment from excessive degradation and pollution. There are excellent reasons for focusing on a state duties paradigm in preference to an individual human right paradigm, which will be taken up in the next chapter. Here, it suffices to observe that adopting either or both rights or duties paradigms under international law can be morally justified and legally feasible.

The case for a universal, individual moral duty toward others respecting the environment is a relatively easy one to make. The health of ecosystems inevitably affects human beings, directly or indirectly. Ecosystems are a shared resource even when divided into parcels of private property; nature respects no legal boundaries. All human beings are affected by the health of the natural environment, because it sustains human life. The legal right to use private property as one wishes does not itself undermine the moral duty to use the property in a manner that maintains

122. William O. Douglas, A Wilderness Bill of Rights 86 (1965).

123. Org. of Am. States, Additional Protocol to the American Convention on Human Rights in the Area of Economic, Social and Cultural Rights, "Protocol of San Salvador," Nov. 14, 1988, art. 11, O.A.S.T.S. No. 69, 28 I.L.M. 156 (1989).

124. U.N. Hum. Rts. Comm'n, Res. 1991/44, Mar. 5, 1991, U.N. Doc. E/CN.4/RES/1991/44.

125. Rio Declaration on Environment and Development, principle 1, 3–14 June 1992, U.N. Doc. A/CONF.151/26 (Vol. I). For more on such rights, *see* Donald Anton & Dinah Shelton, Environmental Protection and Human Rights (2011); Human Rights and Climate Change (Stephen Humphreys ed., 2011); Alan Boyle, *Human Rights and the Environment: Where Next?*, 23 Eur. J. Int'l L. 613 (2012); Alexandre-Charles Kiss, *Peut-on définir le droit de l'homme à l'environnement?*, 1976 Rev. Juridique de l'Environnement 15; Alexandre-Charles Kiss, *Le droit à la conservation de l'environnement*, 2 Rev. Univ. des Droits de l'Homme 445 (1990); Dinah Shelton, *Human Rights, Environmental Rights, and the Right to Environment*, 28 Stan. J. Int'l L. 103 (1991). *But see* Gunther Handl, *Human Rights and Protection of the Environment: A Mildly Revisionist View*, *in* Human Rights and Environmental Protection 117 (Antônio Augusto Cançado-Trindade ed., 1992).

126. *See* James W. Nickel, *The Human Right to a Safe Environment*, 18 Yale J. Int'l L. 281 (1993).

the basic health of the natural environment for the benefit of all presently living persons and future generations. It would be theoretically possible to impose an individual legal duty toward the environment—many municipal laws already regulate certain forms of environmental abuse on public and private land alike, such as toxic waste dumping or contributing excessively to air pollution, and other laws encourage environmentally responsible behaviors on private land by, for example, subsidizing solar energy or discouraging fresh water wastage. Other municipal laws may protect wildlife—again, including those that wander onto or inhabit private property—from harm.[127]

In principle, there is no reason that international law cannot reflect such a moral duty by imposing legal duties on individuals to use private and public lands responsibly for the benefit of human beings and wildlife. In fact, both universal individual and state duties to protect and preserve the environment with reference to individual rights or the rights of future generations have made their way into various international environmental declarations and instruments. As noted the Stockholm Declaration alludes to the "responsibility" of "man" toward the environment. Principles 4 and 5 of the Earth Charter also posit duties on "the peoples of the Earth" to protect the environment and educate future generations about the importance of ecology,[128] as did the 1989 Hague Declaration on the Environment.[129] Duties toward the environment have also made their way into many state constitutions.[130] Some scholars have argued in favor of a responsibilities approach to balance the tendency of human rights law to privilege human life and flourishing above the long-term sustainability and health of the "natural community."[131] As with other moral duties, whether good reasons exist for imposing *international* legal duties on individuals remains a point of controversy.

C. CONCLUSION

Every individual is already enmeshed in a network of moral and legal duties to other individuals, groups, humankind as a whole, and animals. Individuals also may have moral duties to themselves. Business organization have many of the same moral and legal duties to others. Some of these duties—admittedly, limited to abstinence from participating in the most egregious atrocities—have already been

127. For example, in the United States, the Endangered Species Act prohibits taking endangered or threatened wildlife, including on private land. 16 U.S.C. § 1538 (2015).

128. Earth Charter, principles 4–5, Mar. 2000, *at* http://www.earthcharter.org.

129. Declaration of the Hague on the Environment, Mar. 11, 1989, *available at* http://www.nls.ac.in/CEERA/ceerafeb04/html/documents/lib_int_c1s2_hag_230300.htm. The Hague Declaration was endorsed by twenty-four heads of state or their representatives.

130. As of 2012, ninety-two countries had incorporated a right to a healthy environment into their national constitutions. David R. Boyd, The Environmental Rights Revolution: A Global Study of Constitutions, Human Rights, and the Environment (2012).

131. *E.g.*, Prudence Taylor, *From Environmental to Ecological Human Rights: A New Dynamic in International Law?*, 10 Geo. Int'l Envtl. L. Rev. 309, 310 (1998).

recognized as international legal duties. It is therefore not a tremendous conceptual leap to add to the mix individual and corporate international legal duties with regard to fundamental values.

It may be observed that the foregoing typology omits any discussion of duties to one or more gods. The omission is intentional. Assuming *arguendo* that there were coherent reasons for believing such duties exist, they are nonetheless irrelevant to the discussion here. The faith-based nature of such duties makes them insusceptible of reasoned analysis, and the epistemological problems of determining the content of such duties make it impossible to attract a universal consensus about them. Any attempt to *legally* impose universal duties toward one or more gods would in any event violate the human right to freedom of religion and conscience of anyone dissenting from the consensus view about what such duties are. No person, group, or state has the right or ability to authoritatively determine what each individual's duties toward a god would be. The international community, if it could somehow agree on the content of such duties, can claim no greater authority on this point than any individual state. Therefore, each individual must determine for himself what duties he has toward his god or gods, and such duties are therefore best analyzed as if they were duties to oneself.

The next chapter will examine two separate uses of international legal duties as an alternative or supplementary paradigm to IHRL. It will first discuss whether supplementing IHRL with a broader corpus of direct individual and corporate duties would further the goals of a stable and efficient world public order based on dignity. That question raises a variety of moral, legal, and practical issues for consideration. It will then discuss the advantages and disadvantages of a paradigm shift from individual rights to state duties for the protection of fundamental human (and, again, other) interests.

2

Duties and Rights as Alternative Paradigms

International human rights law is embedded within a network of local, state, regional, and international systems of value articulation and protection. The various values encoded in human rights law fall within a protected sphere of life, liberty, equality, and other human interests upon which the state may infringe only with a showing of sufficient interest and a balance of state needs with the needs of the individual. The concept of rights is an exercise in what H.L.A. Hart called ascriptive language;[1] international law does not describe preexisting human rights, but assigns them to persons in pursuit of the existing and aspirational values of the international community. But rights are not the only conceptual means available for the value expression. Imposing a set of universally applicable, fundamental duties could serve at least some of the same values through a different but complementary mechanism. This chapter will explore the idea of fundamental duties as a substitute for or a supplement to the concept of human rights.

IHRL currently provides for mostly individual or group rights against the state. Every human right consequently entails a state duty toward the right holders. But IHRL itself imposes no formal obstacle to supplementing state duties with private duties. Chapter 1 discussed the movement for supplementing IHRL with an international code, whether binding or precatory, of fundamental individual or business firm duties. It then analyzed the types of obligees toward whom a person might owe a moral or legal duty. The discussion should have made clear that there is a wide variety of obligees to whom a person (or business firm or state) might owe such duties.

Scholarly and political reactions to the suggestion of incorporating private duties into IHRL have so far been based on shallow analyses of the ethical implications of omitting private duties from IHRL, and of the social context in which IHRL operates. Such analyses are in particular plagued by a paradox: the same commenters who oppose the individual duties paradigm frequently support imposing IHRL duties on private business firms. The rejection of individual duties as a supplement to IHRL might be fully justifiable, but not for the reasons that the opponents of individual duties typically invoke. These arguments will be analyzed in greater detail in

1. *See* H.L.A. Hart, Essays in Jurisprudence and Philosophy 21, 23–26 (1983); H.L.A. Hart, *The Ascription of Responsibility and Rights*, 49 Proc. Aristotelian Soc'y 171 (1949).

this chapter. In addition, as Chapter 1 made clear, the distinction between private and corporate duties under IHRL cannot be justified on moral grounds. Whether it can be justified on practical grounds deserves more thorough consideration.

Finally, a question not raised by the movements for individual and corporate duties, but which is of great interest, is why IHRL has generally adopted an individual and group rights paradigm instead of a state duties paradigm. If the *lex lata* of IHRL dictates that, outside the realm of international criminal law, only states hold duties to implement IHRL, why is IHRL not framed from the perspective of the relevant actors (states) rather than the beneficiaries of the duties (individuals and groups)? The final part of this chapter will examine the reasons for and consequences of choosing an individual rights paradigm instead of a state duties paradigm.

A. UNIVERSAL HUMAN DUTIES AS A LEGAL CONCEPT

1. Why Individual Duties?

Thomas Pogge has claimed: "There is nothing important that can be expressed" in terms of duties that cannot equally be expressed as a right; the "essentials of morality can be presented in either idiom."[2] Rhetorically, he is no doubt correct. Instead of saying "all persons have a duty to preserve the environment for future generations," we could say "the environment has a right to preservation" or "future generations have a right to a well-preserved environment." Similarly, we could say "all persons have a right to have themselves act honestly" instead of "all persons have a duty to themselves to act honestly." But are these formulations equivalent in all relevant respects? The preceding chapter shows that they are decidedly not, and indeed that, in some cases, duties can accomplish objectives in a manner that would be ineffective or nonsensical if framed in terms of rights.

Although states are obligated to define and enforce certain individual duties relating to the human rights of others within their jurisdictions, as discussed earlier, legally binding norms are rarely imposed by international law directly on individuals. In public international law, a human right is generally conceived as correlative to a *state* duty rather than an individual or other private duty. Although all individuals, as members of organized groups and societies, and as recipients of the benefits of membership in such societies, hold moral duties toward each other, and although some of these duties are universal, many are codified in municipal laws already. In many countries, for example, private employers have legal duties not to discriminate against others on the basis of race or sex. One might wonder why everyone, including private persons, should not have international legal duties toward other private persons on similar terms. Granted, not all moral duties should be legal duties, but isn't it possible that at least some private moral duties should be elevated to international legal duties?

In a limited way, the international community has already determined that they should. International law incorporates indirect individual duties by

2. Thomas W. Pogge, *O'Neill on Rights and Duties*, 43 Thomas Grazier Philosophische Studien 233, 237 (1992).

imposing on states the obligation to adopt measures in their municipal law to restrain private violations of human rights. As will be discussed in Part III, many internationally recognized human rights have been interpreted as such "positive rights," placing on states a duty to protect the right holder from private infringements of that person's rights. Although an individual who violates another person's internationally recognized human right has not necessarily violated public international law, he may have triggered the state's duty to take reasonable measures to punish and rectify the violation. In such cases, the state can fulfill its positive duties only by enacting legislation deterring and punishing certain private violations of the right, and providing for compensation to the victim. The state assumes the responsibility for legally enforcing individual duties to respect human rights.

Notwithstanding the dicta of the international treaty-monitoring bodies discussed in the previous chapter, which assert that individuals have positive duties under the CEDR and CESCR, if IHRL were to adopt a system of individual duties, it is unthinkable that individuals would owe a broad scope of positive legal duties toward others. Aside from duties arising from special relationships such as family membership or employment (Chapter 1, Section B.1), individual IHRL duties would be exclusively negative. Such duties would be limited to the mainly passive act of respecting the rights of others rather than protecting them from external threats or guaranteeing their fulfillment. Obviously, a norm interpreted to authorize the international community to punish an individual doctor for refusing to provide free medical care to all the needy ill persons who appear at a clinic, or to punish someone who refused to share his food with every hungry person who requested it, would intrude not only on the general system of state municipal regulation, but would make intolerable inroads into the human rights of those subjected to the positive duties. Moreover, the universe of individuals capable of contributing meaningfully to the protection and fulfillment of the human rights of many other individuals will be small in most societies. Jim Nickel points out that positive duties can be reliably fulfilled when the duty holder has "the *sustainable* capacity to respect and uphold the right."[3] Most individuals generally lack the capacity to protect each other from the risks of starvation, violence by others, or other rights deprivations that may arise over time.

Negative universal duties under IHRL are much less problematic. There is no obvious reason that everyone cannot bear a legal duty to refrain from seriously infringing everyone else's human rights. Nickel gives the example of the duty not to torture another, which "can feasibly be borne and fulfilled by all, so this duty can be addressed to everyone."[4] Private duties could theoretically supplement state duties under IHRL either as complementary first-order duties or as contingent duties in case the state fails to come through. In *The Morality of Freedom*, Joseph Raz argues that this latter observation exposes a latent potential of human rights; because a statement of rights does not specify the duty holder, relying on rights

3. James W. Nickel, *How Human Rights Generate Duties to Protect and Provide*, 15 Hum. Rts. Q. 77, 81 (1993).

4. *Id.* at 80.

creates space in which to infer new duties when circumstances change, making rights a more "dynamic" paradigm than duties.[5] In other words, should the state be unable or unwilling to protect or fulfill a positive human right, the duty could be reinterpreted to belong to a business entity, community organization, or private individual as well or instead.

Raz bases his argument on the supposed indeterminacy of the right's correlative duty holder. In the realm of moral rights, the observation about the indeterminacy of the duty holder applies to positive rights only. To say X has a right to condition, action, or omission α leaves indeterminate who must provide α. A negative moral right, in contrast, is universal; to say X has a right to freedom from condition or action β means everyone has a duty not to inflict β on X. Raz's claim is overbroad, but it is correct for some kinds of rights. What Raz does not observe is that the same applies to duties. To say Y has a (positive) duty to provide α leaves indeterminate to whom α must be provided. To say Y has a (negative) duty not to inflict β implies that it must not inflict β on anyone. Rights, then, are not by nature less determinate or more flexible than duties; both can be phrased with greater or lesser precision.

In contrast to Raz, Onora O'Neill views the focus on human rights as pathological, because a sole emphasis on *moral* human rights without reference to *moral* human duties encourages irresponsible claims with no thought for who must fulfill them.[6] What Raz sees as a salutary flexibility that strengthens the ability of right holders to seek redress, O'Neill considers a weakness that may render the right overbroad or vacuous. But moving from moral to legal theory moots the objection to a focus on rights. One important way IHRL differs from moral theory is that certain key metaphysical questions are not up for debate. Law is anchored to traditions and texts that shape and limit the understanding of the relevant concepts—in this case, rights and duties. Raz's claim does reflect the tendency in IHRL instruments to leave the duty holder unspecified. The major treaties list rights, sometimes with a clear implication that the state holds the correlative duty, but more often without implying who bears responsibility for respecting, protecting, or fulfilling the right. The right to seek pardon or commutation for a death sentence,[7] for example, can only be fulfilled by the state. But article 6(1) of the CCPR states: "Every human being has the inherent right to life" without specifying whether private individuals or organizations have a correlative duty to respect that right.

Nonetheless, Raz's interpretive dynamism does not apply in an international legal context. Treaties are agreements between states, and canons of construction limit the permissible interpretations of treaties. Although any interpretation must ultimately reflect the shared intentions of the parties as well as the community policies that subserve a desired public order,[8] confining the universe of permissible sources of interpretation to a limited set of principles serves important public policies. It augments the predictability of the interpretive act's outcome and adds to

5. JOSEPH RAZ, THE MORALITY OF FREEDOM 170–71 (1986).

6. *See, e.g.*, Onora O'Neill, *The Dark Side of Human Rights*, 81 INT'L AFF. 427 (2005).

7. CCPR art. 6(4).

8. *See* MYRES S. MCDOUGAL, HAROLD D. LASSWELL & JAMES C. MILLER, THE INTERPRETATION OF AGREEMENTS AND WORLD PUBLIC ORDER 44–45 (1967).

the legitimacy of the decision process by limiting the interpreter's discretion and, therefore, power to interject subjectivity or arbitrariness into the decision process.

As international lawyers know well, IHRL has routinely been interpreted to impose direct legal duties solely on states, with only a few, narrowly drawn exceptions. In the interpretation of human rights treaties, then, the ability of an authoritative interpreter to displace duties from the usual duty holder—the state itself—onto other or additional parties is limited. This is not merely an accident of history; by its nature, the law must designate a determinate right holder and duty holder in order to fulfill its function of social control. Persons who do not know their duties, or who cannot with reasonable certainty discover the person to whom their rights give rise to claims, cannot invoke the law's powers or protections.

The flexibility Raz perceives in a rights paradigm are not an advantage in international law, then. The state is understood to be the only first-order duty holder by all relevant actors in almost all cases, and the duty cannot easily be shifted elsewhere for convenience. On the other hand, O'Neill's concern for rights run amok translates to the IHRL context no better. The establishment of a right implicates a duty holder automatically: the state. That does not mean international law could not evolve to designate other duty holders, such as individuals—which is rather the point of this discussion—but that it would require an affirmative lawmaking act by the international community or a recognized authority. The established understanding of correlativity between rights and duties in IHRL leaves open the possibility of explicitly identifying new duty holders, even hierarchizing and diversifying the responsibilities of relevant duty holders. It merely means such a development would have to result from a conscious act rather than a creative interpretation of existing instruments and customs.

Raz also observes that a right does not necessarily imply that a single duty rests on a single party alone; multiple parties can hold duties correlative to the same right. Moreover, there is no reason all parties must have the same duty or be called upon in equal priority to act with respect to the right. A contingent duty holder may be required to act only upon the contingency, such as the primary duty holder being unable or unwilling to fulfill the duty. This observation does apply in legal as much as moral theory. Municipal laws commonly allocate joint and several duties, as well as conditional duties, and in theory IHRL could do the same. For example, the correlative of a human right to free primary education is usually thought of as a duty to provide free primary education. The classic interpretation of this duty in IHRL is that the state alone bears the duty, but suppose it were thought desirable to impose an education-related duty on parents as well. If the relevant policy goal is to ensure that all children have a primary education, then imposing on parents a primary duty to provide an education to their children and on the state a contingent duty could trigger the state's duty to provide free primary education only for children whose parents cannot afford to pay for their education, or who refuse to comply with their duties to provide education. Other duties could be different but of parallel stature; for example, if the state has a duty to provide free public education, parents could have a duty to ensure their child's attendance at an educational institution. Whether IHRL is the most appropriate vehicle for imposing private duties of this kind is a separate question, but it is certainly feasible to allocate multiple and varied duties correlative to a single right in this manner.

We have reached a good point to summarize the argument so far. First, some kinds of universal duties under IHRL could feasibly be imposed. For private individuals, these would be exclusively negative duties except where the duty holder has a special relationship with the right holder. The indeterminacy of the moral duty holder is neither a problem nor an advantage in IHRL, because the duty holder must always be specified with reasonable certainty. However, all such duties would need to be enforced by the state to be effectively guaranteed, except in case of the most widespread and systematic human rights violations. Second, such duties need not be held solely or even in primacy by individuals. Individuals could have contingent duties that are conditional or parallel to those held by the state.

Possibility tells us nothing about desirability, though. Given that not all moral duties should be legal duties, we need not seriously consider the various proposals to incorporate individual duties into IHRL, under the ambiguous rubric of "soft law" or anything else, unless there are sufficient reasons for such a revolutionary change. I can discern only one reason that might be at all persuasive, and it relates to O'Neill's observation respecting moral rights. The global *legal* recognition of individual human rights without correlative duties creates an imbalance in individual expectations of right behavior. The absence of any direct imposition of general individual duties in IHRL has interrelated psychological, cultural, and practical consequences. The imbalance arises from a sense of entitlement to a panoply of liberties and benefits from society without a corresponding sense of responsibility for protecting and assisting others in one's society. *Liberté* is exalted, *égalité* and especially *fratérnité* are cast down.

Trust in and willingness to cooperate with others in society is a valuable form of social capital, and the consistent and pervasive abuse of the recognized rights of others will inexorably degrade that social capital. A global system of individual rights without a global system of individual duties encourages individuals to rely on states to act in a morally responsible manner before the international community while exempting individuals from any similar expectation. A state that fails to inculcate in its nationals a broad culture of respect for the human rights of others—and such states are legion—violates no definite norm of international law. The state maintains a formal duty of ensuring that private persons and organizations respect human rights, and its failure through inability or apathy to fulfill the duty to ensure general respect for human rights entails no serious further consequences, unless perhaps a large-scale atrocity should erupt and trigger intervention by the international community. Low-level human rights violations are a constant background noise in most societies to which the formal system of IHRL is all but deaf.

No system of law is perfectly effective, and virtually no system of law relies mainly on formal enforcement methods for what effectiveness it does claim. Psychological expectations of right behavior arise from conscience (self-policing) and culture (contextual social influence). These are the primary motivators for compliance with most laws, including IHRL. A formal system of individual duties might not be as effective as a system of rights as enforceable norms, but it could at least gradually push noncompliant societies toward cultural acceptance of IHRL. The two arguments in favor of an international system of individual duties under IHRL, then, are that such a system might supplement the system of state duties by providing complementary or contingent support for state action, and that, even if not practically enforceable on an international scale, such duties might exert some psychological and cultural influence to restrain individual infringements on human rights and respect the dignity of all persons.

2. Objections to Individual Duties under IHRL

For those who consider these claims to constitute a sufficient prima facie reason for seriously considering incorporating individual duties into IHRL, the next question is whether the challenges or problems that will likely result from the incorporation of individual duties outweigh the benefits. Here, I will examine the most common and credible objections to individual duties under IHRL, then I will suggest my own reasons for disfavoring individual legal duties.

A. Individual Duties Would Be Redundant

One objection sometimes made to proposals to introduce individual duties into IHRL is that such duties are already established by existing IHRL instruments. As noted above, these instruments make various references to individual "responsibilities" to other individuals or the "community," which appears to suggest an intention to establish duties both to other persons and perhaps the state itself. Because duties are already incorporated into various international human rights instruments, the argument goes, there is no need for more.[9]

This objection rather misses the point of the argument for individual duties. The IAC draft Universal Declaration lists specific duties not currently mentioned in existing human rights instruments. For example, no international human rights instrument posits a duty "to behave with integrity, honesty and fairness." It is the merest non sequitur to assert that, if some duties are listed, then no others should be. Even for those duties currently included in international human rights instruments, though, it makes little sense to equate the brief and vague references to duties to a complete set of fundamental and universal human duties. Nebulous references to unenumerated individual duties are no more satisfactory than would be similar references to human rights in the instruments. Can we be certain that any valuable proposal for the recognition of universal duties would add nothing to the vague and unenforceable references to duties in existing human rights instruments? Whatever the failings of the efforts to propose universal duties to date, there is no reason to doubt that an instrument *could* be designed by thoughtful drafters that would elaborate these duties usefully or establish entirely different and better formulated duties. Given how sparely these instruments reference duties, it takes precious little creativity to imagine a more comprehensive and precise instrument.

Moreover, the argument does not really apply to legally binding individual duties, because the "responsibilities" listed in the existing instruments are not intended to be binding, as discussed in Chapter 1, Section A. The inclusion of legally binding

9. *See* Ben Saul, *In the Shadow of Human Rights: Human Duties, Obligations, and Responsibilities*, 32 Colum. Hum. Rts. L. Rev. 565, 581–601 (2001); Amnesty International, Muddying the Waters: The Draft "Universal Declaration of Human Responsibilities"—No Complement to Human Rights, Apr. 2, 1998, at 1–2, AI Index IOR 40/02/98, *available at* http://www.amnesty.org [hereinafter "Muddying the Waters"].

universal individual duties, whether such inclusion is thought desirable or repugnant, would in any case not be redundant of hortatory lists of duties.

B. Rights Render Individual Duties Unnecessary

An argument for the "incoherence" of individual legal duties, made by Stephen Holmes and Cass Sunstein, is that exercising rights themselves sometimes makes right holders more responsible.[10] For example, owning property or raising a child gives individuals an interest in behaving responsibly to preserve the value of the property or promote the best interests of the child, respectively; having a legal right to redress for a private injury entails giving up seeking private vengeance.[11] The word "incoherence" itself is incoherent in this context; Holmes and Sunstein probably meant that such duties would be superfluous.

These arguments are not general ones—most rights give no clear incentives to behave responsibly—and when they do apply, they conflate separate concepts. Having a right does not logically entail exercising the right responsibly, either in theory or in law.[12] More important, no reliable evidence supports that supposition. Property may be left to deteriorate within the right of a property owner, and in many cases an owner exercises that right. A right to seek legal redress for an injury does not substitute for private vengeance; the plaintiff whose right is nullified by an incompetent judge does not gain approval to unleash a hitman on the defendant.

In any case, Holmes and Sunstein's claims are beside the point in an enforceable system of norms. Even if the hypothesis that having rights tends to teach responsibility reflected reality rather than naked optimism, the right to property does not *obligate* the property owner to act responsibly with respect to property, either his own or a stranger's, nor does it give him a direct incentive to do so. The societal effect of a system of rights without duties will predictably undersupply respect for the rights of others. This is especially so because, although human rights may be universal, they are not necessarily socially embedded. In other words, although a person may not self-consistently claim a right to disregard the comparable rights of others, human beings are nonetheless notorious for their inconsistency when self-interest is at stake. The average person may or may not learn responsibility with respect to his own property, but a system lacking duties does not teach him responsibility with respect to the property of others. Whatever incentives a right may give the right holder to act responsibly, then, it would be primarily for self-benefit rather than public benefit, and thus a selfish responsibility rather than a socially conscious one.

C. Individual Duties Would Undermine or Weaken Human Rights

Upon publication of IAC's proposed Universal Declaration of Human Duties, Amnesty International issued a position paper critical of the idea of defining

10. Stephen Holmes & Cass Sunstein, The Cost of Rights 149 (1999).

11. *Id.* at 152.

12. Of course, a legal system may impose a limit on the irresponsible exercise of rights. This is how the *abus de droit* doctrine developed.

fundamental duties.[13] Aside from suggesting that the draft was premature when many human rights laws were going unenforced—a point that attacks the timing of the proposal rather than its merits—Amnesty's main objection appears to have been that the IAC draft undermined human rights "because they refer to specific rights in a weaker manner, leave out important elements of the guarantees or introduce vague and ill-defined concepts."[14] To support its claims, Amnesty pointed out that many rights present in the UDHR were absent from, or vaguer or weaker in, the IAC draft, such as the right to freedom of movement or the right to participate in choosing one's government.[15] These objections have been echoed by many publicists, who in some cases have expanded them to make the general point that the broad imposition of private duties could undermine rights by justifying limitations on those rights in the name of social values.[16]

Similar objections were raised against the ASEAN Human Rights Declaration. The U.N. Human Rights Council's Coordinating Committee, for example, wrote an open letter to ASEAN objecting to its duty provisions:

> With regard to provisions which seek to "balance" rights with individual duties, this is not the wording of international human rights law. Reference to "balancing" in these terms denies the positive dynamic that exists between rights and duties. The creation of an environment where people are able to exercise their human rights is directly linked to the creation of an environment where trust and respect can develop between individuals and groups and between the people and state institutions. In such an environment, duties and responsibilities are able to emerge freely. This is not to say that laws should not be in place to guard against, for instance, defamation of individuals or incitement to hatred. However, advocating a balance between human rights and duties creates much greater scope for Governments to place arbitrary, disproportionate and unnecessary restrictions on human rights.[17]

This statement was tersely echoed by the U.N. High Commissioner for Human Rights: "The balancing of human rights with individual duties is not a part of international human rights law, misrepresents the positive dynamic between rights and

13. Muddying the Waters, *supra* note 9.

14. *Id.* at 4.

15. *Id.* at 4–5.

16. *See, e.g.*, Saul, *supra* note 9, at 602–04; Stéphanie Hennette-Vauchez, *A Human Dignitas? Remnants of the Ancient Legal Concept in Contemporary Dignity Jurisprudence*, 9 Int'l J. Const. L. 32 (2011). Similarly, in response to the United Kingdom's proposal to add private "responsibilities" to its bill of rights, some members of the public criticized the idea of adding a charter of duties because it would devalue human rights by an association with them. Ministry of Justice, Rights and Responsibilities: Developing Our Constitutional Framework: Summary of Responses, Cm. 7860, at 12 (2010) (on file with author).

17. U.N. Human Rights Council, Coordinating Committee of the Special Procedures, Open Letter: ASEAN Human Rights Declaration Should Maintain International Standards (Nov. 16, 2012) (on file with author).

duties and should not be included in a human rights instrument."[18] The Secretary-General of the International Commission of Jurists, an NGO, also responded:

> The idea that all human rights are to be "balanced" against individual responsibilities contradicts the very idea of human rights agreed upon in the 1948 Universal Declaration of Human Rights .... Balancing human rights with responsibilities turns on its head the entire *raison d'être* of human rights.[19]

Most of these objections relate to the concept of universal duties as such rather than their specific implementation in the IAC Declaration. To that extent, the objections are baseless. The codification of universal individual duties is in no manner inconsistent with the notion of universal human rights. There is no inherent conflict between individuals having both rights and duties, either legal or moral. For evidence, it is unnecessary to look farther than existing moral theory and legal practice. All individuals already have both moral and legal duties to all other individuals whose lives they can or do affect. As already discussed, in moral theory, universal human rights inescapably imply universal human duties. As for legal duties, all individuals have legal duties to one another that both limit their own exercise of rights and protect the rights of others at the municipal level. Establishing universal legal duties on the international level would no more inherently undermine universal legal rights than establishing tort duties of reasonable care undermines the right not to be injured by another's negligence at the municipal level. In fact, individual legal duties usually buttress rather than undermine individual legal rights.

With specific reference to the IAC draft, the arguments misconceive the relationship between the duties proposed in the draft and international human rights. The claim that vague *individual* duties, or a neglect of certain individual duties correlative to individual rights, undermines the rights, is a non sequitur. International law cannot weaken the rights by adding duties, unless the duties somehow conflict with the rights. Nothing in the IAC draft suggests that the duties qualify the rights. Although the duties as drafted may lack the specificity of some rights, the draft does not purport to relieve states of the obligation of fully protecting existing human rights. IHRL duties are state duties; the IAC draft proposed to extend some of those duties to individuals. This sufficiently explains why the draft says nothing about individual duties regarding freedom of movement or participation in government. Private individuals do not grant passports or hold scheduled elections. More generally, not every duty of the state under IHRL can or should have a counterpart in the form of individual duties.

As for specific objections to the substance of the IAC's proposed Universal Declaration, the ASEAN Declaration, or the Banjul Charter, these may be perfectly

18. Statement by the High Commissioner for Human Rights at the Bali Democracy Forum, Nov. 7, 2012, *available at* http://www.ohchr.org/EN/NewsEvents/Pages/DisplayNews.aspx?NewsID=12752&LangID=E.

19. Quoted in Amnesty International, Press Release, Postpone deeply flawed ASEAN Human Rights Declaration, Nov. 6, 2012, AI Index PRE01/540/2012, *at* http:// www.amnesty.org/en/for-media/press-releases/postpone-deeply-flawed-asean-human-rights-declaration-2012-11-05.

valid without rejecting the value of codifying human duties. To object to one specific implementation of an idea does not impugn the idea itself.

Finally, it is important to recognize that some impetus for this objection to universal duties reflects suspicion of the motives of the proponents of codifying such duties. Some have pointed out that political elites frequently invoke individual duties in order to undermine or suppress human rights, rather than to complement them.[20] Such elites may try to justify suppressing free speech by invoking a supposed duty to support the state, for example, or to justify the oppression of women by invoking the duty to protect the family. The concern is of course valid, but it does nothing to undermine the case for universal duties *in abstracto*. It merely suggests the need for caution in the conception and phrasing of the duties, and care in defining the relationship between human duties and human rights.

D. Duties Are Not as Forceful as Rights

One aspect of rights that apparently motivates environmental advocates to frame ecological interests in this manner, instead of framing them as duties, is tactical rather than theoretical or substantive: some believe imprecations to perform duties are not as compelling as imprecations to respect rights. Thus, Richard Hiskes:

> Certainly there are other political and moral arguments aplenty that encourage the recognition of an environmental obligation, but those arguments are usually framed using concepts like sacrifice, good citizenship, or stewardship, and invoking a vocabulary from ethics full of righteous-sounding invocations to "care," to recognize a "moral obligation," to "be generous," or "to do one's duty." Surely these are all good words and sentiments, and they are all guaranteed to move environmental policy to the rear of any political agenda or presidential campaign bus. Environmentalism needs a new and more muscular political vocabulary grounded in today's central political ideas of human rights and justice. It must present an argument rooted in these power words of contemporary politics so that it cannot be ignored in any election or by any government.[21]

There are several problems with extending Hiskes's argument to reject an international set of individual duties. The foremost is that such motivations for using rights rhetoric do not rest on a principled rationale. Hiskes openly calls for invoking rights in the service of a political agenda rather than to justify the merits of using rights. Anyone who does not share Hiskes's agenda has no reason to agree that recognizing a concept of environmental rights is appropriate.

Another problem is that Hiskes's argument neglects the possibility that duties could be worded as forcefully as can rights. As noted early, rights are always correlative to duties. There is no semantic advantage to recognizing an individual or group "right to a safe and healthy environment" over recognizing a (state, corporate, individual, etc.) "binding duty to preserve and protect the environment so that it is safe and healthy." If one is concerned that the duty will not confer standing on

20. *See* Saul, *supra* note 9, at 602.

21. Richard P. Hiskes, The Human Right to a Green Future 2 (2009).

specific right holders, that problem is easily solved by specifying the intended beneficiary or beneficiaries of the duties (all individuals within the state's jurisdiction, all individuals everywhere, the environment itself through an official agent, etc.).

Third, Hiskes seeks to codify a moral right to a safe and healthy environment as a legal right, but his argument is based on the alleged rhetorical weakness of moral duties, and not just any moral duties, but the nonbinding kind—supererogatory duties. The counterpart to legal rights is legal duties, not moral duties, much less morally advisable (as opposed to morally mandatory) duties. And just as these moral duties are as "muscular" as moral rights, legal duties may be every bit as forceful as legal rights.

Indeed, the rationale for legal duties is stronger than the rationale for legal rights under Hiskes's own reasoning. He elsewhere notes that, with respect to environmental rights, "the harms and duties to which they respond are emergent (diffuse across groups and time)."[22] If international law were to recognize a universal right to a safe and healthy environment, it would empower only those individuals able to show that the behavior of their own states endangered or harmed them personally and substantially. But an individual will encounter great difficulty showing significant personal harm from global warming, the thinning of the ozone layer, the disappearance of Arctic ice, or oil drilling in a national forest that he has never visited or plans to visit. If a person has a right that the environment at large be preserved, he has no feasible means for vindicating it by himself. Even if he could, as Hiskes points out, many such threats to the environment are not entirely or primarily attributable to any one state, and so he could not necessarily bring a successful human rights complaint against his own government (much less a foreign government). A universal duty to protect and preserve the environment, in contrast, is better adapted to addressing diffuse harms, because the international community as a whole can have a duty to protect and preserve the environment in parallel with state duties, and it is unnecessary to identify an individual beneficiary or group of beneficiaries. States can be obligated to protect and preserve the environment as an absolute duty, or for the protection of all living persons or future generations. Of course, adopting such a duty would no more empower individuals to vindicate a general interest in environmental preservation than would adopting a universal right, but it could empower states to hold each other accountable, supported by fact-finding and pressure by intergovernmental organizations, to fulfill the duties. Moreover, it would clarify the addressee of the duty and the reason for the duty.

E. Moral Duties Are Too Indeterminate and Variable to Sustain Legal Implementation

Ben Saul has argued that moral duties in general have characteristics that make them inappropriate candidates for codification as international law:

> In broad terms, moral duties—as custom—are flexible, local, decentralized, fluid, informal, non-justiciable, particular, heterogeneous, and culturally specific. By contrast, law is frequently the opposite: inflexible, national or

22. *Id.* at 45.

> international, centralized, fixed, formal, justiciable, general, homogenous, and universalizing.[23]

International human rights, he goes on to assert, "are universally applicable; morality is locally variable. Any attempt to codify human morality could violently disturb the inherited, though dynamic and evolving, systems of morality operating in different societies."[24]

It is unclear why Saul equates moral duties with custom. These are of course two separate ideas, and duties reflect custom no more and no less than rights do. The idea of human rights based on universal human dignity was customary in only a few countries before the adoption of the UDHR; it was instead an aspiration that ran distinctly contrary to custom in most of the world. That was precisely why a universalistic moral theory was needed. Saul's attempt to invoke cultural relativity, then, is misplaced. To invoke cultural relativity to oppose universal duties impugns IHRL itself ipso facto. Anyone who accepts universal rights can logically accept universal duties as well.

Suppose we were to refine Saul's objection and begin by pointing out that laws—including international laws—are promulgated publicly by a recognized authority, whereas moral standards are not. Moral standards must arise by reasoning and deduction, and they may reflect local conditions, something a universal law cannot do. Moreover, legal systems establish processes for authoritative interpretation and application of laws; there is no such universally recognized arbiter of morality. Moral rules are consequently subject to dispute in interpretation in ways the law is not.

The first point is not a valid objection unless *all* moral rules are debatable and must be adjusted locally. But we know that is not true. Although there are perhaps rules of international human rights law justifiable on grounds other than that they embody a moral right, most international human legal rights can be justified as the codification of a universal moral right. Again, where there are universal moral rights, there are universal moral duties, so this objection is hardly persuasive. There is no coherent system of moral reasoning that could justify the arbitrary deprivation of another person's life or employment discrimination based on race, for example. Granted, moral theories may differ on when it is appropriate to tell a lie, refuse to act charitably, or break a promise. It would be difficult to develop a theory of sufficiently general appeal to justify adopting universal rules of behavior in such matters. That is one reason for the failure of the IAC's Draft Declaration. But universal negative duties to respect internationally recognized human rights are immune to this particular objection.

F. Most Universal Legal Duties Are Inappropriate Subjects for Public International Law

Accepting that individuals have urgent and universal moral duties toward one another, and that it is feasible and desirable for at least some of these duties to be

23. Saul, *supra* note 9, at 602.

24. *Id.* at 603–04.

enforced legally, does not mean that public international law is an appropriate mechanism for ensuring the performance of the duties. Universal individual duties may be sound in theory and may even be implemented as legal duties in municipal law everywhere in the world without justifying their addition to the corpus of IHRL.

To be clear, the practicalities discussed here relate to the formation and interpretation of international law rather than its enforcement. To my knowledge, nobody has ever suggested the creation of a global or even regional system of enforcement of universal duties. States currently protect human rights from private intrusion primarily through their municipal systems of law, with the state acting as parens patriae for the interests of its nationals against offenses by other private persons. An international system of enforcement of private duties would raise the question of standing: Who but the state may complain of an individual violation of a human rights duty? The obvious answer would be the right holder, but a global enforcement institution for such duties would have to adapt to hearing individual complaints against alleged individual human rights violators on a very small scale. Such a system would quickly—indeed, probably instantly—become disabled by overcrowding. If the answer is instead that the primary privilege of enforcing individual duties would remain with the state or the international community as a whole, then this argues for the continuation of the current enforcement system.

Returning to the idea of an international body of law imposing individual duties, it will help to remind ourselves how a duties doctrine would fit into the international lawmaking system. Structurally, the main body of IHRL is designed as a three-way system of delegation: (1) a delegation of authority from communities of individuals to their state governments, (2) a delegation of authority from states to the international community as an inclusive group for the creation and high-level interpretation of norms, and (3) a delegation of authority and control from the international community back down to states for the application and enforcement of these norms.[25] Although the global system of IHRL uses both the second and third delegations for creating and interpreting human rights, it is by authority of the third step that IHRL normally imposes and enforces human rights duties on individuals. The introduction of direct individual duties would put human duties on par with human rights in the system of creation and interpretation of norms.

Given that universal duties would merely parallel universal rights in this manner, it is not obvious how the recognition of individual duties would pose a serious practical challenge to the existing system of IHRL if states remained the primary enforcers. Duties imposed on state actors would continue to be monitored by other states, intergovernmental organizations, international agencies, and NGOs. If universal individual legal duties were limited to negative duties to other individuals, discrete groups, humankind as a whole, and ecological subjects, the addition of

25. Among other reasons, this dynamic of delegation from bottom to top and back down again explains why the attempts of Verdross, Kelsen, and their followers to trace the source of international law's authority directly upward to a single *Grundnorm* are doomed ab initio. *See* HANS KELSEN, PRINCIPLES OF INTERNATIONAL LAW (1952); ALFRED VERDROSS, GESELLSCHAFT, STAAT UND RECHT (1931); Josef L. Kunz, *The "Vienna School" and International Law*, 11 N.Y.U. L.Q. REV. 370 (1933–1934).

such duties to IHRL would neither be redundant nor weaken human rights protections, and they would be enforceable on the same terms as individual rights.

There is still one pragmatic point to consider, however. The size and power of the state relative to individuals renders human rights violations by the state of general concern to the international community, whereas individual threats to human rights, although potentially severe in certain cases, will not in the normal case rise to the same level of significance for a large number of victims. A state pension law discriminating on the basis of sex or a state police practice of incarceration without access to counsel will inevitably affect a large number of persons in a very significant way. The same cannot be said of an isolated landlord who refuses to rent to a member of a racial minority or a parent who denies his or her child's right to an education out of religious conviction. Such human rights violations are serious without being pervasive. Moreover, in each case some form of alternative relief may remedy or at least ameliorate the effects of the violation. For example, the would-be tenant may find an alternative, nonracist landlord, and the child's other family members or the state itself may intervene to demand vindication of the child's right to education. However, when the state itself violates human rights, the victim may have nowhere else to turn, and the international community offers the most effective chance of recourse.

As with most general observations, there are exceptions to this one. Some kinds of private threats to human rights may be both serious and systematic. Some of these are already incorporated into public international law as war crimes and crimes against humanity. But there are other major private abuses that international law does not punish directly. Culturally embedded or socially accepted abuses, such as female genital mutilation, marginalization of indigenous peoples, and religious discrimination in some parts of the world, may originate from historical practices, common cultural attitudes, or private campaigns rather than the state itself, but they may well have social effects equivalent to state action. Similarly, widespread cultural apathy toward environmental abuses among the general population may collectively seriously compromise the interests of future generations, despite any state efforts to regulate air emissions, water pollution, overfishing, wildlife poaching, and clear-cutting of forests.

Mary Ann Glendon has made a similar point in the more narrow context of U.S. political discourse. She condemns what she views as an exclusive focus on rights as a basis for social interaction and political dialogue:

> [rights talk] promotes unrealistic expectations, heightens social conflict, and inhibits dialogue that might lead toward consensus, accommodation, or at least the discovery of common ground. In its silence concerning responsibilities, it seems to condone acceptance of the benefits of living in a democratic social welfare state, without accepting the corresponding personal and civic obligations .... All of these traits promote mere assertion [of the right] over reason-giving [that a value is worthy of priority].[26]

26. *See* MARY ANN GLENDON, RIGHTS TALK: THE IMPOVERISHMENT OF POLITICAL DISCOURSE (1991). *See also* ONORA O'NEILL, TOWARD JUSTICE AND VIRTUE ch. 5 (1996).

By analogy, the framing of international human rights law in terms of "rights" may seem to dictate at least some tendency toward an egoistic orientation. Glendon's critique does not of course attack rights per se; it rather suggests that an exclusive focus on legal rights neglects the personal and social duties that make liberal rights possible in the first place.[27] It is based on the belief that a purely right-based society has a pathological effect on public beliefs in personal responsibility.[28] Philosophers have also sometimes criticized human rights on similar grounds, arguing for example that their individualistic nature causes the state to neglect other important public goods that might be indivisible and nonexcludable, such as tolerance or charity.[29]

It is true that rights justify the right holder in disregarding the interests of others to some degree, at least if those interests do not rise to the level of countervailing rights. However, whatever the merits of these critiques, if the main value of universal individual duties is their potential influence on cultural attitudes indifferent or hostile to certain human rights, then presumably an appropriate use of such duties would be to counter pathological cultural tendencies. In a society that marginalizes a religious minority, for example, the invocation of a universal duty of nondiscrimination might exert at least psychological pressure on individual members of the society to counterbalance destructive social tendencies and fracture the solidarity of human rights violators by demands for conformity to different norms than those they espouse—specifically, norms and values compatible with human rights. Impulses toward self-righteousness and social acceptance then motivate the private actor to respect the human rights through prosocial virtues such as tolerance and understanding.

Another possible use of universal individual duties could be as a tool to exert pressure on democratic states themselves to comply with human rights duties. Individuals in democratic polities use their states as a kind of psychological buffer between themselves and the victims of their state's human rights abuses. The citizen of a state that discriminates against a minority group, assists in overthrowing a democratically elected foreign government, tortures suspected terrorists, ruthlessly economically exploits poverty-stricken countries, and so forth can sometimes exonerate himself with the thought that responsibility rests with their government, even if he supports or at least does not oppose that government. The comforting illusion of moral blamelessness could not withstand universal individual human rights duties, however. All individuals in democratic societies would be obligated to vote for and support governments likely to sustain human rights, and to oppose governments likely to abuse them. Such a duty would be impossible to enforce, as noted earlier; its sole value would be rhetorical.

That said, the effectiveness of universal duties at such tasks remains speculative at best. More important, because such cultural attitudes and practices are frequently

27. *See, e.g.*, GLENDON, *supra* note 26, at x–xi, 171.

28. *Id.* at 88.

29. *See, e.g.*, Robert Young, *Dispensing with Moral Rights*, 6 POL. THEORY 63 (1978); John Charvet, *A Critique of Human Rights*, *in* HUMAN RIGHTS: NOMOS XXIII, at 31 (J. Rolland Pennock & John W. Chapman eds., 1981); Joseph Raz, *Right-Based Moralities*, *in* THEORIES OF RIGHTS 182 (Jeremy Waldron ed., 1984).

idiosyncratic to a state, group of states, or region within a state, we cannot distinguish on a level of *universal* duties between the kinds of widespread cultural practices that pose a serious threat to human rights and those having significance only in isolated cases. Ultimately, the most precision a declaration of universal duties can hope to achieve is to enjoin all individuals everywhere to respect the human rights of all other individuals, support governments that comply with human rights obligations, and oppose all other governments. Such injunctions are commendable, but they can no more hope to attain the status of binding law that the preambular words of the Universal Declaration.

3. Summary

International human rights law is not blind to individual duties. It is rather selective in the individual duties it imposes, and it imposes them indirectly by requiring the collective representatives of individuals—states—to implement systems of control to curb serious or widespread private abuses of human rights. States, in turn, use criminal justice systems, regulatory measures, and private legal remedies such as tort law to deter, punish, and compensate private violations of human rights. At least some kinds of human rights abuses that tend to be serious, widespread, and urgent have motivated the international community to impose direct individual duties under IHRL and international humanitarian law.

It may seem a dismal bit of bathos to conclude, despite the strong case for universal moral duties, that the international *legal* recognition of direct individual duties would contribute very little toward the progressive realization of a world public order based on dignity. A general injunction to all persons everywhere that each individual is duty-bound to respect the human rights of others may have some marginal value for counterbalancing entrenched cultural practices damaging to human dignity, but it could not be realistically expected to accomplish much more. The news is not so bad, though, because it suggests a point on which the current arrangement of delegation is nearly optimal, with greater public education about human rights and the values underlying them being the only really helpful improvement that can be justified on both theoretical and practical grounds.

B. CORPORATE HUMAN RIGHTS DUTIES AS A LEGAL CONCEPT

Does the same conclusion apply to the possibility of imposing duties directly on business organizations to respect human rights? Business firms stand in substantially the same place as individuals in having moral duties toward individuals. Business organizations, as legal persons acting as agents for natural persons, have moral duties toward those whom their actions affect. They have such duties, not because moral duty is inherent in the concept of a legal person, but rather because legal persons are endowed by the public with certain legal privileges to act in and on society. They are consciously controlled by their officers, and their activities necessarily have moral consequences. It follows that they have at least the same duties to respect human rights as the persons who control them and benefit from their activities. It follows further that business organizations have at least the same legal duties under IHRL that individuals are capable of having.

Indeed, the justification for corporate duties under IHRL is considerably stronger than the argument for individual duties. Many of the difficulties of attributing universal legal duties to individuals do not apply in the same measure to business organizations. The practical objection to individual duties found most cogent above does not apply to MNEs, the business organizations most capable of affecting societies significantly in international affairs. If universal individual duties are generally unnecessary because of the relatively small effect that most isolated human rights abuses have on the enjoyment of human rights, the same generalization does not apply to MNEs. Some MNEs rival the average state in economic power, which they can frequently convert to forms of political influence. In 2013, the average annual profit of the world's biggest fifty publicly traded companies was US$16.9 billion.[30] That is the average profit, not the average income. The same year, there were seventy-eight countries with a gross domestic product (income) below that number.[31] Because of their economic power, the potential of many MNEs to commit human rights abuses rivals or exceeds that of many states. And unlike states, MNEs have no accountability to the local constituencies where they operate. Although many governments are plagued by corrupt officials who put their own interests ahead of those whom they are expected to serve, very few governments pay no attention whatever to the needs and interests of the public. MNEs, in contrast, do not intentionally serve the public weal; their purpose is to accumulate profits by any legal means possible, regardless of whether it does good or ill to local populations. The need to regulate business activity is accordingly greater in general than the need to regulate state activity because the former lack the prosocial incentives and built-in accountability mechanisms of the latter.

The objection that any international enforcement mechanism might be flooded by private claims also carries less weight in the case of MNEs than it does for individuals accused of violating another's human rights. The universe of potential individuals who could be accused of violating duties under IHRL is nearly limitless, whereas there are far fewer MNEs to serve as respondents. Of course, the number of claimants initially determines the potential number of claims, but the overcrowding problem could be managed by two measures. First, similar claims against the same respondent MNE could be consolidated for judicial efficiency. This measure would be less effective for reducing the burden of claims against individuals, because the acts of individuals are far less likely to negatively affect a broad class of persons than acts of a large corporation. Second, the requirement that claimants first exhaust local remedies would likely winnow down the set of cases brought before an international authority to a manageable number.[32]

30. Calculated from profits column of the Forbes World's Biggest Public Companies List, May 2014, *available at* http://www.forbes.com/global2000/list/ (on file with the author).

31. International Monetary Fund, Report for Selected Countries and Subjects, World Economic Outlook, April 2014 (on file with author).

32. *See generally* Silvia d'Ascoli & Kathrin Maria Scherr, *The Rule of Prior Exhaustion of Local Remedies in the International Law Doctrine and Its Application in the Specific Context of Human Rights Protection*, Eur. Univ. Inst. Working Paper LAW 2007/02, ISSN 1725-6739 (2007), *available at* http://cadmus.eui.eu/.

An additional reason that we might consider as practical the idea of imposing human rights duties on MNEs is that the array of enforcement measures that could influence MNEs is broader than that of either states or individuals. Individual human rights violators are largely immune to foreign courts adjudicating human rights violations unless they have assets within the court's reach, travel there themselves, or can be deported by extradition (which may not be available for accused nationals of the requested state[33]). In the case of public officials who abuse human rights, even these avenues are typically blocked by diplomatic immunity. The International Court of Justice affirmed in the *Arrest Warrant* case that sitting state officials maintain full jurisdictional immunity from criminal prosecution in foreign courts, despite allegations of grave human rights violations.[34] MNEs and their officers benefit from no such immunity, and because of their international operations, they are much more likely than are individuals to have a presence or continuous operations in foreign jurisdictions. If they benefit from political or legal protection against allegations of human rights abuses in their home jurisdictions, they will not necessarily receive the same protection in foreign jurisdictions where the alleged abuses occurred.

To be clear, I am not arguing that business organizations have even negative duties *de lege lata* under IHRL. I am also not arguing that business organizations should have such legal duties *de lege ferenda*. To make that argument would require a much more detailed analysis of the kinds of business organizations to which duties should apply, how the duties might apply, the disadvantages of direct liability, potential abuses, and the merits and disadvantages of different enforcement means. My purpose has been the much more limited one of showing that, given that MNEs have moral duties to all persons: (1) that there are strong reasons for regulating the conduct of MNEs insofar as it affects the human rights of currently living persons and future generations; and (2) that the reasons for refraining from applying such duties to individuals are less persuasive in the case of MNEs. Much more could be said on both scores, but as this subject has received a great deal of quite competent discussion in the legal literature, I will let the matter rest there.

C. STATE FUNDAMENTAL DUTIES AS AN ALTERNATIVE TO INDIVIDUAL HUMAN RIGHTS

One very important advantage of a state duties paradigm over a human rights paradigm was suggested in Chapter 1. Some duties, such as duties to oneself or duties *regarding* something or someone, have no correlative right holder. Modern IHRL already includes some such state human rights duties. The Convention on the

33. Some extradition treaties exempt the requested state from an obligation to surrender its own nationals to the requesting state. *Compare* U.S.-Denmark Extradition Treaty, June 22, 1972, 25 U.S.T. 1293, art. 5 (permitting refusal of extradition based on nationality of the accused) *and* Canada-Philippines Extradition Treaty, Nov. 7, 1989, E101341, CTS 1990 No. 36, art. 4(1) (same) *with* Canada-South Africa Extradition Treaty, Nov. 12, 1999, E103348, CTS 2001 No. 20, art. 5 (extradition may not be refused based on nationality).

34. *See* Arrest Warrant of 11 April 2000 (Dem. Rep. Congo v. Belg.), 2002 I.C.J. Rep. 3, para. 54.

Rights of the Child, for example, obligates state parties to take measures to educate parents about child health and nutrition, and to encourage the production and dissemination of children's books.[35] Individual children do not apparently have a right under the treaty to have parents who are educated about health and nutrition or to receive children's books. The state's duty under such provisions *regards* the welfare of children without giving rise to specific individual human rights in those children. However, such duties are something of an exception. Most duties in the IHRL system by far correlate to specific rights.

Because every right entails a correlative duty, the international human rights system is also a general system of state duties with regard to human dignity. Even if international law had incorporated an extensive system of individual duties, it would have to include its present state duties as well to maintain its effectiveness, because states remain the international actors most readily capable of infringing the rights of individuals. State positive duties would also be necessary for pragmatic reasons; individual moral duties often cannot be fulfilled effectively individually. For example, a system of individual duties to feed those unable to obtain sufficient nourishment, or to provide education to children, could serve human interests in no conceivable organized society of any magnitude. Frequently, individual moral duties can be fulfilled effectively only through collective action, and the state is a primary means of organizing political action to fulfill such duties.

IHRL has been fashioned primarily as a system of individual rights correlative to the state duties, but the focus on rights was not inevitable. Indeed, there are good reasons to think that a greater emphasis on state duties would improve both the substance and functioning of the international human rights system. Rights are problematic on several grounds, theoretical and practical. The metaphysical basis for moral rights is highly contestable. IHRL grounds rights in human dignity, but definitions of dignity are problematic, and arguments for why humans have some kind of unique dignity ultimately resort to tautology or morally irrelevant criteria.[36] The difficulty of coherently justifying human dignity on secular grounds creates a fundamental metaphysical weakness in rights, which in turn limits their ability to justify public policy arguments to rights skeptics. In contrast, a fundamental state duties paradigm does not necessarily correlate to any rights and need not be grounded in dignity. It can instead be grounded in less metaphysically contentious reasons, such as interests or utility. Duties have accordingly wider application to policy problems not grounded in a conception of uniquely human fundamental value.

Onora O'Neill made what appears to be a similar observation when arguing that "while claim rights are mirror images of obligations, not all obligations have mirror images. If there are obligations without corresponding rights, it will evidently impoverish moral thinking if one starts with the rights and leaves aside those

35. Convention on the Rights of the Child arts. 17(c), 24(2)(e), G.A. res. 44/25, annex, 44 U.N. GAOR Supp. (No. 49) at 167, U.N. Doc. A/44/49 (1989), *entered into force* Sept. 2 1990.

36. For some interesting observations on this point, see Jeffrie Murphy, *The Elusive Nature of Human Dignity*, 9 HEDGEHOG REV. 20 (2007); Nicholas Wolterstorff, *Response: The Irony of It All*, 9 HEDGEHOG REV. 63 (2007).

obligations not mirrored by rights."[37] O'Neill's conception of "imperfect or incomplete obligations"[38] are not exactly those for which there is no right holder capable of demanding redress. Rather, she has identified two kinds of obligations: (1) duties for which the specific holder of the correlative right is unspecified—virtues such as caring or charity—or rights for which the correlative duty holder is unspecified, such as a universal right to sustenance imposing a universal duty to provide sustenance; and (2) duties for which the holder is specified but there are many ways to interpret and fulfill the duty, and so the right holder cannot demand a specific act in fulfillment of the duty.[39]

On the first point, as Thomas Pogge has commented, there are ways to specify a right that accounts for contingent duties.[40] Contingent moral duties may be difficult to translate into legal duties, because, as I noted earlier, legal rights require a certain definiteness in allocating duties, but the concept of contingent legal duties is certainly not foreign to the law. Multiple duties correlating to a single right are de rigueur, as when both parents of a child have the same duty to care for the child. It is also common for such duties to be hierarchically organized or contingent, as when a surety owes a duty to a creditor to service a debt, but only if the debtor fails to pay. On the second point, a right can be as vague as its correlative duty. A duty to help one's children flourish in the best judgment of the parent, for example, may give the parent broad discretion in interpreting what "flourishing" means and how best to bring it about. But, as Pogge observes, it can easily carry a correlative right to help from one's parents to flourish.[41] Pogge does not anticipate the counterargument that a child may have a different interpretation of the right than the parent, and in practice the parent's interpretation will prevail nonetheless. But there is a ready rejoinder: there are no ethical duties of purely subjective content. There may be many courses of action that can be considered reasonably calculated to lead to the child's flourishing, and many interpretations of what "flourishing" means, but whether an interpretation of this duty falls within the parameters of the duty depends on an *inter*subjective understanding of the duty, not the idiosyncratic interpretations of the duty holder or right holder. A parent who honestly believes malnourishment is an acceptable form of flourishing violates the duty because no society shares that conception of flourishing, just as a child who believes the complete absence of discipline will lead to his flourishing misinterprets his own right for the same reason.

In short, O'Neill's claim is quite different from mine. O'Neill impugns some rights as vague on critical criteria for effective claims. My contention is that duties can accomplish some things that rights cannot because they are not tied to an

37. O'Neill, *supra* note 14, at 97–98.

38. *Id.* at 107; Onora O'Neill, *Environmental Values, Anthropocentrism and Speciesism*, 6 Envtl. Values 127, 133 (1997).

39. *See also* Onora O'Neill, Constructions of Reason 191 (1989); Onora O'Neill, Faces of Hunger 101 (1986).

40. *See* Thomas W. Pogge, *O'Neill on Rights and Duties*, 43 Thomas Grazier Philosophische Studien 233, 241–42 (1992).

41. *See id.* at 239.

assumption of individual human dignity, and therefore can respond to a broader range of values than can rights. Pogge's argument that duties and rights are equivalently effective accordingly does not address my observation.

Not only can a right correlate to multiple duties: a duty can also correlate to multiple rights. This is the normal case in IHRL, where a state owes the same duty to all persons under its jurisdiction. But IHRL actually imposes *dual duties of different characters* to two kinds of right holders that require the same substantive conduct. The duty that a state owes to persons under its jurisdiction is a duty owed to the beneficiary of the right; this is the natural consequence of a rights paradigm that vests the individual with the primary legal interest in the enjoyment of the right. But states also owe a separate and parallel duty to the international community to comply with their international human rights obligations. A state that violates an individual's human right simultaneously breaches its duty to the individual and to the international community.

These parallel duties reflect a distinction between two types: duties *to* someone and duties *regarding* someone. As the typology of duties set forth in Chapter 1, Section B suggests, duties are not necessarily toward individual persons; one may have a duty toward a group of persons, an animal or species of animals, one's self, or even contingent persons such as future generations. Moral or legal duties may be owed directly to their beneficiaries, or they may be owed to someone else. For example, one could have a moral or legal duty toward an animal not to harm it or toward a species not to waste natural resources necessary for its survival, but one could also have a moral duty to oneself not to be cruel or wasteful. In the last case, the moral duty regards the animal or species and benefits them, but it is not directly for their benefit.

The state's direct duty toward the beneficiaries makes the duties correlative to "human rights" in the first place. As holders of these rights, individuals may demand respect, protection, or fulfillment of their rights directly, whether from the states themselves or through international institutions, such as courts and international organizations. They are also entitled to remedies, of which they themselves are the beneficiary, when the right is insufficiently observed. By allowing victims of a human rights abuse to demand and obtain remedies for themselves, IHRL avoids a situation where the abuse is terminated or deterred for the future, but at the cost of the victims obtaining no relief for themselves. Human rights duties toward individuals imply an individual right of remediation for the harm that befell those individuals.

The duty to other states *regarding* the individuals under the state's jurisdiction makes the human rights a component of public international law. There are two major advantages of maintaining IHRL as an international legal relationship. Most obviously, oppressive states may use their power to silence the direct victims of human rights abuses so that only parties not under the state's control—other states and international institutions—can effectively represent the interests of the victims. This is the normal situation in authoritarian dictatorships, theocracies, and other systems of government that, by their very nature, deny human rights systematically. It may even apply in a more representative political system, when the state oppresses a distinct group by popular or elite demand. But in addition, victims of human rights abuses may be motivated or able to demand the cessation and redress of their own grievances only. The "class action lawsuit" is not an accepted procedure in IHRL, although it has some (less potent) analogs. In contrast, the international community has the right to prevent and an interest in preventing a broader pattern of violations by deterring human rights abuses by states.

The conceptual centrality of dual duties to the system of IHRL suggests an important but unasked question about the interests served by IHRL: Why is the body of law framed in terms of rights instead of fundamental state duties in the first place? I mean this not as a historical question, although there are interesting historical reasons for the preference for a rights paradigm. I mean it as both a philosophical and practical question. Certain benefits follow from using a rights paradigm, but there are neglected and important advantages to a state duties paradigm. This section will explore the comparative advantages of rights and duties for protecting fundamental human (and other) interests.

1. Tonal Connotations of Rights and Duties Paradigms

Historically, the preference for a rights paradigm was dictated by the politically and culturally determined philosophical proclivities of the individuals who set the stage for the human rights movement—Thomas Jefferson, Thomas Paine, the Marquis de Condorcet, and other revolutionaries who under the influence of individualistic Enlightenment values rejected authoritarian regimes.[42] The emphasis on rights reflected their perceptions that individual freedom was a paramount value, and governments could not be trusted to refrain from imposing oppressive laws on their citizens. The architects of modern IHRL were greatly influenced by the history of state oppression and disregard of human dignity, but they did not see the moral world entirely through the same individualistic lenses. Much of the postcolonial impetus for human rights revolved around the idea of collective rights—specifically, the rights of colonized peoples to equal treatment based on race and ethnicity, and the related right to freedom from imperialistic domination. As a result, the U.N. Charter and the international bill of rights place special emphasis on nondiscrimination and self-determination as founding principles of the modern world public order.

At the same time, the nonaggression norm that undergirds that order was framed as a duty rather than a right: "All Members shall refrain in their international relations from the threat or use of force against the territorial integrity or political independence of any state, or in any other manner inconsistent with the Purposes of the United Nations."[43] The Charter could instead have established a right to freedom from threat or use of force, which would have aligned better with the emphasis on rights of peoples to self-determination and the individual rights proclaimed in

42. *See generally* Jonathan Israel, Revolutionary Ideas: An Intellectual History of the French Revolution from The Rights of Man to Robespierre (2014); Bernard Bailyn, The Ideological Origins of the American Revolution (1992); Samuel Moyn, The Last Utopia: Human Rights in History (2012).

43. U.N. Charter art. 2(4).

the Universal Declaration of Human Rights. The framers preferred instead to stipulate a *duty* of nonaggression. Why?

It is not possible to know their thinking with certainty, but the likely answer relates to the political events of the time and the different tone conveyed by rights and duties in municipal law. The San Francisco Conference that established the U.N. Charter concluded its work in 1945, at about the same time that the trials of major Nazi war criminals were beginning at Nuremberg, Germany. A right to noninterference by armed force would imply that all states have a duty of nonaggression, and any state victim of aggression could complain of the violation of its rights. Directly proclaiming a duty of nonaggression, in contrast, emphasizes the wrongfulness of aggressive conduct regardless of who is attacked and any right of third states to intervene to protect the victim of aggression. Although the two paradigms seem functionally equivalent in this case, a duty paradigm seems better adapted to the Nuremberg agenda of laying the foundations for both collective security on a global level and the individual criminal responsibility of political elites who engage in or promote armed aggression. To analogize to municipal law (which is the source of most of these new international norms), to breach someone's right gives rise to a duty of cessation of the wrongful conduct and restitution or compensation. To breach one's duty under municipal law, however, may also violate criminal prohibitions and provoke official measures of deterrence and punishment. In other words, in municipal law, although the civil law uses both rights and duties paradigms, criminal justice uses mainly the duties paradigm. By framing nonaggression in terms of duties, the framers of the Charter may have intended to emphasize the wrongfulness and potential criminality of the aggressive use of armed force.

The different tonal connotations of right and duty paradigms may also explain the early framing of IHRL. Postwar political elites strongly resisted accountability for human rights violations; it was only through the heroic efforts of a relatively small group of determined diplomats, philosophers, lawyers, and public figures that the General Assembly adopted even the nonbinding Universal Declaration.[44] It is easy to imagine that any hint of individual criminal liability for political elites under international human rights law would have scuttled any suggestion to frame the Declaration in terms of state duties. Certainly, the Soviet Union and its satellite states would never have accepted individual criminal liability for human rights violations; Soviet governments maintained power only through a systematic campaign of invading the very human rights they pretended to approve. A stipulation of duties does not necessarily imply condemnation and punitive intent, of course. The point is merely that duties hew more closely to the tone of criminal law than do rights.

Aside from the punitive or remedial tones of duties and rights, respectively, promoting fundamental duties sustains a logical and realistic conception of the state's role in protecting human autonomy and dignity. Even the best-intentioned state cannot guarantee human rights against every private incursion. A state will be held responsible only for failing to react to incursions reasonably within its power to prevent or punish. In an important sense, this is true of the state's duties to refrain

44. *See generally* PAUL GORDON LAUREN, EVOLUTION OF INTERNATIONAL HUMAN RIGHTS: VISIONS SEEN (2d ed. 2011).

from violating human rights as well; some interference with human rights will nearly always be viewed as permissible if necessary for a legitimate state purpose. The unrecognized fact is that human rights are, from an international legal perspective, almost always viewed *in practice* from the perspective of the state rather than the right holder, and thus almost always viewed as fundamental state duties rather than individual or group human rights. The rights dimension takes on its greatest significance in municipal enforcement and before those few tribunals empowered to issue authoritative decisions in response to individual complaints, such as the Strasbourg Court and Inter-American Court of Human Rights. Human rights and state duties are of course two sides of the same coin, but they differ in tone in another sense.

Specifically, fundamental state duties suggest more flexibility than available in rights claims in balancing conflicting interests. A right superficially entitles the right holder to demand without qualification the acts or forbearance to which that person has a right. Mary Ann Glendon has argued that, when rights claims oppose other rights claims, the result tends to polarize opinions and encourage "mere assertion [of the right] over reason-giving."[45] Balanced policymaking is of course possible despite a conflict of rights, but rights assertions tend to polarize and legalize policy debates, and in matters affecting the balance of individual rights with the interests of animals, future generations, community values, and other non-individual interests, reasonable minds may come to the conclusion that considered debate on the merits is desirable.

Indeed, the rights paradigm may be thought to imply that having a right means enjoying the right. This is the premise on which several human rights theorists base their arguments,[46] and the "principle of effectiveness" used by the Strasbourg Court reflects a similar philosophy. The equation of having a right and enjoying it is not, however, conceptually necessary, because a *legal* right is nothing more than the ability to invoke someone else's duty. The assumption that all rights imply a correlative duty to ensure the person's enjoyment of the right (which is to say, a duty to "fulfill" the right) does not reflect the general understanding of IHRL. States have no absolute duty to fulfill rights; they satisfy their duties by taking reasonable measures under the circumstances to ensure enjoyment of the rights, subject to such limitations as may be necessary in a democratic society and proportional to the legitimate aims sought, as the formulation usually goes.

A state duty, then, must always be balanced against other state duties. The state has duties to all persons within its jurisdiction, some of them relating to human rights and others to legal entitlements or interests of other kinds. The human rights of a state's nationals and residents will inevitably conflict at some times, which makes a conflict in the state's duties equally inevitable. And rights must be balanced with other interests; all nationals of a state have at least some kind of interest in such subjects as the state's economic growth, national security, reputation in the international community, maintenance of linguistic and cultural traditions, and

45. Glendon, *supra* note 26, at 14.

46. *See, e.g.*, Henry Shue, Basic Rights (2d ed. 1996). This point was made originally by Michael Payne in *Henry Shue on Basic Rights*, 9(2)(5) Essays in Philosophy 3–4 (2008).

preservation of the natural environment. The state's duties to advance these interests will periodically encroach on its duties to respect and protect human rights in some ways.

James Nickel has made a related point, also grounded in the dynamics of the social conception of rights:

> If the language of rights is used loosely in environmental discourse, people may begin to claim rights that are excessively metaphorical and rhetorical. Conversely, if the language of rights is used strictly, people may develop environmental prescriptions that are excessively rigid and that preclude tradeoffs necessary for providing for human needs while trying to work out today's environmental and population crises. Rights claims are not completely immune to tradeoffs, but the language of rights does imply the restriction of tradeoffs; thus, rights language should be used sparingly in a field in which tradeoffs are a necessary part of progress.[47]

As Nickel suggests, the relative rigidity of rights claims adapts them better for some purposes than others. A duties paradigm does not suffer from the same rigidity. These observations do not imply that the rights paradigm is uniformly "stronger" or "weaker" than the duties paradigm, as some have claimed; it merely means that they have different emphases and characteristics. The human rights paradigm tends toward greater subservience to the protected interest by formulating a demand that is not qualified by a need to balance the right with other rights. The rights paradigm suggests that rights are, in Dworkin's famous analogy, "trumps" that *normally* defeat competing considerations.[48] The fundamental state duties paradigm tends toward greater flexibility in public policy precisely because duties may conflict and need to be balanced with each other. That *fundamental* state duties will usually outweigh less pressing state duties does not detract from the recognition that the difference between fundamental and non-fundamental duties more one of degree than kind. The duties paradigm accentuates that the interests protected are not metaphorical trumps at all; sufficiently important competing considerations of public policies may justify limiting such an interest.

Whatever the reason for the choice of a human rights paradigm, the consequences are significant. This will strike many as counterintuitive, because of the apparent symmetry between rights and duties. In law, the correlativity of claim-rights to duties is taken as a given, because rights can have no meaning without some person to whom the claim for satisfaction can be sooner or later addressed.[49]

47. Nickel, *supra* note 3, at 281–82.

48. Ronald Dworkin, *Rights as Trumps*, *in* THEORIES OF RIGHTS 153 (Jeremy Waldron ed., 1984).

49. In ethical theory, some skeptics remain. Joel Feinberg, for example, asserted that rights may exist prior to duties as an ethical matter. JOEL FEINBERG, RIGHTS, JUSTICE AND THE BOUNDS OF LIBERTY 139–40 (1980). Although he makes no theoretical argument for the claim, he does furnish an example: a starving, fatherless infant with a destitute mother in a slum. Surely, Feinberg argued, the child has a right to be fed, and the question of who has the duty to feed the child is epiphenomenal. The main problem with this argument is that, like many philosophical arguments, it reduces to semantics. Rights are a social construction. They do not

As noted, states have duties under IHRL, some of which do not correlate to an individual right. Given that rights must implicate duties, but duties need not implicate rights, there are situations in which duties will resolve a policy problem in ways that a right cannot easily do, such as protecting important environmental values, animal interests, or the interests of future generations of persons.

An examination of two other important differences between rights and duties paradigms will help explain why. The first difference relevant here is that a duties paradigm makes the identity of the duty holder explicit, whereas a rights paradigm tends to leave the identity of the duty holder open. Second and related, because a rights paradigm makes an identified right holder the repository of fundamental values, the right holder's interests must be ascertainable, and the right holder must be capable of claiming its rights either in person or through an agent. There are other differences. For example, most rights can be waived by the right holder, but the waivability of a duty is complicated by the dual nature of state duties under IHRL. For purposes of this discussion, I will focus on these two.

2. Identification of the Relevant Duty Holder and Extent of Its Duties

As Joseph Raz has pointed out, one ambiguity about "human rights" as a legal concept is that nothing about a "right" indicates who holds the correlative duty and how that duty relates to the right. Onora O'Neill has often claimed that rights rhetoric admits a moral claim by the right holder without undertaking the less pleasant task of specifying the correlative duty holder.[50] James Nickel has made the related observation that changing paradigms from rights to duties "moves the debate in the direction of implementation, towards the question of who has to do what."[51]

Consider two alternative formulations of a health norm:

{a} All persons have the right to the highest attainable standard of health.
{b} All states have the duty to provide the highest attainable standard of healthcare to their nationals.

The duty holder is clear in the second alternative only. The example bears out Nickel's point about implementation as well. The duty framing of {b} specifies what the state must do: "provide." It is not a question of abstaining from interfering in the attempts of all persons to seek healthcare; to fulfill its duty the state must take positive measures to supply healthcare.

It is true that legal statements of human rights have usually omitted specification of the duty holder. However, O'Neill's and Nickel's points are not really about the

exist independent of human cognition. Therefore, they cannot precede duties so long as duties are conceptually tied to rights (which they are). Feinberg's argument is really just an indirect way of saying that he thinks rights protects interests so important that *somebody* ought to fulfill them.

50. *E.g.*, O'Neill, *supra* note 6, at 97–101.

51. Nickel, *supra* note 3, at 85.

limitations of the concept of rights, but limitations on the form they usually take in philosophical arguments and political claims. Statements of rights do not inherently omit specification of the duty holder or the extent of his or her duties. Indeed, specifying the duty holder in IHRL is at all events unnecessary, because by default the duty holder is understood to be the state, unless otherwise specified.

The duties paradigm also leaves open the door to an expansion of individual criminal liability for certain human rights violations by private persons who do not act on behalf of the state. For example, the International Criminal Tribunal for Rwanda tried and convicted radio broadcasters and newspaper editors who encouraged genocide in Rwanda, despite their lack of official position in the Rwandan government.[52] And, as discussed in Chapter 1, Section A, by omitting explicit mention of the duty holder, a rights paradigm opens the door to aggressive interpretations such as those of the Committee on Economic, Social, and Cultural Rights and the Committee on the Elimination of Racial Discrimination, which has intimated that individuals, communities, and corporations already have such duties. The designation of duties greatly reduces the ability of decision-making authorities to hold new parties accountable for violations of protected rights.

Semantically as well, rights are not necessarily vaguer than duties. Alternative {a} above could easily be rephrased to specify the duty holder:

> {a1} All persons have the right to be provided the highest attainable standard of healthcare by their states of nationality and residence.

The rephrasing of {a} achieves the same specificity as {b} with regard to the duty holder and the extent of the duty. The passive phrasing is awkward, however, and if a legal instrument contemplates multiple duty holders and duties, Nickel's preference for duties over rights is indeed justified on semantic grounds.

Regarding the typical vagueness as to the extent of the state's duty in the rights paradigm, Nickel's point is also well taken. The lists of human rights found in the major international instruments frequently include no specific limitations or qualifications to the right. If we continue the example above, the CESCR's right to the "highest attainable standard of physical and mental health" (article 12) nowhere implies that the state may condition the use of its health resources on responsible behavior (e.g., not engaging in unreasonably dangerous hobbies or refraining from tobacco use). The rights paradigm provides a blunt instrument for coping with conflicting public policies, leaving the difficult task of reconciling overlapping rights, or rights that clash with important public interests, to the ad hoc decisions of human rights authorities.

In contrast, duties tend to promote greater sensitivity to such conflicts and more nuanced moral reasoning. A case in point are claims by maximalist philosophers to a right to subsistence. Henry Shue, for example, claims that the "basic right to subsistence" imposes a moral duty on the citizens of "affluent" states to ensure the survival and security of starving and physically threatened persons worldwide.[53]

52. *See* Prosecutor v. Nahimana, Barayagwiza & Ngeze, Int'l Crim. Trib. for Rwanda, Case No. ICTR-99-52-T, Judgment of Dec. 3, 2003.

53. SHUE, *supra* note 46.

Shue may have borrowed this idea from Locke's theory of "right to surplussage"[54] and applied it internationally.[55] Subsistence is surely a core human interest, but the maximalist conclusion does not necessarily follow from that premise. Reframing the value as a duty makes clear the weak points in the chain of reasoning. The counterpart of a universal right to subsistence is not a universal duty to redirect one's resources to anyone starving anywhere in the world up to the point of self-starvation.[56] There are several assumptions underlying that conclusion, one of which is that all duties corresponding to the subsistence right are of equal strength and priority.

There is no need to rehearse here the practical and ethical problems of such "pure impartiality."[57] The point is that a general ethical theory of respect for equal human dignity can ground a hierarchy of moral duties to different individuals or groups. The position that all persons have equal rights based on equal dignity does not logically dictate that all persons and groups have identical *duties* toward each other. As noted in Chapter 1, special relationships among individuals justify different moral demands, and therefore different legal duties. Even if moral rights are conceived as absolute, moral duties need not be.[58] A child may have an absolute right to subsistence, but the duty of his parents is a first-order duty. The duty of his state of nationality may be a contingent duty, which is greater than the duty of a foreign state (a multiply contingent duty), and so forth. This does not mean that the failure of someone with a superior duty to perform that duty excuses someone with a lesser duty from performing his own duty. It does mean that the dynamics of duties are more complex than a simple statement of rights might lead one to believe.

It is because human rights instruments focus on the interests of the right holder rather than specific expectations of the duty holder that international authorities have had to invent or import equitable doctrines to interpret the extent of state duties under IHRL. Drawing on analogies to municipal law, international human rights authorities have generally held that the state's duty is not to guarantee a result—that is, not to guarantee enjoyment of the right—but rather to take reasonable measures to prevent violations. The International Court of Justice,[59]

54. 1 John Locke, Two Treatises of Government § 42 (1689).

55. Shue also seems to have borrowed from Peter Singer's maximalist argument that individuals have a moral obligation to use their resources to ensure the subsistence of all persons in the world, up to the point where their own subsistence is minimal for survival. *See* Peter Singer, *Famine, Affluence, and Morality*, 1 Philos. & Pub. Affairs 229 (1972). Singer's argument, unlike Shue's, focuses on individual moral duties.

56. Shue, *supra* note 46, at 114–18. For similar arguments, see Garrett Cullity, The Moral Demands of Affluence 99 (2004); Peter K. Unger, Living High and Letting Die: Our Illusion of Innocence (1996).

57. Brian Barry, Justice as Impartiality 217–33 (1995); Alan Gewirth, *Ethical Universalism and Particularism*, 85 J. Phil. 283 (1988).

58. Richard Miller makes a similar point in *Beneficence, Duty and Distance*, 32 Philosophy & Pub. Affairs 357–83 (2004).

59. *See, e.g.*, Application of the Convention on the Prevention and Punishment of the Crime of Genocide (Bosnia-Herz. v. Serbia & Montenegro), Judgment, 2007 I.C.J. Rep. 43, para. 430.

Inter-American Court of Human Rights,[60] European Court of Human Rights,[61] and various treaty-monitoring bodies have all adopted similar "due diligence" standards for human rights duties.[62] There is no textual basis for this standard; the authorities have inferred it from general principles of jurisprudence. The extent of the diligence required to satisfy the state's obligation must be highly dependent on the facts of each case, which gives the duties paradigm a space for highly flexible, and therefore less predictable, interpretation. Direct statements of duties tend to invite greater precision in the type and extent of expectations for the duty holder's conduct, and accordingly discourage absolutist claims without the need for creative interpretation by human rights decision authorities.

3. Ascertainment of Interests of the Right Holder and Right Claiming

For there to be a right, there must be an identifiable right holder, and only someone who has a right (or that person's legitimate agent) can realistically claim the benefit of the right. By definition, universal human rights are held by every human being, so there is no question of identification of the right holder. When the interest does not relate to an identifiable right holder, however, rights become problematic. As Chapter 1 discussed, a person (including a state) may have several kinds of free-floating moral duties without any person necessarily being identifiable as a right holder. In such cases, human rights not only fail to protect the relevant moral value, they may operate as positive impediments to the protection of that value by elevating individual interests above other interests.

Chapter 1 pointed out that persons (including states) may owe duties that are directed neither to other states nor to individuals within their jurisdiction. At a minimum, the state owes human rights-related duties to its constituency that are not easily claimable as individual rights, such as duties to promote economic growth, to preserve the natural environment, to expand the frontiers of scientific knowledge, or to provide national security. Such duties are necessary to establish general social conditions conducive to the enjoyment of human rights.

International human rights treaties do indeed sometimes eclipse the concept of individual rights by emphasizing state duties regarding such general conditions. The human right to the highest attainable standard of physical and mental health in the CESCR, for example, although framed as an individual right, is in practice elaborated through a series of institutional duties imposed on the state to adopt general measures for the prevention and treatment of illness rather than to ensure

60. Velásquez Rodriguez v. Honduras, 1988 Inter-Am. Ct. H.R. (ser. C) No. 4, ¶ 172 (July 29, 1988).

61. Bevacqua & S. v. Bulgaria, App. No. 71127/01, Eur. Ct. H.R. (June 12, 2008).

62. *E.g.*, Committee against Torture, General Comment No. 2, para. 18, U.N. Doc. CAT/C/GC/2 (Jan. 24, 2008); Committee on the Elimination of Discrimination against Women, General Recommendation No. 19, 11th Sess., 1992, para. 9, U.N. Doc. A/47/38 at 1 (1993), *reprinted in* Compilation of General Comments and General Recommendations Adopted by Human Rights Treaty Bodies, U.N. Doc. HRI/GEN/1/Rev.6 at 243 (2003).

each individual's healthcare needs are everywhere and always satisfied.[63] It is difficult to see, for example, how an individual could ever have standing to complain of his or her state's failure to observe the duty to improve "all aspects of environmental and industrial hygiene."[64]

Earlier, I contended that IHRL imposes on states dual duties, toward the individual right holders and toward other states, and that the latter duties reflects the character of human rights law as public international law, as opposed to municipal law. Although some state duties under public international law are owed to specific states only, such as treaty duties owed only to other treaty parties or duties to prevent transboundary pollution owed to neighboring states under customary law, many international legal obligations are owed to the international community as a whole in the character of obligations *erga omnes*. The duties that states owe each other under customary IHRL are *erga omnes* obligations.

The distinction between duties *toward* someone and duties *regarding* someone suggests an important advantage of the duties paradigm, because it is also possible for a state to owe a human rights duty to the international community without the necessity of identifying a right holder who can claim his right. For example, states owe a legal duty to other states not to harm the Antarctic environment or kill endangered whales for food; a state that pollutes Antarctica or allows extensive whale hunting does not violate its legal duty toward a continent or animal, but toward other states. In municipal practice, criminal and regulatory laws are frequently conceived this way as well. An individual owes a (municipal) legal duty to the state not to commit a crime within the state's jurisdiction regardless of whether the crime would violate the rights of any individual. Similarly, a legal duty not to litter is not conceived as a duty toward the environment itself or even the specific persons who will suffer the effects of the littering, but rather as duties to the state or one of its administrative subdivisions.

One of the key advantages of a duties paradigm, then, is its ability to offer protection to fundamental values that are not exclusively individualistic. The preponderance of human rights claims brought by individuals tends to skew the jurisprudence toward those cases involving relatively direct injuries to identifiable individuals. Of course, duties have very substantial disadvantages over rights for protecting some kinds of interests. First, a right holder has a direct interest in enforcing the right and receiving compensation or other remedies for its breach. It would be possible to designate an ombudsman or agent to represent the interests of those whose interests are affected by the nonperformance of a duty. But there are many practical problems with such an expedient, as will be discussed in the context of specific state duties. Agency without supervision and control by the beneficiary is a perilous basis for the enforcement of fundamental values.

A right holder can also waive his rights in cases where the waiver grants greater benefits than the enforcement of the right. For example, in those cases where an accused criminal knows himself to be guilty and the evidence against him weighty, it may serve his interests better to accept a reasonable plea bargain than to risk a

63. CESCR art. 12.

64. *Id.* art. 12(2)(b).

much greater penalty following a fair trial. If the state had a duty to grant a fair trial to all without the possibility of the intended beneficiaries waiving that right, such an advantage would be forfeited.[65] Finally, as Allen Buchanan has observed, right holders have a direct incentive, by claiming violations of their rights, to bring public and official attention to noncompliant state behavior.[66]

Rights also have different distributive consequences than do duties. If we adapt Buchanan's example of the right to nourishment, if the state owes an obligation to take reasonable measures against hunger during a famine, it does not follow that every hungry individual has a claim against the state. Reasonable measures may leave some individuals hungry. In contrast, a universal right to nourishment leads to the conclusion that every individual left hungry after reasonable measures have been taken has a valid claim against the state,[67] which, depending on the circumstances, may or may not be a desirable result.

And yet, as I have argued, some important interests, including those bearing on human dignity, are not reducible to direct individual interests. In other words, some interests that we might wish to prioritize decisively are not tied either to identifiable, individual human beings or to cohesive groups of human beings. To protect such interests, we have to choose between trying to force them into the Procrustean bed of a rights paradigm or to rely instead on the flexibilities of a duties paradigm.

The interests most frequently considered to reflect fundamental values relate to animals, the natural environment, and future generations. Frequently, the three are considered together as intimately tied. Diverse reasons explain this nexus, but underlying them all is the recognition that the human beings presently living are not the only legitimate subjects of serious moral concern by the international community, and by some lights they are not always the most pressing concerns. Claims that rights are the appropriate way to protect these interests remain controversial. A person can agree that an animal should not be treated cruelly, or the interests of future generations should equal or trump those of the present generation on many important issues, without believing that animals have a right to freedom from cruelty or that future generations have a right to enjoy the same or better standard of living as the present generation. There are good reasons to believe the idea of direct ecological rights or future generation rights will never be accepted by a majority of the public, or even perhaps a large number of thoughtful persons.

Aside from the question of values, there are practical problems with attributing rights to animals, the natural environment, and future generations, and there are in addition metaphysical problems with attributing rights to the latter two. It is worth exploring whether using a duties paradigm would solve the problems posed by such rights and would present any significant advantages over rights.

65. On this point, see Joel Feinberg, Rights, Justice and the Bounds of Liberty 156–58 (1980); Theodore M. Benditt, Rights 45–50 (1982); Allen Buchanan, *What's So Special about Rights?*, 2 Soc. Philos. & Pol'y 61, 79–80 (1984).

66. Buchanan, *supra* note 65, at 64–65.

67. *Id.* at 74.

A. Duties toward Animals

As discussed above, the arguments for nonhuman animals having at least some moral rights is quite strong, at least if one bases the belief in human rights on either dignity or interests. If animals have moral rights, then humans as moral actors have ethical duties to respect those rights. Recognizing international legal rights for animals adds two complications, however. First, if rights reflect the interests of the right holder, then the content of most animal rights will be contentious. Animals have the same interest in avoiding suffering as do human beings, so the case for a right to freedom from unnecessary suffering is easy to make. Animals also have the same interest in living and reproducing that humans have, but a right to life is especially likely to meet opposition from human beings. Killing animals is rarely necessary to human survival. If animals have a *right* to life, then eating animals cannot be justified by a strong carnivorous human preference. Killing animals for research is equally unjustifiable, and killing them for entertainment is of course totally out of the question. Beyond these rights, it is not entirely clear what rights animals would have.[68]

In short, attributing moral rights, and a fortiori legal rights, to animals poses difficult metaphysical challenges. Undertaking the laborious task of crafting even a minimally satisfactory theory seems unnecessary to accomplish what should be the real goal, which is consideration for the crucial interests and dignity of animals, and a willingness to make sacrifices to protect those interests. When we are dealing with public international law, the goal would have to be even more circumscribed, because the universality of international law, the challenge of enforcing its rules, and the ponderousness of its enforcement institutions all counsel against detailed and context-insensitive rules about the human treatment of animals, however desirable such rules may be in theory.

Even if we can agree on the content of animal rights, however, a second complication arises. Animals cannot represent themselves in claiming their rights. This is not an insurmountable problem, but it is an unavoidably problematic one. Who should have standing to speak for animals? Nobody naturally can claim to speak for them, and animals have no capacity to choose their own agents or to assert claims themselves. In practice, the primary guarantors of legally recognized human rights are state governments, and international organizations with a more (e.g., the European Court of Human Rights) or less (e.g., the U.N. Human Rights Committee and Human Rights Council) loosely supervisory capacity over them. But the state does not universally speak for right holders, principally because most human rights claims are asserted against governments themselves. When individuals or groups of individuals assert their human rights, they may generally speak for themselves through agents they have chosen, and they thereby put themselves in opposition to the state.

68. Perhaps animals have the same interest in liberty that human beings have. Give any wild animal a choice between living in the perilous wild and a cage where it will be reliably fed, protected, and given medical care, and most will instinctually prefer to live in the wild. Do animals have a right to freedom of movement? Martha Nussbaum has advanced a strong argument as to why they should. *See* Martha C. Nussbaum, Frontiers of Justice 337, 376–77, 392, 398–99 (2006).

Joel Feinberg has argued that an agent can represent animals in the same way that agents represent infants and the mentally incompetent.[69] For human individuals, a guardian from within the infant's family is usually appointed. If no such person is available, the state will typically appoint a guardian at its own expense. But even if states could be persuaded to adopt bureaucratic innovations to protect animal rights, the guardian position would raise some tricky problems. One present in many agency relationships is moral hazard. It would be difficult to guarantee that states would appoint an agent whose interests, despite being those of a human being, aligned with those of other animals, or who could sublimate his own interests as a human being in favor of those of animals. How can we guarantee the guardian will not succumb to agency risks, the avoidance of which are one of the primary advantages of individual rights?[70] Even an objective agent may experience difficulty overcoming her personal and cultural biases and idiosyncratic views to represent organisms with many interests very unlike her own.

There are also problems of scope. Should the same guardian have standing to represent the rights of domesticated animals, animal companions, wildlife, or all of them? Even within categories, representation would also be complicated by the fact that, unlike a legal guardian for a single child or mental incompetent, the animal guardian would presumably represent the interests of many animals with potentially diverse or conflicting interests. Predatory carnivorous animals may have interests quite different from prey animals. It may not be exceptionally difficult to imagine what interests a domesticated dog or cat or horse might have, but what a wild coyote, feral lovebird, or migratory goose might claim as its rights requires an objectivity and imagination that few could confidently claim. As Martha Nussbaum has observed, "it is likely that all our empathetic imagining of the experiences of animals is shaped by our human sense of life."[71]

Finally, there is the question of powers. Appointing an agent does not resolve the question of whether the agent would be limited to facts gathering and influencing international and municipal policies in favor of animal rights through education and persuasion, somewhat like the U.N. High Commissioner for Human Rights, to propose animal rights conventions to the U.N. General Assembly, or to bring animal rights claims before international decision-making authorities.

In short, if attributing moral rights to animals raises problems of theory, attributing legal rights to them raises additional problems of practice. Fundamental state duties regarding animals offer some significant advantages over animal rights. If animals do not have moral rights, it does not necessarily follow that there are no fundamental moral duties toward animals.[72] The idea of fundamental state duties regarding animals lacks some of the rhetorical punch of animal rights, and as

69. Joel Feinberg, *The Rights of Animals and Unborn Generations*, *in* PHILOSOPHY AND ENVIRONMENTAL CRISIS 43, 46–48 (William T. Blackstone ed., 1974).

70. *See* Allen Buchanan, *Liberalism and Group Rights*, *in* IN HARM'S WAY 1, 13 (Jules Coleman & Allen Buchanan eds., 1994).

71. NUSSBAUM, *supra* note 68, at 353.

72. Taimie Bryant, *Animals Unmodified: Defining Animals/Defining Human Obligations to Animals*, 2006 U. CHI. LEG. F. 137 (2006).

discussed it suggests greater flexibility in how states protect animal interests, but it also solves the knottiest problems with animal rights. A person can have moral duties toward animals without animals having a correlative right against human beings. Although reasonable minds may still differ on exactly what fundamental duties states have toward animals beyond protection from unnecessary suffering, there is no metaphysical objection to state duties toward animals. We need not enter into recondite debates about whether animals have dignity, whether their interests give them rights, and whether human interests may ever trump those rights. The interests of animals beyond protection from unnecessary suffering would be established through the normal means of international political negotiation taking account of all relevant interests—human, animal, and ecological.

From a practical perspective, the flexibility of duties offers weaker protection to animal interests, but it has some countervailing advantages. The conceptual rigidity of rights would not necessarily serve animal interests across the board. The natural environment is the crucible of amoral evolution, which can occur only through competition for resources. Animal interests are likely to conflict on some important points. Many invasive species of wildlife, from the brown tree snake to the black rat, and from the house sparrow to the Burmese python, destroy native species and threaten human health. The extinction or depletion of top predators such as tigers, wolves, and crocodiles may save a few human and other animal lives, but it will predictably lead to overpopulation and starvation of former prey species. The domestication of animals improves their evolutionary chances by guaranteeing their long-term reproduction. Human efforts to manage invasive species, reintroduce predators, cull prey species, and use domestic animals for work or meat raise complex policy issues that would be further complicated by resorting to claims about inalienable animal rights. Again, the point is not to deny animal have such rights, but to point to the advantages of a more flexible state duties paradigm.

State duties also pose no agency problem; states could establish duties toward animals using the same techniques by which they establish duties toward persons. True, the concept of animal rights has an additional practical advantage, because the recognition of rights would make it positively necessary to appoint a representative for animal interests. Yet, the idea of state duties does not preclude the appointment of an international guardian or ombudsman to represent the interests of animals. His role would merely be to advise and help states fulfill their duties toward animals rather than to demand the rights of animals. Again, the point is not that duties are superior to rights for dealing with animal interests, it is merely that the two paradigms have different strengths and weaknesses.

B. Duties toward Future Generations

As noted, some philosophers have argued that future generations can have rights against the present generation. This claim faces a basic metaphysical challenge, because what does not exist cannot have a present right.[73] No doubt future generations will have the same rights when they are born that presently living persons

73. For more on the conceptual difficulties of attributing rights to future generations, see Feinberg, *supra* note 65, at 180–82.

now have. If the basis of rights is dignity or interests, then rights are contingent, as someone who does not yet exist has neither dignity (present fundamental value as an end unto himself) nor interests yet. Without entering deeply into this debate, it suffices to say that the metaphysics of such rights is contentious.

Even if future generations could have rights, determining the content of those rights would be problematic as well. The "rights" of future generations would necessarily be collective rights. Different persons in the group of "future generations" will inevitably have different expectations about what their heritage should be and the balance of interests it should reflect. Some will wish to prioritize leisure and economic wealth, others greater economic equality, others a pristine environment, still others a more educated cohort, etc. There will undoubtedly be some common ground—probably nobody will advocate the apocalyptic decimation of the natural environment or indebtedness to the point of economic collapse—but beyond this minimum, there is no reason to expect future generations to have viewpoints much less diverse than the current generations. There is, in short, no way to know precisely what rights future generations will want or to consolidate their interests except at an exceedingly general level.

As with animal rights, future generation rights face the problem of agency. It would be meaningless to speak of future generation *legal* rights unless future generations could travel backward in time and claim them, or somehow their interests could be represented responsibly and foresightfully in the present. The proposal for representing animal rights—the appointment of a guardian for future generations—has been made by publicists[74] and was even made by a state government in 1992 at the preparatory meetings for the Rio Earth Summit. Malta suggested creating a guardian to vindicate the "interests" (not rights) of future generations:

> We declare that each generation has, in particular, the responsibility to ensure that in any national or international forum, where it is likely that a decision be taken affecting the interests of future generations, access be given to an authorised person appointed as "Guardian" of future generations to appear and make submissions on their behalf, so that account be taken of the responsibilities stated in this Declaration and the obligations created thereby.[75]

The proposal failed to attract a consensus among states that already consider themselves, rightly or wrongly, the best representatives of the interests or rights of their own future generations.

An agent for future generations would have to deal with many of the same problems as would an agent for animals, mutatis mutandis. Unlike in cases of guardians ad litem for children or the mentally incompetent, where a guardian will be appointed who has no conflict of interest with his principal, every living human being has some personal interest or ideology implicated by decisions that would

74. *See* Christopher D. Stone, Should Trees Have Standing? Law, Morality, and the Environment ch. 5 (3d ed. 2010).

75. Malta National Report Submitted by the Government of Malta to the World Summit on Sustainable Development, Aug. 2002, at 82 (on file with author).

affect future generations.[76] Resources spent on (as opposed to invested in) improving the lives and comfort of existing persons may diminish the availability of resources for future generations. A guardian cannot dictate how to resolve a conflict of interests between current and future generations; he or she can only advocate for the interests of the latter. Having a representative is different from having an enforceable right.

As before, a fundamental state duties paradigm avoids the problems of the rights paradigm. Duties of intergenerational justice could be based on several philosophical grounds. One theory is that the Earth and its resources do not belong to presently living persons in the first place: they are held in trust for future generations. On such a premise, states have fiduciary duties to preserve (and, if possible, improve) the common heritage of humankind for the benefit of future generations. This specific theory is reflected in many of the cultural property, environmental, and related treaties and declarations already established in international law.

Alternatively or in addition, some have argued that we exist in a community of reciprocity with future generations.[77] Future generations will share the genetic code of the present generation and inherit all that it has, including its history. The psychological desire to be remembered well by history is one aspect of the present interest that can be served by future generations. We therefore derive an intangible benefit from the security and prosperity of future generations that could justify duties to behave in a manner that benefits future generations. Such arguments support state duties toward future generations without necessitating the attribution of rights to the generations.

Translating such moral duties into fundamental state duties involves no conceptual leaps. As noted, states already consider themselves the guardians of the interests of future generations, so accepting fundamental duties toward them follows naturally. There are in any case some jurisprudential precedents for holding states to such a duty. For example, the International Court of Justice implicitly attributed to states duties respecting future generations in its advisory opinion on the legality of nuclear weapons. After noting the danger such weapons pose to mankind and the natural environment, the Court held that the international law of armed conflict requires states to "take account of . . . their ability to cause damage to generations to come" in deciding when and how to use nuclear arms.[78]

The challenge is getting states to think in a more cosmopolitan manner about fundamental duties toward future persons. With only minor exceptions, IHRL is currently bound by jurisdictional doctrines that encourage states to spend their resources on protecting the interests of their nationals—the persons who compose the state, justify its existence, and have immediate privity with it. The division of

76. Christopher Stone relied on this analogy to make his case for environmental guardians, but he failed to account for the inevitable conflict of interest in the latter case. *See* STONE, *supra* note 74, at 8.

77. *See, e.g.*, Martin P. Golding, *Obligations to Future Generations*, 56 THE MONIST 85 (1972); AVNER DE-SHALIT, WHY POSTERITY MATTERS (1995).

78. Advisory Opinion on the Legality of the Threat or Use of Nuclear Weapons, 1996 I.C.J. REP. 226, para. 36.

the peoples of the world into states with primary human rights duties for their own nationals is justified by administrative efficiency and the human need for a socially accepted identity, but such values do not preclude other duties based on long-term, shared human interests, such as cultural and environmental preservation. Fundamental state duties to protect these interests need not be limited to future generations of the state's nationals alone, and the global nature of such interests gives reasons to prefer global duties.

c. Ecological Duties

The proposal to appoint a guardian to represent the environment faces precisely the same problems as proposals to appoint agents for animals and future generations. The challenges of agency may seem to be moot, however, if all individuals already benefit from a human right to a safe and healthy natural environment.[79] In that case, the beneficiaries of the right may employ municipal and international mechanisms of rights enforcement in support of human interests in the environment, and the problems of representation, bias, moral hazard, and uncertainty about the interests of the principal do not arise.

However, by itself, a universal human right regarding the natural environment is insufficient to protect the crucial underlying interests for both conceptual and practical reasons. Without rehearsing all of the reasons the human rights paradigm falls short in protecting environmental interests, I will here mention two important objections. The first is that threats to the environment by their nature harm more than one individual. Some such threats, such as global warming and the thinning of the ozone layer, have species-wide implications. Although groups of right holders may seek to vindicate their legal rights at the international level, there may be no sufficient incentive to form a cohesive advocacy group, and it is possible that no one individual or group of individuals will have sufficient incentive to shoulder the cost of vindicating the rights of everyone—another problem of collective action.[80] Nothing in these observations suggests that an individual human right to a safe and healthy environment could not frequently vindicate the individual's interest and even the environmental problem for everyone affected by it, but it does suggest that an individual's rights frequently will not provide adequate incentives to bear the costs of fully vindicating the right.

Even in those cases in which an individual is willing to shoulder the burden of vindicating a community right, he faces the problem of standing. When an individual's or community's well-being has been directly and exceptionally affected by environmental damage or degradation, it is possible to impute standing to the individual or community before a national or international tribunal to enforce the

79. *See generally* Dinah Shelton, *Human Rights, Environmental Rights, and the Right to Environment*, 28 Stan. J. Int'l L. 103 (1991); Prudence E. Taylor, *From Environmental to Ecological Human Rights: A New Dynamic in International Law?*, 10 Geo. Int'l Envtl. L. Rev. 309 (1998); John H. Knox, *Human Rights, Environmental Protection, and the Sustainable Development Goals*, 24 Wash. Int'l L.J. 517 (2015).

80. *See* Mancur Olson, The Logic of Collective Action: Public Goods and the Theory of Groups (1971).

right.[81] However, the U.N. Human Rights Committee has declared that not everyone has standing to vindicate the human rights set forth in the International Civil and Political Covenant worldwide.[82] If automobile emission standards in Ruritania seem too high to a national of Freedonia, possibly resulting in an increase in global warming, the Freedonian national has no legal basis for requiring Ruritania to increase its emission standards. An individual human right to a safe and healthy environment goes only so far in protecting ecological values.

The second problem is in some ways the flip side of the first. It is possible that no individual or group will perceive any interest *at all* in vindicating serious environmental problems. Despoliation of the sensitive Antarctic environment, for example, would immediately affect no human population, because none permanently lives there. Similarly, human blindness about or apathy toward environmental degradation could result in underenforcement of the right. It is possible that no individual or group of individuals with sufficient influence would step forward to complain that his or her or the group's specific human right is violated by the extinction of a living species that turns out in hindsight to have been an ecological linchpin. The disappearance of certain bacteria, fungi, corals, insects, or plants may dangerously unbalance the ecosystem without any person perceiving himself to have a fundamental interest in preserving them. It is even possible that many serious long-term threats to the environment will not trigger any individual or group's sense of personal injury. For example, many persons live in deserts that, without highly environmentally destructive technologies, could not sustain human habitation. As of this writing, 4.3 million persons live in and around Phoenix, Arizona, which is not equipped to sustain significant human life without pathogenic air pollution, enormous waste of energy for cooling, depletion of groundwater, evaporation of fresh water inefficiently transported by open-air canals, and large-scale destruction of extremely sensitive wildlife habitats.[83] Far from wishing to protect the environment from such activities, virtually all directly interested persons seem intent on continuing the devastation or increasing it in an ever-expanding radius. The legal mechanism by which an individual could vindicate his human right to a safe and healthy environment would not necessarily address such issues before disaster strikes and the opportunity to protect the individual environmental right is beyond redemption. Alternatively, the gradual degradation of the environment may not rise to a level of interference with any individual's rights until irreversible damage has been done. Future generations may suffer from environmental damage that did not bother any living person at the time.[84]

81. Regional human rights tribunals as well as the U.N. Human Rights Committee have recognized the standing of individuals or communities specially affected by a harmful environmental practice to seek exoneration of the right to a clean environment. *See* Francesco Francioni, *International Human Rights in an Environmental Horizon*, 21 Eur. J. Int'l L. 41, 50–54 (2010).

82. Brun v. France, U.N. Hum. Rts. Comm. Commun. No. 1453/2006, para. 6, U.N. Doc. CCPR/C/88/D/1453 (2006) ("[N]o person may, in theoretical terms and by *actio popularis*, object to a law or practice which he holds at variance with the Covenant.").

83. *See* William deBuys, *Could Phoenix Soon Become Uninhabitable?*, The Nation, Mar. 14, 2013, *at* http://www.thenation.com.

84. *See* Timo Koivurova, Book Review, 106 Am. J. Int'l L. 437, 439 (2012).

Given that individual rights to a safe and healthy environment cannot adequately protect collective interests in the environment, the interests of future generations, or the interests of wildlife in the environment, the only other right-based option is the one proposed by Christopher Stone and discussed in Chapter 1—attributing rights to the natural environment itself, or some features of it. We already established that such a right was metaphysically incoherent, and in any case it faces the same practical obstacles as the idea of future generation rights does. The natural environment has no opinions, desires, or ability to suffer or experience pleasure. It is an abstraction. The same is true of natural features such as forests, streams, and mountains, and living organisms that lack sentience such as trees. If they have interests, they cannot express them, and no one person is legitimately capable of speaking for the natural environment or any feature of it.

Once again, fundamental state duties provide a potential solution to most of the insufficiencies of the rights paradigm. Mary Midgley raises the idea of ecological moral duties, but not because forests and lakes have rights. She seems to believe that, as social beings living in an ecosystem in which each part, whether biological or geological, interrelates, human beings owe some sort of duty of care to non-sentient beings as well as their habitats.[85] Midgley's idea, if I have interpreted it correctly, boils down to an argument for a duty arising from the derivative interest of living or sentient beings in their environment. We must accept that such a duty binds persons or their agents (including states) universally if we accept that living things have an interest in living and thriving that merits respect, as we ourselves hope to live and thrive. A fundamental state duty to protect and preserve the natural environment avoids the agency problem of ascribing rights to inanimate matter or conceptual abstractions. More important, it can obligate states to take measures for the preservation of collective rights and future interests in a way that individual human rights cannot.

The imposition of mutual, fundamental duties for the preservation of the environment is of course already part of the agenda of international environmental law. Treaties such as the Framework Convention on Climate Change and its protocols, the Convention on Long-Range Transboundary Air Pollution, the Convention on Biological Diversity, and the various conventions on the marine environment and living resources impose both general and specific duties for the preservation of the natural environment. In theory, at least, the international community has a relatively developed practical capability to demand respect for ecological interests, either through direct pressure or institution building. Such duties may not yet be recognized as fundamental in the sense of meriting exceptional weight in the way that rights do. The difference between such environmental treaties and a fundamental state duty to preserve and protect the environment is that the former are voluntary and mutable, whereas the latter would require exceptional weight to be given to environmental interests, perhaps on par with or even superior to internationally recognized human rights. Voluntary treaties for the protection of the environment are undersubscribed, underprotective, and underenforced. Fundamental state duties would better reflect the urgency of the values at stake while avoiding the

85. Mary Midgley, Animals and Why They Matter 90–91 & n.2 (1983).

pitfalls of individual human rights. Attributing duties to states to respect an important value such as environmental protection would raise the value's priority without implicating conceptual or practical challenges of the kind associated with appointing a guardian to represent environmental rights or relying solely on individual rights to protect community values of exceptional importance.

PART TWO

Nondiscrimination and Substantive Right Claiming Paradigms

Part I of this book dealt with a basic structural question about public international law: To what extent can and should international law promote core community values by recognizing fundamental individual, corporate, and state duties instead of, or in addition to, individual human rights? This Part examines another aspect of the structure of international law: To what extent can and should international law promote core community values by prohibiting states from discriminating among different groups of persons, or different kinds of activities, as opposed to establishing substantive rights applicable to all persons equally?

Nondiscrimination as a human right has been much discussed,[1] but to most international lawyers, it will not seem obvious to ask this question at all. The nondiscrimination right has been a core component of human rights doctrine for so long that it seems an inevitable and integral part of the system. But the nondiscrimination right differs from and interacts with substantive human rights in exceptional ways with important theoretical and practical consequences. As Allen Buchanan observed a decade ago: "For the most part, international lawyers

1. *See, e.g.*, EGBERT W. VIERDAG, THE CONCEPT OF DISCRIMINATION IN INTERNATIONAL LAW (1973); WARWICK A. MCKEAN, EQUALITY AND DISCRIMINATION UNDER INTERNATIONAL LAW (1983); Dinah Shelton, *Prohibited Discrimination in International Human Rights Law*, *in* THE DIVERSITY OF INTERNATIONAL LAW: ESSAYS IN HONOUR OF PROFESSOR KALLIOPI K. KOUFA 261 (Aristotle Constantinides & Nikos Zaikos eds., 2009); Anne Bayefsky, *The Principle of Equality or Non-discrimination in International Law*, 11 HUM. RTS. Q. [HUM. RTS. L.J.] 1 (1990).

and others professionally concerned with human rights, to the extent that they have examined the theoretical grounding of human rights at all, have not utilized the rich philosophical literature on egalitarianism."[2] With few exceptions,[3] ten years has not changed much on that score. Much less have international human rights lawyers attempted to ground the rights to nondiscrimination and equal protection of the law specifically in ideal egalitarian theory.

The reverse is equally true. Philosophers have developed sophisticated ideal egalitarian theories of human rights without a nuanced understanding of the difficulties of translating them to a workable international legal regime. Yet, any attempt to operationalize an egalitarian theory in the world public order should be informed by the technical limitations and tendencies of the system and the practical consequences of implementing the theory. The relationship between a nondiscrimination paradigm and a substantive rights paradigm forms a critical component of such an understanding, because in the world public order, the nondiscrimination right functions within and synergizes with a matrix of highly varied substantive legal rights.

International human rights instruments do not entirely gloss over the differences between substantive rights and nondiscrimination paradigms. Human rights conventions indeed tend to treat universal substantive rights as existing in a category distinct from the right against arbitrary discrimination. The latter is sometimes viewed as complementary, but otherwise unrelated, to the various substantive rights codified in the major human rights treaties. Of course, nondiscrimination is also a substantive right in the sense that it represents a claim on the state to treatment as advantageous as (or no more disadvantageous than) that afforded to others in similar circumstances. In that limited sense, the right to freedom from discrimination is no different from the right to freedom from torture or the right to privacy.

2. Allen Buchanan, *Equality and Human Rights*, 4 Pol., Philos. & Econ. 69, 70 (2005).

3. Notably Samantha Besson, *The Egalitarian Dimension of Human Rights*, *in* Law, Science, Technology: Plenary Lectures Presented at the 25th World Congress of the International Association for Philosophy of Law and Social Philosophy 19 (Ulfrid Neumann et al. eds., 2013). Besson justifies human rights as based on equal moral status, *id.* at 49–50, and necessary to protect those interests tied to equal political membership whose disrespect would deny inclusion in the political community to the right holder. *Id.* at 34. Thus, Besson views human rights and political equality as "mutually constitutive." *Id.* at 36. Allen Buchanan has also taken up his own gauntlet to some extent. *See* Allen Buchanan, The Heart of Human Rights 139–52 (2013).

The right against discrimination differs, however, in several crucial respects. Most prominently, other rights all have a semantically circumscribed subject matter. We may not be able to say with certainty exactly what conduct constitutes "torture" or what is denoted by "privacy" in every case, but the international community's shared subjective understandings of these terms gives us some crude sense of the requirements it imposes on the state. Whatever the outer boundaries of the right against torture, for example, at a minimum it encompasses freedom from the deliberate, enforced infliction of serious physical pain not intended for the benefit of the subject or the prevention of immediate harm to a person directly being attacked or threatened by the subject. The nondiscrimination right differs from other human rights because the concept of discrimination per se does not presuppose any theory about which specific benefits or freedoms a group of persons should have.

In contrast, the right against discrimination tells us almost nothing about what the state is forbidden to do, without the further development of facts. Initially, it depends on evidence that a distinction was made between persons based on divergent characteristics. Distinctions themselves in public policy are unobjectionable and indeed necessary in any legal system; discrimination must therefore refer to a specific kind of distinction. Nor are distinctions—even those harming a specific class of persons—inherently or intrinsically unethical in the way that torture is, if the distinction can be justified. In the human rights context, then, discrimination carries two connotations: "significantly detrimental" and "arbitrary." Because discrimination by definition results in a difference in treatment, and some treatment is normally bound to be less beneficial or more detrimental than others, that addition does not add much to our comprehension of the term, other than the understanding that discrimination having a trivially negative effect on any group of persons or class of activities is unlikely to violate the right.

As early as Aristotle, it has been recognized as a fundamental maxim of justice that like cases should be treated alike.[4] Differences in treatment between groups in similar situations violate this maxim, and are what IHRL calls "arbitrary" distinctions. The "arbitrary," or more properly "unjustified," qualification for distinctions prohibited by IHRL adds a more helpful limitation. An early draft of the UDHR actually included the word "arbitrary" as a qualification

4. *See* ARISTOTLE, NICOMACHEAN ETHICS, Book V.3 (W.D. Ross trans., 1925) (350 B.C.E.); *see also* H.L.A. HART, *Positivism and the Separation of Law and Morals*, *in* ESSAYS IN JURISPRUDENCE AND PHILOSOPHY 49, 81 (1983).

to "discrimination," but it was soon removed as redundant; most delegates understood discrimination as a legal term to encompass only arbitrary distinctions by definition.[5] Only unjustified discrimination is forbidden by IHRL, meaning that only discrimination based on intergroup differences that are irrelevant to the state's policy, that cannot be justified as necessary and proportionate to a legitimate aim, or that fail to treat like cases alike qualify as arbitrary. Distinctions between persons in different situations, of course, are not necessarily unjustified. The "likeness" of different cases calls for the exercise of judgment about their relevant characteristics and degree of similarity, but this is only saying that the analysis of arbitrariness in discrimination is no simpler than the analysis determining which invasions of privacy or restrictions on freedom of expression are justified by other moral considerations.

Because the human right against discrimination embodies a fundamental principle of justice that is neutral as to substantive content, it can be considered an indispensable right. Whatever else one's moral or political theory may stipulate, the principle of nondiscrimination must be observed if it is to be coherent, although questions of interpretation and implementation will inevitably engender controversy. The ethical dimension of discrimination depends on historical, cultural, economic, political, and other social conditions relating to the class of persons or activities against which discrimination is directed. It also depends on the form discrimination takes, who is doing the discriminating (the state, large sectors of private society, or isolated individuals), and the consequences of the discrimination for both the subjects of discrimination and society as a whole. Harmful, arbitrary state discrimination is pervasive in almost all societies, but it is not always considered a human rights violation.

The juridical challenge posed by a human right against arbitrary discrimination, then, is in tailoring the right to regulate, within the vast universe of public and private distinctions and discriminatory behavior, only the set of discriminatory acts that seriously compromises a just public order based on human dignity. This challenge has proved sufficiently formidable in IHRL doctrine that nondiscrimination doctrine remains fragmented and frequently inconsistent. Not from ignorance of its importance, though. Since the United Nations General Assembly adopted the UDHR in 1948, the right against

5. Dinah Shelton, *Prohibited Discrimination in International Human Rights Law*, *in* THE DIVERSITY OF INTERNATIONAL LAW: ESSAYS IN HONOUR OF PROFESSOR KALLIOPI K. KOUFA 261, 276 (Aristotle Constantinides & Nikos Zaikos eds., 2009) (citing U.N. Doc. E/CN.4/99 (May 24, 1948); U.N. Doc. E/CN.4/82/add.8 (May 6, 1948); U.N. Doc. E/CN.4/SR.52, at 6, 8 (May 28, 1948)).

discrimination has held a central place in IHRL.[6] It is one of only two rights specifically mentioned (three times, in fact) in the preamble to the U.N. Charter.[7] It is found in most national constitutions,[8] and is one of the few rights included in all three conventions in the international bill of rights[9] and all of the major regional human rights conventions.[10]

It is also one of the very few human rights around which several whole treaties revolve.[11] The earliest of these is the Convention on the Elimination of All Forms of Racial Discrimination (1965), which condemns racial discrimination and requires states to take active measures to mitigate racism within their societies. The Convention on the Elimination of All Forms of Discrimination against Women, adopted fourteen years later, does the same for sex and gender. Another treaty, the Convention on the Rights of Persons with Disabilities, focuses significantly on preventing and remedying government and social discrimination against persons with disabilities,[12] and a regional treaty in

6. *See* Paul Gordon Lauren, Evolution of International Human Rights: Visions Seen 183–84 (2d ed. 2011) ("In each and every one of these proposals [for U.N. human rights commitments in its founding documents], nondiscrimination was seen as absolutely essential to any provision about international human rights."); *see also id.* at 159.

7. "To reaffirm faith in . . . the equal rights of men and women of nations large and small . . . . To develop friendly relations among nations based on respect for the principle of equal rights . . . . and in promoting and encouraging respect for human rights and fundamental freedoms for all without distinction as to race, sex, language, or religion." U.N. Charter, pmbl.

8. *See, e.g.*, Const. of Arg. arts. 37, 43 (1994); Const. of Braz. arts. 3(IV), 5(XLI), 7(XXXI) (2001); Const. of Can. art. 15 (1989); Const. of Egypt art. 40 (2007); Const. of France art. 1 (1958); Const. of Ger. art. 3 (2009); Const. of India arts. 14–16 (2007); Const. of Japan arts. 14, 44 (1946); Const. of Mex. arts. 4, 123(VII) (1917); Const. of Pol. arts. 32–33, 60 (1997); Const. of Rus. arts. 19, 37 (1993); Const. of S. Afr. arts. 9, 36 (1996); U.S. Const. amend. XIV.

9. The "international bill of rights" refers to the UDHR, CPPR ("Recognizing that these rights derive from the inherent dignity of the human person"); and CESCR.

10. ECHR, art. 14; ACHR, arts. 1(1), 24; Additional Protocol to the American Convention on Human Rights in the Area of Economic, Social and Cultural Rights ("Protocol of San Salvador"), Nov. 17, 1988, art. 3, 28 I.L.M. 161 (1989); Banjul Charter, arts. 2, 18(2); EU Charter arts. 21, 23; ESC arts. 20, pt. V art. E. The U.N. Convention against Torture also defines as prohibited torture severe pain or suffering that is intentionally inflicted "for any reason based on discrimination of any kind." Convention against Torture and Other Cruel, Inhuman or Degrading Treatment or Punishment art. 1, Dec. 10, 1984, 1465 U.N.T.S. 85.

11. Among the other such rights are those protecting against genocide and torture. *See* Convention on the Prevention and Punishment of the Crime of Genocide, Dec. 9, 1948, 78 U.N.T.S. 277; Convention against Torture and Other Cruel, Inhuman or Degrading Treatment or Punishment, Dec. 10, 1984, 1465 U.N.T.S. 85.

12. Convention on the Rights of Persons with Disabilities, Dec. 13, 2006, arts. 3–7, 12, 2515 U.N.T.S. 3.

the Americas specifically deals with discrimination based on disability.[13] The ubiquity of the nondiscrimination right bespeaks its significance and flexibility. The Inter-American Commission on Human Rights went so far as to describe nondiscrimination as "the backbone of the universal and regional systems for the protection of human rights,"[14] and the Inter-American Court asserted that it is part of *ius cogens*.[15] The nondiscrimination right is, in short, sui generis among human rights.

This Part will discuss some consequences of the nondiscrimination right's unique attributes. The most consequential of these is its availability as a paradigm for claiming a wide variety of human rights violations. In other words, most human rights violations may be framed as acts of unjustified discrimination as an alternative, or in addition, to reliance on the substantive rights specifically recited in international treaties. This is entirely different from suggesting that claiming a violation of the nondiscrimination right is equivalent to claiming a violation of a substantive right. On the contrary, the differences between the two kinds of claims will be illuminated in some detail in the coming chapters. It is instead to say that there is a nondiscrimination claiming paradigm that generally stands as a conceptually viable alternative to the substantive rights-claiming paradigm in the great majority of cases.

13. Inter-American Convention on the Elimination of All Forms of Discrimination against Persons with Disabilities, June 7, 1999, OAS Doc. AG/RES.1608, *available at* http://www.oas.org.

14. Gonzales v. United States, Inter-Am. Comm'n on Hum Rts., Rep. No. 80/11 (July 21, 2011), para. 107.

15. Advisory Opinion on Juridical Condition and Human Rights of Undocumented Migrants, Sept. 17, 2003, Ser. A, No. 18, para. 101.

3

Nondiscrimination as a Claiming Paradigm

A. TWO METHODS OF VALUE PROTECTION

All international human rights instruments codify a series of substantive rights. These rights are universal in the sense that respect for them is considered necessary to protect the dignity of all persons and to foster conditions that will help to ensure them an opportunity of achieving comfort, enlightenment, happiness, and other conditions that lead to their flourishing as individuals and members of an organized society. In theory, universal rights apply to all persons regardless of race, sex, political opinion, religious belief, age, class, disability, or other distinction, because human rights are premised on the equal moral status of all persons.[1] Entitlement to the rights is automatic by membership in the human species. The rights are "substantive" in the sense of having at least some definite content expressing a purportedly fundamental human interest served by the right. Any interest can theoretically support a right; the variety of interests capable of expression in the form of rights is, subject to the previous Part's discussion, virtually unlimited. But only those interests of sufficient importance to the world community attract sufficient consensus to rise to the status of rights. Most rights are phrased to protect a single, specific interest or group of related interests, such as the interest in freedom from torture, in a fair trial, or in the ability to seek and obtain employment.

All major international human rights treaties also codify nondiscrimination rights of one form or another. These forms range from very specific, substance-delimited nondiscrimination rights, such as a right to freedom from racial discrimination in inheritance laws;[2] to a positive right for the state to take remedial measures to combat private discrimination on some ground, such as sex;[3] to a very broad right to equal protection of the law.[4] Each instrument in the international bill of rights, and the three broad regional human rights treaties (the European

1. *See* Samantha Besson, *The Egalitarian Dimension of Human Rights*, *in* Law, Science, Technology: Plenary Lectures Presented at the 25th World Congress of the International Association for Philosophy of Law and Social Philosophy 29–30 (Ulfrid Neumann et al. eds., 2013).

2. *E.g.*, CERD art. 5(d)(vi).

3. *E.g.*, CEDAW art. 10.

4. *E.g.*, UDHR art. 7; CCPR, art. 26.

Convention, American Convention, and Banjul Charter), contains a nondiscrimination right of this latter, general type, in addition to a litany of universal substantive rights and sometimes more specific nondiscrimination rights.

The reason for the general nondiscrimination right's ubiquity lies in a unique trio of characteristics. First, the nondiscrimination right is inherently comparative, allowing it to address inequities beyond the reach of substantive rights phrased in absolute terms. A right to a fair trial, for example, is lexically indeterminate about the procedures and conditions that would satisfy "fairness," but the concept of fairness implies that some minimum standards must be met to satisfy the right. An authoritative interpreter of the right must infer that minimum based on general principles of law, moral reasoning, the political and economic needs of society, and other relevant criteria. From this he may infer, for example, that such a right encompasses competent legal representation and an equal opportunity to present one's case. A nondiscrimination right, in contrast, calls on the decision authority to resort to comparison with a similarly situated group that supplies an objectively ascertainable standard of reference. This analysis will not necessarily resort to lexical definitions, philosophical theories of justice, or analogies to municipal legal systems. It will instead rely on a relativistic analysis of the similarities and differences between the victim group and a reference group, and evaluation of the necessity and appropriateness of a distinction between them.

Second and related, is the point mentioned earlier that the nondiscrimination right need not be limited to any specific subject matter. Substantive rights are assigned by definition to protect specified interests, such as the interest in sustenance, education, or freedom of movement. The general nondiscrimination right, in contrast, is neutral as to the interests served, so long as they are served equivalently to the interests of the comparison group. It thereby responds in a neutral way to the problem identified by James Madison in *The Federalist* papers: "In all cases where a majority are united by a common interest or passion, the rights of the minority are in danger."[5] The nondiscrimination right denies the majority the right to allocate to itself benefits denied to the minority.[6] A nondiscrimination right can potentially protect almost any threatened interest of the right holder and, depending on its interpretation, potentially protects against unfavorable treatment in matters beyond the scope of other human rights.

Third, because substantive human rights are universal, they apply to all persons everywhere. The set of beneficiaries of the nondiscrimination right is limited in any case of practical application, but nonetheless indeterminate a priori as to the identity of the beneficiaries. In principle, the nondiscrimination right is universal in the sense of applying to all persons, because every person has characteristics that may be used as a basis for discrimination. But in practice claims under the nondiscrimination right always depend on the claimant's identification with a limited class of persons. In other words, to say that everyone has a right against discrimination does not mean that, when Albert invokes the right in response to some

5. THE FEDERALIST NO. 10 (James Madison).

6. It equally denies the right of an empowered minority to allocate to itself benefits denied to a disempowered majority.

state measure, Betty can successfully invoke the same right in reaction to the same measure. That means the nondiscrimination right can be tailored to protect only specific classes of persons, and these classes can be expanded or contracted to adapt the right to changing political and social needs.

The relative resources required to ensure the effective enjoyment of the right differ as well. Positive substantive rights span the spectrum from very to only trivially costly. Examples of the former include duties to provide education, healthcare, or sanitary water to the population, which obligate the state to expend very considerable resources to build facilities, train and hire personnel, and regulate the operation of the resulting institutions. Examples of the latter include negative duties to protect the freedom of expression or the right to form a labor union. In many such cases, the most significant threats to the right come from the state itself, and protecting individuals from private infringements calls for little more than legislation and a minor dedication of the state's police and judicial powers to preventing occasional abuses of the rights.

A positive nondiscrimination right, such as that implemented in Europe and the United States,[7] generally calls for much more extensive commitment to intervene in private transactions, because private discrimination may be as prevalent as, or more prevalent than, government discrimination in any given society. To comply with a positive obligation, the state must at a minimum promulgate laws prohibiting private discrimination in politically and economically significant situations and enforce those laws through judicial and policing measures. The sheer number and diversity of politically and economically significant private actors—business firms, universities, local governments, homeowners' associations, landlords, restaurants, hotels, etc.—requires the state to maintain an efficient judicial system to resolve a potentially very large number of discrimination disputes.

One important way in which substantive and nondiscrimination rights do *not* differ is that, although either kind of right might be phrased in absolute terms,[8] both inevitably require balancing the right with conflicting human rights or societal interests. All international human rights authorities have approved derogations from rights when the measure is necessary and proportionate to the state's legitimate interests. Most countries with significant human rights traditions interpret the rights as implying similar limitations.[9] Of course, the standard for testing the permissibility of limitations on human rights is far from undeviating. Sometimes, certain

7. Defrenne v. Sabena (No. 2), Eur. Ct. Justice Case 43/75 (Apr. 8, 1976), 1976 E.C.R. 455; 42 U.S.C. §§ 2000e *et seq.*

8. *See, e.g.*, CEDAW art. 1 (defining discrimination to mean "any distinction" based on sex); National Minorities Convention art. 4 (prohibiting "any discrimination" based on national minority group membership).

9. *See, e.g.*, Australian Hum. Rts. Comm'n, Human Rights Brief No. 4: Lawful Limits on Fundamental Freedoms (Mar. 8, 2006), *at* http://www.hreoc.gov.au/human_rights/briefs/brief_4.html#3_neccessary; Canadian Charter of Rights & Freedoms, Part I of the Constitution Act, 1982, Schedule B to the Canada Act 1982 (U.K.), 1982, ch. 11, art. 1; Basic Law: Freedom of Occupation, 1454 Sefer Ha-Chukkim (10 March 1994) at 90 (Isr.); Const. of S. Afr. art. 36(1); Pickering v. Board of Educ., 391 U.S. 563, 568 (1968). *See generally* Armand L.C. de Mestral et al., The Limitation of Human Rights in Comparative Constitutional Law (1986).

substantive rights are considered more vulnerable to state abuse than others, and so demand a more urgent state interest and exacting demonstration that the measure is necessary to serve that interest. However, insofar as discriminatory measures affect these vulnerable interests, the same demanding standard typically applies.[10]

Despite a certain uniformity of jurisprudence by national and international authorities on these aspects of human rights, the kinds and extent of protection of rights differ very significantly on a regional and national level. It is well known that different countries may interpret the same human right in radically different ways. Less understood is the significant divergence in the application of the nondiscrimination right. In discrimination analysis, the focus rests on the state's justification for distinguishing between the injured class and society at large. As Schwarzenberger observed:

> Arbitrariness in any form is—or ought to be—abhorrent to *homo juridicus*. His whole professional outlook is dominated by the attitude that, in the eyes of the law, equal situations require equal remedies.
>
> Yet, anybody who is acquainted with the techniques by which judicial precedents are applied and distinguished is aware of the element of subjectivity which is inseparable from deciding, even on a judicial level, what situations are supposed to be equal.[11]

Adjudicating substantive rights can be essentially reduced to an exercise in defining the scope of the human right at issue and balancing it against the state's goals and means. The same is true of nondiscrimination rights analysis, but this latter entails further comparing two allegedly like groups and evaluating the legitimacy and cogency of the state's rationale for distinguishing between them.

B. THE INTERNATIONAL LEGAL DEFINITION OF DISCRIMINATION

The usual doctrinal analysis of the nondiscrimination right begins with a definition of prohibited discrimination that incorporates the concept of arbitrariness. In the Strasbourg Court's terminology, discrimination is deemed to occur when there is (1) different treatment of persons or groups in relevantly the same or similar situations,[12] and (2) that difference has no "objective and reasonable justification."[13]

10. *See, e.g.*, Smith & Grady v. United Kingdom, 29 Eur. H.R. Rep. 493, para. 89 (2000) ("[W]hen the relevant restrictions concern 'a most intimate part of an individual's private life,' there must exist 'particularly serious reasons' before such interferences can satisfy the requirements of Article 8(2) of the Convention.") (quoting Dudgeon v. United Kingdom, 4 Eur. H.R. Rep. 149, paras. 52, 59 (1982)).

11. Georg Schwarzenberger, International Law and Order 100 (1971).

12. D.H. v. Czech Rep., 47 E.H.R.R. 3, para. 175 (2008); *accord* Willis v. United Kingdom, 35 E.H.R.R. 21, para. 48 (2002).

13. *See* Rasmussen v. Denmark, 7 E.H.R.R. 371 (1985); *Belgian Linguistics Case*, Eur. Ct. Hum. Rts. Judgment of July 23, 1968 (merits), 1 E.H.R.R. 252, para. 10 (1968) ("*si la distinction*

A justification will be considered objective and reasonable if the measure pursues (2a) a legitimate aim, further defined as an aim "necessary in a democratic society" for the public welfare,[14] and (2b) there is "a reasonable relationship of proportionality between the means employed and the aim sought to be realized."[15] The regional human rights tribunals and other institutional international authorities have adopted very similar tests, sometimes with minor differences in terminology, but always to the same purport.[16] We will begin by examining each component of the definition in turn.

1. Similar Situations

The converse of Aristotelean justice is that unlike cases ought not to be treated alike. As a general rule, if two groups are found sufficiently dissimilar, a measure that distinguishes between the groups will accordingly not be considered discriminatory. Merit-based admissions to a university, for example, will frequently result in less intelligent, intellectually ambitious, or diligent applicants being denied opportunities for higher education, but such admissions policies are not discriminatory if they deny admission to applicants whose relevant characteristics are sufficiently dissimilar to those of admitted applicants. Of course, which characteristics

manque de justification objectif et raisonnable"); Norris v. Ireland, 13 E.H.R.R. 186, paras. 41, 44 (1989).

14. This qualification originates in CCPR article 21 ("No restrictions may be placed on the exercise of this right other than those imposed in conformity with the law and which are necessary in a democratic society in the interests of national security or public safety, public order (*ordre public*), the protection of public health or morals or the protection of the rights and freedoms of others.") and CESCR article 4 ("the State may subject such rights only to such limitations as are determined by law only in so far as this may be compatible with the nature of these rights and solely for the purpose of promoting the general welfare in a democratic society.").

15. *Belgian Linguistics Case*, 1 E.H.R.R. 252, para. 10 (1968).

16. *E.g.*, Toonen v. Australia, U.N. GAOR, Hum. Rts. Comm., 50th Sess., Comm'n No. 488/1992, at 226, paras. 8.3–8.4, U.N. Doc. U.N. Doc CCPR/C/50/D/488/1992 (1994) ("The Committee interprets the requirement of reasonableness to imply that any interference with privacy must be proportional to the end sought and be necessary in the circumstances of any given case."); Herrera-Ulloa v. Costa Rica, Inter-Am. Ct. H.R., Case No. 12.367, Judgment of July 2, 2004, para. 123 ("[T]he restriction must be proportionate to the legitimate interest that justifies it and must be limited to what is strictly necessary to achieve that objective."); Committee on Economic, Social and Cultural Rights, General Comment No. 20, paras. 10, 13, Comm. No. E/C.12/GC/20 (May 25, 2009), 49 E.H.R.R. SE10 (2009); Tanganyika Law Society v. Republic of Tanzania, Afr. Ct. Human & Peoples' Rts., App. No. 009/2011, Judgment of June 14, 2013, para. 106.1 ("restrictions on the exercise of rights . . . must be necessary in a democratic society; they must be reasonably proportionate to the legitimate aim pursued."); Committee on the Elimination of Racial Discrimination, General Recommendation No. 30, para. 4, 64th Sess., U.N. Doc. CERD/C/64/Misc.11/rev.3 (2004) ("[D]ifferential treatment based on citizenship or immigration status will constitute discrimination if the criteria for such differentiation, judged in light of the objectives and purposes of the Convention, are not applied pursuant to a legitimate aim, and are not proportional to the achievement of that aim.").

are relevant and which persons or groups are objectively different from each other is a flashpoint for disputes. Similarity must be judged in social context and in light of the purpose of the measure. A Catholic and a Muslim may be similar with regard to the right to healthcare needs but dissimilar with regard to the right to employment, if the employment is as a church leader.

A perennial question relating to similar situations in discrimination analysis is whether, if the sex of an insured person reliably predicts risk, it is permissible for the underwriter to charge males and females different insurance rates. There is no obvious biological reason that males and females face different risks of accidents; males and females have the same physical and mental equipment necessary for safe driving. But in practice they do differ in many countries, because men tend to drive more recklessly than women. On this question, the Court of Justice of the European Union (CJEU) has held that sex discrimination in insurance premiums could not be justified under the Charter of Fundamental Rights of the EU, because it resulted in unequal treatment of persons in comparable situations.[17] Some have argued to the contrary that, because the evidence established that men and women are in fact differently situated with respect to certain risk factors, a sex-based distinction in insurance is justified; to mandate equal premiums would treat persons in unequal situations as if they were equal.[18] The debate is edifying, because it illustrates how differences in a *mutable* factual situation can alter the status of groups. In this case trends in male versus female driving behavior can justify different treatment despite the superficial appearance of similarity between the groups.

Although the CJEU rejected the distinction, the problem with a rigid view of similarity of situation is easily revealed by reductio ad absurdum. Suppose females *never* caused automobile accidents, and every male caused an automobile accident every three years without fail, entirely due to differences in driving behavior. If the CJEU were to continue to insist that insurance companies charge the same rates for male and female drivers, it would be penalizing good driving and subsidizing bad driving—which is to say, discriminating against good drivers—for the sake of preserving an appearance of nondiscrimination based on sex. By similar *reductio*, the CJEU's position if adopted as a general rule could justify prohibiting using *any* risk factors in assessing insurance premiums, such as age or history of driving while intoxicated.

Yet, the position that the prohibition of discrimination based on *any* ground is always justified if the groups stand in factually distinct situations is equally untenable. It would mean that, if race, height, or homosexuality reliably predicted a risk factor by even a small amount—say, 2 percent—such characteristics could justify differential premiums. Even more troubling would be a modification of presumption of innocence in a criminal trial if it were shown, for example, that a specific race factually correlated to a higher crime rate. Demographic factors not directly related to causation penalize members of the disfavored group despite the fact that any given individual within the group may diverge a great deal from the average.

17. Association Belge des Consommateurs Test-Achats ASBL v. Council of Ministers, Judgment of Mar. 1, 2011, Case No. C-236/09 (Ct. Just. Eur. Union).

18. *See, e.g.*, Jakob Cornides, *Three Case Studies on "Anti-Discrimination,"* 23 Eur. J. Int'l L. 517, 531–34 (2012).

As usual when two extreme positions rely on logic leading to extreme results, a better policy lies somewhere between. The greater the predictive power of group membership and the greater its weight in the prediction, the more convincing the rationale for allowing distinctions, whether public or private, among groups. Ultimately, the persuasiveness of this argument turns on questions of fact, specifically, how consistent and significant sex is in predicting risk factors, especially in comparison with factors more directly related to driving risk, such as driving experience, past accidents, age, or a record of moving violations.

The social contextuality of similarity analysis can easily lead a human rights authority to rely on trivial distinctions between groups to approve arbitrary discrimination, or to overlook meaningful distinctions to deny a discrimination claim. In *van der Mussele v. Belgium*, for example, the Strasbourg Court held that lawyers obligated by law to work for the indigent without pay were not similarly situated to other professions who were not so obligated.[19] Without analysis, the Court concluded that "differences as to legal status, conditions for entry to the profession, the nature of the functions involved, the manner of exercise of those functions" justify the distinction.[20] Without published reasoning, it is unclear whether the Court was stumbling around in tautology or had some implicit theory as to why members of the legal profession and not, say, doctors, dentists, psychotherapists, or pet groomers should be required to donate labor to the indigent. The Strasbourg Court's decision might have been less unsatisfactory had the Court related its views about the social and economic uniqueness of the legal profession more coherently to the realities of the case and the role of lawyers in Belgian society compared to that of similar professions that labor under no comparable legal obligations.

It is possible that some minority groups with no meaningful differences from the majority group exist, but they are few. The usual example is race; except in purely historical or artistic representations, no cogent argument can support a distinction in treatment between races. Similarly, in almost any society at almost any time, persons whose given name begins with "A" are similarly situated with persons whose given name begins with "B," because such distinctions rarely if ever reflect significant social meaning. But most distinctions between groups requires some analysis to justify a judgment of similarity or difference. One cannot conclude a priori whether overweight and ideal weight persons, or urban and suburban residents, are similarly situated for all purposes. Overweight or ideal weight persons may not be similarly situated in societies with a strong and pervasive bias respecting body size, and they are certainly not similarly situated respecting their candidacy for the position of fighter jet pilot, but it would be difficult to justify any difference in respect of their freedom of speech. Urban and suburban residents may not be similarly situated with respect to their transportation needs, but they are similarly situated with respect to the need for competent representation in a criminal trial.

The need to evaluate both the measure and the distinction in social context has led to some knotty problems. Dinah Shelton has pointed out that the Human Rights

19. 6 E.H.R.R. 163 (1984).

20. *Id.* para. 46.

Committee has viewed residents of different Australian states and territories as *not* similarly situated with respect to lengths of statutes of limitations, while the Inter-American Commission on Human Rights has viewed juveniles in different U.S. states as similarly situated with respect to sentencing laws.[21] Although it would not be difficult to imagine plausible reasons for distinguishing the two cases, such divergences do suggest the difficulty of forming doctrine on a global scale with consistent results. Unless states are afforded very considerable deference, such determinations call for informed and sophisticated analysis of each state's social context in the course of applying the nondiscrimination right in international practice.

2. Legitimate Aim

The most politically sensitive of the questions involved in discrimination analysis is the legitimacy or necessity of the state's aim, because it requires the human rights authority to evaluate whether the state's public policy is consistent with liberal democratic values. In undertaking this task, human rights authorities are left somewhat to their own devices, because international human rights law does not articulate a coherent political theory about how human rights and public policies should be balanced in a "democratic society." It does not mandate any specific balance between protecting individual freedoms and entitlements versus promoting civic morality, social cohesion, environmental protection, preservation of culture, economic growth, or other social policies. It merely opens the door to such balancing.

The Strasbourg Court has interpreted "necessary" to mean a "pressing social need" to interfere with the human right in question.[22] Aside from suggesting that the threshold for discrimination is a high one, this merely rephrases the issue. It offers no real guidance about whether, for example, a ban on same-sex public displays of affection could be justified by a policy of teaching puritanical public morals to children, or limitations on the distribution of foreign motion pictures could be justified by a policy of preserving a national culture or language. At least some plausible arguments could be adduced on each side of such debates, and the Strasbourg Court itself has tended to defer to state judgments on such questions using the "margin of appreciation" doctrine when European states have not formed a consensus on the scope of the right.[23] The Strasbourg Court accordingly often

21. Dinah Shelton, *Prohibited Discrimination in International Human Rights Law*, *in* The Diversity of International Law: Essays in Honour of Professor Kalliopi K. Koufa 261, 282 (Aristotle Constantinides & Nikos Zaikos eds., 2009).

22. Handyside v. United Kingdom, 1 E.H.R.R. 737, para. 48 (1976); Dudgeon v. United Kingdom, 4 E.H.R.R. 149, para. 51 (1982).

23. *See, e.g.*, *Handyside*, 1 E.H.R.R. 737, paras. 48–49 (1976). Burden v. United Kingdom, 47 E.H.R.R. 38, para. 60 (2008). *See generally* Andrew Legg, The Margin of Appreciation in International Human Rights Law (2012). The Strasbourg Court's use of the margin has, however, come under some trenchant criticism. *See* Eyal Benvenisti, *Margin of Appreciation, Consensus, and Universal Standards*, 31 Int'l L. & Pol. 834 (1999); Aaron Xavier Fellmeth, *State Regulation of Sexuality in International Human Rights Law and Theory*, 50 Wm. & Mary L. Rev. 797, 904–06 (2008).

refuses to find a violation of the Convention when a critical mass of European states has not yet converged on a certain human rights practice.[24] In the context of positive rights, the margin has been even broader to allow the state very great discretion to determine how to allocate its scarce resources for the protection and advancement of human rights. One author has even suggested that in practice the margin invalidates only those state policies that are flatly arbitrary or do not even satisfy a modest threshold of protection for the right,[25] although this view is debatable.

To the extent that the state's justification for interfering with a human right relies on assertions of fact—for example, that the discrimination in question averts a threat to public morality or a cultural institution, the authority may evaluate the evidence and reject the necessity of a measure unlikely to achieve its purported goal. For example, in *Dudgeon v. United Kingdom*, the Strasbourg Court relied on evidence that Northern Ireland's criminal prohibition on consensual homosexual intercourse had been underenforced to reject its alleged necessity; the United Kingdom had produced no evidence that the recent underenforcement had damaged the community's moral fabric.[26] A measure manifestly ineffective at achieving its intended result cannot be necessary to achieve that result.

Similarly, in *O'Donoghue v. United Kingdom*, the respondent state charged a significant fee to any immigrant not married with Church of England rites, allegedly to prevent sham marriages.[27] In finding that the discriminatory treatment failed the test of necessity, the Court observed that the United Kingdom had adduced no evidence that the measure effectively reduced sham marriages.[28] In *Salgueiro da Silva Mouta v. Portugal*, the Strasbourg Court similarly found a Portuguese court's decision to award child custody to a vindictive and unstable mother based entirely on the father's homosexuality was disproportional, because the state could produce no evidence that a parent's homosexuality posed any risk of harm to the child.[29]

Although in *Dudgeon*, the state's public justification was the preservation of morals, from another perspective the legislation at issue qualified as flatly opposite to the necessity criterion because it served a function repugnant to liberal democratic values. It reflected and promoted hatred against homosexuals as a class based purely on cultural biases and religious bigotry. Legislation defining a group's core self-expression as immoral suggests intolerance of the group itself. Mere animus toward a group cannot render discriminatory measures "necessary in a democratic society," because expressing hatred of a group is not only unnecessary in a democratic society, it is destructive of its values of respect for equal human dignity and tolerance of harmless differences. In the rare cases in which discriminatory treatment was clearly based on historical racism, then, the Strasbourg Court has

24. *See, e.g.*, Engel v. Netherlands, 1 E.H.R.R. 747, paras. 59, 72 (1979–1980); Rasmussen v. Denmark, 7 E.H.R.R. 371, para. 40 (1985).

25. Besson, *supra* note 1, at 91–92.

26. Dudgeon v. United Kingdom, 4 E.H.R.R. 149, para. 60 (1981).

27. Eur. Ct. Hum. Rts., App. No. 34848/07, Judgment of Dec. 14, 2010.

28. *Id.* paras. 89, 102.

29. Salgueiro da Silva Mouta v. Portugal, 31 E.H.R.R. 47, paras. 28, 36 (2001).

understandably felt it unnecessary to even consider whether the toleration of public persecution could meet a pressing social need.[30]

In practice, international human rights authorities have frequently approved as legitimate distinctions based purely on historical biases. One prominent example is the case of adoption by same-sex couples. As late as 1992, the European Commission on Human Rights considered it legitimate to discriminate against same-sex couples in adoption decisions even in the absence of reliable evidence that same-sex couples make less fit parents than different-sex couples,[31] and in 2002, the Strasbourg Court approved discrimination in adoption decisions against single homosexuals (as opposed to single heterosexuals), apparently in both cases based on deference to prevailing social biases.[32] That the Court soon reversed itself[33] does not undermine the point that human rights authorities encounter great difficulty in overcoming their cultural and personal biases to objectively evaluate the "necessity" of state measures. It merely shows that they can indeed overcome them in time. In any case, such decisions can hardly be reconciled with any coherent human rights doctrine.

In short, the distinction between racism, sexism, and other forms of group bias on one hand, and the pursuit of more facially legitimate public policies on the other, is not always self-evident. The systematic oppression of a group from feelings of cultural or religious superiority may reflect the state's vision of the good life. To adjudicate the legitimacy of imposing such a vision on society by law or tolerance of widespread social discrimination inevitably requires a developed theory of political morality and an understanding of the social dynamics of the relevant state. Some forms of unjustifiable discrimination are very popular and culturally rooted in some states, and their prohibition may provoke a strong popular backlash. In most cases, requiring the state to bear the burden of producing sound evidence supporting the need for discrimination to achieve a legitimate aim would dispose of the question, if human rights authorities are willing to reject discriminatory state measures that are backed by broad popular support.

A final point about necessity analysis bears some emphasis. The Human Rights Committee has rejected "mere administrative convenience" as a legitimate reason for discriminating against a group.[34] Similarly, in the *O'Donoghue* case mentioned above, the Court did not accept the United Kingdom's argument that a general marriage prohibition on certain kinds of immigrants could be justified by the expense or administrative burden of inquiring into the facts of each proposed marriage to determine whether it was genuine or a marriage of convenience.[35] Although it is impossible to posit an a priori rule about how much inconvenience and expense the state must tolerate to avoid discriminating, and no human rights authority

30. *See, e.g.*, Yordanova v. Bulgaria, Eur. Ct. Hum. Rts. App. No. 25446/06, Judgment of Apr. 24, 2012.

31. Kerkhoven & Hinke v. The Netherlands, App. 15666/89 (1992).

32. For an analysis of this case, *see* Fellmeth, *supra* note 23, at 869–72.

33. E.B. v. France, 47 E.H.R.R. 21 (2008).

34. *See* Shelton, *supra* note 21, at 261, 284.

35. *O'Donoghue v. United Kingdom*, Eur. Ct. Hum. Rts., App. No. 34848/07, Judgment of Dec. 14, 2010, paras. 22 & 89.

has tried, it appears that avoiding minor expenses, difficulties, and delays in the administration of social services would not by itself justify discriminating against a group. We can at least conclude that necessity and mere convenience are at opposite ends of the justification spectrum.

3. Proportionality

Proportionality is generally understood to mean that the measure does not discriminate more than is reasonably necessary to accomplish the measure's legitimate aims. Most national and international human rights authorities employ some sort of balancing test to identify state distinctions that violate the nondiscrimination right. An early formulation of this test is found in the Universal Declaration:

> In the exercise of his rights and freedoms, everyone shall be subject only to such limitations as are determined by law solely for the purpose of securing due recognition and respect for the rights and freedoms of others and of meeting the just requirements of morality, public order, and the general welfare in a democratic society.[36]

Although the Declaration's provision offers little guidance on what kinds of limitations on rights might be justifiable for such purposes as "the just requirements of morality," etc., the words "solely for the purpose" and "requirement" suggest an expectation that laws limiting rights be narrowly tailored to impinge minimally on the right. The U.N. Human Rights Committee; Committee on Economic, Social, and Cultural Rights; Strasbourg Court; and Inter-American Court of Human Rights have each adopted similar balancing tests,[37] and national constitutional courts also frequently rely on a proportionality test in weighing human rights against state interests, including interests in distinguishing between groups of persons or classes of activities.[38]

The evaluation of the necessity requirement may blend into the proportionality analysis when the state is unable to show that a discriminatory measure is necessary. If there is no sound evidence that the measure is effective at accomplishing its goal, any significant discrimination is disproportionate to its aim.[39] The U.N. Human Rights Committee used reasoning precisely identical to the Strasbourg Court's in *Dudgeon* in finding a criminal prohibition on sodomy to be disproportionate rather than pursuant to an illegitimate aim. The criminal prohibition on

36. UDHR art. 29(2).

37. *See, e.g.*, Toonen v. Australia, U.N. GAOR, Hum. Rts. Comm., 50th Sess., Commc'n No. 488/1992, at 226, U.N. Doc. A/49/40 (Sept. 21, 1994); Committee on Economic, Social and Cultural Rights, General Comment No. 20, para. 13, Commc'n No. E/C.12/GC/20 (May 20, 2009), 49 E.H.R.R. SE10 (2009).

38. *See* Dieter Grimm, *Proportionality in Canadian and German Constitutional Jurisprudence*, 57 U. Toronto L.J. 383, 389 (2007); Alec Stone Sweet & Jud Mathews, *Proportionality Balancing and Global Constitutionalism*, 47 Colum. J. Transnat'l L. 72 (2008).

39. *See, e.g.*, A. v. United Kingdom, Eur. Ct. Hum. Rts. App. No. 3455/05, Judgment of Feb. 19, 2009, paras. 20, 190.

sodomy was unreasonable, the Committee concluded, because it did not serve the purported goal of preventing the spread of HIV. It observed that "no link has been shown between the continued criminalization of homosexual activity and the effective control of the spread of the HIV/AIDS virus," and some evidence showed that criminalization was in fact counterproductive, because it drove the conduct underground and deterred public education and medical diagnoses and treatment.[40]

If the measure does accomplish its goal but has discriminatory effects, the human rights authority must evaluate how well tailored the measure is to the legitimate aim sought. Generally, only the least discriminatory means available will be proportionate to the aim; superfluous discrimination is always disproportionate absent unusual circumstances. A proportionality analysis must account for the nature of the distinction and the effects of differential treatment. Any given ground for the discrimination may have a greater or lesser correlation to the policy goal sought, and the measure should be carefully tailored accordingly.

In *Palau-Martinez v. France*, for example, the Strasbourg Court faced a municipal court judgment denying a mother custody over her children based on her intention to raise them as Jehovah's Witnesses. The state's intention of protecting the children's well-being was of course a legitimate aim, but the Court found the denial of custody a disproportionately discriminatory measure, because the municipal court had failed to undertake any evidentiary investigation as to the effect of the mother's religious convictions on the best interests of the children.[41] Abstract reasoning and assumptions could not justify discrimination based on religion in a matter so fundamental as the right to family life. Consideration of the children's best interests should have been based on concrete evidence rather than mere assumption, surmise, or stereotype about the consequences of the mother's religious convictions.

The Inter-American Court has adopted a similar test using some of the same terms. In an advisory opinion, it summarized the test as follows:

> No discrimination exists if the difference in treatment has a legitimate purpose and if it does not lead to situations which are contrary to justice, to reason or to the nature of things. It follows that there would be no discrimination in differences in treatment of individuals by a state when the classifications selected are based on substantial factual differences and there exists a reasonable relationship of proportionality between these differences and the aims of the legal rule under review. These aims may not be unjust or unreasonable, that is, they may not be arbitrary, capricious, despotic or in conflict with the essential oneness and dignity of humankind.[42]

40. Toonen v. Australia, Comm. No. 488/1992, Decision of Mar. 31, 1994, U.N. Doc. CCPR/C/50/D/488/1992, para. 8.5.

41. Palau-Martinez v. France, Eur. Ct. Hum. Rts. No. 64927/01, Judgment of Dec. 16, 2003, para. 42.

42. *Legal Status and Human Rights of the Child*, Inter-Am. Ct. Hum. Rts., Advisory Opinion OC-17/02 of Aug. 28, 2002, OAS Ser. A, No. 17, para. 47, *quoting* Proposed Amendments to the Naturalization Provisions of the Constitution of Costa Rica, Inter-Am. Ct. Hum. Rts., Advisory Opinion OC-4/84, Ser. A, No. 4 (Jan. 19, 1984), para. 57.

The Court has not yet elaborated in detail how the proportionality test should be interpreted. In the *Undocumented Migrants* advisory opinion, for example, the Court ignored suggestions from several amici curiae that only a "least restrictive means" test would satisfy the proportionality requirement,[43] despite the evident suitability of such a rule for minimizing infringements of human rights while allowing the state to pursue its legitimate aims to the extent possible. In this context, a "least discriminatory means" test would have the same advantages. The Court may have intended to signal that some (presumably minor) discrimination would be tolerated in pursuit of legitimate state aims despite the fact that less discriminatory means were available, if more discriminatory measures offered important advantages or avoided other harms. However, such considerations are compatible with a "least discriminatory means" test, as long as the relevant "means" effectuate a goal that encompasses the advantages or avoids the harms in question.

C. CONTEXTUAL FACTORS IN DISCRIMINATION ANALYSIS

The legitimacy and proportionality of a distinction between groups necessarily vary according to the context and facts of each case. In this section, five key factors relevant to most discrimination cases will be analyzed. The first, the grounds for discrimination, may be decisive in some cases. IHRL uses three different approaches to defining prohibited grounds for discrimination: (1) In a few international treaties and declarations, the nondiscrimination right may be invoked exclusively by a defined class of persons, such as women, national minorities, or persons with disabilities. (2) In most treaties and declarations, an exemplary list of prohibited grounds is followed by a residual category, such as "other status," which leaves the door open to a wide range of bases for invoking the nondiscrimination right. (3) A few instruments, which focus on specific prohibited grounds of discrimination, such as CEDR and various U.N. General Assembly declarations on religious discrimination,[44] prohibit only or primarily the discrimination that forms the subject matter of the treaty.

In the first class of instruments, the initial question must be whether the claimant qualifies as a member of the protected class. Article 4(1) of the Council of Europe's Framework Convention for the Protection of National Minorities states:

> The Parties undertake to guarantee to persons belonging to national minorities the right of equality before the law and of equal protection of the law. In this respect, any discrimination based on belonging to a national minority shall be prohibited.[45]

43. Advisory Opinion on Juridical Condition and Human Rights of Undocumented Migrants, Sept. 17, 2003, Ser. A, No. 18.

44. *E.g.*, G.A. Res. 36/55 (Nov. 25, 1981); G.A. Res. 63/181 (Mar. 16, 2009).

45. ETS No. 157, *entered into force* Feb. 1, 1998 [hereinafter CoE National Minorities Convention].

The Convention purposely does not define the term "national minority,"[46] so there is room for debate about which groups of persons qualify for protection. However, by its terms the Convention is intended mainly to apply to racial, ethnic, and cultural groups, and it is at least beyond dispute that any such group must comprise less than a majority of the state. Such instruments may provide no grounds for complaint by majority group members who are victims of discrimination in favor of minority group members. Some human rights authorities are more inclined than others to limit the right to specific grounds or classes of persons, causing significant variability in the application of the nondiscrimination right.

The more general nondiscrimination provisions of the second class, in contrast, either do not mention specific prohibited grounds of discrimination, or else they list classes for illustrative purposes rather than to limit the scope of the right. Equal protection of the law clauses exemplify the former. For example, the Arab Charter provides in article 11: "All persons are equal before the law and have a right to enjoy its protection without discrimination."[47] The EU Charter of Fundamental Rights laconically provides in article 20: "Everyone is equal before the law."[48] The ACHR has a similar provision (article 24): "All persons are equal before the law. Consequently, they are entitled, without discrimination, to equal protection of the law." National constitutions sometimes include similar provisions that do not specify prohibited grounds for "unequal protection." For example, the Polish constitution states: "Polish citizens enjoying full public rights shall have a right of access to the public services based on the principle of equality,"[49] and the U.S. Constitution provides: "No State shall . . . deny to any person within its jurisdiction the equal protection of the laws."[50] Nothing in these clauses limits their protections to discrimination on grounds of race, religion, or other specific category.

In the third class of instruments, the scope of the prohibition is relatively narrow and well defined, and so the question of prohibited grounds is largely answered ab initio. Because the ground of discrimination is a group characteristic and not membership in a specific class, qualification to raise a claim is usually not contentious. The CEDR does not condemn discrimination based on membership in a certain race, nor do the U.N. declarations on religious discrimination prohibit discrimination against a limited class of religions, and so no person need demonstrate

46. *See* CoE National Minorities Convention, Explanatory Report, para. 12.

47. Arab Charter on Human Rights, League of Arab States Council Res. 5437 (102nd sess.), Sept. 15, 1994, *reprinted in* 18 Hum. Rts. L.J. 151 (1997).

48. Charter of Fundamental Rights of the European Union, Mar. 30, 2010, art. 20, EU Doc. 2010/C 83/02, *available at* http://eur-lex.europa.eu.

49. Const. of Poland art. 60 (1997).

50. U.S. Const. amend. XIV, sec. 1. Although the Fourteenth Amendment applies only to U.S. states, the Supreme Court has interpreted the Fifth Amendment's due process clause as conferring the same nondiscrimination duty on the federal government. *See* Bolling v. Sharpe, 347 U.S. 497 (1954).

membership in a specific race or religion to benefit from the respective instrument's protections.

The second important factor in nondiscrimination analysis is the relative importance and vulnerability of the interest affected by the measure. The interests protected by the nondiscrimination right are not uniform in perceived importance. National and international human rights authorities vary significantly in their assessments of which interests are entitled to protection from discrimination and which are not. In some cases, such as article 14 of the ECHR, this is a function of the human rights instrument itself, which may limit its protections to certain enumerated rights ("the rights and freedoms *set forth in this Convention*"). In other cases, such as equal protection clauses, the instrument seems to suggest that the right applies with respect to all laws. In practice, human rights authorities vary in their interpretations of open nondiscrimination rights, construing some interests as more vulnerable or sensitive to discrimination than others.

The third factor evaluates the consequences of the discrimination, both for the individual right holder and the society as a whole. Notwithstanding the absence of any textual hierarchy of moral interests underlying the nondiscrimination right, some reasons for discrimination are more morally acceptable than others, and these former tend to attract legal approval. Because objections to discrimination must be justified on consequentialist rather than deontological grounds, the justification is always weighed against the nature and importance of the protected interest. To the extent they conflict, the interests underlying this justification must be weightier than the interests of both society and the subjects of discrimination in equal treatment. For this reason, the question of rectification of historical oppression or prejudice through reverse discrimination, or "affirmative action," entails certain doctrinal complexities.

The fourth factor is the source of the threat to the right. There is no uniform global interpretation with regard to the extent to which the state must protect right holders against private discrimination or general situations of social inequality. In other words, a general nondiscrimination right does not determine a priori whether the state is bound to prevent or rectify private discrimination. This ultimately boils down to a distinction between negative and positive discrimination rights, and so this factor is closely tied with the questions dealt with in Part III of this book.

The final factor is intent. Although intent to discriminate may be inherently blameworthy, an innocent intent resulting in disparate treatment between classes of persons in similar situations can impair human dignity and the enjoyment of human rights as well. Human rights authorities have dealt variably with the intent factor, with some viewing intent to discriminate as a virtual prerequisite to a finding of violation, and others viewing it as a weighty factor or conditionally relevant factor. Each of these factors will be evaluated in turn.

1. Prohibited Grounds

> It occurred to him that all strongly accentuated classes ... divided men into two kinds: their own kind—and those without. To the clergyman there were clergy and laity, to the Catholic there were Catholics and non-Catholics,

> to the negro there were blacks and whites, to the prisoner there were the imprisoned and the free, and to the sick man there were the sick and the well.[51]

As noted earlier, by their semantic and conceptual nature alike, substantive rights tend to be self-limiting, but this does not mean they have no synergies. In practice, many substantive rights are interlinked; the enjoyment of each right may be helpful—in some circumstances necessary, as will be discussed in Chapter 5, Section D—to the enjoyment of others. Nevertheless, as a matter of shared culture and linguistics, each right has a conceptual dominion, if a fluid one. Few jurists would interpret a right to sustenance, for example, to include the right to cross-examine witnesses in a trial, and few would interpret a right to privacy to include the right to the sustenance necessary to enjoy that privacy. A jurist who steps outside the boundaries of a right's intersubjectively determined dominion will be seen as failing in his interpretive task.

It was noted earlier that the nondiscrimination right differs in that in its most general formulation it lacks any definite subject matter. As with substantive rights, and indeed all legal concepts, the nondiscrimination right exists within a shared culture and linguistic framework, but its boundaries in terms of the substantive interests it serves are underdetermined by both. Nondiscrimination is not defined by, and therefore not limited to, the human interest in self-expression, education, or a family life. It is defined instead by the most abstract human interest in justice, and specifically in being treated with dignity equal to that of other, similarly situated persons. In this context, equal dignity means that no individual's life, freedom, and happiness can be valued more than any other's, unless the individual acts in such a manner as to undermine his own dignity, by, for example, committing a crime of great moral turpitude, attempting to devalue the equal rights of others, or bargaining away a right voluntarily. In consequence, the nondiscrimination right's scope can encompass a great deal of interpretive discretion.

One very important underdetermined aspect of the nondiscrimination right is the basis for which discrimination is permissible or impermissible. Although some human rights instruments specify prohibited grounds of discrimination, such as race, language, or sex, they do not always explicitly clarify whether these grounds are inclusive and exemplary, or exclusive. If they are not exclusive, are all grounds of arbitrary discrimination prohibited equally, or are some more acceptable than others? Many theorists assume that the nondiscrimination and equal protection rights are designed to protect only members of socially and structurally disadvantaged or vulnerable groups.[52] But that is not the theory adopted by many human rights authorities. Theories about the prohibited grounds of discrimination could be arrayed on a spectrum between two dystopian poles, from a comprehensive prohibition on all grounds of arbitrary discrimination at one extreme to a highly selective number of prohibited grounds, predetermined and unvarying, at the other. No

51. F. Scott Fitzgerald, The Beautiful and Damned 327 (Penguin Classics ed. 2004) (1922).

52. *See, e.g.*, Besson, *supra* note 1, at 47–48.

national or international human rights authority consistently interprets the state's duty as falling at either extreme, but authorities do vary substantially in the point along that spectrum at which they locate state duties.

A. The Open Approach

Toward the more liberal side of the spectrum are the interpretations advanced by two U.N. treaty bodies, the Human Rights Committee and Committee on Economic, Social, and Cultural Rights (ESCR). The covenants they administer provide open lists of prohibited grounds for discrimination. The CPPR states in article 2(1):

> Each State Party to the present Covenant undertakes to respect and to ensure to all individuals within its territory and subject to its jurisdiction the rights recognized in the present Covenant, without distinction of any kind, such as race, colour, sex, language, religion, political or other opinion, national or social origin, property, birth or other status.

The CESCR contains similar language:

> The States Parties to the present Covenant undertake to guarantee that the rights enunciated in the present Covenant will be exercised without discrimination of any kind as to race, colour, sex, language, religion, political or other opinion, national or social origin, property, birth or other status.[53]

Both committees read the "or other status" language as opening the door to an interpretation prohibiting discrimination on unlisted grounds of an unspecified nature. In General Comment 18, the Human Rights Committee interpreted the CPPR article (2)(1) nondiscrimination right as forbidding discrimination on other grounds not enumerated specifically in the Covenant.[54] With regard to states in which private discrimination prevails based on unlisted grounds, the Committee has accordingly recommended measures to combat discrimination to fulfill the state's article 2 duties.[55] Similarly, the Human Rights Committee determined in several cases that discrimination based on other statuses or activities not listed in the Covenant, such as age[56] or attendance at a public versus private

53. CESCR, art. 2(2). In addition, article 3 of both covenants commit state parties to a positive duty to "ensure the equal right of men and women to the enjoyment of all economic, social and cultural rights set forth in the present Covenant."

54. U.N. Hum. Rts. Comm., General Comment No. 18: Nondiscrimination, para. 11, 37th Sess., Nov. 10, 1989, U.N. Doc. HRI/GEN/1/Rev.1 at 26 (1994); 2 Hum. Rts. Comm. 1990 Report, Annex VI, paras. 6–7, U.N. Doc. HRI/GEN/1/Rev.9, Vol. I, Pt. II.

55. *See, e.g.*, 1 Report of the Human Rights Committee, U.N. GAOR, 65th Sess., Supp. No. 40, at 25, 43, 185, U.N. Doc. A/65/40 (Vol. I) (Mold., Rus. Fed., San Marino).

56. Love v. Australia, U.N. Hum. Rts. Comm., Comm. No. 983/2001, 2 Hum. Rts. Comm. 2001 Report, Annex X, Sec. O, para. 7.2.

school,[57] must be justified by reasonable and objective criteria and adopted for a legitimate purpose.

The Committee on ESCR also interprets the Covenant's residual "other status" qualification in article 2(2): "this list is not exhaustive and other grounds may be incorporated in this category."[58] The Committee's observations on "other status" indicate a willingness to expand the category considerably to encompass such considerations:

> The nature of discrimination varies according to context and evolves over time. A flexible approach to the ground of "other status" is thus needed to capture other forms of differential treatment that cannot be reasonably and objectively justified and are of a comparable nature to the expressly recognised grounds in art. 2(2).[59]

Neither the Human Rights Committee nor the Committee on ESCR has offered more detailed formal guidance on the kinds of grounds that might justify a finding of prohibited discrimination. The general phrasing of the right and its interpretation to this point leaves unspecified the circumstances under which discrimination based on age, disability, caste, sexual orientation, wealth, marital status, parentage, country of residence, prior criminal conviction, physique, food allergies, etc. would be considered suspect or prohibited. The most specific guidance on this point is found in the optional protocols to the covenants authorizing individual communications. For example, the Optional Protocol to the CCPR requires the author to allege that the difference in treatment is attributable to his status as a member of a distinct group.[60] Although some view the distinct group requirement as different from an allegation of arbitrary action or abuse of discretion,[61] the line between them is conceptually blurry, as will be discussed later. In any case, the theories underlying the doctrinal interpretations of both committees remain unarticulated.

In practice, not all grounds of discrimination are treated equally by human rights authorities. Race has frequently been considered by human rights authorities as the least justifiable ground for discrimination.[62] A distinction based on race must satisfy a goal of exceptional importance to society, and the discriminatory measure must be strictly necessary to achievement of that goal. Similarly, human rights authorities have tended to treat sex as a presumptively, if less reliably, illegitimate

57. Blom v. Sweden, U.N. Hum. Rts. Comm., Comm. No. 191/1985, A/43/40, at 211 (1988).

58. Committee on Economic, Social and Cultural Rights, General Comment No. 20, para. 15, Comm. No. E/C.12/GC/20 (May 20, 2009), 49 E.H.R.R. SE10 (2009).

59. *Id.*, paras. 15–16.

60. B.d.B. v. The Netherlands, U.N. Hum. Rts. Comm. Comm. No. 273/1989, U.N. Doc. Supp. No. 40 (A/44/40), at 286 (1989).

61. *E.g.*, Shelton, *supra* note 21, at 261, 281.

62. *See* Hilary Charlesworth, *The Concept of Equality in International Law*, *in* LITIGATING RIGHTS: PERSPECTIVES FROM DOMESTIC AND INTERNATIONAL LAW 143 (Grant Huscroft & Paul Rishworth eds., 2002).

basis for social distinctions,[63] and the Inter-American Court of Human Rights has repeatedly held that the interests of children warrant special protection from discrimination.[64] The Committee on ESCR has more generally emphasized protection for social groups that are "vulnerable and have suffered and continue to suffer marginalization,"[65] although it has never suggested that nondiscrimination rights are confined to such groups.

The Strasbourg Court and Inter-American Court take a similar view of the grounds for discrimination. Article 14 of the European Convention codifies the general nondiscrimination right:

> The enjoyment of the rights and freedoms set forth in this Convention shall be secured without discrimination on any ground such as sex, race, colour, language, religion, political or other opinion, national or social origin, association with a national minority, property, birth or other status.[66]

Article 1(1) of the ACHR provides:

> The States Parties to this Convention undertake to respect the rights and freedoms recognized herein and to ensure to all persons subject to their jurisdiction the free and full exercise of those rights and freedoms, without any discrimination for reasons of race, color, sex, language, religion, political or other opinion, national or social origin, economic status, birth, or any other social condition.

Like the U.N. Committees, the European human rights authorities and Inter-American Court have interpreted "other status" and "any other social condition" to leave open the possibility of claiming discrimination on grounds not listed in the ECHR or ACHR. The *travaux préparatoires* of Protocol No. 12 to the ECHR make clear that the article 14 list was not intended to be exhaustive,[67] a position that the Strasbourg Court has many times confirmed.[68] The European Commission

63. *See* Rebecca J. Cook, *The International Right to Nondiscrimination on the Basis of Sex*, 14 Yale J. Int'l L. 161 (1989).

64. *E.g.*, Case of the "Street Children" (Villagrán Morales), Inter-Am. Ct. Hum. Rts., Judgment of Nov. 19, 1999. Ser. C, No. 64, para. 146; Case of Gómez Paquiyauri Bros., Inter-Am. Ct. Hum. Rts., Judgment of July 8, 2004, Ser. C, No. 110, para. 162; Case of Bulacio, Inter-Am. Ct. Hum. Rts., Judgment of Sept. 18, 2003, Ser. C, No. 100, para. 133.

65. Committee on Economic, Social and Cultural Rights, General Comment No. 20, para. 27, Comm. No. E/C.12/GC/20 (May 20, 2009), 49 E.H.R.R. SE10 (2009).

66. The EU Charter contains a very similar, but not identical, provision in article 21(1): Any discrimination based on any ground such as sex, race, colour, ethnic or social origin, genetic features, language, religion or belief, political or any other opinion, membership of a national minority, property, birth, disability, age or sexual orientation shall be prohibited.

67. See Protocol No. 12 to the Convention for the Protection of Human Rights and Fundamental Freedoms art. 1, CETS No. 177, *signed on* Nov. 4, 2000, Explanatory Report para. 20 (June 26, 2000), *available at* http://conventions.coe.int/Treaty/en/Reports/Html/177.htm.

68. *See, e.g.*, Mouta v. Portugal, 31 E.H.R.R. 47, para. 28 (2001).

on Human Rights and Strasbourg Court have accordingly rejected as arbitrary distinctions based on a wide variety of unlisted grounds, including profession, marital status, employment status, place of residence, confinement (in the case of prisoners), holding of a military commission, and even, in a few cases, behavior, such as whether a union member participated in a strike.[69]

The Inter-American Court has interpreted ACHR article 1 in like manner:

> 84. [W]hen interpreting the words "any other social condition" of Article 1.1 of the Convention, it is always necessary to choose the alternative that is most favorable to the protection of the rights enshrined in said treaty, based on the principle of the rule most favorable to the human being.
>
> 85. According to Article 1(1) of the American Convention, the specific criteria by virtue of which discrimination is prohibited do not constitute an exhaustive or limitative list, but merely illustrative. Indeed, the wording of said article leaves open the criteria with the inclusion of the term "any other social condition," allowing for the inclusion of other categories that have not been explicitly indicated. Consequently, the Court should interpret the term "any other social condition" of Article 1.1 of the Convention in the context of the most favorable option for the human being and in light of the evolution of fundamental rights in contemporary international law.[70]

One telling example of how these interpretations have extended the grounds of the nondiscrimination right is the case of sexual orientation. None of the major international human rights instruments, except the EU Charter of Fundamental Rights (article 21),[71] explicitly includes sexual orientation as a prohibited ground for discrimination, but both the Inter-American Court and Strasbourg Court have interpreted sexual orientation as a prohibited "other status" in some circumstances.[72]

There are notable advantages to leaving the prohibited grounds of discrimination open. By including a list of exemplary prohibited grounds, the human rights instruments clarify which grounds are least justifiable and set a baseline for the kinds of grounds that should not be used for distinguishing between classes of persons and activities. Even the concept of "distinct group" is exceedingly fluid.

69. *See* Anne F. Bayefsky, *The Principle of Equality or Nondiscrimination in International Law*, 11 HUM. RTS. Q. [HUM. RTS. L.J.] 1, 69 (1990).

70. Riffo v. Chile, Judgment of Feb. 24, 2012, paras. 84–85. The OAS General Assembly has also implied that the ACHR extends to unlisted grounds such as sexual orientation by annually condemning discrimination based on sexual orientation or gender identity. *See, e.g.*, OAS Doc. AG/RES. 2653 (XLI-O/11), Human Rights, Sexual Orientation and Gender Identity, 4th plen. sess., June 7, 2011; OAS Doc. AG/RES. 2600 (XL-O/10), Human Rights, Sexual Orientation and Gender Identity, 4th plen. sess, June 8, 2010.

71. Charter of Fundamental Rights of the European Union, Mar. 30, 2010, art. 21, EU Doc. 2010/C 83/02, *available at* http://eur-lex.europa.eu.

72. *See, e.g.*, Mouta v. Portugal, 31 E.H.R.R. 47, para. 28 (2001); Riffo v. Chile, Inter-Am. Ct. Hum. Rts., Judgment of Feb. 24, 2012, *available at* http://www.corteidh.or.cr/docs/casos/articulos/seriec_239_ing.pdf.

Semantically, any persons who share some common feature, preference, or activity could be called a distinct group simply by tautology. Birdwatchers, claustrophobics, persons whose name begins with "D," residents of Brooklyn, vegans, and occasional video game players could all be described as belonging to a distinct group. Unless a state measure is strictly universal or entirely random in its application to persons potentially subjected to it, an argument could be made that the measure affects a distinct group. A list of prohibited statuses provides guidance on the kinds of grounds on which discrimination is presumptively unjustified.

In practice, international human rights jurisprudence generally comports with something akin to the U.S. strict scrutiny standard when state discrimination is based on the categories of race, sex, ethnicity, and national origin. Under that standard, a distinction must be narrowly tailored to serve a "compelling government interest."[73] Although human rights authorities do not distinguish categorically between discrimination based on some grounds rather than others, they have used the proportionality test to balance legitimate state goals with rights based on their relative importance and sensitivity, keeping in mind the vulnerability of the class claiming its rights have been violated and the gravity of the threat to the right.

The Strasbourg Court's jurisprudence in particular evidences greater concern with some grounds of discrimination than with others. For example, the Strasbourg Court has held several times that "very weighty reasons" must justify a difference in treatment based on race,[74] sex,[75] or birth within marriage ("legitimacy").[76] Similarly, discrimination based on sexual orientation relates to private intimate conduct and, as such, requires "particularly serious reasons by way of justification."[77] But the Court has not used equally strong language with respect to every ground for distinction. For example, states that distinguish in their legal treatment of different property sizes or types have been held to enjoy a wide margin of appreciation in adopting regulations,[78] and the Court has equally given states a wide margin of appreciation in certain discriminatory religious policies.[79]

73. Perry Educ. Ass'n v. Perry Local Educators Ass'n, 460 U.S. 37, 45 (1983).

74. *See, e.g.*, D.H. v. Czech Rep., 47 E.H.R.R. 3, paras. 175–76 (2008).

75. Schuler-Zgraggen v. Switzerland, 16 E.H.R.R. 405, para. 67 (1993); *accord* Petrovic v. Austria, 33 E.H.R.R. 14, para. 37 (2001).

76. Camp & Bourimi v. Netherlands, 34 E.H.R.R. 59, para. 38 (2000).

77. S.L. v. Austria, 37 E.H.R.R. 39, para. 36 (2003); L. & V. v. Austria, 36 E.H.R.R. 55, para. 44 (2003).

78. *See, e.g.*, Chabauty v. France, Eur. Ct. Hum. Rts. App. No. 57412/08, Judgment of Oct. 4, 2012, para. 50; Nilsson v. Sweden, Eur. Ct. Hum. Rts. App. No. 11811/05, Decision on Admissibility of Feb. 26, 2008, *available at* http://hudoc.echr.coe.int/sites/eng/pages/search.aspx?i=001-85409 ("[T]he Court recognises that the State enjoys a wide margin of appreciation with regard both to choosing the means of enforcement and to ascertaining whether the consequences of enforcement are justified in the general interest for the purpose of achieving the objective of the law in question [relating to land use].").

79. *Compare* Sahin v. Turkey, 44 E.H.R.R. 5 (2007) *with* Lautsi v. Italy, 54 E.H.R.R. 3 (2012).

B. The Closed List Approach

The U.S. approach offers an enlightening contrast in the form of a human rights system focusing discrimination analysis on a tightly circumscribed and hierarchically organized set of prohibited grounds.[80] The United States has a long history of discrimination jurisprudence, with prohibitions on certain kinds of discrimination in the federal and state constitutions and legislation. The main federal constitutional provision, enshrined in the Fourteenth Amendment, is an "equal protection" form of nondiscrimination provision. It provides that no state may "deny to any person within its jurisdiction the equal protection of the laws."[81] As such, the Fourteenth Amendment on its face applies not just to discrimination based on race or sex, but on any grounds that results in a denial of equal protection of the laws. In fact, the concept of "equal protection" could reasonably be interpreted to relate to equality between individuals rather than groups, a far more expansive concept than nondiscrimination based on membership in a distinct group.

The U.S. Supreme Court has usually interpreted the Fourteenth Amendment as far more constrained in scope than a plain reading would dictate, however. The Court interprets the Amendment's open language as primarily prohibiting discrimination on grounds of race, national origin, sex, and religion, with an extremely weak residual nondiscrimination right based on other grounds. The resulting jurisprudence establishes a hierarchical system of classes of protection that treats discrimination based on some class memberships as presumptively requiring strong justification, and discrimination based on others as a nearly unlimited prerogative of the state.

Discrimination based on race, national origin, and religion sit atop the hierarchy. In balancing the methods and goals for accomplishing state purposes, the state is supposed to bear a heavy burden of justifying such discrimination. In principle, as mentioned earlier, any discrimination based on either ground is presumed illegitimate unless the state can show that the discrimination was "necessary" and "narrowly tailored" to effect a governmental purpose of "overriding" importance.[82] The phrasing of this strict scrutiny test differs slightly from discrimination doctrine as

80. The United States does not stand alone in a class-based approach to human rights. Canada, for example, in its Charter of Rights and Freedoms, Constitution Act, 1982, Schedule B, pt. I, art. 15, as well as its Human Rights Act 1985, R.S., 1985, c. H-6 pt. I, § 3, defines certain classes as protected from discrimination. On a purely textual level, the U.N. Charter also states as its purpose the protection of a limited set of groups from arbitrary discrimination, although the phrasing has little legal significance. *See* U.N. Charter art. 1(3).

81. U.S. Const., amend. XIV, § 1. This language is reflected in several human rights conventions, but the conventions often include additional language clarifying prohibited grounds for discrimination. Many U.S. states have similar constitutional provisions, but some go into greater detail and specify grounds on which discrimination will not be tolerated, such as gender or race. *See generally* Stanley H. Friedelbaum, *State Equal Protection: Its Diverse Guises and Effects*, 66 Alb. L. Rev. 599 (2003). Nonetheless, state courts rarely depart greatly from federal equal protection practice. *See id.* at 629.

82. McLaughlin v. Florida, 379 U.S. 184 (1964) (race); Oyama v. California, 332 U.S. 663, 645–46 (1948) (national origin).

interpreted by international human rights authorities such as the Strasbourg Court and Human Rights Committee, but the main concepts are essentially identical.

Immediately below these classes sit sex and (inconsistently) the marital status of one's parents, discrimination based on which must usually satisfy reduced but still substantial skepticism. Although the precise phrasing of the standard varies somewhat from case to case, such classifications have generally been held to require the state to show that the discrimination serves "important governmental objectives" and must be "substantially related to the achievement of those objectives."[83] This intermediate scrutiny does not precisely correspond to any IHRL doctrine, and so appears superficially inconsistent with the dominant interpretations of the ECHR, ICCPR (International Covenant on Civil and Political Rights), and CEDAW (Convention on the Elimination of all Forms of Discrimination against Women). In practice, however, international human rights authorities have frequently shown elevated skepticism of distinctions on sex and legitimacy grounds.

Since the time when these "protected classes" were established many years ago, the U.S. Supreme Court has not considered it necessary to recognize other presumptively invalid bases for government discrimination. As a result, other distinctions, such as those based on wealth, age, or mental disability, are not considered constitutionally "suspect" and are instead presumed legitimate despite any showing of a harmful effect.[84] Long ago, the Court did recognize that discrimination based on criteria other than membership in a protected class can be sufficiently arbitrary and harmful to violate the right to equal protection of the laws.[85] Over the years, however, the Court has shifted its jurisprudence decisively toward extreme deference to the legislative and executive branches, resulting in a very strong presumption in favor of the constitutionality of government distinctions among different persons and classes of persons.[86] Such distinctions receive "rational basis" review, meaning that the Court will approve any arbitrary distinction against unprotected classes that is rationally related to some legitimate government purpose.

In practice, rational basis doctrine represents a near abdication of judicial review. Except for occasional and highly unpredictable uses of the rational basis review to strike down legislation deemed arbitrary or invidious,[87] the Constitution

83. Craig v. Boren, 429 U.S. 190 (1976) (sex); Trimble v. Gordon, 430 U.S. 762, 766–69 (1977) (parentage). *But see, e.g.*, United States v. Virginia, 116 S. Ct. 2264 (1996) (holding that the state, when seeking to justify a gender-based classification, must demonstrate an "exceedingly persuasive justification"); Matthews v. Lucas, 427 U.S. 495 (1976) (applying a "reasonably related" test to discrimination based on the marital status of one's parents).

84. *E.g.*, Massachusetts Bd. of Ret. v. Murgia, 427 U.S. 307, 313–14 (1976) (per curiam) (age); Harris v. McRae, 448 U.S. 297, 323 (1980) (wealth); City of Cleburne v. Cleburne Living Ctr., Inc., 473 U.S. 432, 435 (1985) (mental disability).

85. *See, e.g.*, Douglas v. California, 372 U.S. 353, 357–58 (1963), *quoting* Griffin v. Illinois, 351 U.S. 12, 17 (1956); Harper v. Virginia Bd. of Elections, 383 U.S. 663, 668 (1966).

86. *See, e.g.*, Federal Commun. Comm'n v. Beach Communs., Inc., 508 U.S. 307, 314–15 (1993); *see* Laurence H. Tribe, American Constitutional Law § 16-2, at 1442–43 (2d ed. 1988).

87. *See, e.g.*, Romer v. Evans, 517 U.S. 620 (1996); U.S. Dep't of Ag. v. Moreno, 413 U.S. 528, 534 (1973); *see generally* Gayle Lynn Pettinga, Note, *Rational Basis with Bite: Intermediate Scrutiny by Any Other Name*, 62 Ind. L.J. 779 (1987).

as interpreted by the Court affords little or no protection to the human rights of persons subjected to arbitrary and harmful discrimination based on membership in any but the handful of classes considered suspect. The Court interprets the term "rational" in its broadest sense and has shown itself reluctant to imply that the legislature or president has acted irrationally except when no explanation, even a purely hypothetical one, is possible for the discrimination beyond animus toward the group affected or purely random lawmaking.[88] In many cases, the Court has stretched the limits of rationality to encompass overinclusive, underinclusive, and illogical measures discriminating against unprotected classes, including "speculation unsupported by evidence or empirical data."[89] As a result, the Court has upheld discriminatory laws that are clearly and arbitrarily intended to favor one group over others because the basis for the discrimination was not race, national origin, religion, or sex.[90]

The Court's explanations for the heightened scrutiny afforded to some classifications and not to others have varied. In some cases, the greater sensitivity to race has been explained by the "history of purposeful unequal treatment"[91] or "unique disabilities on the basis of stereotyped characteristics not truly indicative of their abilities."[92] Although the rationales for heightened scrutiny might seem doctrinally appealing, the Court has not applied them with any meaningful consistency; the same reasoning would justify strict scrutiny of discrimination based on many grounds, such as sex, sexual orientation, religion, socioeconomic status, and political affiliation, all of which the Court has declined to examine closely in interpreting the equal protection clause.

Another explanation offered was that certain minority groups are "discrete and insular" and in need of "extraordinary protection from the majoritarian political process."[93] This rationale, too, is helpful but problematic; the social, political, or economic dispossession of a class of persons does not require minority status; women have long needed protection from the majoritarian political process, and not only are they not a minority, they are the precise opposite of insular.[94] Even more telling, in the case of South Africa during the long apartheid era, it was the black majority and not the small white minority that required the most protection

88. *See, e.g.*, Lawrence v. Texas, 539 U.S. 558 (2003).

89. *Beach Commc'ns*, 508 U.S. at 315.

90. A classic example is *McGowan v. Maryland*, 366 U.S. 420, 444–50 (1961), in which the Court upheld a Sunday closing law clearly intended for the unconstitutional purpose of promoting Christianity based on a fictitious "legitimate" governmental purpose of providing for a uniform statewide day of rest. The Court failed to explain why mandating a uniform day of rest was a legitimate governmental purpose, especially given the disadvantages of all persons trying to use the same limited recreational facilities at once, and business firms wasting resources through uniformly unoccupied buildings.

91. United States v. Carolene Prods. Co., 304 U.S. 144, 152–53 n.4 (1938).

92. Massachusetts Bd. of Ret. v. Murgia, 427 U.S. 307, 313 (1976) (per curiam).

93. *Id.*

94. *See* Kerrigan v. Commissioner of Pub. Health, 957 A.2d 407, 441–44 (Conn. 2008).

from oligarchic political processes. Similarly, it would be difficult to characterize atheists[95] or children born out of wedlock[96] as "insular" groups, but they too are and have historically been subjected to various forms of majoritarian oppression in the United States and elsewhere.[97] The inconsistencies in U.S. equal protection cases and ultimate incoherence of the justification for class categories in a long-standing democracy with a highly developed constitutional jurisprudence demonstrate the difficulties of a rigid system limiting protection to a few select groups.

Like most constitutional doctrines, the hierarchical class approach has not gathered complete consensus. Justice Stevens was known to observe that "there is only one equal protection clause,"[98] meaning that there is no textual basis for granting some groups strict protection against discrimination and others virtually none at all. Scholars have repeatedly impugned the hierarchical, closed list approach as generating more problems than it solves,[99] and there is some evidence that the categories themselves are gradually disintegrating.[100] Discrimination based on sexual orientation provides a salient and recent example of the inconsistencies in the Supreme Court's application of its own jurisprudence. The Court has never held that discrimination against sexual minorities must be justified as necessary to fulfill a compelling government purpose. Nor has it applied intermediate scrutiny to discrimination based on sexual orientation; the Court's formal position is that sexual orientation-based discrimination need only satisfy a rational basis test. Yet, the California Supreme Court, applying equal protection analysis at the state level, has observed that homosexuals satisfy all of the criteria of a suspect class, and discrimination

95. In colonial North America, failure to attend church twice a day was punished as a crime. *See* James A. Cox, *Bilboes, Brands, and Branks*, Colonial Williamsburg J., Spring 2003. Although oppressions on atheists were gradually relaxed over 200 years, as recently as the mid-twentieth century some states forbade atheists from holding public office. *See* Torcaso v. Watkins, 367 U.S. 488 (1961) (overturning a provision of the Maryland constitution requiring a religious oath of office). On contemporary U.S. discrimination against atheists, *see generally* Greta Christina, *Atheists Fight Discrimination Too*, Salon, Aug. 9, 2012, *at* http://http://www.salon.com/2012/08/09/4_reasons_atheists_have_to_fight_for_their_rights_salpart/.

96. *See* Aaron X. Fellmeth, *Nondiscrimination as a Universal Human Right*, 34 Yale J. Int'l L. 588, 590–91 (2009). The most complete, albeit now rather dated, study of discrimination on the basis of legitimacy is Vieno V. Saario, *Study of Discrimination against Persons Born out of Wedlock*, U.N. Doc. E/CN.4/Sub.2/265/Rev.1 (1967). The Strasbourg Court has disapproved legitimacy of birth as a basis for discrimination in some cases. *See, e.g.*, Marckx v. Belgium, 2 E.H.R.R. 330 (1980); Inze v. Austria, 19 E.H.R.R. 394 (1988).

97. For an extended argument on the debilities of using the discreteness and insularity of a group as a proxy for the need for constitutional protection against discrimination, *see* Bruce A. Ackerman, *Beyond* Carole Products, 98 Harv. L. Rev. 713, 724 (1985).

98. Craig v. Boren, 429 U.S. 190, 211 (1976) (Stevens, J., dissenting).

99. *See, e.g.*, Suzanne B. Goldbert, *Equality without Tiers*, 77 S. Cal. L. Rev. 481, 484–91 (2004); Jeffrey M. Shaman, *Cracks in the Structure: The Coming Breakdown of the Levels of Scrutiny*, 45 Ohio St. L.J. 161 (1984); Eugene Volokh, *Freedom of Speech, Permissible Tailoring and Transcending Strict Scrutiny*, 144 U. Pa. L. Rev. 2417 (1996).

100. *See* Calvin Massey, *The New Formalism: Requiem for Tiered Scrutiny?*, 6 U. Pa. J. Const. L. 945, 946 (2004).

against them must accordingly meet strict scrutiny.[101] Soon, U.S. state and federal courts were issuing conflicting decisions on whether sexual orientation discrimination had to meet strict scrutiny, intermediate scrutiny, or rational basis review.[102]

The problematical nature of the protected class approach similarly motivated the Obama administration in 2011 to take the extraordinary step of refusing to defend in court section 3 of the Defense of Marriage Act (DOMA), which codifies discrimination against same-sex married couples by uniformly denying their marital status under federal law. The president and attorney general concluded that discrimination based on sexual orientation should face a "more heightened [*sic*] standard of scrutiny," which standard, they concluded, the DOMA failed to satisfy.[103] Interestingly, the attorney general did not state his opinion about the precise level of scrutiny applicable to such discrimination. Indeed, he made no effort to justify the use of a heightened review at all, possibly in the hope of avoiding a legal debate on the appropriate standard. In 2013, the Supreme Court finally held state bans on same-sex marriage unconstitutional, and it similarly did so without clearly invoking heightened scrutiny. It merely repeated prior holdings that distinctions based purely on animus toward a politically unpopular group cannot be considered to serve a "legitimate" purpose that would survive constitutional challenge.[104]

The Court's enumeration of prohibited grounds of discrimination do not exhaust the protections of the U.S. human rights system, however. Beginning in the 1960s, Congress began enacting statutory prohibitions on discrimination that apply only to specific classes of persons. Most prominently, the 1964 Civil Rights Act prohibits discrimination on grounds of race, color, religion, or national origin in places of public accommodation such as restaurants or hotels.[105] It also prohibits discrimination in federal financial assistance based on race, color, or national origin.[106] Congress further prohibited public and private employment and housing discrimination based on race, color, religion, sex, or national origin.[107] Later, Congress passed laws prohibiting employment discrimination against persons aged forty or older,[108] pregnant,[109] or having disabilities,[110] and further prohibiting discrimination in

101. *In re* Marriage Cases, 183 P.3d 384, 440–41 (Cal. 2008).

102. *See, e.g.*, SmithKline Beecham Corp. v. Abbott Labs., 740 F.3d 471 (9th Cir. 2013) (strict scrutiny); Varnum v. Brien, 763 N.W.2d 862, 882 (Iowa 2009) (intermediate scrutiny); Glossip v. Missouri Dep't of Transp. & Highway Patrol Emp. Ret. Sys., 411 S.W.3d 796 (Mo. 2013) (rational basis).

103. Office of the U.S. Attorney General, Statement of the Attorney General on Litigation Involving the Defense of Marriage Act, Feb. 23, 2011.

104. United States v. Windsor, Slip Op. 12-307 (June 26, 2013), 570 U.S. __ (2013).

105. 42 U.S.C. § 2000a (2015).

106. *Id.* § 2000d.

107. *Id.* §§ 2000e-2, 3604–3606.

108. 29 U.S.C. §§ 623, 631 (2015).

109. Pub. L. 95-555 (Oct. 31, 1978), 92 Stat. 2076, *codified as amended at* 42 U.S.C. § 2000e (2015).

110. 42 U.S.C. §§ 12103–12213 (2015).

federal financial assistance based on disability.[111] In 1993, Congress required courts to give discrimination based on religious beliefs and practices the highest level of scrutiny whenever government action imposes a substantial burden on religious exercise.[112]

These U.S. civil rights statutes omit any mention of discrimination based on other grounds, including membership in other groups commonly or historically subjected to social, economic, or political disadvantage in the United States. No federal statute generally forbids discrimination based on youth, sexual orientation, political affiliation, marital status, parental status, birth out of wedlock, or poverty and economic status.[113] Private business organizations and city and state governments are free to discriminate arbitrarily on these grounds, subject to the substantive rights of individual members of the groups and the inconsistently applied rational basis approach, unless the state government has happened to adopt a constitution or legislation more expansive than federal law. The result in the United States is pervasive governmental and social discrimination based on popular prejudices and political convenience. Even within protected classes, courts have frequently weakened constitutional and statutory protections. For example, the U.S. Supreme Court was able to reconcile the constitutional right to equal protection of the laws with a state disability insurance scheme that discriminated against health issues caused by pregnancy, but not with comparable health issues affecting only men.[114] Similarly, the U.S. Court of Appeals for the Ninth Circuit, sitting *en banc*, felt comfortable concluding that a casino could, without violating the Civil Rights Act's prohibition on sex-based discrimination, demand that its employees conform to gender stereotypes[115] by requiring women to wear makeup and style their hair.[116] When courts are blind to gender discrimination despite established doctrinal disapproval, much less secure are the rights of groups that do not benefit from any form of heightened scrutiny.

111. 29 U.S.C. §§ 706, 794 (2015).

112. Religious Freedom Restoration Act of 1993, Pub. L. 103-141, § 2, 107 Stat. 1488, *codified at* 42 U.S.C. §§ 2000bb to 2000bb-4 (2015).

113. There are scattered U.S. federal laws prohibiting various forms of discrimination in some circumstances, such as marital status or parenthood of a minor, and much stricter restrictions on discrimination apply to federal employees, but, as stated, there are no general prohibitions on discrimination based on status other than those discussed here.

114. *See* Geduldig v. Aiello, 417 U.S. 484, 497 (1974).

115. By "sex," I mean the innate biological characteristic that determines reproductive capabilities. Generally, the female sex is defined by the presence of XX chromosomes and the male by XY, and "intersex" persons have genetic abnormalities such as XXY chromosomes or a mixture of cells with XX and XY chromosomes. By "gender," I mean the socially constructed, culturally accepted stereotypes that any given society identifies with one or the other sex. *See* American Psychological Association, Guidelines for Psychological Practice with Lesbian, Gay, and Bisexual Clients, Feb. 18-20, 2011, Introduction, *available at* http://www.apa.org/pi/lgbt/resources/guidelines.aspx.

116. Jespersen v. Harrah's Operating Co., 444 F.3d 1104 (2006) (en banc). For an interesting analysis of this case and its implications, *see* Zachary A. Kramer, *The New Sex Discrimination*, 63 Duke L.J. 891 (2014).

Any deficiencies in U.S. nondiscrimination legislation and inconsistencies in U.S. nondiscrimination jurisprudence are not necessarily inherent to the closed list approach, however. Some are clearly idiosyncratic to the U.S. implementation. A closed list offers maximally clear guidance on the prohibited grounds for discrimination by explicitly enumerating those grounds and excluding all others. In theory, such a list could be altered by legislation periodically to include new grounds or remove obsolete grounds. Added grounds could address evolving social prejudices, whereas changes in demographics or the distribution of political and economic power could render old grounds unnecessary. This approach involves some significant disadvantages, however, which will be discussed in the next section.

More promising is the hierarchization of grounds for discrimination. The U.S. Supreme Court jurisprudence explaining its chosen hierarchy, and congressional choices about what kinds of discrimination to elevate to the top of that hierarchy, may not provide a coherent justification for the judicial decisions actually made, but poor implementation does not necessarily impugn the potential value of establishing some kind of hierarchy. Indeed, it may seem that the value of hierarchization is independent of whether the list of prohibited grounds is open or closed. As noted earlier, several human rights authorities have suggested that some grounds of discrimination, such as race, ethnicity, and sex, are more suspect than others.[117] Regarding race and ethnicity, the Strasbourg Court has even spoken in absolutes: "no difference in treatment which is based exclusively or to a decisive extent on a person's ethnic origin is capable of being objectively justified in a contemporary democratic society built on the principles of pluralism and respect for different cultures."[118] European Union jurisprudence seems headed in the same direction.[119] Ironically, the more rigid hierarchization of the U.S. system makes *less* sense when applied to a closed list. The more grounds for discrimination a system treats as potentially incompatible with human rights, the more pressing is the need for firm guidance on the justifiability of any given distinction. A short list of prohibited grounds needs a less nuanced doctrine of justification because it relies on arbitrary bright lines rather than thoroughly reasoned policies that account for nuances of the social context in which the prohibition operates.

In any case, a hierarchy of some kind has notable advantages, because some grounds for distinctions among members of society and their activities are nearly always and everywhere irrational and harmful, while others could easily be logical and beneficial, depending on circumstances. As human rights authorities have sometimes recognized, it is the rare state measure that could justify discrimination based on race, ethnicity, birth outside of marriage, marital status, sex, gender,

117. *See, e.g.*, Karner v. Austria, Eur. Ct. Hum. Rts., Case No. 40016/98, July 24, 2003, paras. 34–43 (holding there is a "narrow" margin of appreciation when the state discriminates based on sex or sexual orientation).

118. Sejdić v. Bosnia and Herzegovina, Eur. Ct. Hum. Rts. Case Nos. 27996/06 & 34836/06, Judgment of Dec. 22, 2009, para. 44; *accord* Timishev v. Russia, Eur. Ct. Hum. Rts. Case Nos. 55762/00 & 55974/00, Judgment of Dec. 13, 2005, para. 58.

119. *See* Mark Bell, Anti-discrimination Law and the European Union 32 (2002); Mark Bell & Lisa Waddington, *Reflecting on Inequalities in European Equality Law*, 28 Eur. L. Rev. 349 (2003).

sexual orientation, religious conviction, or political opinion. Distinctions based on wealth, age, and disability will be justifiable in some cases and not in others. Distinctions based on an individual's chronic antisocial behavior will in some cases not only be generally justifiable, but mandatory for the proper functioning of the state. The difficulty, of course, lies in arranging the hierarchy in a manner consistent with equal human dignity and uninfluenced by the prejudices of popular opinion or the biases of political and legal elites—a challenge to be taken up later.

As noted, the closed list has the virtue of offering relatively clear guidance to the state and, when applicable, private actors, regarding the prohibited grounds of discrimination. As always in law, reasonable certainty about the forms of conduct permitted and prohibited benefits all duty holders. Frederick Schauer has hypothesized that courts may tend toward such firm rules in service of a desire "to conserve their decisional resources and thus to make unimportant (to them) decisions more routinized," and to discard irrelevant information that might prove distracting.[120] Although this rationale probably depicts some kinds of judicial cognition accurately, it does not entirely explain the U.S. Supreme Court's reliance on formal rules in the context of fundamental civil rights against discrimination. Judicial preferences on human rights questions rarely rate as weak or unimportant. Indeed, the policy issues at stake are so important that judges may wish to reduce their own discretion to avoid accusations of politicization. A judge conscious of his or her official role as a declarer of preexisting law rather than a progenitor of original law may consider the risks of an open list of prohibited bases for discrimination to invite criticism by civil society and the political branches. International human rights tribunals may not feel the same pressure because their specific role and mandate is to develop and apply quintessentially vague human rights standards. They are expected to elaborate these standards and, qua authoritative human rights decision-makers rather than general courts, to interpret them in a manner consistent with human dignity and sound ethics. International human rights tribunals accustomed to interpret and apply generally phrased rights have less reason to shy away from assuming broad discretion in dealing with a nondiscrimination right.

Whatever the rationale for the adoption of the closed list of prohibited grounds in the United States, its inflexibility comes at a high cost to the meaningful enjoyment of the nondiscrimination right. The human capacity to attribute importance to minor distinctions between persons—what Freud called the narcissism of petty differences—has few limits.[121] The ability of states and private actors to invent reasons to distinguish between groups and inflict harms and disadvantages on disfavored ones does not always correspond to any rational or preconceived set of criteria. The nondiscrimination right cannot act as a bulwark against arbitrary oppression based on artificial distinctions if corralled into a cleanly defined doctrine of very limited scope. The Supreme Court has sometimes accordingly chaffed at the rigidity of its own doctrine, inventing the concept of "substantive due process of law" to fill in where its narrow equal protection doctrine constrains it too

120. *See* Frederick Schauer, *The Tyranny of Choice and the Rulification of Standards*, 14 J. Contemp. Legal Issues 803, 813 (2005).

121. Sigmund Freud, Civilization and Its Discontents 58–63 (1930).

tightly, and occasionally invoking a test that weighs "the congruence and proportionality between the injury to be prevented or remedied and the means adopted to that end,"[122] in a serendipitous echo of international human rights doctrine. Yet, perversely, the Court has sometimes used this test not to exercise the independent judgment so often displayed by the Strasbourg Court, but rather to strike down legislative attempts to rectify preexisting social discrimination.[123]

Another problem with the closed list is that judgments about which classes are worthy of protection tend to reflect an idiosyncratic view of human rights. Ironically, the classes that political elites or public sentiment may view as having no right to equal treatment are frequently the very same classes most likely to need such protection. Majoritarian or elite bias against such groups, and popular cultural apathy toward or support of social or legal discrimination against them, may equally blind national and even international human rights institutions to the need for protection. The very designation of some grounds for discrimination as arising from "protected classes" seems from a rhetorical standpoint to suggest "special treatment" in favor of the subject group rather than a universal privilege against arbitrarily imposed disadvantages. The irony is that the need for special protection arises precisely because the subject groups are perceived to suffer exceptional prejudice. "Perceived" is the key word here. The choice of grounds upon which distinctions are considered presumptively illegitimate reflects culturally and politically influenced judgments about which groups are worthy of, and in need of, protection.

A case in point is *Vos v. The Netherlands*, in which the Human Rights Committee considered a social insurance scheme that granted disability benefits to disabled widowers but not to disabled widows.[124] The government's defense was that the system reflected prevailing employment patterns in which men tended to earn the primary household income, and the Committee concluded that this explanation was based on objective and reasonable criteria.[125] But a system that grants advantages only to couples conforming to discriminatory social stereotypes (here, the working man and housewife) reinforces those very stereotypes by creating systemic disincentives to realign social patterns according to the needs of the individuals. The Committee's approval of a sexist state policy therefore not only failed to rectify a situation of unequal treatment for equally situated disabled persons, but discouraged women from working and men from playing homemaker roles according to their personal proclivities and capabilities. As Anne Bayefsky observed, the policy "bore the hallmarks of classic stereotyping of women with its accompanying consequences of degradation and second-class status."[126]

By allowing states to rely on sex as a proxy for the fact of being a primary income-earner, human rights authorities not only allow the state to reinforce a pattern of

122. City of Boerne v. Flores, 521 U.S. 507, 520 (1997).

123. *See* Kenji Yoshino, *The New Equal Protection*, 124 HARV. L. REV. 747, 771–72 (2011).

124. U.N. Hum. Rts. Com., Communication No. 218/1986/ U.N. Doc. A/44/40 (1989).

125. *Id.* para. 12.

126. *See* Bayefsky, *supra* note 69, at 15.

economic discrimination, they dilute the nondiscrimination right to reflect the gender stereotypes of the authorities themselves. The Committee failed in *Vos* to recognize the basic point of anti-discrimination law: the *present fact* of entrenched patterns of social and economic discrimination in a state cannot justify reinforcing or rewarding the pattern through government policies. Although this misunderstanding is not universal among all human rights authorities at all times and places, it is a recurrent problem among even the most enlightened and progressive of them.[127] The Committee's failure to perceive the sexism of the Netherlands policy no doubt reflected the attitudes of Committee members at the time.[128] Objectivity in discrimination analysis presents a unique challenge for human psychology. The very common trait of self-confidence in one's own objectivity is no substitute for laborious efforts to develop the trait of sensitivity to one's arbitrary cultural and personal biases.

The problem has not evaporated with the social unacceptability of racism and sexism; it has merely gone sub rosa, with more overt patterns of discrimination shifting toward new groups, such as Muslims and homosexuals. Recently, one European public official even intimated in the *European Journal of International Law*, in the face of centuries of vicious persecution as well as pervasive contemporary discrimination against and stereotyping of homosexuals, that homosexual perceptions of discrimination are merely falsely induced by state-sponsored awareness-raising campaigns.[129] It is precisely because even well-intentioned political and legal elites frequently share popular stereotypes and biases about minority groups, and selective blindness to discrimination against them, that human rights authorities need to exercise their fact-gathering powers and uncomfortable introspection into their own prejudices to evaluate the true extent and consequences of state or social discrimination.

On the other hand, an open list of grounds carries its own problems. It is possible, for example, that the proliferation of discrimination claims based on unconventional grounds could distract from remedies for the most serious forms of discrimination.[130] States have limited resources for redressing claims of human rights violations. To the extent only some claims will be realistically addressed, the most pervasive and debilitating forms of discrimination should be privileged, which is to say, given hierarchically superior status, as compared to less serious forms of discrimination. Human rights authorities called upon to evaluate potentially limitless grounds for discrimination will necessarily devote less time to the most pervasive and invidious forms of discrimination.

This argument has the most force in states where some forms of discrimination markedly dominate over others. Its force is reduced, however, by the fact that,

127. *See id.* at 22–23 (recounting examples in the Strasbourg Court).

128. Even at this writing in late 2014, only four of the Committee's eighteen members are women.

129. Jakob Cornides, *Three Case Studies on "Anti-Discrimination,"* 23 Eur. J. Int'l L. 517, 519 (2012).

130. *See, e.g.*, Richard Thompson Ford, The Race Card: How Bluffing about Bias Makes Race Relations Worse 176 (2008).

in most societies that maintain severe forms of discrimination, others are equally pervasive, or nearly so, but receive less attention for political or cultural reasons. No society labors under just one or two major popular prejudices. Interests against discrimination on these less visible grounds may be no less worthy of urgent protection, but it is the fallible perception of political elites that guides the prioritizing of one form of discrimination over others. A more objective system for prioritizing group discrimination claims, combined with an open list of prohibited grounds, could contribute to avoiding the pitfalls of unconscious bias. This subject will be taken up at the end of this chapter.

2. The Protected Interest

For the same reason that the grounds of discrimination are underdetermined by the right itself, the right does not specify the interests from which a state or private measure is forbidden to derogate. Nothing in a nondiscrimination right inherently suggests that a denial of equal housing rights on prohibited grounds such as race violates the right, but a discourteous income tax audit by state officials on prohibited grounds such as race does not. Remember that a substantive right tends to define the broad outlines of the protected interest by specifying its subject matter; a nondiscrimination right may or may not do so. As will be discussed, the consequences of the choice to identify or leave open the catalog of interests to be protected are significant.

Nondiscrimination in Identified Rights

Many international human rights instruments explicitly confine the protection against discrimination to the specific rights enumerated in the instrument. Anne Bayefsky referred to such provisions as "subordinate," in the sense that the discrimination right relates to listed rights only. A better term might be "dependent," in that the nondiscrimination norm is not hierarchically inferior to the substantive rights listed in the convention. In contrast, independent nondiscrimination provisions confer a freestanding right against arbitrary distinctions with respect to interests not listed in the treaty as a protected human right.[131] Both kinds appear in some of the major international human rights instruments. The nondiscrimination provisions in the international bill of rights illustrate the dependent kind:

> Everyone is entitled to *all the rights and freedoms set forth in this Declaration*, without distinction of any kind, such as race, colour, sex, language, religion, political or other opinion, national or social origin, property, birth or other status.[132]
>
> Each State Party to the present Covenant undertakes to respect and to ensure to all individuals within its territory and subject to its jurisdiction *the rights recognized in the present Covenant*, without distinction of any kind, such as

131. *See* Bayefsky, *supra* note 125, at 3.

132. UDHR art. 2 (emphasis added).

> race, colour, sex, language, religion, political or other opinion, national or social origin, property, birth or other status.[133]
>
> The States Parties to the present Covenant undertake to ensure the equal right of men and women to the enjoyment of all economic, social and cultural *rights set forth in the present Covenant.*[134]

Similarly, the Convention on the Rights of the Child article 2(1) and ECHR article 14 contain dependent nondiscrimination rights.

Ironically, the terms of the dedicated anti-discrimination treaties are sometimes *more* ambiguous regarding the scope of the equal treatment right. The CEDAW and CEDR, for example, define the nondiscrimination right as protecting the exercise or enjoyment of "human rights and fundamental freedoms in the political, economic, social, cultural or any other field of public life."[135] The treaties might have defined the right more expansively to encompass the exercise or enjoyment of all "benefits and freedoms granted or protected by law." However, the conventions then somewhat confusingly expand on state obligations to encompass prohibitions against "all" discrimination and promoting equal rights in any legislation.[136]

Given the expansiveness of some human rights instruments, dependent provisions may seem to impose at most a minor limitation on the nondiscrimination right. Equal enjoyment of the conventional rights does unquestionably provide great benefits to everyone within the jurisdiction of the adopting state. However, dependent provisions are in fact much less constraining of arbitrary discrimination than independent ones. Radical inequalities in state treatment are possible consistent with such nondiscrimination provisions, as illustrated in the European jurisprudence. The Strasbourg Court has long interpreted article 14 of the ECHR to have "no independent existence since it has effect solely in relation to 'the enjoyment of the rights and freedoms' safeguarded by the treaty's substantive provisions."[137] The limitation of the nondiscrimination right to cases where the applicant has already

133. CCPR art. 2(1) (emphasis added). In interpreting the CCPR, the Human Rights Committee has said that:

> the term "discrimination" as used in the Covenant should be understood to imply any distinction, exclusion, restriction or preference which is based on any ground . . . and which has the purpose or effect of nullifying or impairing the recognition, enjoyment or exercise by all persons, on an equal footing, *of all rights and freedoms.*

U.N. Hum. Rts. Comm., General Comment No. 18: Nondiscrimination, para. 7, 37th Sess., Nov. 10, 1989 (emphasis added). The Committee apparently intended an unstated qualification to this expansive language limiting it to rights and freedoms set forth in the CCPR.

134. CESCR art. 3 (emphasis added).

135. CERD art. 1; CEDAW art. 1.

136. CERD art. 2; CEDAW art. 2.

137. Schalk & Kopf v. Austria, 53 E.H.R.R. 20, para. 89 (2011); Willis v. United Kingdom, Eur. Ct. Hum. Rts. Case No. 36042/97, para. 29 (2002).

alleged a violation of a substantive right guaranteed by the Convention has led one jurist to qualify the right as "almost parasitic" and conclude: "The nondiscrimination provision has been at least to some extent a second-class guarantee over much of the period in which the Convention has been in force."[138]

A few examples can illustrate the deficiencies of a dependent nondiscrimination right. Suppose a Council of Europe member state were to adopt a law requiring all female children to be given one of fifty names traditional in the state's dominant culture. The ECHR provides no fundamental human right to absolute freedom in choosing a child's name, or else a parent would be free to choose an insulting name for his or her child.[139] Although it would be hard to argue the law's consistency with the substantive right to family life, assume *arguendo* that the law is considered consistent with that right. A dependent discrimination provision would logically grant the parents no relief, because the discriminatory provision ex hypothesi violates no substantive right. Similarly, the ECHR provides for no human right to public transportation services. Technically, a state measure allowing only persons of a specific race or gender to ride the subway would not violate article 14. By its own terms article 14 is operative only when taken in conjunction with another article of the Convention establishing a human right or fundamental freedom.

In practice, the Strasbourg Court has sometimes mitigated the effects of article 14's limited scope with compensating doctrines. In some cases, without actually interpreting article 14 to prohibit discrimination in all state measures generally, the Court has expanded article 14 to apply to discrimination that does not technically violate a listed human right, but that relates to the subject matter of a human right in some way. In its own words, the "application of Art. 14 does not necessarily presuppose the violation of one of the substantive rights protected by the Convention. It is necessary but it is also sufficient for the facts of the case to fall within the ambit of one or more" articles of the Convention.[140] A state that grants a benefit or imposes some burden "within the ambit" of a protected right may not discriminate arbitrarily. The Court has accordingly sometimes interpreted the European Convention to prohibit arbitrary discrimination in matters not specifically listed as a protected human right, such as adoption or employment in a specific profession.

For example, in *Abdulaziz v. United Kingdom*,[141] one of the applicants was a lawful permanent resident of the United Kingdom who had later married a foreign

138. Luzius Wildhaber, *Protection against Discrimination under the European Convention on Human Rights—A Second-Class Guarantee?*, 2 Baltic Y.B. Int'l L. 71, 72, 82 (2002).

139. In some countries, parents are forbidden to give their children insulting or offensive names. *See, e.g.*, Births, Deaths, and Marriages Registration Act of 1995, Pub. Act No. 16, § 18(8) (Mar. 31, 1995) (N.Z.); Namnlag SFS 1982:670, § 34 (Sweden). *See also* Jonathan Lis, *Israeli Panel to Debate Bill Banning "Insulting" Baby Names*, Ha'aretz, Jan. 1, 2012, *at* http://www.haaretz.com/print-edition/news/israeli-panel-to-debate-bill-banning-insulting-baby-names-1.404804. *But see* Gillette v. Schroeder, 49 Conn. L. Rep. 405 (Conn. Super. Ct. 2010) ("There is no law in Connecticut concerning the naming of a child. A parent is free to misspell the name, utilize a unique variety of pronunciations, choose a name not matching the child's gender or select one's favorite automobile, planet or breakfast cereal as the child's name.").

140. E.B. v. France, 47 E.H.R.R. 21, para. 47 (2008).

141. 7 E.H.R.R. 471 (1985).

national not resident in the United Kingdom. When the United Kingdom denied permanent residence to the spouse, the couple complained of a violation of the article 8 right to family life as well as a violation of article 14 taken in conjunction inter alia with article 8. The Strasbourg Court rejected the claim that article 8 requires state parties to allow the immigration of any alien who marries a resident,[142] but it nevertheless held that a state may not discriminate arbitrarily on grounds of sex in granting immigration rights.[143] Similarly, in *Schmidt v. Germany*, the Court held that it was consistent with the article 4 prohibition on forced labor to require citizens to serve at a local fire department or else to pay a levy, but that article 14 prohibited the state from requiring men and not women to pay the levy.[144] In *Petrovic v. Austria*, the Court recognized that the ECHR did not guarantee fathers a right to a parental leave allowance when their wives gave birth, but held nonetheless that granting such allowances to wives alone constituted arbitrary discrimination in violation of article 14 taken with article 8.[145] In *E.B. v. France*, it recognized the absence of a substantive human right to adopt a child, but held nonetheless that discrimination based on the prospective adoptive parent's sexual orientation violated article 14 of the ECHR taken with the article 8 right to privacy and family life.[146] This is not to say the Strasbourg Court has been consistent in applying article 14 in this manner; it has not. But the Court is clearly aware of the problems caused by a narrow reading of a dependent nondiscrimination right, and has sometimes applied a judicial correction to what is undoubtedly a serious deficiency in article 14's underlying concept.

One approach sometimes adopted by the Strasbourg Court is to vary the skepticism with which discrimination is viewed in proportion to the importance of the human right that the discrimination threatens. The Court has adopted this approach, for example, when states have discriminated based on sexual orientation because of the perceived importance of privacy and family life.[147] Human rights authorities make the best use of the nondiscrimination right when they require states to offer more convincing justifications for discrimination that threatens a fundamental value important to survival, a dignified existence, personal identity, or the meaningful exercise of a wide range of other rights and freedoms.

Optional Protocol No. 12 to the Convention, signed in 2000, eliminates the limitations of article 14 by expanding its scope to "[t]he enjoyment of any right set forth by law" and prohibiting any arbitrary governmental discrimination generally.[148] "Any right," in this case, includes benefits that are not Hohfeldian claim-rights, but privileges and powers as well. In other words, the Protocol effectively converts the

142. *Id.* para. 68.

143. *Id.* paras. 71, 79–82.

144. Schmidt v. Germany, 18 E.H.R.R. 513 (1994).

145. Petrovic v. Austria, 33 E.H.R.R. 14 (2001).

146. E.B. v. France, 47 E.H.R.R. 21 (2008).

147. *See* Fellmeth, *supra* note 23, at 923–24.

148. Protocol No. 12 to the Convention for the Protection of Human Rights and Fundamental Freedoms art. 1, CETS No. 177, *signed on* Nov. 4, 2000.

ECHR's nondiscrimination provision from a dependent right to an independent one for those states that have adopted it. Under Protocol No. 12, it does not matter whether there is a human right to ride the subway; access to the subway is a privilege granted by law and, as such, subject to the nondiscrimination principle. But Protocol No. 12 has been ratified by only eighteen states as of 2016—which number excludes all of the major European powers except Spain and the Netherlands.[149]

On their plain terms, conventional equal protection provisions such as CCPR article 26 also propound independent rights, because they apply to "laws" rather than "human rights." Although CCPR article 2 obligates states to respect and ensure "the rights recognized in the present Covenant, without distinction of any kind," article 26 includes no limiting reference to the rights of the Covenant:

> All persons are equal before the law and are entitled without any discrimination to the equal protection of the law. In this respect, the law shall prohibit any discrimination and guarantee to all persons equal and effective protection against discrimination on any ground such as race, colour, sex, language, religion, political or other opinion, national or social origin, property, birth or other status.

Superficially, nondiscrimination and equal protection seem like two sides of the same coin, with both principles prohibiting the state from making arbitrary distinctions based on prohibited grounds. Bayefsky once interpreted them that way,[150] and in an early case the Committee itself treated CCPR article 26 as coterminous with article 2.[151]

However, the recent trend is toward interpreting equal protection clauses as being independent. The Human Rights Committee has interpreted article 26, which has no counterpart in the CESCR, to recognize a rather different right:

> In the view of the Committee, article 26 does not merely duplicate the guarantee already provided for in article 2 but provides in itself an autonomous

149. In any case, the Protocol's advisability in the context of the European human rights regime remains doubtful. Article 3 of the Protocol effectively treats articles 1 and 2 as an amendment to the Convention. The Strasbourg Court already suffers from chronic docket overcrowding; the further addition of recourse to the Court for the very wide class of cases covered by Protocol No. 12 may undermine the Court's ability to respond to serious rights violations in a timely manner. The value of the principles of Protocol No. 12 is beyond question; the feasibility of relying on the Strasbourg Court as the enforcer of a substantially expanded body of human rights law is not, at least without strong guidance and elaboration about the kinds of considerations that will render distinctions in the national laws and policies of states inconsistent with human rights.

150. *See* Anne F. Bayefsky, *The Principle of Equality or Nondiscrimination in International Law*, 11 HUM. RTS. Q. [HUM. RTS. L.J.] 1, 2 n.1 (1990).

151. I.M. v. Norway, U.N. Hum. Rts. Comm. Case No. 129/1982, para. 5, Hum. Rts. Comm. 1983 Report, Annex XXVII (dismissing the claim of a Norwegian alleging race-based discrimination in tax benefits and the allocation of low-rent housing, because these are not benefits included as rights in the Covenant).

> right. It prohibits discrimination in law or in fact in any field regulated and protected by public authorities. Article 26 is therefore concerned with the obligations imposed on States parties in regard to their legislation and the application thereof. Thus, when legislation is adopted by a State party, it must comply with the requirement of article 26 that its content should not be discriminatory. In other words, the application of the principle of non-discrimination contained in article 26 is not limited to those rights which are provided for in the Covenant.[152]

Thus, the Committee has now come to consider article 26 as establishing a broader right against unequal treatment in any state-granted or -protected interest. The critical moment came in two 1987 cases dealing with claims of sex discrimination in Dutch social security benefits. In these cases, the Committee held that the equal treatment right of article 26 applies even to state action that does not implicate a right listed in the Covenant, unless the unequal treatment is based on "reasonable and objective criteria."[153]

The Inter-American Court reads the ACHR's article 24 in parallel to the Human Rights Committee's interpretation of the equal protection provision of the CCPR. According to the Inter-American Court:

> Article 24 of the American Convention prohibits discrimination, by law or de facto, not only with regard to the rights enshrined in said treaty, but also in regard to all laws approved by the State and their application. In other words, if a State discriminates in the respect for or guarantee of a right contained in the Convention, it will be failing to comply with its obligation under in [sic] Article 1(1) and the substantive right in question. If, on the contrary, the discrimination refers to unequal protection by domestic laws, the fact must be analyzed in light of Article 24 of the American Convention.[154]

The foregoing discussion suggests some policy reasons for treating the equal protection right of CCPR article 26 as having a scope and signification different from the nondiscrimination right of article 2. Equality "before the law" implies that the law itself may not discriminate impermissibly, but it does not necessarily imply a duty to prohibit private discrimination, because private acts are not attributable to "the law." The "equal protection of the laws" language could reasonably be read the same way. The law "protects" accused criminals from the arbitrary power of the state and individuals given statutory or other legal powers by the state. It does not necessarily protect all persons from private acts detrimental to them as members of a group or

152. U.N. Hum. Rts. Comm., General Comment No. 18: Non-discrimination, para. 12, 37th Sess., Nov. 10, 1989.

153. Broeks v. The Netherlands, U.N. Hum. Rts. Comm. Case No. 172/1984 (1987); Zwaan-de Vries v. The Netherlands, U.N. Hum. Rts. Comm. Case No. 182/1984 (1987).

154. Riffo v. Chile, Am. Ct. Hum. Rts., Judgment of Feb. 24, 2012, para. 82; *see* Barbera ("Corte Primera Contencioso Administrativo") v. Venezuela, Am. Ct. Hum. Rts., Judgment of Aug. 5, 2008, Ser. C, No. 182, para. 209.

persons having some particular characteristic. This is instead the purpose of the positive aspect of the nondiscrimination right, as the "ensure" language suggests.

In other words, the most credible reading of the respective provisions is one of complementarity. The article 2 nondiscrimination right obligates states not only to respect all enumerated human rights without discrimination as to the right holder's race, sex, or other status, but to ensure that these rights may be enjoyed without private impairment. States therefore undertake the positive duty to prohibit private impairment of the human rights recognized by the Covenant. The article 26 equal protection right adds a duty not to discriminate arbitrarily between classes of persons in any of the state's public measures, but it does not include any duty to protect individuals from private discrimination with regard to interests not qualifying as human rights. From this perspective, the equal protection right extends to a broader range of state acts (including those not infringing a specific listed human right). The two duties differ not only in their scope; the nondiscrimination rights is a positive right, whereas the equal protection right is a negative one. The equal protection right in this reading is more circumscribed than the nondiscrimination right in some ways and broader in others.

Another potential difference between a nondiscrimination right and an equal protection right is that the "equality before the law" language seems to tie in to the due process and fair trial right of the Universal Declaration and CCPR.[155] "Before" the law implies that the right kicks in when a person is brought before a court or other regularly constituted tribunal to answer charges of an illegal act, whether civil or criminal. Both instruments even repeat the "equality" language in their fair trial provisions. UDHR article 10 states: "Everyone is entitled *in full equality* to a fair and public hearing by an independent and impartial tribunal, in the determination of his rights and obligations and of any criminal charge against him." CCPR article 14(1) begins: "All persons shall be equal before the courts and tribunals." These provisions could be read to imply that "equal protection" demands the most exacting standards in the administration of justice compared to other forms of social control, in which the state may have some valid justification for discrimination, or at least benefit from some (albeit limited) discretion in determining when discrimination is justified.

3. The Individual and Social Consequences of Discrimination

The nondiscrimination right departs from the classic liberal individual rights paradigm in important ways. In some cases, as with ethnic discrimination, it superficially resembles a group right, but ultimately all discrimination claims are asserted by or on behalf of individuals as victims. Although discrimination is based on some characteristic shared among multiple individuals, it is important to recognize that these individuals may not share a common identity in any meaningful sense. Obese persons and atheists suffer discrimination in many societies, but they are not socially cohesive groups.[156] Because it does not require a common identity as a

155. UDHR arts. 10 & 11; CCPR arts. 9 & 14.

156. This may partly explain why, in evaluating a claim of discrimination based on body weight under the Charter of the Fundamental Rights of the European Union, the Court of

precondition to protection, the nondiscrimination right is as much an individual right as any substantive right.

Yet, because discrimination always relates to a shared characteristic, by its nature it potentially affects a class of persons rather than the individual victim alone. A person who suffers harm from an isolated instance of ill will is not experiencing discrimination based on status or group membership so much as based on individual idiosyncrasies. Discrimination in a legal sense is a social—or rather, antisocial—phenomenon that reflects elite or popular prejudices against the group. This can take the form of a widespread, entrenched cultural bias against a group, or significant political or economic disempowerment of the group's members, or both.

Communitarian critiques sometimes accuse human rights law of ignoring unequal power relations in society precisely through this kind of preoccupation with individuals. Individual rights may not be the most efficient or effective mechanism to address more general social injustices. However, the social effects of the nondiscrimination right do tend to vindicate claims based on group characteristics. As such, a thoroughly enforced nondiscrimination right could redress social, political, and economic forces that create or sustain power imbalances between groups. The compatibility of a state measure with IHRL depends to some degree on the measure's social consequences, regardless of whether we are talking about a substantive human right or the nondiscrimination right. But a violation of an individual's substantive right may affect nobody but himself.

In contrast, an evaluation of the social consequences of discrimination is integral to nondiscrimination analysis. Bound up in the dynamics of alleged discriminatory treatment are preexisting social, political, and economic inequalities in the affected society, because discrimination claims allege unfair disadvantages to whole group of which the claimant is a representative member. Differential treatment of groups is, of course, inevitable in any state measure. A progressive income tax takes a different percentage of the wealth of some groups than others (in each case, persons in a certain income category). A flat income tax differentiates between groups, because it affects the well-being of those with lower income more than those with higher income due to the diminishing marginal utility of income.[157] In fact, any income tax at all differentiates the group of persons with income (subjected to a levy) from the group without income (not subjected). Human rights analysis of discrimination involves a comparison of the relative treatment of different but "similarly situated" social groups. To speak of "arbitrary" discrimination, then, means a distinction that is not arbitrary for the individual (which is inevitable), but rather that is arbitrary in its *societal effect*, and therefore morally unjustifiable on a social level.

Justice of the European Union posed the question as one of discrimination based on disability rather than treating obesity as a prohibited ground for arbitrary distinctions. *See* Fag og Arbejde v. Kommunemes Landsforening, Ct. Just. Eur. Union, Case C-354/13, Judgment of Dec. 18, 2014, Celex No. 613CJ0354.

157. On this point, *see* Michael Argyle, *Causes and Correlates of Happiness*, *in* WELL-BEING: THE FOUNDATIONS OF HEDONIC PSYCHOLOGY 353 (Daniel Kahneman et al. eds., 1999); Ed Diener, Ed Sandvik, Larry Seidlitz & Marissa Diener, *The Relationship between Income and Subjective Well-Being: Relative or Absolute?*, 28 SOC. INDICATORS RES. 195, 204 (1993); Ruut Verhoven, *Is Happiness Relative?*, 24 SOC. INDICATORS RES. 1, 10 (1991).

A. Justified Distinctions

Public and private discrimination based on stereotypes and biases irrationally devaluing certain groups of persons violate core liberal moral canons of equal respect for human dignity. Distinctions with a rational basis, in contrast, not only refrain from offending human dignity, but may be necessary to proper respect for human dignity. A common consequentialist argument justifying distinctions in treatment of different classes of persons as a societal good is that certain forms are objectively cost-justified. The most common example, alluded to earlier, is the insurance industry, for which such attributes as sex and age play an important role in assessing risks from serious health disorders or automobile accidents. If older individuals are more likely to develop serious ailments, and young men are more likely to engage in risky driving, then the case is certainly stronger for allowing private distinctions on grounds such as age and sex.

Even when there is a relatively strong correlation between such attributes and social reality, however, there may be reasons in some cases for not embracing such discrimination uncritically. Even rational distinctions can create social externalities not captured by the benefits of the distinction. As illustrated by the *Vos* case, rational distinctions can create or perpetuate broader negative social effects when accompanied by irrational social perceptions. Usually, the Strasbourg Court has rejected justifications for discrimination based on social gender role preferences. It has held, for example, that male employees could not be denied the same parental leave rights as female employees, because men are stereotypically assumed to be the primary income earners and women the primary caregivers, even if in fact the stereotype reflects a general trend in gender roles.[158]

Admittedly, the suppression of rational private distinctions not only sacrifices any efficiency benefits of such distinctions, it also intrudes on the freedom of private actors.[159] Whether and when the costs and benefits of suppressing rational private distinctions overshadow the costs of permitting them depends much on the characteristics of the distinguishers and the subjects of distinction, and the social context in which it all occurs. Allowing automobile insurers to charge higher rates to male drivers is unlikely to stigmatize the male sex or create an economic underclass of men. On the other hand, allowing employers to refuse to hire a minority race in a society already suffused with racist attitudes, because the minority race has a much higher crime conviction rate, would be quite likely to further stigmatize the group and perpetuate an underclass. IHRL cannot maintain its commitment to the preservation of human dignity by adopting simplistic rules permitting states to tolerate private discrimination in a predefined set of circumstances and prohibiting it in others. Accounting for social context will inevitably require weighing and balancing diverse factors, some of the most important of which will be discussed at the end of this chapter. Justice is an inefficient process.

Such social externalities suggest that, if a factual correlation between a group characteristic and its perception is based principally on "social laws" or cultural beliefs

158. *E.g.*, Markin v. Russia, 56 E.H.R.R. 8 (2013).

159. *Cf.* Larry Alexander, *What Makes Wrongful Discrimination Wrong? Biases, Preferences, Stereotypes, and Proxies*, 141 U. Pa. L. Rev. 149, 172 (1992) (making the same observation with respect to moral injunctions).

about human nature or group characteristics, such preferences generally cannot justify discrimination. Even if "the entire point of many jobs"—mostly jobs involving interpersonal relations—"is to elicit the appropriate reaction" from customers, for example,[160] the state should not ignore the sociocultural externalities caused by deferring to private preferences. Discrimination based on public perceptions may seem rational in the short run, but it is likely to reinforce stereotypes or the subordination of disfavored groups, creating a vicious circle that ultimately denies the equal protection of the laws to group members. If the state were to defer to private business firms catering to a social preference for male doctors or female airline attendants, for example, the public would tend to be exposed to doctors and attendants of solely that gender. Because human beings have a strong psychological tendency to prefer the familiar to the unfamiliar,[161] exposure to doctors and airline attendants of a single sex will reinforce the very preference that caused the discrimination in the first place, and will breed succeeding generations with similar or stronger preferences.[162]

Larry Alexander doubts the morality of uniformly forbidding immoral discrimination inter alia on Utilitarian grounds. The consequences of *failing* to account for social prejudices could themselves create immoral consequences, he observes. He uses Wertheimer's example of the failure to assign a black police officer to an inner city beat, where he might be more effective than a white officer culturally associated with racist oppression. If community prejudices make the black officer more effective than a white officer, then failure to discriminate against the white officer may result in more crime against innocent third parties. "Sometimes disregarding immoral reactions," Alexander concludes, "may itself be immoral."[163]

If we accept a consequentialist premise, this perspective seems unobjectionable. The problem is that it assumes a static model of society. It ignores the long-term effects of discriminatory practices. The private discrimination that underlies moral prejudices, in Alexander's view, is or should be treated as immutable, or at the very least we should be willing to trade short-term pragmatic gains for long-term social costs. International human rights law does not share that assumption, at least with respect to race and sex. As noted, both the CERD and the CEDAW require states to take positive measures to combat racism and sexism, respectively, and to promote tolerance and understanding through education and similar measures.[164] For example, CEDAW mandates that states pledge:

> To modify the social and cultural patterns of conduct of men and women, with a view to achieving the elimination of prejudices and customary and all other

160. Alan Wertheimer, *Jobs, Qualifications, and Preferences*, 94 Ethics 99, 101 (1983).

161. *See* Robert B. Zajonc, *Attitudinal Effects of Mere Exposure*, 9 J. Personality & Soc. Psych. 1 (1968); Henri Tajfel & Michael Billic, *Familiarity and Categorization in Intergroup Behavior*, 10 J. Experimental Soc. Psych. 159 (1974); Robert F. Bornstein, *Exposure and Affect: Overview and Meta-analysis of Research, 1968–1987*, 106 Psych. Bull. 265 (1989).

162. In the rare cases in which customer preferences actually oppose accepted stereotypes, this argument does not apply.

163. Alexander, *supra* note 159, at 172.

164. CERD, arts. 2, 7; CEDAW, arts. 2–5, 10–14.

> practices which are based on the idea of the inferiority or the superiority of either of the sexes or on stereotyped roles for men and women.[165]

These instruments are based on the recognition that cultures are dynamic and evolving, and that human rights law plays an important role in that evolution. Accordingly, it accepts that both state and individual freedom to discriminate can and should be limited with respect to race and sex precisely because discrimination on these grounds cannot rationally be justified. In other words, they pursue a utopian vision of state intervention to alter individual prejudices and discrimination even at some short-term costs. If we accept that this project is feasible, then the argument that it would be immoral for the state to oppose discrimination having some immediate immoral consequences proves too much. The immediacy of the consequences is not the litmus test of the morality of the measure, even on consequentialist grounds. The certainty and magnitude of the consequences are, however. These cannot be assumed a priori to weigh against intervening in private discrimination, even if intervention has some immediate immoral consequences, such as (using Wertheimer's example) a higher crime rate in the short term.

As Alexander has observed, irrational proxy discrimination also imposes social costs that are not justified by equivalent or greater social benefits.[166] Foremost among these costs is behavior toward the stereotyped group that demeans group members and puts them at an arbitrary disadvantage relative to nonmembers. These consequences affect both the discriminators and their subjects. If the state does not disapprove private discrimination, it is possible that persons viewing the discrimination will assume such biases and stereotypes are socially acceptable, which tends to reinforce and entrench the pattern of discrimination. More generally, the all-too-human habit of thinking simplistically—of relying on irrational stereotypes and prejudices—will not be discouraged. Insofar as all human beings have a moral interest in developing and elevating their cognitive and moral capabilities, punishing irrational stereotypes and prejudices serves even their own interests.

As for the subjects of discrimination, the advantages of legal prohibitions are self-evident. Such discrimination reduces the status and quality of life of the targeted group in the best case, and in the worst can lead to seriously repressive or even violent private or public organized behavior. For example, the nearly global persecution suffered by unpopular minorities such as homosexuals all too frequently leads to private mob violence against them even today. In some places, it also leads to state repression by laws criminalizing homosexuality or censoring discussions of human sexuality not approved by religious authorities.[167] Alexander further cautions:

> Members of the group whose sense of personal identity is very much bound up with such membership, by observing so few other members in particular roles,

165. CEDAW art. 5(a).

166. *See* Alexander, *supra* note 159, at 169–70, 194–95.

167. *See generally* Aaron Xavier Fellmeth, *State Regulation of Sexuality in International Human Rights Law and Theory*, 50 Wm. & Mary L. Rev. 797, 814–24, 843–47 (2008).

> may conclude erroneously that those roles are unrealistic aspirations and fail to develop talents that would be individually and socially rewarding.[168]

The result can be a cycle of cultural stagnation within the discriminating society, as members of the subject group avoid disfavored activities and are accordingly further stereotyped as unsuitable for such activities. The arguments in favor of allowing objectively arbitrary distinctions based on cultural norms or social laws rather than factual differences in capabilities between groups, then, tend to rest on tenuous premises.

B. Distinctions to Counter Discrimination: Affirmative Action

Both the CEDR and CEDAW provide that states taking special measures to rectify social patterns of discrimination based on race and sex, respectively, do not violate the nondiscrimination right. Article 1 of CEDR includes the following provision:

> Special measures taken for the sole purpose of securing adequate advancement of certain racial or ethnic groups or individuals requiring such protection as may be necessary in order to ensure such groups or individuals equal enjoyment or exercise of human rights and fundamental freedoms shall not be deemed racial discrimination, provided, however, that such measures do not, as a consequence, lead to the maintenance of separate rights for different racial groups and that they shall not be continued after the objectives for which they were taken have been achieved.[169]

CEDAW has a similar clarification:

> Adoption by States Parties of temporary special measures aimed at accelerating de facto equality between men and women shall not be considered discrimination as defined in the present Convention, but shall in no way entail as a consequence the maintenance of unequal or separate standards; these measures shall be discontinued when the objectives of equality of opportunity and treatment have been achieved.[170]

These provisions suggest that certain forms of affirmative action would be included among acceptable measures of redress for members of groups that suffer systematic discrimination or that have inherited a legacy of disempowerment or disadvantage caused by past discrimination. They are permissive rather than mandatory.

Although the treaties mostly require procedural equality in legal measures and equal access to resources, some provisions do imply a positive obligation to adopt affirmative action when necessary to advance women and racial minorities

168. Alexander, *supra* note 159, at 194–95.

169. CEDR art. 1(4).

170. CEDAW art. 4(1).

to a position of complete equality. For example, Article 3 of CEDAW provides in relevant part:

> States Parties shall take in all fields, in particular in the political, social, economic and cultural fields, all appropriate measures, including legislation, to ensure the full development and advancement of women, for the purpose of guaranteeing them the exercise and enjoyment of human rights and fundamental freedoms on a basis of equality with men.[171]

The CEDAW Committee has accordingly recommended the use of affirmative action to remedy societal inequalities.[172]

The international bill of rights neither requires nor endorses affirmative action as a remedy for social inequalities, but human rights authorities have also interpreted the nondiscrimination duty to encompass affirmative action. The ECOSOC Committee has endorsed affirmative action by interpreting the prohibition on discrimination in the Covenant to require remedial measures for groups that have suffered "historical or persistent prejudice,"[173] presumably including private prejudice on a societal scale. The U.N. Human Rights Committee similarly reads the CPPR to obligate states to implement affirmative action:

> The Committee also wishes to point out that the principle of equality sometimes *requires* States parties to take affirmative action in order to diminish or eliminate conditions which cause or help to perpetuate discrimination prohibited by the Covenant. For example, in a State where the general conditions of a certain part of the population prevent or impair their enjoyment of human rights, the State *should* take specific action to correct those conditions. Such action may involve granting for a time to the part of the population concerned certain preferential treatment in specific matters as compared with the rest of the population. However, as long as such action is needed to correct discrimination in fact, it is a case of legitimate differentiation under the Covenant.[174]

The Committee has interpreted the articles 3 and 26 rights to equal treatment in a similar manner.[175] In contrast, in the European human rights systems, affirmative action has been viewed not so much obligatory as permissible under defined circumstances.[176]

171. CEDAW art. 3.

172. Comm. on the Elimination of Discrim. against Women, General Recommendation No. 5, 7th Session, U.N. Doc. A/43/38, at 109 (1988).

173. Committee on Economic, Social and Cultural Rights, General Comment No. 20, para. 8(b).

174. U.N. Human Rights Committee, General Comment No. 18: Non-discrimination, para. 10 (emphasis added).

175. U.N. Human Rights Committee, General Comment No. 4, para. 2 (1981).

176. *See* Olivier de Schutter, *L'action affirmative comme instrument de la lutte contra les discriminations en Europe*, *in* AFFIRMATIVE ACTION: DES DISCOURS, DES POLITIQUES ET DES PRATIQUES EN DÉBAT 127, 138–55 (Marco Martiniello & Andrea Rea eds., 2004).

Although affirmative action distinguishes between groups in a way that harms some, an affirmative action program, if properly implemented, would not violate the nondiscrimination right. This is not a metaphysical observation, although Gregory Vlastos has defended the position that needs-based variations in treatment are in the most important sense a perfect form of equal treatment.[177] Instead, I am merely observing that affirmative action does not necessarily violate the right because it may not be "arbitrary" in the sense used in international law.[178] Whatever one's views about any specific implementation of an affirmative action program, if the goal of such a measure in general is progress toward equal human dignity and equal opportunity for the enjoyment of human rights among all persons, then it seems self-evident that an affirmative action program could be designed to comport with those purposes. Affirmative action may address structural social inequalities among groups that persist based on past discrimination against a group despite a current situation of formal legal equality. Such a corrective mechanism would not necessarily qualify as arbitrary.

Of course, an affirmative action program could also be designed to elevate, for example, a select few women or minority group members to (or beyond) a level of equality while leaving the average woman or minority group member at the same (or worse) level of inequality. Such is the criticism sometimes leveled at such measures in the United States and elsewhere. But this is a practical objection to specific features of specific programs. If an affirmative action program arbitrarily benefits a few individuals in a disadvantaged group without addressing the underlying social inequality, such a program might be considered arbitrary, although in a society with extreme disparities in opportunity and wealth, it may actually comport with general social trends and create a kind of perverse cross-gender or cross-racial equalization while increasing stratification within the gender or race category. In any case, this presents a problem of implementation rather than principle.

As noted, the effect of state measures distinguishing between groups must be evaluated in the social context. IHRL accordingly approves affirmative action to the extent that it remedies imbalances caused by historical oppression, widespread social biases, or other impersonal forces creating an imbalance of rights and benefits. As Olivier de Schutter has pointed out, persistent and widespread stereotypes about a group may create a self-fulfilling prophecy. Despite formal legal equality, a social stereotype may condition the perceptions of a group, including the self-perceptions of group members, to shy away from ambitions or investment in acquiring skills necessary to succeed in fields of action contrary to the stereotype.[179] When a society has few female graduate students, for example, few parents may think to encourage graduate education as a goal for their daughters, and women

177. *See* Gregory Vlastos, *Justice and Equality*, *in* Theories of Rights 41 (Jeremy Waldron ed., 1984).

178. The criticism of positive discrimination sometimes advanced, that proponents of such discrimination are "unable to make a principled decision about what groups shall be compensatorily advantaged," William B. Griffith, *Equality and Egalitarianism: Framing the Contemporary Debate*, 7 Can. J.L. & Jurisprudence 5, 17 (1994), is no more a valid objection to affirmative action programs than the claim that human rights do not self-define their own content, and so it is difficult to balance conflicting human rights in a principled way.

179. *See* de Schutter, *supra* note 176, at 132.

themselves may believe graduate school unattainable. Without affirmative action, the progress of equality might proceed at a glacial pace.

Objections to affirmative action by members of a historically dominant group—claims of "reverse discrimination"—tend to ring false precisely because they depend on an individual's grievance being hermetically sealed away from this social context. In the United States, for example, the claim of a white male that an affirmative action denied him employment "because of" his group membership,[180] even if true, ignores the relatively privileged position he now enjoys in life through historical injustices that his claim ignores. Taking the broader social context into account, he was denied employment "in spite of" his group membership as much as because of it, and what outrages him is the complete unfamiliarity of the experience of disadvantage that form the normal, living background for members of less privileged groups. Although nondiscrimination doctrine protects individual rights, it does not aim at atomistic individual justice: it aims at social justice.

A more serious objection is that, if affirmative action elevates less privileged group members to positions for which they are not qualified, they will paradoxically reinforce the very stereotypes and prejudices that discourage achievement by members of that group.[181] Such a problem is of course entirely possible, at least in the short term. But the objection is directed more toward a specific implementation of affirmative action than the concept itself. Affirmative action that provides early advantages to underprivileged groups in order to help them secure the skills and attributes for success later in life, but then tapers off its advantages as the beneficiaries approach work life, could greatly mitigate the concern about self-defeating preferentialism.

In short, nothing about the general concept of affirmative action programs is theoretically inconsistent with the nondiscrimination right, which is why such measures have been so widely endorsed in international instruments and by their authoritative interpreters. For example, the U.S. delegation reported favorably on affirmative action in its interpretation of article 1 of the American Convention on Human Rights:

> [D]istinctions have been accepted which benefit disadvantaged groups such as Hindu outcasts, American Indians, or Negros who suffer the effects of past discrimination. The same principle of common-sense adjustment has been recognized for children, the ill, the handicapped, etc., where differing needs and responsibilities call for differing treatment which aims at equalizing the situation for the individual.[182]

Although the United States did not ultimately ratify the ACHR, it apparently considered affirmative action consistent with the nondiscrimination obligation, which the ACHR treats no differently from the one found in the international bill of rights.

180. *See, e.g.*, Martin v. Wilks, 490 U.S. 755 (1989).

181. *Cf.* de Schutter, *supra* note 176, at 132.

182. Report of the U.S. Delegation to the Inter-American Specialized Conference on Human Rights, Apr. 22, 1970, 9 I.L.M. 710, 714 (1970).

In contrast, the interpretations of these international human rights instruments as positively requiring affirmative action relies on an aggressive interpretation of the language. Although CEDAW does imply some duties of affirmative action, no provision of the CEDR or the international bill of rights plainly requires states to adopt a compensatory policy. However desirable more active measures might be to redress inequalities, subjective interpretations of IHRL instruments that misaligned with state expectations threaten to undermine the authority of the interpreter and deter the adoption of new international instruments strengthening human rights.

4. Source of the Threat

Part III of this book explores the distinction between negative and positive human rights in some detail. Here, it suffices to observe that the nondiscrimination right can be either one. In the preceding discussion, I observed that international human rights authorities have tended to interpret the nondiscrimination right as a positive right, and argued that its positivity was one factor distinguishing that right from the right to the equal protection of the laws. However, municipal human rights authorities have not uniformly considered nondiscrimination rights to be positive, at least as a general rule.

A negative nondiscrimination duty prohibits the state from making certain arbitrary distinctions between classes of persons and behavior, without the additional (positive) duty to protect individuals from arbitrary discrimination by private actors. A positive right might also require the state to adopt a program of rectifying broad patterns of social discrimination; affirmative action promotes the enjoyment of a positive right. Both negative and positive rights correlate to a state duty, but the negative right leaves private discrimination unredressed. As noted in Part I, neither private business firms nor private individuals are generally bound by IHRL, so they are free to discriminate except to the extent prohibited by municipal law. However, because international law imposes positive duties on the state, IHRL regulates private behavior indirectly.

The CEDR, CEDAW, and Banjul Charter require states to take certain measures to deter private discrimination, but the nondiscrimination provisions found in the international bill of rights, ECHR, and ACHR do not explicitly obligate states to take positive measures to protect individuals against private discrimination. The Pact of San José, for example, provides:

> The States Parties to this Convention undertake to respect the rights and freedoms recognized herein and to ensure to all persons subject to their jurisdiction the free and full exercise of those rights and freedoms, without any discrimination for reasons of race, color, sex, language, religion, political or other opinion, national or social origin, economic status, birth, or any other social condition.[183]

183. ACHR art. 1(1).

However, by distinguishing between an obligation "to respect" the rights and freedoms and an obligation "to ensure to all persons . . . the free and full exercise of those rights and freedoms," the provision strongly implies a positive as well as a negative duty. Similarly, the European Convention states:

> The enjoyment of the rights and freedoms set forth in this Convention shall be secured without discrimination on any ground such as sex, race, colour, language, religion, political or other opinion, national or social origin, association with a national minority, property, birth or other status.[184]

Here, the use of the phrase "shall be secured" in preference to "shall be respected" or "observed" suggests a positive duty to prevent impairments to the rights, whatever their source, public or private. A right can only be "secured" if its exercise is adequately protected. The CCPR similarly strongly suggests a positive right:

> All persons are equal before the law and are entitled without any discrimination to the equal protection of the law. In this respect, the law shall prohibit any discrimination and guarantee to all persons equal and effective protection against discrimination on any ground such as race, colour, sex, language, religion, political or other opinion, national or social origin, property, birth or other status.[185]

Although the requirement that the law "prohibit" discrimination could conceivably be interpreted to include discriminatory state action only, the words "guarantee . . . equal and effective protection against discrimination" implies a positive duty to take measures to protect against private discrimination. If the state were obligated solely to refrain from discrimination in its own actions, the "prohibition" would suffice, and no further "guarantee" would be necessary. The language of "guarantee," like "ensure" and "secure," directs the attention to the importance of the meaningful exercise of the right rather than the source of its impairment.

International authorities have accordingly inferred positive obligations from the provisions. The Human Rights Committee in its general comment on article 26 of the CCPR stated: "The right to equality before the law and freedom from discrimination protected by Article 26 requires states to act against discrimination by private, as well as public agents in all fields."[186] In *Nahlik v. Austria*, the Committee expanded further on this interpretation of articles 2 and 26:

> Under articles 2 and 26 of the Covenant the State party is under an obligation to ensure that all individuals within its territory and subject to its jurisdiction are free from discrimination, and consequently the courts of the States parties are under an obligation to protect individuals against discrimination, whether

184. ECHR art. 14.

185. CCPR art. 26.

186. U.N. Human Rights Committee, General Comment No. 28, para. 31, Compilation of General Comments and General Recommendations Adopted by Human Rights Treaty Bodies, U.N. Doc. HRI/GEN/1/Rev.1 at 38 (1994).

this occurs within the public sphere or among private parties in the quasi-public sector of, for example employment.[187]

Using similar reasoning, the Inter-American Commission on Human Rights and Inter-American Court have inferred positive obligations from ACHR articles 1 and 24.[188] Finally, the Committee on Economic, Social and Cultural Rights interprets the CESCR's prohibition on discrimination as obligating states to protect individuals from private discrimination as well, without however publishing any explanation to support its interpretation.[189]

Notwithstanding these generalizations, a discrimination claim's persuasiveness depends in practice a good deal on whether it is directed against the state or a private actor. The state itself is typically held to a higher standard of nondiscrimination than are business organizations, and both are held to a much higher standard than individuals. The same is true for substantive right violations, but to a very different degree and for some different reasons. Four reasons stand out as justifying holding the state to a stricter standard of neutrality than private actors.

First, prohibitions on private discrimination cut into the business owner's or organization member's freedom to associate with persons of his or her own choosing. This point carries the most weight for individuals. The fact that, in distinguishing between classes of persons, private actors may be exercising their own human rights—for example, to privacy, property, freedom of association, and freedom of expression—makes discrimination disputes especially challenging and sometimes abstruse. Such freedoms, especially privacy and association, are important aspects of personal development and identity, and necessary for the pursuit of the individual's idiosyncratic conception of the good life. A woman who demands a female gynecologist, a director who insists on casting a black man as Othello, or a madrasa that refuses to hire a non-Muslim night guard do not have obviously morally deplorable preferences.

Such freedoms also carry considerable weight for social organizations whose purpose is precisely to develop individual capabilities, to pursue desirable social connections, and to promote political goals. It carries much less weight for business organizations, however, whose purpose is commercial rather than political or social. The state authorizes business organizations to be formed not to facilitate the exercise of personal freedoms, but to promote commerce. It carries still less weight for very large business organizations, whose owners are least likely to come into personal contact with customers and employees. Many countries accordingly restrict the ability of employers, universities, landlords, hotels, and other public accommodations to discriminate on the basis of race, national origin, sex, religion,

187. Nahlik v. Austria, Comm. No. 608/1995, Decision on Admissibility, para. 8.2, U.N. Doc. CCPR/C/57/D/608/1995 (1996).

188. Morales de Sierra v. Guatemala, Inter-Am. Comm'n Hum. Rts., Rep. No. 4/01, Case 11.625, Jan. 19, 2001, para. 54; Advisory Opinion on Juridical Condition and Human Rights of Undocumented Migrants, Sept. 17, 2003, Ser. A, No. 18, paras. 146–56.

189. Committee on Economic, Social and Cultural Rights, General Comment No. 20, para. 11, Comm. No. E/C.12/GC/20 (May 20, 2009).

or other grounds.[190] At the same time, in some countries, private civic and religious organizations are exempted because of the personal nature of the associations.[191]

It carries no weight whatsoever in the case of the state, whose moral interests are all derivative and that has no rational interest in discrimination (which is by definition arbitrary). Although states must always analyze the legitimacy and proportionality of a measure affecting human rights, states do not have conflicting human rights of their own. Adopting or refraining from a measure that affects the human rights of some persons may in turn affect the human rights of others, but frequently these cases are easy. Censorship rarely comes into question as a legitimate measure except in the rare case that it would protect the privacy, reputation, or health and safety of others. Torture, unfair trials, and denial of the right to basic education virtually never come into question as legitimate measures.

Second, the greater economic and political power of the state justifies applying a more rigorous standard of rationality and impartiality to its behavior, because the power of an actor directly affects its ability to harm groups through arbitrary distinctions. In all states, the government ranks among the most powerful actors, if it is not the single most powerful actor. Government employment and budget make up a considerable portion of the total employment and income everywhere.[192] It makes sense to hold the state, as an actor of unusual influence over the economy and power distribution of society, to a higher standard of rationality and impartiality than most private actors. In consequence, government distinctions should be justified with more convincing and weighty reasons than private discrimination requires. Similarly, large business firms tend to have much greater power—economic and in extreme capitalist societies political—than private individuals and less political and economic power than the state. The case for requiring states to hold large business firms as a class to an intermediate standard is, consequently, a strong one. However, even relatively small actors such as small business firms and isolated landlords may significantly impair the equal rights of group members subjected to discrimination if private discrimination is sufficiently widespread.

A point distinct from but related to the first is that discrimination by private collectivities, such as business organizations or civic groups, tends to affect the subject of discrimination much more than discrimination by individuals. If many persons refuse to socialize with adherents of Zoroastrianism and invite them to dinner, they may be damaging the interests and dignity of Zoroastrians, but much less

190. *See, e.g.*, Ley 045 Contra el Racismo y Toda Forma de Discriminación, Law 7372010 (Bolivia); Allgemeine Gleichbehandlungsgesetz, Aug. 14, 2006, Dir. 402-40, BGBl. I, at 610, 615 (Ger.); Promotion of Equality and Prevention of Unfair Discrimination Act, Act. No. 4 of 2000 (S. Afr.); Equality Act, 2010 c. 15 (U.K.); 42 U.S.C.A. §§ 2000a *et seq.*, 12103–12213 (2015); 29 U.S.C. §§ 621 *et seq.* (2015).

191. *See, e.g.*, U.K. Gov't Equalities Office, "Myth-Busting: The Equality Bill and Religion," Jan. 10, 2010 (on file with author); 42 U.S.C. § 2000a(e) (2015); Boy Scouts of Am. v. Dale, 530 U.S. 640 (2000) (holding that private organizations have a constitutional right to exclude homosexuals from membership).

192. *See* Salvatore Schiavo-Campo, Giulio de Tommaso & Amitabha Mukherjee, An International Statistical Survey of Government Employment and Wages, World Bank Rep. No. WPS1806, Aug. 31, 1997.

so than a restaurant that refuses to hire or serve Zoroastrians. Individuals have a much stronger claim on controlling their personal associations than do business firms, whose economic activities are by definition impersonal. The consequences of discrimination vary according to the political, economic, and social power of the discriminators, as well as the prevalence of the discrimination among smaller actors. Very powerful discriminators can affect the lives and prospects of the subject of discrimination more effectively than powerless discriminators.

Third, and least weighty of the reasons for holding the state to a higher standard of compliance, is that compliance with nondiscrimination laws may be costly. IHRL generally uses open lists of prohibited grounds of discrimination, and it forbids incidental discrimination as well as intentional discrimination. Actors with considerable economic resources are better able to bear the costs of implementing nondiscrimination education and compliance programs and defending dubious lawsuits claiming unlawful discrimination. Although any sizable private actor may be capable of bearing the costs of compliance and defense, the state government, as frequently the most powerful economic actor in any given state, is the most capable of it.

Finally, the state formally represents the entirety of its people. As such, official state positions on social issues frequently reflect social attitudes, and, even if they do not, they are capable of influencing those attitudes, sometimes very effectively. When the state discriminates against a group in legislation or other official measures, it tends to both reflect and signal the acceptability of that discrimination publicly. Such signaling may reinforce or exacerbate private social trends of bias, stereotyping, and prejudice. When the average private individual or organization discriminates against a group, it carries no such implication. The public influence of observed private discrimination depends on multiple factors, but an important one is the status or influence of the discriminator. Of course, private discrimination, if widespread or perpetrated by prestigious actors, can be extremely damaging to its victims. But even when a prejudice is widespread, there is no reason to hold the state to a *lower* standard than the one private persons must meet. In all cases, the importance of the state government and its role as the representative of its citizens justifies exacting scrutiny of its distinctions between classes of persons in its legislation and executive acts to prevent bias and irrationality from inflicting disadvantages on groups arbitrarily.

5. Intention to Discriminate

It is a truism that directed behavior tends to be much more effective at achieving a goal than serendipity. Someone who actively seeks to discriminate against some group will surely succeed, and so a showing of intention to discriminate always weighs heavily toward finding a violation of the human right against discrimination. When the state in particular directs its powers to discriminate against a specific group, its coercive means of social control guarantee a significant negative impact on the group's enjoyment of fundamental rights and public benefits.

It would be a rare state measure that serves a pressing need in a democracy by specifically targeting a vulnerable, disempowered, or minority group for harm or denial of benefits, especially if the group were defined by an immutable or involuntary trait. The closest case that comes most readily to mind is disenfranchisement of convicted criminals. In a few countries and U.S. states, convicted criminals are denied their right to vote even after having served their sentences,[193] a practice that in most of Europe would be considered to violate the human right to participation in government.[194] The political disempowerment of convicted criminals is viewed by some as a potentially legitimate consequence of their refusal to comply with the rules of minimum acceptable behavior established by the society's laws. Intentional discrimination against an already disempowered group under such circumstances is arguably rational and morally defensible.[195] In most cases, though, intentionally discriminatory measures tend to have a greater negative impact on the target group than measures intended to affect groups neutrally.

The more difficult question is whether a state measure pursuing a legitimate aim that has incidental or unintended discriminatory effects violates the nondiscrimination right. In the United States, the Supreme Court for some time considered the absence of a primary intent to discriminate to exonerate the government in all but the most extreme cases: "Proof of racially discriminatory intent or purpose is required to show a violation of the Equal Protection Clause."[196] Superficially neutral measures that have a systematically negative effect on a single race or sex—so-called "disparate impact" measures—were not considered to violate the nondiscrimination right even if their effects on a group is severe, sustained, and foreseeable in several cases.[197] The U.S. Congress reversed this doctrine in some areas,[198] and the Supreme Court has recently interpreted other statutes as affirming a prohibition on disparate impact measures in certain cases unless the discrimination is justified as necessary for some legitimate purpose,[199] but the general rule remains.

International human rights law does not defer to the state's good or neutral intentions. Both direct and indirect discrimination fall within the relevant prohibitions.

193. For the United States, *see* Jean Chung, The Sentencing Project, Felony Disenfranchisement: A Primer (Aug. 2015), *at* http://sentencingproject.org/doc/publications/fd_Felony%20Disenfranchisement%20Primer.pdf. *See also* Richardson v. Ramirez, 418 U.S. 24 (1974) (upholding such laws). Very few other countries impose post-sentence voting restrictions. *See* Brandon Rottinghaus, *Incarceration and Enfranchisement: International Practices, Impact and Recommendations for Reform*, June–July 2003, *at* http://felonvoting.procon.org/sourcefiles/RottinghausDisenfranchisement.pdf.

194. *See, e.g.*, Hirst v. United Kingdom (No. 2), App. No. 74025/01, Judgment of Oct. 6, 2005 (finding a blanket denial of the right to vote to all felons while serving time violates the human right to vote under ECHR Protocol No. 1).

195. For a nuanced analysis of this issue, *see* Mary Sigler, *Defensible Disenfranchisement*, 99 Iowa L. Rev. 1724 (2014).

196. Village of Arlington Heights v. Metro. Housing Dev. Corp., 429 U.S. 252, 265 (1977).

197. *See, e.g.*, Washington v. Davis, 426 U.S. 229, 239–42 (1976); City of Boerne v. Flores, 521 U.S. 507, 511 (1997).

198. *See, e.g.*, Religious Freedom Restoration Act of 1993, Pub. L. 103-141, 107 Stat. 1488, 42 U.S.C. § 2000bb (2015); Civil Rights Act of 1991, Pub. L. 102-66, 105 Stat. 1071, *codified as amended at* 42 U.S.C. § 2000e-2 (2015).

199. *See* Texas Dep't of Housing & Community Affairs v. The Inclusive Communities Project, Inc., 133 Sup. Ct. 46 (2014).

The language of the CERD,[200] CEDAW,[201] and other treaties containing nondiscrimination provisions[202] define prohibited discrimination as those distinctions having the "purpose or effect," or sometimes simply the "effect," of nullifying or impairing protected rights. The U.N. General Assembly's Declaration on the Elimination of All Forms of Intolerance and of Discrimination Based on Religion or Belief uses identical language in defining discrimination based on religion.[203] These instruments employ the disjunctive ("or"), or omit mention of "purpose" altogether, precisely to disqualify intention to discriminate as a necessary precondition to finding a human rights violation.

International human rights authorities have accordingly found measures that harm disempowered, vulnerable, or minority groups to violate the nondiscrimination right despite the absence of discriminatory intent.[204] The Human Rights Committee has interpreted the CCPR to ban policies that have the unintended effect of discriminating.[205] A domestic measure causing a disparate impact on similarly situated groups may violate the nondiscrimination right whatever the legislature's intent may have been. The Committee has in fact expressly rejected the contention that nondiscriminatory intent exonerates a legislature from liability for a de facto discriminatory measure: "a violation of article 26 can also result from the discriminatory effect of a rule or measure that is neutral at face value or without intent to discriminate."[206] However, the Committee has qualified this point by observing that "rules or decisions with [a disparate] impact do not amount to discrimination if they are based on objective and reasonable grounds."[207] The European Union and the Strasbourg Court have adopted a similar view. The institutions of the former have interpreted nondiscrimination rules to shift the burden of showing the appropriateness and necessity of the measure to achieve a legitimate aim when a measure has a disparate impact on employees based on sex.[208] The latter wrote in *Hoogendijk v. The Netherlands* that "the Court considers that where a general policy

200. CERD art. 1.

201. CEDAW art. 1.

202. *See, e.g.*, ILO Convention concerning Discrimination in Respect of Employment and Occupation (No. 11), art. 1(a), 362 U.N.T.S. 31; Convention against Discrimination in Education, art. 1, 429 U.N.T.S. 93.

203. U.N. G.A. A/RES/36/55, art. 2(2) (Nov. 25, 1981).

204. *See* U.N. Economic & Social Council, Analytical Study of the High Commissioner for Human Rights on the Fundamental Principle of Non-discrimination in the Context of Globalization, U.N. Doc. E/CN.4/2004/40, para. 12.

205. U.N. Hum. Rts. Com. General Comment 18, para. 7, U.N. Doc. CCPR/C/21/Rev. 1/Add. 1 (1989).

206. Althammer v. Austria, Comm. No. 998/2001, para. 10.2, U.N. Doc. CCPR/C/78/D/998/2001 (Aug. 8, 2003); *accord* Simunek v. Czech Rep., U.N. Hum. Rts. Comm. Comm. No. 516/1992, 2 Hum. Rts. Comm. 1995 Report, Annex X, sec. K, para. 11.7.

207. *Althammer*, Comm. No. 998/2001, para. 10.2.

208. *See* Olivier de Schutter, *Three Models of Equality and European Anti-discrimination Law*, 57 N. Ire. Legal Q. 1, 10, 13, 36 (2006); de Schutter, *supra* note 176, at 16–17, 25.

or measure has disproportionately prejudicial effects on a particular group, it is not excluded that this may be regarded as discriminatory notwithstanding that it is not specifically aimed or directed at that group."[209] It is interesting that the Court said "not excluded . . . may be regarded," leaving the door open to finding a violation while also maintaining the possibility that a disproportionately prejudicial measure would *not* violate article 14 if the intent were honest.

The typical justification for prohibitions on indirect discrimination is that they are necessary to counter devious attempts to circumvent the direct prohibitions. Discriminators may after all use seemingly innocuous characteristics that correlate to prohibited classifications such as race or sex—a minimum educational qualification or possession of a driver's license might serve—to discriminate based on the prohibited category.[210] In such cases, it may be very difficult to prove intent to discriminate. But this reason is based on a misunderstanding of how bias typically operates. Authority to find discrimination in the absence of specific evidence of discriminatory intent is necessary, not just because such evidence may be nonexistent or carefully concealed, but because the intention to discriminate may be systematic without being conscious, and thus intentional. Psychological studies consistently demonstrate that much stereotyping and bias occurs unconsciously.[211] Requiring a showing of intent leaves potentially widespread and invidious unconscious discrimination unremedied. A prohibition on indirect discrimination will typically be necessary to counter systematic institutional and social biases.[212]

In practice, it may sometimes be difficult for an international human rights authority, typically removed at least one step from the society and culture of the state being examined, to perceive accurately and objectively the subtleties of social inequalities and social psychological biases in every country under examination. The challenges of indirect discrimination claims require human rights authorities to examine not just the specific facts of an allegedly discriminatory act, but to bring in demographic, statistical, and other social science evidence into their evaluation, because a facially neutral policy may disadvantage a minority group due to factual or perceived differences between the minority and majority groups.[213] A facially neutral measure may differ in discriminatory effects over time and in

209. Hoogendijk v. The Netherlands, Eur. Ct. Hum. Rts. Case 58641/00, Decision on Admissibility of Jan. 6, 2005, para. 2.

210. de Schutter, *supra* note 208, at 9.

211. Mazarin R. Banaji & Anthony R. Greenwald, Blind Spot: Hidden Biases of Good People (2013); Kevin Durrheim, *Implicit Prejudice in Mind and Interaction*, *in* Beyond Prejudice: Extending the Social Psychology of Conflict, Inequality and Social Change 179 (John Dixon & Mark Levine eds., 2012); Mark Chen & John A. Bargh, *Nonconscious Behavioral Confirmation Processes: The Self-Fulfilling Consequences of Automatic Stereotype Activation,* 33 J. Experimental & Soc. Psych. 541 (1997); Mahzarin R. Banaji, Curtis Hardin & Alexander J. Rothman, *Implicit Stereotyping in Person Judgment*, 65 J. Pers. & Soc. Psych. 272 (1993).

212. *See* de Schutter, *supra* note 208, at 34.

213. *See* de Schutter, *supra* note 176, at 20–21, 27–31. However, de Schutter is mistaken in arguing that separation-of-powers concerns are based on the necessity of the judge examining statistical evidence, as opposed to "juridical" evidence. *Id.* at 30. Judges examine statistical evidence in many kinds of cases, such as environmental law claims and mass tort claims. The

different societies, so that a more expansive, context-sensitive inquiry will usually be necessary. The human rights authority correcting indirect discrimination must, as de Schutter has observed, condemn seemingly neutral measures and demand a more nuanced policy of different treatment for differently situated persons.[214]

Requiring a showing of discriminatory intent (not necessarily *primarily* discriminatory intent, as the U.S. Supreme Court has done) does have the virtue of reducing the need to second-guess whether a facially neutral measure was motivated by bias or ill will. Because an intent to discriminate makes actual discriminatory effects much more likely and demonstrates publicly the acceptability of bias against the target group, human rights authorities have an easy time detecting the most obvious and harmful distinctions. There is no need to undertake the delicate balancing of interests involved in assessing the legitimacy and proportionality of a measure.

To the extent that examining the discriminatory effects of a well-intended state measure requires human rights authorities to second-guess the wisdom of the measure and its alternatives, disparate impacts may be pragmatically unavoidable. For example, persons living in rural communities may be required to travel a greater distance to attend schooling or receive healthcare than their urban counterparts. Although in some states public transportation can ameliorate the inequality in access, many developing countries have expansive and sparsely inhabited territories that would make universally available school buses or health clinics unsustainable. A disparate impact on poor country-dwellers, even a substantial one, must be accepted in such cases as inevitable by any workable nondiscrimination doctrine.[215]

In practice, the risks of excessive intervention are mitigated by doctrines that require some deference to the state in making distinctions between groups. As de Schutter has observed, "*une des missions du juge à qui est confiée la garde de l'existence de non-discrimination est alors de s'imposer de telles limites, qui ne lui sont pas fournies de l'extérieur.*"[216] This is precisely what human rights authorities have done. The Strasbourg Court uses proportionality analysis as well as the margin of appreciation to avoid interpretations that would create a potentially unbounded mandate to strike down legislation distinguishing between different classes of persons. The Inter-American Court has not officially adopted a deference

character of a decision as juridical does not turn on the nature of the evidence, but on the availability of positive law standards for evaluating that evidence, whatever its nature may be.

De Schutter also errs in claiming that prohibitions on direct discrimination guarantee "formal" equality whereas prohibitions on indirect discrimination guarantee "economic and social" equality. *Id.* at 25. Both forms of discrimination implicate social and economic equality. For example, a ban on allowing women to vote or hold executive positions in a corporation is a direct form of discrimination with very pronounced social, political, and economic consequences. It would be more accurate to say that the direct discrimination prohibition addresses intentional or overt forms of discrimination, whereas its counterpart addresses unintended (incidental) or covert forms of discrimination.

214. de Schutter, *supra* note 176, at 36–37.

215. *Cf.* Allen Buchanan, *Equality and Human Rights*, 4 Politics, Philos. & Econ. 69, 76 (2005).

216. de Schutter, *supra* note 176, at 44.

doctrine[217] and, in practice, the Inter-American Court and Commission defer to state policies somewhat less than the Strasbourg Court, sometimes fomenting criticism of excessive activism,[218] but by invoking Strasbourg Court precedents, as the Inter-American Court has often done, the latter has indirectly incorporated some of the former's deference. Even when the Inter-American commissioners and judges have not relied on European precedents, they have frequently taken care to decide cases on narrow grounds when highly political questions of uncertain legal application were involved, or else avoided such issues altogether.[219] The Human Rights Committee has similarly stated its intent to defer to state decisions on the allocation of economic resources unless it makes distinctions that are "manifestly discriminatory or arbitrary": "it is not for the Committee to re-evaluate the complex socio-economic data and substitute its judgment for that of the legislature of States parties."[220] In the absence of evidence of intent to discriminate, then, the evidence and effect of a distinction's disparate impact must be sufficiently pervasive and severe to suggest the workings of unconscious but invidious bias, or perhaps ignorance of or indifference to the systematic negative consequences of the measure.

Such deference to state discretion can easily go too far. In the *Cossey* judgment, for example, the Strasbourg Court insisted that "attachment to the traditional concept of marriage" supports denying marital rights to persons of the same sex.[221] More recently, it reaffirmed in *Schalk and Kopf* that the "deep-rooted social and cultural connotations" of marriage in a society justify a margin of appreciation that allows continued discrimination against homosexuals."[222] Restricting rights to those traditionally recognized or culturally acceptable may vindicate the hopes of states that adhere to a human rights instrument with an expectation that their cultures will be protected in a form of social stasis. Yet, such a view is susceptible of undermining the entire system of human rights. Arranged child marriages, oppressive caste systems, clitoral mutilation, and other practices utterly abhorrent to human dignity can be justified on precisely the same grounds. Any coherent system of human rights must accept the logic of the nondiscrimination right in the

217. *See* Liliana Valina, *El Margen de Apreciacion de los Estados en la Aplicación del Derecho Internacional de los Derechos Humanos en el Ambito Interno*, *in* LA APLICACIÓN DE LOS TRATADOS SOBRE DERECHOS HUMANOS POR LOS TRIBUNALES LOCALES 173, 180–81 (Martin Abregu & Christian Courtis eds., CELS 1997).

218. *See* Manuela Picq, *Is the Inter-American Commission of* [*sic*] *Human Rights Too Progressive?*, ALJAZEERA.COM, June 9, 2012.

219. An example of the latter is *Baby Boy v. United States*, Case No. 2141, Inter-Am. Comm'n H.R. Rep. No. 23/81, OEA/Ser.L/V/II.54, doc. 9 rev. 1 (1981), in which the Inter-American Commission avoided the question of whether a fetus in utero was "protected life" under article 4.1 of the ACHR by noting that the drafters of the Convention had deliberately left this matter to state discretion.

220. Oulajin & Kaiss v. The Netherlands, U.N. Hum. Rts. Comm. Comm'ns Nos. 406/1990 & 426/1990 (Oct. 23, 1992), U.N. Doc. CCPR/C/46/D/406/1990 and 426/1990 (1992).

221. Cossey v. United Kingdom, 13 E.H.R.R. 622 (1991).

222. Schalk & Kopf v. Austria, 53 E.H.R.R. 20, paras. 62, 108–09 (2011).

face of contrary traditions, no matter how culturally entrenched. What makes the nondiscrimination right most valuable as a norm without substantive content is its potential to compel political elites to abandon harmful and irrational prejudices inherited from a less enlightened age. Deference to state policies should be confined to morally neutral or arguable questions that do not undermine the coherence of the legal doctrine. The Strasbourg Court has abused the margin of appreciation in some cases in which discrimination, in the above example based on sexual orientation, for any social benefit whatsoever is both morally indefensible and inconsistent with nondiscrimination doctrine generally.[223]

D. RATIONALIZING NONDISCRIMINATION DOCTRINE

It may be helpful to recapitulate the five key factors in discrimination analysis: (1) whether the distinction must be based on prohibited grounds, generally meaning membership in a class of persons subject to special protection; (2) whether the interest harmed by the distinction relates to a recognized human right as opposed to a more general interest in the equal application of state measures; (3) whether the distinction carries the requisite social consequences in terms of (a) the distribution of resources and burdens on various social groups, and (b) the political, economic, and social position of the affected group relative to society; (4) whether the distinction originates from the state or a private actor, and, in the latter case, the relative political, economic, and social power of the private actor; and (5) whether the discrimination is intentional or coincidental to a legitimate purpose.

Human rights authorities rarely give full consideration to all five factors in the same case and, when they do consider any given factor, they do not always provide an explicit analysis of the relevant community policies. In some cases, the reasoning published by human rights authorities has simply been tautological or a priori, as when the Strasbourg Court justified heightened scrutiny of sex discrimination because "the advancement of the equality of the sexes is today a major goal" of the Council of Europe.[224] A thorough analysis is especially critical for the persuasiveness of a nondiscrimination decision, because the conflicting interests of the state and private actors involved in nondiscrimination claims frequently make such nondiscrimination cases politically and socially sensitive as well as morally complex. Here, I will suggest some doctrinal refinements to the analysis of nondiscrimination factors that I believe could render the right more predictable, uniform, and effective at protecting equal human dignity.

1. Prohibited Grounds

As discussed, the disadvantages to a closed list of prohibited grounds for discrimination, as in U.S. equal protection jurisprudence, is excessive rigidity and a consequent diminution of meaningful protection against a wide variety of arbitrary state measures. At the same time, an open list of prohibited grounds offers little

223. *See* Fellmeth, *supra* note 23, at 873–919.

224. Abdulaziz v. United Kingdom, 7 E.H.R.R. 471, para. 80 (1985).

guidance about the extent to which different grounds for distinctions may be justified as serving a legitimate need. It is not enough to rely on intuitions about which stereotypes are legitimate, to defer to the state's own biases and stereotypes, or to put forward ad hoc theories about which kinds of social needs are pressing and what kinds of measures are proportionate to serving them. Human psychological blindness to one's own biases and prejudices cannot be overcome without firmer assistance.

When prohibited grounds are listed in the instruments, they tend to share either or both of two core features: (1) they are immutable characteristics, such as race, sex, birth, or disability; or (2) they are characteristics commonly perceived as central to a person's intellectual or cultural identity, such as religion, political opinion, caste, or language. This is not to say that such distinctions are never permitted—there are almost always acceptable bases for distinctions in at least some cases—it merely means that distinctions based on these grounds are generally presumed illegitimate absent some valid justification. I will call these features *identity characteristics* here.

The importance of certain traits and activities to an individual's identity is frequently proclaimed in human rights instruments and declarations. For example, the U.N. General Assembly's Declaration on the Elimination of All Forms of Intolerance and of Discrimination Based on Religion or Belief begins by "*Considering* that religion or belief, for anyone who professes either, is one of the fundamental elements in his conception of life and that freedom of religion or belief should be fully respected and guaranteed."[225] This statement seems to reflect the individual's interest in understanding himself, psychologically constructing an account of the world for his own guidance and comfort, and securing a predictable place in society generally. Whether a characteristic being a "fundamental element" of one's "conception of life" is the best or most complete grounding for a distinction between identity and nonidentity characteristics will be taken up later.

Immutable identity characteristics, or those very difficult to alter, merit special consideration because they have an intrinsic connection to human dignity. Such characteristics—sex, gender, race, ethnicity, sexual orientation, national origin, etc.—have no bearing on the equal dignity of human beings, but they typically are very important to the self-conception of the individual and his understanding of his role in society. Generally, a person's identity gives him a psychological anchor for self-esteem, understanding of the world and his place in it, and the pursuit of his conception of a good life. Even when the individual does not personally conceive of these traits as central to his identity, society may perceive them as significant and vary its treatment of the individual according to its perception of them. Arbitrary distinctions based on such characteristics demean and disadvantage their victims based on whom they are, frequently for no better reason than the discriminator differs from his victim in some way important to the discriminator's own identity. In a dignity-based moral system such as the one that undergirds international human rights law, moral judgments about a person are based on that person's choices and behavior rather than their innate or immutable characteristics. The immutable characteristic of belonging to the *Homo sapiens* species is, after all, the basis for human rights in the first place. Distinctions based on such characteristics

225. *See, e.g.*, U.N. G.A. A/RES/36/55, pmbl. (Nov. 25, 1981).

cannot usually be justified on moral grounds and are especially pernicious to the individuals themselves when used as the basis for some legally or socially imposed disadvantage.

Grounds sufficiently dissimilar to those listed, such as hairstyle, music preference, or proclivity to smoke cigars, do not generally benefit from the same presumption. Distinctions based on such acquired characteristics and activities are thought not to interfere with the person's identity in the same manner as distinctions based on innate or immutable identity characteristics. Of course, the distinction drawn here will strike some as artificial. Many persons consider their clothing or choice of music to be extremely important to their identity. Things one likes and does and owns, however temporary or mutable, certainly do figure into most person's identity in some way, either to themselves or to others.

Where a feature or activity falls along the identity and voluntariness spectrums varies among individuals in their social context, then. Although what people do and think and enjoy may be malleable and changeable, they can color a person's identity greatly. Characteristics indifferent to some individuals may be critical to others; just as one person may define herself primarily by her race and sex, another may define his "very essence" as being a virgin and a poet.[226] Impressions about which features and activities define a person's identity most centrally are ultimately subjective. It may be that these characteristics are culturally determined or idiosyncratic rather than innate, but a culturally determined or idiosyncratic trait may serve a person's self-conception as much as a permanent trait might.

The importance of some mutable characteristics to individual identity suggests a justification for the default position of individual liberty upon which political theories of liberal democracy are based, but it does not refute the general importance of permanent traits or suggest that state policies discriminating against everything one does that is important to one should be presumed illegitimate. General trends of belief in some characteristics as important to one's identity, and social perceptions about the importance of such characteristics to identity in others, matter more than any one individual's personal self-perceptions, because discrimination is a social phenomenon. A convicted felon may be considered a "criminal" based on a single act for which he received the full prescribed punishment, even though he may obey the law for his entire life thereafter. The winner of an Olympic medal in gymnastics is considered an Olympian thirty years after the last time she touched a balance beam. The list of such long-term statuses is presumably short, and the labeled person, for his part, may not personally identify with the act. A convicted felon is very unlikely to consider "criminal" as being part of his identity, and an erstwhile Olympian may (at least privately) consider herself a trainer or dancer or whatever else rather than some kind of lifelong athletic laureate. The social consequences for the labeled person can be significant nonetheless. As long as the characteristics and acts are widely viewed as identity-defining in social context, discrimination based on them are likely to reflect potentially problematic cultural tropes rather than rational analysis of the character and value of the individuals.

Because many (certainly not all) prohibited grounds of discrimination are characteristics shared by more or less cohesive groups, such as ethnic or religious

226. *See* John Barth, The Sot-Weed Factor 628 (1967).

communities, one might conclude, as Joseph Raz has done, that such grounds should be prohibited because discrimination on the basis of such characteristics is "more common" and harms the self-esteem of group members qua members.[227] While acknowledging that discrimination based on height, lack of a sense of humor, or other grounds is as likely to be unjust as discrimination based on membership in a marginalized race, religion, or other distinctive culture, Raz justifies the special treatment of such groups partly because discrimination against the group as such "distorts their ability to feel pride in membership in groups[,] identification with which is an important element of their life."[228]

Raz is right to point out the negative feelings that discrimination based on one's personal characteristics provoke. However, to the extent Raz's premises are accurate,[229] I think these factors are only loosely related to the reason discrimination on such grounds is undesirable. It seems to me that Raz is trying to shoehorn the ethical consequences of discrimination into a theory that rights "depend on" collective goods. This rather misses the point. The problem with discrimination has less to do with the interests of the distinctive group than with the disadvantage and suffering caused to the individual by the discrimination. The discrimination is a personal attack on arbitrary grounds related to (perceived or actual) group characteristics. When a distinction is justified by facts and a legitimate purpose, it may not be an attack at all. The point is not that the group suffers; groups cannot suffer, only individuals can. Acts causing unjustified suffering are presumptively unethical, and because discrimination causes arbitrary suffering by definition, the discrimination is morally unjustified regardless of whether based on membership in a discrete and insular minority or some trait such as height. This is why human rights jurisprudence is no less concerned with discrimination based on age, illegitimacy, and other factors that have no relationship to culture or "membership" in a group.

As for pride, IHRL does indeed consider the importance of group membership, but not quite as Raz conceives it. It is true that ethnicity is important to an individual's identity, but it is not the only such characteristic. As noted, IHRL focuses on a broader set of identity characteristics in discrimination analysis, and the rationales for each choice of prohibited grounds are not uniform. Discrimination based on disability, for example, is certainly not prohibited because it distorts the pride of persons in being disabled. It is prohibited because (and only when) it treats as relevant a characteristic that is objectively irrelevant to the person's human dignity and flourishing.

Discrimination not based on identity characteristics may be equally arbitrary and fundamentally harmful to a person if the characteristics are largely beyond that person's control. Poverty and superficial physical appearance are two examples of these characteristics, harmful discrimination based on which is likely to impair the victim's sense of self-worth. We may refer to these features as *involuntary characteristics*.

227. Joseph Raz, The Morality of Freedom 254 (1986).

228. *Id.*

229. Although race, sex, and ethnic discrimination are very common, there may be other kinds of discrimination that are equally or even more common. This is an empirical question that cannot be assumed away.

Involuntary characteristics may include identity characteristics if they are immutable or difficult to change. Obviously, many distinctions can be justified based on involuntary characteristics. Attributes such as physical strength and intelligence are to a degree involuntary, but they support justifiable social and political distinctions. The point is not that there should be a presumption against distinctions based on involuntary characteristics, but rather that the fact that a characteristic is involuntary should weigh somewhat against the validity of such distinctions.

The features and activities that furnish grounds for legal distinctions can be placed on two spectra between, first, those considered to fundamentally define the character and identity of most persons (e.g., ethnicity, religion, language, or political opinion) and those considered peripheral to a person's core identity (e.g., favorite color or sports team), and, second, between those maximally voluntary (e.g., association membership or precise place of residence) and those entirely involuntary (e.g., caste, race, or baldness). Where a feature or activity falls along the identity spectrum is to some extent culturally and individually determined. At different times and in different cultures, sex and race may be at the extreme identity-forming end of the spectrum or closer to the middle, and tattoos may be at the extreme periphery of identity or closer to the identity-forming end. State regulation and social pressures alike affect different groups and persons differently in different cultures. If a subset of persons have strong physiological propensities toward obesity, discrimination against the obese may be expected to hit them harder than other obese persons, just as discrimination against tattooed persons will affect persons of Samoan and Māori descent far more than hipsters pursuing a fad.

It follows that there is no timeless and universal list of grounds on which discrimination may be judged categorically justified or unjustified. The personal traits and behaviors that qualify as involuntary or identity characteristics will vary between cultures and over time. This observation does not necessarily justify deference to state judgments about what grounds of discrimination should be permissible; it instead suggests that an evaluation of such measures should be sensitive to the specific social context in which such judgments are made and not based on a priorism or intuitive assumptions about human nature.

Although equal protection clauses do not use exemplary lists of prohibited grounds for discrimination, many nondiscrimination treaty provisions, such as article 2 of both the CCPR and CESCR, do include such lists. The difficulty in relying on an exemplary list without a theory of justification is that human rights authorities will tend to succumb to their own biases and stereotypes and may not understand the importance of social context for assessing the effects of class-based distinctions. Without an organized effort at objectivity and contextual understanding, the evaluation of the legitimacy of a distinction and the proportionality of the measures taken necessarily reflects merely the subjective opinions of the decision-makers. Such opinions will inevitably appear unconvincing to any of the intended audience who does not share the same assumptions and biases as the decision-maker.

Equally important, without a reasoned basis for evaluating the consistency of distinctions with IHRL, such decisions furnish no ground for treatment as a precedent. In *Gallego Díaz v. Spain*, for example, the U.N. Human Rights Committee rejected an equal treatment claim by a Spanish migrant worker who received less favorable social security benefits pursuant to a bilateral treaty with Switzerland, where he had worked, than would have been granted under other bilateral treaties to which Spain was a party.[230] Rather than engaging the question of why "country of employment" was not a prohibited ground of discrimination in social security benefits for a migrant worker, the Committee merely noted that the author of the communication "has not shown how this distinction is based on the race, colour, sex, [etc.] or other status of these migrant workers."[231] It is certainly the case that country of employment is not a "status," but then, neither is language or political opinion. No doubt the Committee could have justified its decision, but its sparse reasoning failed to support that decision and gave no aid to those interpreting the communication as a precedent. The Committee might instead have pointed out that country of employment is neither related to the author's identity nor an involuntary characteristic of the author, and that the author was not a member of an especially vulnerable or historically disempowered group (Spanish nationals working in Switzerland, presumably). From these facts, the Committee could have analyzed the legislation's legitimacy of aim and proportionality of means with substantial deference to the state's employment policy choices. If made sufficiently explicit, a reasoned decision of this kind would have broadcast guidance on what grounds for discrimination are more or less acceptable, and enhanced the legitimacy of the decision and the Committee itself.

Ad hocism in evaluating grounds for discrimination has another pitfall as well. Forms of discrimination logically inconsistent with accepted IHRL principles may nonetheless escape condemnation by human rights authorities if the authorities share the biases that led to the discrimination in the first place, or when they lack a coherent theory that would strengthen their resolve to challenge state practices that benefit from popular support but cannot withstand doctrinal or policy scrutiny. As mentioned earlier, the lack of such a theory has led the Strasbourg Court, for example, to recognize that homosexuals have an equal right to privacy and family life in the abstract[232] while denying them the right to marry on equal terms with heterosexuals.[233] The Human Rights Committee, arguably relying on an implicit margin of appreciation doctrine,[234] has repeated the same contradiction.[235]

At the same time, an unbounded universe of potential group members does pose challenges to a coherent nondiscrimination doctrine. A particularly refractory example will illustrate. Numerous psychological studies have documented a "halo effect," which is a common cognitive trait that causes individuals to unconsciously think more highly of, and associate greater abilities and virtues to, physically attractive persons of the opposite sex than to normal or unattractive persons, under most

230. U.N. Hum. Rts. Com., Comm. No. 988/2001, U.N. Doc. CCPR/C/82/D/988/2001 (2004).

231. *Id.* para. 7.3.

232. *See* Fellmeth, *supra* note 23, at 808–09.

233. *See, e.g.*, Schalk & Kopf v. Austria, 50 E.H.R.R. 20 (2011); Gas & Dubois c. France, Eur. Ct. Hum. Rts., No. 25951/07, Judgment of Mar. 15, 2012.

234. *See* Markus Schmidt, Book Review, 10 HARV. HUM. RTS. L.J. 333, 338 (1997).

235. *See* Joslin v. New Zealand, U.N. GAOR, Hum. Rts. Comm., 57th Sess., Comm. No. 902/1999, U.N. Doc. A/57/40, at 214, para. 8.3 (July 17, 2002). For a discussion of the Committee's reasoning, see Fellmeth, *supra* note 23, at 862–63.

circumstances.[236] The consequences of this bias on a social level are the systematic and arbitrary elevation of opportunities and salaries to attractive persons entirely independent of merit, such as higher grades in school, better job prospects and evaluations, higher salaries, and reduced chance of some kinds of criminal convictions.[237] Some efforts have been made in a few regions to prohibit some kinds of appearance discrimination by law,[238] and several publicists have called for positive legal measures to neutralize such forms of bias.[239] Although the arguments made in the legal and social science literature so far have not been strong, the legitimacy of the concern cannot reasonably be doubted; personal pulchritude is rarely if ever a valid measure of either merit or need. Political, social, or economic advantages conferred by a state government or private entity on that basis cannot be justified as necessary, legitimate, or even rational. Personal appearance is, moreover, perceived as important to individual identity in almost all societies, and is to a great degree involuntary for almost all persons.[240]

Extending the human right against arbitrary discrimination to traits such as attractiveness would carry certain complications. The problem is clearly not that discrimination based on appearance fails to rise to a social injustice.[241] Any systematic and arbitrary bias—and plentiful social science evidence indicates that human reactions to differences in appearance qualify as such—creates some level of social injustice. Rather, one challenge is identifying cases in which attractiveness actually influenced a decision on the allocation of benefits, risks, or burdens. Another lies in accurately assessing the extent of the improper influence. Although some forms of appearance-based discrimination will be so blatant as to invite condemnation, such as the notorious 1966 Chicago municipal law forbidding maimed individuals from

236. *See, e.g.*, Michael T. French, *Effects of Physical Attractiveness, Personality, and Grooming on Academic Performance in High School*, 84 Labour Econ. 373 (2009); Gerald R. Adams, *Racial Membership and Physical Attractiveness Effects on Preschool Teachers' Expectations*, 8 Child Study J. 29 (1978); Karen Dion & Ellen Berscheid, *Physical Attractiveness and Peer Perception among Children*, 37 Sociometry 1 (1974); David Landy & Harold Sigall, *Task Evaluation as a Function of the Performers' Physical Attractiveness*, 29 J. Personality & Soc. Psych. 299 (1974); Karen Dion et al., *What Is Beautiful Is Good*, 24 J. Personality & Soc. Psych. 285 (1972).

237. *See* Mark V. Roehling, *Weight-Based Discrimination in Employment: Psychological and Legal Aspects*, 52 Personnel Psych. 969 (1999); Kristie M. Engemann & Michael T. Owyang, *So Much for That Merit Raise: The Linkage between Wages and Appearance*, The Regional Economist, Apr. 2005, at 10, *available at* http://research.stlouisfed.org/publications/regional/05/04/appearance.pdf.

238. *See* Deborah L. Rhode, The Beauty Bias: The Injustice of Appearance in Life and Law 16, 132, 135 (2011); Debra L. Gimlin, Body Work 127 (2002); Sandra Solovay, Tipping the Scales of Justice 129 (2000).

239. *See, e.g.*, Rhode, *supra* note 238, at 154; Bonnie Berry, Beauty Bias 121 (2007).

240. The possibility of using cosmetic products and surgery to conform to cultural stereotypes of beauty is irrelevant here. The most effective techniques lie beyond the financial reach of the great mass of humanity. Even for those who can afford them, it would offend human dignity for international human rights law to encourage individuals to take medical risks and spend limited resources to gratify arbitrary social prejudices.

241. Ford, *supra* note 130, at 159.

appearing in public,[242] proposals to gather and evaluate this information would invite an extreme form of regulatory or judicial intervention in both government and private decision-making. The human rights authority would assume the role of supervisor of governmental measures and private practices that operate to the detriment of any identifiable segment of society. This is at once an empowering and perilous role for that authority.[243]

The alternative, of compensating for the bias by systematically disadvantaging notably attractive persons, suggests the *Harrison Bergeron* scenario,[244] or less hyperbolically Rawl's difference principle, which requires rectifying inequalities of "natural endowment" in service of a theory of social justice.[245] Yet, prohibiting appearance discrimination is not the same as leveling down natural strength or intelligence or co-opting it for the benefit of society. Intelligence begins as a natural endowment that will tend to advantage its possessors in every society because of its objectively functional nature. To a point, more intelligence renders a person more capable in almost every circumstance. Pulchritude, in contrast, is culturally relative—different societies at different times view different characteristics, such as the size of lips or eyes, length of neck, color of skin, fatness or thinness, hair color, foot size, etc. as indicators of beauty. And, once a standard of beauty is established, it serves no reliable social function except the attraction of the opposite sex. It does not directly contribute to childbearing or childrearing ability, productivity, problem-solving, or any other survival skill. When personal appearance influences important social decisions to which it is irrelevant, such as employment or promotion, appearance discrimination is as arbitrary and harmful as any other kind.

I mentioned earlier that some human rights authorities have consciously or unconsciously accorded additional weight to identity and involuntary characteristics in their analyses of prohibited grounds of discrimination. The African Court on Human and People's Rights' first decision on merits, *Tanganyika Law Society v. Tanzania*, illustrates one such instance.[246] Tanzania had amended and interpreted its constitution to require that only members of a recognized political party could seek election to a high government post. The applicants, independent candidates for political office, were denied the ability to run for office, and claimed violation of the Banjul Charter on grounds of freedom of association, the right to participate in government, and arbitrary discrimination. The court held for the applicants on all three grounds. In finding that Tanzania had violated articles 2 (nondiscrimination) and 3(2) (equal protection) of the Charter, the court determined that the discrimination was based on political opinion—a ground explicitly listed in article 2.[247]

242. *See* Marcia Pearce Burgdorf & Robert Burgdorf, Jr., *A History of Unequal Treatment: The Qualifications of Handicapped Persons as a 'Suspect Class' under the Equal Protection Clause*, 15 Santa Clara L. 855, 863–64 (1975).

243. Aaron X. Fellmeth, *Nondiscrimination as a Universal Human Right,* 34 Yale J. Int'l L. 588, 594 (2009).

244. *See* Kurt Vonnegut, Welcome to the Monkey House 7 (Dial Press ed. 1968).

245. John Rawls, A Theory of Justice 100 (1971).

246. Tanganyika L. Soc'y v. United Rep. of Tanz., Afr. Ct. Hum. & People's Rts., Apps. No. 011/2011 & 009/2011, Decision of June 14, 2013.

247. *Id.* para. 119.

It would have been difficult for the African Court in the *Tanganyika Law Society* case to justify the finding of arbitrary discrimination based on the fact that the constitution required membership in a political party, because like-minded persons can presumably always form their own political party (and, in the case, one applicant actually did), except either when their political ideas are so idiosyncratic that they cannot reasonably find others who share them, or when the party certification requirements are extremely burdensome.[248] A distinction between members of a political party and independent candidates can be justified as legitimate and proportional in a democracy on several grounds. For example, if political parties must state a campaign platform, affiliation with a party helps to inform the public about the candidate's political views. In addition, endorsement by a party increases the chance that the candidate will appeal to some portion of the public, which prevents ballots from becoming crowded with candidates lacking significant public support. And there are other reasons. These may not be overwhelming arguments, but they at least suggest that Tanzania's distinction rested on a plausible basis.

The real problem was substantive—the state law compelled individuals who wished to exercise one right (participation in government) to exercise another right (freedom of association) in a manner to which they objected. In effect, the Tanzanian constitutional amendment conditioned the exercise of one right on the infringement of another. It is much more difficult to justify this policy as proportional to the ends sought.

Tanzania's distinction was not really based on political opinion; it arose from a related but distinct characteristic: party membership. Party membership is a matter of public affiliation; it expresses a person's identity just as political opinion does, but in a different way. Political opinion and party membership are both a matter of conscience, but party membership is additionally a matter of association, and others are likely to judge a person by his choice of associates—*noscitur a sociis eiusdem generis*. Political opinion is an important matter of individual conscience, and for most thoughtful persons relates to personal identity. The importance of the rights of conscience and political association to personal identity justified the Court's rejection of the measure as discriminatory.

In several cases, the Strasbourg Court has shown restraint in scrutinizing discrimination based on grounds not closely tied to the identity of the petitioner. *Chassagnou v. France* and *Chabauty v. France* involved the right to property protected by article 1 of the first protocol to the ECHR. In *Chassagnou*, the claimants were landowners subject to the *Loi Verdeille*, which required owners of small properties to band together in a municipal hunting association by which all members of the association must allow all other members to hunt on their lands, to the extent possible without interfering with normal use of the property.[249] As committed members of an anti-hunting movement, however, the claimants objected to the use of their land for this purpose. The Court held that the *Loi Verdeille* violated the substantive property right under article 1 of ECHR Protocol I and the right of association under article 11, but it also found a violation of the nondiscrimination right. According to the Court, "since the result of the difference in treatment between

248. In that case, Tanzania had adopted regional representation requirements, but these were not exceedingly onerous.

249. Chassagnou v. France, 29 E.H.R.R. 615 (2000).

large and small landowners is to give only the former the right to use their land in accordance with their conscience, it constitutes discrimination on the ground of property, within the meaning of Article 14 of the Convention."[250]

In *Chabauty*, the claimant was also a landowner whose relatively small property was included in a compulsory land-pooling scheme for hunters.[251] The claimant was entitled to hunt anywhere on the pooled land, like other landowners within the communal association. Only landowners who held a large amount of land or who objected to hunting "as a matter of personal conviction" could exempt their property from communal hunting rights. The claimant, who held a hunting permit and did not object to hunting in general, did not have sufficiently large land holdings, but still wished to exclude other members of the association from his land. He claimed that the distinction between large landowners (who need not conscientiously object to hunting to be excluded from the hunting associations) and small landowners (who did need to so object) constituted prohibited discrimination. This time, the Court rejected the discrimination claim, noting the government's argument that owners of small land holdings could only effectively hunt by pooling property, whereas large properties could sustain hunting without such pooling.[252] The Court found the revised *Loi* to have a reasonable relationship of proportionality to the legitimate aim of promoting sustainable game management. Moreover, the Court determined that France should have a "significant" margin of appreciation, given the property right at stake.

The point is not that the Strasbourg Court drew an arbitrary distinction between one form of discrimination (conscientious objections to hunting versus self-interested objections) and another (large land holdings versus small land holdings). Those distinctions are at least defensible. It is rather that an open nondiscrimination right makes both claims plausible unless some criteria are adopted to consistently distinguish more justifiable from less justifiable grounds.

A hierarchy of some kind, then, is inevitable, with distinctions based on involuntary identity characteristics, such as race, sex, sexual orientation, class, ethnicity, national origin, and physical appearance irrelevant to any distinction the state or a public accommodation could make, with very few exceptions. The relevance of other characteristics is situational, but the more important the characteristic is to the perceived identity of a person, and the less voluntary the characteristic is, the stronger must be the measure's need in order to justify a distinction. Distinctions based on age or religion, for example, should have to meet a high threshold of justification. Discrimination based on such characteristics hits the subject especially hard because it attacks who they are and thereby denies their equal human dignity.

Such factors as historical oppression of a group, or widespread bias against or stereotyping of the group, also call into question the legitimacy of distinctions that disadvantage members of the group or reinforce stereotypes about them. Groups that suffer a present disadvantage caused by past discrimination require special protection, as the Strasbourg Court has recurrently held with regard to such vulnerable

250. *Id.* para. 95.

251. Chabauty v. France, App. No. 57412/08, Judgment of Oct. 4, 2012.

252. *Id.* paras. 34–38, 43, 47.

groups in Europe as Roma populations.[253] Distinctions harmful to such groups should also face a presumption of illegitimacy because even private discrimination on a significant social scale can have devastating psychological, economic, cultural, and even health consequences. Discrimination against disempowered groups is especially problematic because its targets tend to have only limited means to combat the discrimination through the dissemination of corrective information, the exercise of political or economic leverage, or the ability to persuade through social influence. There may be many persons biased against the very wealthy, or against professional politicians, in a state, but there will generally be no need for legal intervention to protect them against private discrimination, because they already have sufficient means to protect their own interests.

2. The Interests Protected

Dependent nondiscrimination provisions are common in international instruments. The emphasis on nondiscrimination in the protection of human rights is easy to understand; if these most fundamental interests do not receive equal protection, much less can the state be expected to act even-handedly in quotidian legislation and law enforcement measures. An independent clause also protects human rights against arbitrary discrimination, but it subjects all state measures to the rigors of nondiscrimination analysis as well.

It is also easy to see why there has been a strong movement toward using equal protection provisions, supplementary treaties, or simply expansive interpretations so that the nondiscrimination right guarantees not just the equal enjoyment of human rights, but also protection against state measures arbitrarily harming vulnerable or disempowered groups more generally. Human rights tend to relate to the interests most fundamental to human dignity, and so discrimination in the respect or protection of human rights is almost always an exceptionally serious failing. Nonetheless, human rights do not encompass the entire universe of important human interests implicating human dignity. The interest in equal treatment under the law, which is to say in social justice, is universal and far from trivial.

The expansive possibilities of the protected rights approach become especially evident when applied to positive rights to fulfillment—that is, rights that impose on the state a duty to assist the right holder in obtaining a meaningful benefit of the right. A systematic program of discrimination in the legislative allocation of benefits to which nobody has a right could easily create a severe imbalance in political power, wealth, and social status between groups. The modern state grants innumerable benefits and advantages to defined classes of persons that are denied to other classes of persons. Sometimes these benefits and advantages are adopted in pursuit of legitimate and rational public policies. Sometimes they distribute rewards arbitrarily. The arbitrary distribution of police protection, government appointments, tax benefits, or commercial subsidies could in some circumstances create, buttress, or exacerbate social inequalities detrimental to equal human dignity. Presumably nobody has a general human right to state subsidies, but if a state grants subsidies exclusively to a specific religious sect or ethnic group to the exclusion of others, it

253. *See, e.g.*, D.H. v. Czech Rep., 47 E.H.R.R. 3 (2008).

seems to me that the equal dignity of group members, and their ability to flourish, would certainly be compromised. In tacit recognition of this risk, the European Court of Human Rights has held that the nondiscrimination obligation of article 14 ECHR applies to negative and positive substantive rights alike.[254]

Of course, human dignity does not demand universal equal treatment in all state legislation and law enforcement, nor could a uniformly egalitarian system respect human dignity. A coal miner and an electronics engineer specializing in solar cells each have a dignity-based interest in employment, but a state subsidy given to solar energy research that systematically decreases coal mining employment for the purpose of protecting the environment could not reasonably be called arbitrary. If states were subjected to discrimination claims for every policy decision differentially affecting an identifiable group of persons, legislation and law enforcement would quickly become deadlocked. As the Strasbourg Court recognized long ago, if every distinction could support a claim of arbitrary discrimination:

> One would, in effect, be led to judge as contrary to the Convention every one of the many legal or administrative provisions which do not secure to everyone complete equality of treatment in the enjoyment of the rights and freedoms recognised. The competent national authorities are frequently confronted with situations and problems which, on account of differences inherent therein, call for different legal solutions; moreover, certain legal inequalities tend only to correct factual inequalities.[255]

A case in point is *Haraldsson v. Iceland* before the Human Rights Committee.[256] The authors were fishermen who had suffered discrimination in the granting of property rights to fishing quotas in Icelandic waters. The government had granted one group of fishermen an alienable property right to a free share of the fishing quota, while other fishermen had no such right and were required to buy or lease a quota from one of the endowed group. In examining the compatibility of the law with article 26 of the Covenant, the Committee rather skipped over the fact that the authors did not belong to a vulnerable group; the endowed fishermen had merely been active during a certain three-year period, and the others had not. The government's distinction was arbitrary, to be sure, but it did not specially prey upon the weak or helpless, or exacerbate a serious social problem.

The Committee did conclude that the affected rights were "equivalent to those of property," which presumably means that in granting a property right in a common resource to an arbitrary group of private individuals, the state was depriving nonmembers of the group of a property right. The sparseness of the Committee's

254. *See, e.g.*, Belgian Linguistics Case, 1 E.H.R.R. 252 (1968). Indeed, in one case, the Strasbourg Court held that the state might be required to discriminate in favor of a group in a situation significantly different from the majority. *See* Thlimmenos v. Greece, 31 E.H.R.R. 15, para. 44 (2001). The *Thlimmenos* case follows the logic of anti-discrimination jurisprudence quite soundly. However, the Strasbourg Court has since retreated from this position. *See* Chapman v. United Kingdom, 35 E.H.R.R. 18 (2001).

255. Belgian Linguistics Case, 1 E.H.R.R. 252 (1968).

256. Comm. No. 1054/2002, 2 Hum. Rts. Comm. 2008 Report, Annex V, sec. G.

reasoning unfortunately left open an interpretation that virtually any state-granted material benefit could fall within the scope of a protected human right to property. In concluding that the measure was unreasonable, the Committee was undoubtedly on firm footing. However, it is difficult to see how the case illustrates a violation of the nondiscrimination right unless every state legislative or executive measure that results in an arbitrary dissemination of different benefits or burdens to different groups in the population violates the same right. For this reason, the independent nondiscrimination right should be used conservatively, mainly with regard to distinctions on the grounds identified earlier, to progressively abate social conditions that contribute to or sustain correlations between group membership and policies that are democratic and egalitarian or meritocratic, and consistent with human dignity.

3. Public and Private Discriminators

The exercise of discriminatory behavior by powerful social actors—the wielders of economic leverage, social influence, and political control—necessarily degrades the dignity and worsens the life prospects of the victims of discrimination more than discrimination by weak groups or isolated individuals. Indeed, the discriminatory or egalitarian attitudes of such powerful actors as governments, multinational corporations, and socially inclusive private organizations may have an important effect on encouraging similar attitudes among less influential actors.[257]

The relative power of the respondent is therefore a critical factor in determining the social effects, and therefore the proportionality, of the distinction being made. The state, as an actor of superlative coercive and economic power, should bear the heaviest burden of justifying socially unbalancing or arbitrary distinctions. It is also justifiable to require the state to regulate discriminatory behavior of politically, socially, and economically powerful groups.

It is more difficult to justify obligating the state to regulate discrimination by smaller private actors unless the discrimination at issue is a widespread social phenomenon. As Larry Alexander has observed, the social effects of private discrimination depend on many factors and are not uniform in all states at all times.[258] Holding all else equal, the greater the social effect of private discrimination, the more easily a prohibition can be justified. The "all else" that may not be equal includes, for example, the degree of the prohibition's intrusion on the discriminator's rights and the externalities that may arise from enforcement of an anti-discrimination right. In cases of less severe, private social discrimination and stereotypes, human rights authorities would be justified in requiring states at most to engage in noncoercive measures of persuasion. Some such duties are included in the CEDR and CEDAW to supplement outright prohibitions on private discrimination in access to such important resources as education, housing, employment, and public services. However, there is no reason, in cases of less socially destructive forms of discrimination, persuasive measures could not stand alone as sufficient to address the problem from a human rights standpoint.

257. *See* Joey T. Cheng et al., *Two Ways to the Top: Evidence That Dominance and Prestige Are Distinct Yet Viable Avenues to Social Rank and Influence*, 104 J. PERS. & SOC. PSYCH. 103 (2013).

258. Alexander, *supra* note 159, at 163.

4. Intention to Discriminate

There are no credible arguments against evidence of intent to discriminate continuing to create a strong presumption that a distinction is unjustified under IHRL, but human rights authorities have rightly considered the *absence* of such intent irrelevant. Whatever the merits of making intent a precondition to a finding of discrimination, they do not outweigh its deficiencies in protecting against harmful state measures. What the U.S. Supreme Court's approach ignores is that the primary goal of the nondiscrimination right is not to combat overt prejudices among legislators or even private citizens (although that is *a* goal). The primary goal is to prevent or rectify the harm resulting from discrimination, whether conscious or not. The nondiscrimination right does not exist to punish morally repugnant purposive action, but to safeguard human dignity on an equal basis. It achieves this goal best by counterbalancing sub rosa as well as overt biases and stereotypes.

A conscious intent to discriminate is for those purposes largely epiphenomenal. The primary relevance of intent is that it supplies indirect evidence that a distinction is socially harmful, because those who seek to discriminate consciously usually do so in conformity to popular stereotypes and biases rather than idiosyncratic personal preferences. Discrimination is much more problematic when it reflects societal devaluation of the victim group rather than isolated cases of malice.

The technical immateriality of intent explains why IHRL prohibits facially neutral measures having substantial discriminatory effects. A state that systematically disadvantages a group in pursuit of what it believes to be a neutral policy could be overlooking, reinforcing, or exacerbating entrenched social inequalities. As Dinah Shelton has observed:

> Structural factors can lead certain groups to fall behind the rest of society, regardless of formally equal treatment or a prohibition of direct discrimination. As a result, consistency of treatment may fail to ensure the broader aims of equality, if applied on its own without taking into account differences as well as similarities within the population.[259]

Group stereotypes in particular tend to result from unconscious beliefs about the characteristics or proper role of group members.[260] A policy of ignoring unconscious discrimination effectively eviscerates the right, paving the proverbial road to hell with good, or at least not demonstrably bad, intentions.

259. Shelton, supra note 21, at 261, 262.

260. *See* John A. Bargh, Mark Chen & Lara Burrows, *Automaticity of Social Behavior: Direct Effects of Trait Construct and Stereotype Activation on Action*, 71 J. Personality & Soc. Psych. 230 (1996); Mahzarin R. Banaji & Anthony G. Greenwald, *Implicit Social Cognition: Attitudes, Self-Esteem, and Stereotypes*, 102 Psych. Rev. 4 (1995); Mahzarin R. Banaji, Curtis Hardin & Alexander J. Rothman, *Implicit Stereotyping in Person Judgment*, 65 J. Personality & Soc. Psych. 272 (1993).

4

Interchangeability and Complementarity of Substantive and Nondiscrimination Paradigms

With these characteristics of the nondiscrimination right in mind, it becomes easier to analyze the dynamics of substantive and nondiscrimination rights as alternative or complementary paradigms for the protection of human dignity. In this chapter, I will discuss the extent to which the two paradigms may be used as alternatives, most prominently at the enforcement stage, for protection against identical threats, as well as the limits on the interchangeability of the two paradigms for that purpose. I will then discuss the more general systemic consequences to the system of international human rights of using one paradigm or the other. Finally, I will evaluate the ways in which the two paradigms conflict and, more commonly, synergize in the system of IHRL for the protection and promotion of human dignity.

A. THE EXTENT AND LIMITS OF EQUIVALENCE

There are classes of claims that can be asserted only as a violation of a substantive right or only as a violation of the nondiscrimination right. In the former category are claims based on substantive rights that are more or less universally violated by a state measure, so that no specific group is treated more or less favorably than any other. If a state were never to inform any arrested person of the criminal charges, the only proper claim would be a violation of the substantive right to such information.[1] If all arrests were made without providing charging information, no distinction is being made between any class of persons,[2] and consequently no claim of a violation of the nondiscrimination right would be credible.

In the latter category are state measures that discriminate without denying any person's substantive human rights. This is possible because a state measure may distinguish arbitrarily between classes of persons in providing some benefit to

1. ICCPR art. 9(2).

2. Except, of course, persons who are arrested and those who are not, but presumably persons in the latter category do not need or want to know why they have not been arrested.

which all persons are not entitled, or imposing a burden to which all persons are legally susceptible—interests typically protected by an equal protection right, as discussed in Chapter 3, Section C.2. For example, if a state were to grant a subsidy to men but not women purchasing automobiles, there could be no claim to the violation of any substantive right. Nobody has the substantive human right to assistance in purchasing an automobile, and so an appropriate claim would invoke the nondiscrimination right.

In those few human rights regimes in which discrimination claims must be based on a substantive human rights violation, such as the ECHR sans Protocol No. 12, claims that can invoke only purely substantive rights and claims that invoke only the right against discrimination are extremely rare. This is not to say that they are entirely equivalent in these regimes; the point is that most human rights violations potentially involve both kinds of rights. Even in independent nondiscrimination regimes, the nondiscrimination right tends to overlap with substantive human rights claims, although to a diminished extent. The extent and limits of this equivalence are the subject of this section.

1. General Substitutability

Most claims of discrimination relate either to denials of equal protection of a human right, or to matters within the ambit of a human right, or at a minimum to measures that carry implications for the exercise of a human right. As a result, more often than not, claims of human rights violations could be framed as either prohibited discrimination or an infringement of a substantive right. Three hypothetical scenarios can illustrate the strong pattern of overlap in substantive universal rights and nondiscrimination rights:

{A} A national ethnic minority group seeks to stage a public parade to promote the rights of the group. The state government denies the permit on grounds of "*ordre public*." Permits are regularly granted for parades by the majority group.

{B} In a state that subsidizes private hospitals, a nonprofit hospital associated with a minority religious sect applies for a subsidy and is denied because the state has a policy of separation between religion and state. No religious hospital has ever successfully obtained a subsidy in the state.

{C} A state maintains a bifurcated primary educational system in which children with low standardized test scores are put in a trade school of inferior quality, while children with higher scores are put in a university-preparatory academic program. The incomes, employment benefits, and prestige of graduates of trade schools are decidedly lower than those of graduates of the preparatory program.

Scenario {A} recites a classic discrimination fact pattern; the immediate claim would seem to relate to an arbitrary distinction based on ethnicity. It is equally evident that a claim could be made out for a violation of the universal rights to freedom of expression and assembly. Obviously, the rights themselves are quite different, but the group could potentially vindicate its immediate interests from a practical perspective (securing permission for the parade) by successfully invoking either right.

The general right to freedom of expression and assembly requires the state to grant the group a parade permit under reasonable circumstances. The nondiscrimination right requires the state to grant the group a parade permit on the same terms on which it grants such permits to similarly situated groups.

The same analysis of alternative substantive and nondiscrimination claims applies to scenario {B}, with one complication. Because no religious hospital has ever received a subsidy, the discrimination claim effectively amounts *not* to a claim that the applicants were singled out for discrimination based on their specific religious beliefs, but rather to a claim that the entire class of religious groups are the subject of discrimination. In other words, these facts give the scenario more the look and feel of a claim that a universal right to freedom of religion and conscience has been violated. Clearly, the group members have suffered discrimination on the basis of their religious convictions, but not because of any specific religious beliefs. In order to reframe the universal right claim as a discrimination claim, then, it is necessary to establish that "persons offering services based on their religious beliefs" as a whole be considered a class eligible for protection as such.

The closer affinity of scenario {B} to a substantive human right violation partly relates to the fact that it is usually much easier to discriminate against a small minority group than a large minority group, because the latter are often more likely to have the political and economic resources to resist discrimination, and so the state may be expected to hesitate to make a distinction that might seriously harm such an influential group. Partly it is because the larger the group, the more likely it will be to include the political elites who make decisions relevant to human rights in the first place. A legislator who is a religious zealot is obviously much more likely to persecute atheists or members of other religions than to persecute religious persons in general, for example. And partly it is because, considering scenarios {A} and {B} in light of the framework discussed in Chapter 3, Section D, a smaller and more discrete group is more likely to be able to claim historical oppression or discrimination based on identity or involuntary characteristics. None of these are absolutes; they are merely reasons that more general distinctions are usually less suspect than more specific distinctions. In any case, scenario {B} does maintain facts sufficient to support a discrimination claim, although it may be weaker than that in scenario {A}.

Scenario {C} recites a classic fact pattern relating to the denial of the universal substantive right to public education. If the state has a positive duty to provide public education, and a plausible claim can be made that a trade school education does not satisfy the minimum standard required by human rights law, the students may be facing a denial of the substantive right to education. Yet, here too is a distinction, this time between students with high and low standardized test scores. This claim can be framed as a violation of a nondiscrimination right, but it is far weaker than the claim of scenario {A}, and also weaker than the claim of {B}. Academic aptitude is no more involuntary than most traits; it relates somewhat to intelligence and early social advantages such as educated parents, but it also relates to motivation and discipline. Neither of these are immutable or identity traits. Even intelligence cannot be considered a typical identity trait, because intelligence runs a spectrum without firm and easily perceptible distinctions between its degrees, except toward the extremes.

Students with low test scores per se would consequently face a difficult challenge making out a credible claim of historical oppression or that they are being subjected to the distinction because of greater political, economic, or social vulnerability than high test scorers. A discrimination claim can still be made, but it faces the defense that the distinction is necessary and proportional to the goal of allowing every student to attain his maximal academic potential, which would not be possible if all students were given the exact same education regardless of intelligence, study habits, and motivation. The more obvious claim would be based on a denial of the students' substantive right to education by reason of placement in a school of insufficient quality, if such is the case for trade schools.

However weak the discrimination case may be in scenario {C}, nothing about the fact pattern precludes a discrimination claim. The tendency of discrimination claims to accompany substantive right violation claims in so many cases is no coincidence. An exercise in imagining a nondiscriminatory violation of a substantive human right will tend toward the fantastical. If we continue the example of a right to primary education, a state that provides no subsidized education could not prevent the wealthy from obtaining private education for their children, except in a dystopian state that positively prohibited schooling. In any other case, the availability of education to the wealthy could be considered not only a violation of the right to education of all others, but an instance of discrimination based on wealth. If there is after all a substantive human right to primary education, the state's failure to provide subsidized or free primary education discriminates against the poor, because the right will be meaningless for anyone who cannot afford to buy his or her children a private education. Similarly, a state that adopts Islam as an official religion not only violates the substantive right to freedom of religion, it also discriminates against non-Muslims (and Muslims with dissenting views or those who wish to live in a secular state). Most human rights cases accordingly give the claimant an option of asserting both a substantive human right violation and a discrimination claim. In such cases, a human rights authority must decide whether to focus on the substantive right claim, the discrimination claim, or both.

A case in point is *V.C. v. Slovakia*, in which a Roma woman giving birth in Slovakia was allegedly deceived and frightened by hospital staff into agreeing to sterilization.[3] The Strasbourg Court found Slovakia's actions to violate the applicant's substantive rights—specifically, the article 3 right to freedom from inhuman or degrading treatment and the article 8 right to family life, because the Court was convinced the applicant's consent was not free and fully informed. But the problem was not that the hospital had a general practice of sterilizing patients without their free and informed consent. The problem was that special measures had not been taken to ensure the full informed consent of members of a minority group that the Court considered vulnerable in Slovakia. In other words, although the Court found a violation of substantive rights, all of its concerns actually centered on discrimination based on the applicant's Roma ethnicity. Nonetheless, the Court declined to separately determine whether the facts justified an article 14 discrimination claim.[4]

3. Eur. Ct. Hum. Rts. App. No. 18968/07, Judgment of Nov. 8, 2011.

4. *Id.* paras. 176–80. In dissent, Judge Mijović argued powerfully that the essence of the claim was discrimination based on the applicant's Roma ethnicity. The fact that she was "marked

Both claims were plausible despite the Court's choice to address only the substantive claim.

Such a choice can be especially difficult when the claim does not fit squarely within either a substantive right or the discrimination category. The Strasbourg Court has resorted to jurisprudential sleights-of-hand from time to time when dealing with claims that arguably fell outside the scope of both a clear substantive right and the article 14 nondiscrimination right, in order to strengthen or dismiss a claim, according to its preference. For example, in several claims of state discrimination against sexual minorities, including the criminalization of same-sex intercourse and refusal to allow homosexuals to enlist in the military, the Strasbourg Court relied on the article 8 right to privacy alone and concluded that the article 14 right against discrimination does "not give rise to any separate issue."[5] The assertion that dismissal of a homosexual from military service violates the right to privacy rather than a right against discrimination is somewhat counterintuitive. Surely sexual orientation is a matter of private life, but military organizations interfere with the intimate lives of their members as a matter of course. They may prohibit sexual intercourse between officers and enlisted persons, they may regulate contact with a recruit's family, and they may censor the recruit's mail, all without being considered to violate a human right.

The real explanation for this rather strained reasoning may lie in the different consequences of substantive right violations and discrimination violations of the Convention. The declaration of a substantive right violation calls on the human rights decision-maker to expand or contract the scope of the right itself; adjudicating a violation of the nondiscrimination right does not necessarily affect the scope of a substantive right. It merely requires a judgment of whether an unjustified difference in treatment has occurred between two similarly situated classes of persons.

This surmise is supported by a statement of an erstwhile President of the Strasbourg Court, who has observed that judges on the Court may prefer to classify violations as falling under the substantive provisions of the Convention (such as article 8) rather than the article 14 nondiscrimination right because they believe the protections of substantive rights to be stronger.[6] In the military enlistment cases, for example, a decision to rely on article 8 taken in conjunction with article 14 would merely have nullified the arbitrary exclusion of homosexuals from military service. The Court's decision to rely on article 8 alone may be taken to require the state to justify *any* exclusion of any person from military service based on his or her private acts. Following its logic would mean that a state decision to exclude sadomasochists and recreational drug users would be put to the test of necessity to serve

out" for sterilization due to her Roma origin made it a case appropriate for resolution under article 14, in his opinion.

5. *E.g.*, Lustig-Prean & Beckett v. United Kingdom, 29 E.H.R.R. 548, paras. 106–09 (1999); Dudgeon v. United Kingdom, 4 E.H.R.R. 149 (1982); Smith & Grady v. United Kingdom, 29 E.H.R.R. 493 (2000).

6. Statement of Luzius Wildhaber at Realistic Idealism in International Law: A Conference in Honor of W. Michael Reisman, Panel IV, Apr. 24, 2009, New Haven, CT.

a legitimate state purpose. The state may be capable of justifying such exclusions, but the exclusion would have to be justified with adequate reasons.

The Strasbourg Court has not been alone in facing a quandary over whether borderline claims relate to a substantive right or the nondiscrimination right. *Meyer v. Nebraska*[7] and *Pierce v. Society of Sisters*,[8] two U.S. Supreme Court civil rights decisions from the 1920s, furnish exemplary cases of alternative claims. In *Meyer*, the State of Nebraska had outlawed teaching foreign languages to young children following the close of the First World War. The real intention behind the law was discriminatory—to hinder the spread of knowledge of the German language. In *Pierce*, Oregon had made it a misdemeanor for parents to send their children to private schools, the motivation in that case being to deter Catholic education. Had the U.S. Supreme Court recognized a broad concept of human rights at the time, the plaintiffs challenging the Nebraska and Oregon laws would have faced a theoretical choice between claiming a violation of substantive rights (freedom of expression, right to education, and cultural rights) or simply complaining of discrimination based on ethnicity and national origin (*Meyer*) or religion (*Pierce*)—a Fourteenth Amendment Equal Protection Clause claim. The problem with a discrimination approach at the time was that the Supreme Court did not recognize a broad right against discrimination on grounds of ethnicity, national origin, or religion. Instead, the Court resorted to a concept of "substantive due process" in each case. The substantive due process right invented by the Court maps to a limited degree to the human right to privacy as developed by modern international human rights authorities.[9] It encompasses the basic assumption of human autonomy, requiring the state to justify serious interferences with behavior traditionally considered personal because of its attenuated connection to an identifiable public interest. The Court has limited the concept to encompass only those rights a majority of justices in any given case considers "implicit in the concept of ordered liberty,"[10] or to "principles of justice so rooted in the traditions and conscience of our people as to be ranked as fundamental."[11] Such a vague and subjective basis for civil rights has proven unpopular with those justices who consider themselves committed to highly textual approaches to the Constitution, as a result of which the doctrine has become, if not moribund, then infrequently invoked.

At the same time, since the 1940s, U.S. nondiscrimination doctrine has developed to fill in some of the gap left by an anemic privacy right. In the 1972 case *Police Department of Chicago v. Mosley*,[12] the Supreme Court considered a state

7. 262 U.S. 390 (1923).

8. 268 U.S. 510 (1925).

9. The Strasbourg Court has defined the right as "encompassing, *inter alia*, aspects of an individual's physical, psychological and social identity such as the right to personal autonomy and personal development, [and] the right to establish and develop relationships with other human beings . . . ." V.C. v. Slovakia, Eur. Ct. Hum. Rts. App. No. 18968/07, Judgment of Nov. 8, 2011, para. 138.

10. Palko v. Connecticut, 302 U.S. 319, 325–26 (1937).

11. Snyder v. Massachusetts, 291 U.S. 97, 105 (1934).

12. 408 U.S. 92 (1972).

act that arguably violated both a substantive free speech right and a nondiscrimination right. After Mosley had begun picketing outside a high school to allege race discrimination in the school's hiring policies, the city adopted an ordinance prohibiting the peaceful picketing of any school unless the school was involved in a labor dispute. Mosley's main argument was that the ordinance violated his substantive right to freedom of speech—a claim that reflected the Court's past tendency to view abridgments of free speech on public property on grounds of content as presumptively requiring a strong justification[13]—but the Court preferred to annul the law based on Mosley's alternative equal protection claim. The equal protection clause, the Court held, prohibits the state from selecting "which issues are worth discussing or debating in public facilities." It concluded:

> There is an "equality of status in the field of ideas," and government must afford all points of view an equal opportunity to be heard. . . . Selective exclusions from a public forum may not be based on content alone, and may not be justified by reference to content alone.[14]

The Court's focus on equal protection in that case suggests suspicion that the City of Chicago's selective restriction on picketing represented a form of discrimination based on the content of Mosley's speech—in other words, a veiled attempt to silence the message itself. A nondiscrimination claim—in this case, against the speaker's political beliefs—fits the facts about as well as a claim that the speaker's right to freedom of expression had suffered impairment.

In the following year, in *Roe v. Wade*, the Court did the reverse, holding that a state abortion prohibition violated the "substantive due process" right to liberty rather than the prohibition on discrimination against women.[15] Although the antiabortion laws clearly affected women most directly, the Court refrained from deciding the case on equal protection grounds. The Court has for many years now vacillated between the two approaches without method. In *Lawrence v. Texas*, for example, the Court invalidated a state law criminalizing homosexual intercourse as violating fundamental liberties rather than on equal protection grounds.[16] The Court in *Lawrence* recognized that a nondiscrimination (equal protection) claim would have been "tenable," but nonetheless chose to strike down the law as an unwarranted invasion of privacy.[17] Yet, only a few years later, the Court struck down a federal ban on same-sex marriage principally on equal protection grounds.[18] *Roe*, *Lawrence*, and *Windsor* could be reconciled if the Court in each had chosen to decide the case on both theories, but it selected one or the other for reasons of

13. *See, e.g.*, Hague v. Congress of Indus. Org., 307 U.S. 496 (1939).

14. *Mosley*, 408 U.S. at 96.

15. Roe v. Wade, 410 U.S. 113 (1973).

16. Lawrence v. Texas, 539 U.S. 558, 578–79 (2002).

17. *Id.* at 574.

18. United States v. Windsor, Slip Op. 12-307 (June 26, 2013), 570 U.S. __ (2013).

judicial economy.[19] One might wonder why in that case the Court does not simply stick with one theory, substantive due process or equal protection, for cases posing very similar questions. Whatever the explanation, it is political and not doctrinal.

The important point is that these cases illustrate that, in practice, violations of perfect substantive and nondiscrimination rights are relatively rare. State measures of social control must inevitably be based on personal or behavioral characteristics, because they are designed to encourage some kinds of (hopefully prosocial) behavior and discourage other (hopefully antisocial) kinds. Social control measures accordingly differentiate between classes of persons, such as persons who act unsafely, threaten the reputation of others, donate charitably, protest in the streets, have better or worse vision, or suffer from disabilities. When a state arbitrarily censors free speech or tortures persons, it almost always selectively silences a certain class of speech content (e.g., religious dissent, racist speech, political opposition) or selectively tortures a certain class of persons (e.g., political opponents, accused terrorists, criminals). It is the relatively rare case in which a human rights authority hears a claim that the state has violated a substantive right without the basis for an additional allegation of discrimination. For this reason, the Strasbourg Court so frequently states that, although it finds a substantive violation and the applicant has claimed discrimination, "it is not generally necessary for the Court also to examine the case under Article 14, though the position is otherwise if a clear inequality of treatment in the enjoyment of the right in question is a fundamental aspect of the case . . . ."[20] Apparently, the Court sometimes views, or represents that it views, substantive claims and nondiscrimination claims as closely related. Or, as Justice Kennedy wrote in *Lawrence v. Texas*: "Equality of treatment and the due process right to demand respect for conduct protected by the substantive guarantee of liberty are linked in important respects, and a decision on the latter point advances both interests."[21]

It is less universally the case that nondiscrimination claims relate to a substantive human right, although the great majority do. A claimant strengthens his discrimination claim by tying it to a substantive right precisely because an independent nondiscrimination provision has such potentially limitless scope. For example, a discrimination claim based on the fact that the state gives tax subsidies to some kinds of charities (say, charities organized in a certain business form) and not to others has relatively little appeal, because it does not relate to the fundamental dignity concerns that ground IHRL. Independent claims might invoke a departure from strict principles of equity and social justice, and these cannot be ignored, because any injustice affronts human dignity to some degree. But the degree matters. International human rights law in an imperfect world is mainly concerned with the rules necessary to guarantee the minimum regard for human dignity. Although in time IHRL may progress toward greater concern for social justice in

19. Occasionally, the Court has invalidated a measure based on both liberty and equal protection grounds, *see, e.g.*, Loving v. Virginia, 388 U.S. 1, 12 (1967), but such cases are exceptional.

20. Dudgeon v. United Kingdom, 4 E.H.R.R. 149, para. 67 (1981); *accord* Lustig-Prean & Beckett v. United Kingdom, 29 E.H.R.R. 548 (2000).

21. 539 U.S. 558, 575 (2002).

the quotidian operations of the state, international law will inevitably *prioritize* social injustices of either a more severe cast or greater scale.

As a result, nondiscrimination claims that relate to a recognized human right have a stronger basis in IHRL than bare claims of arbitrary difference in treatment, even in independent nondiscrimination regimes such as those with equal protection of the law clauses. In the charitable tax subsidy example, a state offering subsidies to religious charities and not secular charities, or the reverse, implicates dignity concerns because they affect the rights to freedom of conscience and religion to a nontrivial degree. Similarly, social injustices that do not directly violate a human right but that affect important human concerns or very large numbers of persons sustain more persuasive claims even in independent nondiscrimination regimes than relatively minor injustices.

2. Limits on Substitutability

The availability of both types of claims in response to a state measure does not imply that the respective rights are equivalent. Although the Strasbourg Court often likes to say, once it has found a violation of a substantive right, that discrimination claims raise no new issues, in fact approaching a human rights claim from a nondiscrimination perspective differs in several quite important respects from approaching it from a substantive rights perspective. Even in the vast range of cases in which substantive and nondiscrimination rights overlap, nondiscrimination rights and universal substantive rights are not interchangeable, and claims based on the two kinds of rights may carry radically different implications.

In most cases, a claim based on a universal right tends to be more expansive than a claim of arbitrary discrimination. For example, the invocation of CCPR article 21's right to peaceful assembly *in abstracto* may go so far as to claim with textual support that a state is never justified in preventing a group of persons from assembling peacefully, no matter the time, place, or cause they espouse, with the usual exceptions. The state bears the burden of proving that any significant restriction imposed on peaceful assembly is justified on objective and reasonable grounds, necessary in a democratic society for protecting the state's legitimate interests. To frame a human rights claim as a violation of CCPR article 2 or 26 respecting the right to peaceful assembly entails making the more limited assertion that the state has impermissibly restricted the right to freedom of assembly based on religion, political affiliation, or other prohibited grounds of discrimination. The claim need not go so far as to posit an unimpeded right to peaceful assembly; it must merely demonstrate that, without a legitimate and rational justification, restrictions imposed on one class were arbitrarily not imposed on another.

In other cases, a claim of arbitrary discrimination may be more expansive than a claim of a substantive human right violation. As discussed in the previous chapter, if the nondiscrimination right is interpreted to extend not only to discriminatory violations of recognized human rights, but to all arbitrary and harmful distinctions in state measures generally, the universe of nondiscrimination rights will be a broader one than the universe of substantive rights. The nondiscrimination right becomes in that case a kind of super-right that protects against a very wide range of substantive right violations, while adding a set of claims not based on any substantive right violation.

Yet, even in the area of overlap, discrimination claims may offer strategic advantages otherwise unavailable to the claimant. If we continue the example above, a state may advance a plausible justification for a restriction on peaceful assembly for the protection, say, of *ordre public*, but it may not use that justification if it allows assembly in like circumstances to some groups and not to others based on prohibited grounds. In other words, the maximum freedom granted to a favored class sets the lower limit on the freedom that must be granted to all classes, including disfavored ones. If the state grants exceptional freedoms to any class, it has effectively expanded the scope of the human right at issue or, to put it conversely, it has limited its own ability to restrict that freedom to this extent. Otherwise, the state's discrimination undermines the universality of the substantive right.

The advantages of framing human rights claims as a matter of discrimination rather than a substantive right violation were evident in *Religionsgemeinschaft der Zeugen Jehovas v. Austria*.[22] The case arose because Austrian law distinguished at the time between registered religious "societies" and religious "communities." Only a "society" received certain substantial government-granted benefits, including freedom from mandatory military or civilian service, reduced taxes or tax exemptions, and other advantages. Jehovah's Witnesses had applied to the Austrian government for registration as a religious society, but its application was consistently refused over a period of twenty years. Although the Austrian government approved the Jehovah's Witnesses as a "community," other, larger religious groups successfully registered as societies and enjoyed the benefits of this classification.

The Jehovah's Witnesses claimed violations *inter alia* of ECHR articles 9 (guaranteeing freedom of thought, conscience, and religion) and 14 (freedom from arbitrary discrimination). The Austrian government countered that it could not be accused of violating the substantive freedom of religion, because it had not interfered with the group's ability to practice its religion; no government recognition is necessary for any Austrian to practice his or her religion publicly or privately. As for discrimination, the Austrian government argued that a long waiting period was necessary to ensure "that the competent authority could verify during this period of time whether the religious community was ready to integrate into the existing legal order, in particular whether it performed unlawful activities as a consequence of which legal personality had to be withdrawn," and refusal based on the insufficient size of the applicant's sect was intended to ensure monitoring of a society's duties, such as teaching in private schools.[23]

The Strasbourg Court noted that Austria grants substantial benefits to those groups designated as religious "societies" that facilitate the pursuit of their "religious aims," and that these benefits are denied to religious groups not registered as societies, such as religious communities. The Court held that the delay in registration violated article 9,[24] and in addition that, by favoring some religious groups over others, Austria had violated article 14 taken in conjunction with article 9.[25]

22. 48 E.H.R.R. 17 (2009).

23. *Id.* paras. 84–86.

24. *Id.* paras. 78–82.

25. *Id.* paras. 98–99.

The dissenting judges agreed with the Austrian government that, in the absence of interference with the group's exercise of religious observance, no claim of religious discrimination could be made out. But, by choosing to promote some religions through granting the benefits of a registered society while denying these same benefits to other religions, Austria was found to have discriminated without "objective and reasonable justification" against the Jehovah's Witnesses. The Court effectively required Austria to choose between granting no special advantages to any religious group and granting the same advantages to all religious groups, regardless of size.

Zeugen Jehovas is a classic case of discrimination rather than an interference in the universal right to freedom of religion. The applicants adduced no facts to show that Austria interfered in their ability to practice their religion. To support framing the claim as an interference in the universal right, the Court stated:

> While religious freedom is primarily a matter of individual conscience, it also implies, *inter alia*, freedom to "manifest [one's] religion" alone and in private or in community with others, in public and within the circle of those whose faith one shares. Bearing witness in words and deeds is bound up with the existence of religious convictions. Since religious communities traditionally exist in the form of organised structures, art.9 must be interpreted in the light of art.11 of the Convention, which safeguards associative life against unjustified state interference. Indeed, the autonomous existence of religious communities is indispensable for pluralism in a democratic society and is, thus, an issue at the very heart of the protection which art.9 affords.[26]

The Strasbourg Court, unable to sustain the claim of a violation of article 9 alone with any very cogent explanation, resorted to a different right—the right of association under article 11—to create a new and quite expansive right to state recognition of and assistance in organizing religious communities. Besides providing an excellent illustration of the Court turning a textually negative right into a positive one (a subject taken up in Part III of this book), it also transformed a discrimination claim into a claim that a universal right had been violated. The discrimination claim was tricky, because the applicants had not been denied a human right to religion, association, or freedom of conscience; they had been denied certain benefits, to which they had no plausible claim of a human right, that were granted to certain other religious groups. The Court majority was unwilling to limit itself to treating discrimination as a kind of curtailment of religious freedom insofar as some religious groups suffered disadvantage relative to other religious groups; that case was rather weak.

The *Zeugen Jehovas* case also illustrates how relying on a substantive rights paradigm requires the authority to assess the meaning of the right and to define its content as the expression of a universal value. In so doing, the authority transmits public information useful to all right holders about the scope of their rights, and it shapes expectations about the uses and limits of state authority. When human rights authorities interpret a substantive right, they do so for every right holder, and every right holder gets the benefit of, for example, an expansive interpretation

26. *Id.* para. 61 (footnotes omitted).

of the right. There is usually no comparable need to elaborate on the scope of the right as such when assessing a nondiscrimination claim, because the latter relies on comparison between factual cases involving different treatment.

Relying on a universal substantive right sacrifices the ability to make fine distinctions about uniform rules that affect various groups of persons differentially. By definition, a universal substantive right treats all right holders as having some identical kinds of interests. But a right will tend to affect differently situated persons differently. This is the source of Anatole France's witticism about how the law impartially forbids both the rich and the poor to sleep under bridges.[27] Declaring a universal human right to sleep under bridges might be fatuous, but forbidding all persons equally to sleep under bridges discriminates against the dispossessed in their exercise of the right to shelter. Relying on a nondiscrimination paradigm requires human rights authorities to emphasize the factual disparities in the status and power of different groups in society, and to rectify the disparities when they reach the point of degrading human dignity. This is one of the most important differences between substantive rights and nondiscrimination paradigms.

3. The *Ius Cogens* Question

A conceptually unrelated point of difference between the nondiscrimination right and substantive human rights is that some have characterized only the former as *ius cogens*[28] while treating only selected other substantive human rights, such as the prohibitions on torture, slavery, or genocide, as nonderogable. A state may choose to opt out of some customs either unilaterally or by treaty, and in these cases *ius cogens* performs the function of identifying rules of sufficient importance to stand beyond the legal authority of states to alter or from which to exempt themselves.

Without prejudice to the question of the general content of *ius cogens*, it is worth considering that the reasoning that justifies the qualification of nondiscrimination as *ius cogens* applies with equal force to the entire body of IHRL. Some jurists and publicists have indeed taken the position that the entire body of human rights law, or at least the UDHR, is *ius cogens.*[29] Such assertions are easy to make and hard to prove, but the reasons for wishing to develop a *ius cogens* that includes at least the most basic human rights is understandable. If any set of norms deserves special

27. Anatole France, Le lys rouge 117–18 (Calmann-Lévy ed., Paris, 1923) (1894).

28. *E.g., Juridical Condition and Rights of the Undocumented Migrants*, Advisory Opinion OC-18/03, Inter-American Court of Human Rights (ser. A) No. 18 (2003), paras. 100–01; Antônio Augusto Cançado Trindade, Jus Cogens: *The Determination and Gradual Expansion of Its Material Content in Contemporary International Case-Law*, 35 Curso de Derecho Internacional Organizado por el Comité Jurídico Interamericano 16–18 (Organization of American States, Washington, D.C. 2008); Ian Brownlie, Principles of Public International Law 513 & n.4 (3d ed. 1979); Egon Schwelb, *Some Aspects of International Jus Cogens as Formulated by the International Law Commission*, 61 Am. J. Int'l L. 946, 953, 956 (1967).

29. *See, e.g.*, Southwest Africa Cases, 1966 I.C.J. Rep. 298 (Judge Tanaka, dissenting); Karen Parker & Lyn Beth Neylon, Jus Cogens: *Compelling the Law of Human Rights*, 12 Hastings Int'l & Comp. L. Rev. 411 (1989).

supremacy over voluntary treaties and customary practice for ethical reasons, they must include the norms minimally necessary to preserve human dignity and the chance of flourishing. It does not follow, however, that *only* rules establishing individual entitlements deserve special supremacy, because equally important interests may not be individually claimable. This was the basis for my argument in Part I in favor of focusing on states duties in some cases.

Assuming *arguendo* that only some substantive human rights qualify as *ius cogens* and others do not (e.g., the right to paid holidays or the right against attacks on reputation), should the nondiscrimination right nonetheless be included among these privileged few? The Inter-American Court of Human Rights apparently thinks so. Its rationale is that equality before the law is "linked to the essential dignity of the individual" and "the whole legal structure of national and international public order rests on it and it is a fundamental principle that permeates all laws."[30] The Court might more properly have said that the nondiscrimination principle is essential for ensuring respect for the human dignity that grounds the whole legal structure of international public order, including (and most especially) IHRL. Yet, one might think that all human rights are essential for ensuring respect for human dignity, so that would leave no basis for giving special status to the nondiscrimination right. It seems to me that a state that censors the news, thereby intending to derogate from the obligation to respect free expression, or that refuses to assist starving children, thereby derogating from the obligation to provide sustenance, abridges human dignity and violates international law no less or more than if it selectively sought to deny women or a racial minority the right to vote.

It may be that, when a state violates a substantive human right selectively, discriminating against a specific group, it compounds the violation by disrespecting the target group, but I have never seen and cannot imagine a persuasive argument that, in a discriminatory denial of a fair trial, the discriminatory aspect is somehow *semper et ubique* worse than the denial of a fair trial in terms of its consequences for the individual claimant. The same point applies a fortiori with regard to independent nondiscrimination rights. These relate to equal treatment with regard to interests less pressing than substantive human rights, and so independent nondiscrimination rights generally carry less moral weight than a right to equal treatment with regard to substantive human rights.

4. Group Rights and Discrimination

Perhaps the strongest nexus between substantive rights and nondiscrimination rights is found in discussions about group rights. One of the fundamental motivating forces behind the international human rights movement was the desire among colonized peoples for independence and equal treatment. This impetus shaped human rights ideology by making both self-determination and nondiscrimination core features of the modern regime of international law. Self-determination is not an individual human right; it relates to a communal interest in freedom from outside interference. Individuals have no right to self-determination in the sense used in international law.

30. *Juridical Condition and Rights of the Undocumented Migrants*, Advisory Opinion OC-18/03, Inter-American Court of Human Rights (ser. A) No. 18 (2003), paras. 100–01.

It is the right of a "people" to choose its own political status. That interest is of course based on an individual human interest, specifically in participation in government and in cultural and community life for the formation and expression of one's identity, and for the enjoyment of the benefits of membership in a more or less cohesive group. But only a people as a collective entity may coherently claim the right.

Respecting the right to self-determination is mentioned in the U.N. Charter as one of the main purposes of the organization,[31] and it is referenced in both the CCPR and CESCR.[32] As the self-determination right illustrates, the concept of group rights does not necessarily relate to nondiscrimination. Nondiscrimination rights apply to arbitrary differences in treatment, which may or may not be based on membership in a cohesive group. A nondiscrimination right may be based on any perceived characteristic of an individual, whether physical or intellectual, as illustrated earlier through the examples of persons with disabilities and persons born out of marriage.

Nonetheless, group rights necessarily invoke differences between personal characteristics, whether social, cultural, physical, or geographical. A "people" in the special sense that term is used in IHRL is more than a set of persons with shared history and culture though. The group members must also identify themselves as belonging to a discrete and relatively cohesive organization. Membership in a "people" is a social-psychological phenomenon. In a society composed of persons having five different hair colors, or persons dressing in myriad ways, those persons with green hair or who wear hats are only a "group" if socially perceived as a distinct group. Typically, that means at least having a specific group name. Persons-with-green-hair and persons-who-like-to-wear-hats are not "groups" in this sense; "greenies" and "hatters" might be groups. The determination of whether someone is a "greeny" (e.g., someone who has teal-colored hair) or a "hatter" (e.g., someone who wears a head bandanna) is determined by shared subjectivities in the relevant society and not by any objective criteria.

Aksu v. Turkey illustrated some of the challenges of mapping group rights onto the nondiscrimination right in the European human rights system.[33] In *Aksu*, a Roma applicant claimed that government-funded publications about "gypsies" had defamed the Roma people in violation of the rights to freedom from discrimination (article 14 ECHR) and protection of his private life (article 8). On the substantive claim, the Court accepted in principle that stereotyping of a group could rise to a violation of article 8 by spreading negative views of the group and damaging its sense of identity and the self-worth and confidence of its members.[34] However, the Court rejected the applicant's article 14 claim, finding "that the case does not concern a difference in treatment, and in particular ethnic discrimination, as the applicant has not succeeded in producing *prima facie* evidence that the impugned publications had a discriminatory intent or effect."[35]

31. Charter of the United Nations arts. 1(2), 55, June 26, 1945, 59 Stat. 1031, 3 Bevans 1153.

32. CCPR art. 1; CESCR art. 1.

33. 56 E.H.R.R. 4 (2012).

34. *Id.* paras. 54, 58.

35. *Id.* para. 45.

The Strasbourg Court's treatment of the applicant's nondiscrimination claim is unexpected. The applicant had accused the Turkish Ministry of Culture of spreading negative stereotypes about a group to which the applicant belongs. The most obvious conclusion is that, if the allegations were true, Turkey had engaged in discrimination based on ethnicity by spreading negative stereotypes of a vulnerable group in violation of article 14. Instead, the Court held that a publication "allegedly affecting the identity of a group to which the applicant belonged" thereby harmed his private life, in the sense of his sense of self-worth and social identity.[36] In other words:

> [A]ny negative stereotyping of a group, when it reaches a certain level, is capable of impacting on [*sic*] the group's sense of identity and the feelings of self-worth and self-confidence of members of the group. It is in this sense that it can be seen as affecting the private life of members of the group.[37]

To arrive at that conclusion, the Court made a strange assumption. Because the Court's decision was not based on discrimination, it had to adopt the position that the wrongful act was Turkey's failure to protect the privacy (in the sense of the reputation) of the group by not suppressing the offending publication. Hence, the Court referred to "the group's sense of identity" rather than each group member's sense of identity by reason of his or her affiliation with the group.

There are two problems with the Court's approach. First, it is unclear how a group can have a privacy interest in its reputation. The Roma are not a corporate community; they are individuals sharing a common characteristic (Roma ethnicity, culture, and language). The Roma as a "group" cannot have an interest in social position, reputation, or self-respect; individual persons of Roma (or any other) ethnicity, however, have an interest in not being devalued due to their membership in that group. Indeed, if groups did have corporate privacy rights, then it would be conceivable that the group's right to privacy could in some circumstances trump an individual group member's right to privacy, which runs contrary to the very idea and purpose of individual human rights.

Second and related, even if a group could have an interest in maintaining its own reputation, the legal basis on which the Strasbourg Court is authorized to protect a group's reputation is unclear. The ECHR includes no mandate to maintain the social status or self-esteem of groups as corporate entities. There is a European Framework Convention for the Protection of National Minorities, but its provisions primarily apply to individual rights to equal treatment and protection and promotion of the individual's cultural or ethnic identity, not to group interests per se, and in any case Turkey was not a party to that Convention.

The Court could instead have based this part of its reasoning on the more straightforward premise that a government-sponsored publication portraying negative stereotypes about a group thereby discriminates against each group member by degrading (or trying to degrade) his social standing based on his identity as a group member. Discrimination against the group directly affects the privacy rights

36. *Id.* para. 60.

37. *Id.* para. 58.

of group members; it does not affect the privacy of the group and, through the group derivatively, its members.

Recognizing the intermediation of the group was still necessary, but not because the group has a right at stake. If the group as such has no human right to privacy, the individual group member's right to privacy can nonetheless be offended by an attack on the member's association with, or characteristics shared with, the group. Individuals cannot be stereotyped; only a group can be stereotyped. Individuals suffer harm by association with a group that has been negatively stereotyped. It follows that the Court erred in holding that the propagation of a negative stereotype about a group was not discrimination. By definition, a stereotype rests on a distinction made between the group and other groups or the rest of society, when that distinction attributes certain characteristics (in this case, offensive characteristics) only or disproportionately to the group targeted.

A different claim is that groups, because of their cohesion, merit special consideration not available to persons sharing common characteristics. This claim may take either of two forms. The first is that some groups have important cohesive social functions that give every member of the group a greater interest in ensuring that the interests of other group members are taken into account in public policy decisions.[38] No doubt this observation is empirically accurate for some kinds of groups, but it is irrelevant to international human rights law analysis. If human rights are universal, then everyone everywhere has an interest in the rights of others being enjoyed, and any derivative rights should be universal as well. Even if *A1* has a greater interest than *B* in ensuring that *A2*'s interests are advanced, it does not follow that *A1* and *A2* have a collective right to something unavailable to *B*. An interest in another person's rights or interests might give rise to a *procedural* right to intervene for the protection of that other person's rights or interests (*ius standi*), but it does not necessarily create new substantive rights or change the nature of the nondiscrimination right.

The second argument is that, insofar as group membership benefits its members, group members have a collective interest in preserving the group through special rights designed to maintain these benefits. No one member of the group may have an interest sufficiently strong to justify granting special benefits to the group, but the aggregate of interests of the group may justify conferring a right on the group as a whole. In Joseph Raz's explanation:

> A collective right exists when the following three conditions are met. First, it exists because an aspect of the interest of human beings justifies holding some person(s) to be subject to a duty. Second, the interests in question are the interests of individuals as members of a group in a public good and the right is a right to that public good because it serves their interest as members of the group. Thirdly, the interest of no single member of that group in that public good is sufficient by itself to justify holding another person to be subject to a duty.[39]

38. *See* David Miller, *Group Rights, Human Rights and Citizenship*, 10 Eur. J. Philos. 178, 179 (2002).

39. *See* Joseph Raz, The Morality of Freedom 208 (1986).

Raz's view seems to find confirmation in some nonbinding U.N. declarations. For example, the preamble to the U.N. Declaration on the Rights of Indigenous Peoples purports to "recogniz[e] and reaffirm[] that . . . indigenous peoples possess collective rights which are indispensable for their existence, well-being and integral development as peoples."[40] These include "the right to self-determination. By virtue of that right they freely determine their political status and freely pursue their economic, social and cultural development."[41] The right of "peoples" to self-determination is promoted elsewhere as well.[42] The U.N. Declaration on the Rights of Persons Belonging to National or Ethnic, Religious and Linguistic Minorities proclaims state duties to protect the interests of minority groups without establishing individual rights in some articles. Article 1, for example, would obligate the state to "protect the existence and the national or ethnic, cultural, religious and linguistic identity of minorities within their respective territories and shall encourage conditions for the promotion of that identity."[43] Article 4 would require states to

> take measures to create favourable conditions to enable persons belonging to minorities to express their characteristics and to develop their culture, language, religion, traditions and customs, except where specific practices are in violation of national law and contrary to international standards.[44]

The phrasing is unfortunate; no individual could have a moral right to the "development" of the culture, language, or religion to which he belongs. Development means change over time, and it is difficult to see how a person can have an interest in the change over time per se of a social institution, unless the institution itself is *against* that person's interests. For example, it is easy to see how women have an interest in the "development" of atavistic cultural or religious practices that deny them equal treatment. Change of a beneficial institution, in contrast, could be neutral or go either way. It could promote their individual interests or harm them.

Of course, many persons believe they have an interest in the *continuation* of their culture. Perhaps that is what the General Assembly really meant by "development." More accurately, perhaps development of a culture means its adaptation to changing circumstances to ensure the survival of its basic institutions and practices. Suppose we amended the declaration to make this more acceptable assertion. Can a person have a right to a continuation of his culture? If so, group members could argue for imposing a positive duty on the state to help group members protect traditional practices from social or technological changes.

The problem with this argument is that it implies a group right to reverse discrimination even in the absence of a group history of suffering discrimination. The 1972 U.S. Supreme Court case *Wisconsin v. Yoder* illustrates a problem with

40. G.A. Res. 61/295, pmbl. (2007).

41. *Id.* art. 3.

42. CCPR art. 1; CESCR art. 1.

43. G.A. Res. 47/135, Annex, art. 1 (1992).

44. *Id.* art. 4(2).

this reasoning. In that case, the Court held that the group religious rights of the minority Amish population in the United States entitled the group to deprive their children of mandatory secular education after age fourteen.[45] The Court considered that the right of the children to education must yield to the *group* right to religious exercise. Although the Court emphasized the importance of religious conviction to its holding,[46] the group aspect of the holding was crucial to its reasoning. The Court continually emphasized the Amish "way of life," "church-oriented community," and "Amish faith community" in justifying giving the Amish special latitude in determining the education of their children.

Allowing special rights for minority groups in this manner privileges the interests of parents in perpetuating their culture over what might be the individual interests of their children (in the case of *Yoder*, to education and exposure to diverse viewpoints).[47] It also puts members of the (here, non-Amish) majority at a comparative disadvantage. Persons who are not members of a communal religious order who wish to educate their children in a manner contrary to state education laws for secular reasons, for example, are forbidden to do so merely because their conviction does not stem from mystical beliefs shared by a group. The problem with the *Yoder* decision was not necessarily its outcome; it was its failure to analyze these two consequences of the decision: potential impairment of the individual interests of the children, and the arguable unfairness of giving special rights to one group of parents on the basis of religious beliefs rather than other, perhaps more empirically based, heartfelt convictions. The lesson here is that the recognition of group rights frequently tends to imperil individual interests and rights of potentially equal or greater weight.

It may be possible nonetheless that some moral rights cannot fit comfortably within an individual rights paradigm, as Raz suggests, and should be protected as collective rights. However, it is difficult to imagine a good of the kind Raz describes that cannot be accommodated by an individual legal right. Self-determination—his own example—may be broken down into conventional individual rights, such as the right to own property, to participate in government, and to form associations. It is true that an individual cannot meaningfully exercise a group right to self-determination, but if all individual human rights are observed, a cohesive group will be able to exercise de facto self-determination for most relevant purposes. Similarly, it is certainly the case that the right to practice one's own culture, language, or religion is a meaningful right only in a group context, but there is no need for a separate group cultural right as long as the individual rights to freedom of conscience, expression, and association are protected, as they are in IHRL.[48] The CCPR and CESCR, for example, make such rights explicitly individual. CCPR article 27 provides:

> In those States in which ethnic, religious or linguistic minorities exist, *persons* belonging to such minorities shall not be denied the right, *in community with*

45. Wisconsin v. Yoder, 406 U.S. 205 (1972).

46. *Id.* at 215.

47. *Id.* at 241 (Douglas, J., dissenting).

48. UDHR arts. 18–20, 27; CCPR arts. 18–19, 21–22, 27.

> *the other members of their group*, to enjoy their own culture, to profess and practise their own religion, or to use their own language.[49]

CESCR article 15 also states in relevant part: "The States Parties to the present Covenant recognize the *right of everyone*: (a) To take part in cultural life . . . ."[50] These provisions reflect a recognition that individual group members have interests in such matters sufficient to justify some degree of group autonomy. As noted, the Council of Europe in 1995 concluded a Framework Convention for the Protection of National Minorities that purports to establish protections for "national minorities" while shrewdly refraining from defining that key term. The Convention asserts that the protection of such minorities "forms an integral part of the international protection of human rights,"[51] but treats such rights mainly as individual rights rather than group rights.

Of course, these individual rights will not necessarily protect subgroups of society from assimilation or even extinction, but when individual interests do not aggregate to protect cultural cohesiveness and continuation, we might naturally ask on what basis we should continue to preserve the culture. There may be a cogent answer, but it is not enough simply to assume that, because some individuals have some interest in the preservation of group cohesion and continuation of its traditional practices, those interests should prevail over contrary individual or society-wide interests. Minority groups that deny individuals the right to speak a majority language in order to preserve the minority language, for example, make sense only if the individual has a right to exit the group and freely speak whatever language he or she wishes. As Michael Reisman has noted, "The rights of group formation and the tolerated authority of group elites over their members extend insofar as they are indispensable for the achievement of individual rights. They cannot be justified if their effect is to abridge or limit basic individual rights."[52] Deviations from individual rights do not themselves deny the right of association; they require the group to adjust its practices. The goals of preventing discrimination against group members and promoting their interests as group members cannot justify derogating from the individual substantive rights of these same group members.

B. LEGAL IMPLICATIONS AND SYSTEMIC CONSEQUENCES OF THE CHOICE OF PARADIGMS

As discussed earlier, some kinds of human rights claims fit squarely within only one paradigm. In the unusual case that a human rights violation affects an entire population relatively uniformly, a discrimination claim will be untenable. Pervasive air pollution that affects all residents of the state does not implicate discrimination;

49. CCPR art. 27 (emphasis added).

50. CESCR art. 15(1) (emphasis added).

51. Framework Convention for the Protection of National Minorities art. 1, Feb. 1, 1995, 2152 U.N.T.S. 243.

52. W. Michael Reisman, *Autonomy, Interdependence, and Responsibility*, 103 YALE L.J. 401, 416 (1993).

all human beings have to breathe. The very young, very old, and persons suffering from lung ailments may be affected disproportionately, but it would be difficult to make out a persuasive claim that they are the victims of discrimination, for several reasons. Most obviously, the differential effect of air pollution on different groups cannot result from intentional discrimination. Although a government may tolerate toxic levels of air pollution, none intends for it to cause harm. Air pollution is not a state measure itself; it is an externality resulting from state measures pursuing pathological public policies. But more important, the costs and difficulties of mitigating air pollution undermine the argument that pollution control measures are a proportionate response to discrimination against those particularly vulnerable to it. The claim that toxic levels of pollution violate the substantive rights to health and a healthy environment of the population as a whole has greater appeal. Also as discussed, the converse applies as well. A violation of an independent nondiscrimination right or equal protection right need not violate a substantive human right. As noted earlier, though, such cases are unusual; most human rights violations could be framed under either nondiscrimination or substantive rights paradigm.

A human rights authority facing a choice between applying one or the other paradigm will find that it affects more than the strength of the claimant's case. Decisions systematically favoring a particular paradigm, or that employ both paradigms in tandem, cumulate to influence not only human rights doctrine and the structure of the IHRL system, but the very political culture of the society they affect. This section will analyze the consequences of choosing one paradigm over the other when claiming a human rights violation. It then will explore how the two paradigms may complement each other to afford broader protection to the dignity interests at stake.

1. The Substantive Rights Claiming Paradigm

The choice of relying on a substantive rights claim has several important consequences. Except in the unusual case that a claim falls squarely and obviously within the scope of a right, the evaluation of a substantive right violation claim will require the human rights authority to define and interpret the right to ascertain whether the claim properly asserts a violation. In other words, the analysis of a substantive right violation frequently calls on the human rights authority to delimit the right's boundaries and thereby develop IHRL doctrine for that specific right. For example, suppose a state denies a person accused of a crime the right to depose or interview the victim—the sole witness in the case—prior to trial in order to determine what he will say in his courtroom testimony.[53] Article 14(3)(e) of the CCPR provides for the right of the accused to "examine, or have examined, the witnesses against him and to obtain the attendance and examination of witnesses on his behalf under the same conditions as witnesses against him." In determining whether the state has violated article 14 of the CCPR, a human rights tribunal or other authority will have to decide whether the right to examine a witness includes the right to know before trial what the witness intends to claim, or whether the right to an in-trial

53. This is in fact the case in some U.S. states. *See, e.g.*, ARIZ. CONST. art. II, sec. 2.1; ARIZ. REV. STAT. § 13-4433(B) (2013); CAL. CONST. art. I, sec. 28(b)(5) (2016).

confrontation without preparation to refute inaccurate or false testimony suffices as an "examination."

Because substantive rights correlate to the minimum duties that the state must fulfill, finding a substantive right violation frequently implies that the state must expand the sphere of liberties or the benefits to which the public is entitled. A state measure invalidated for violating a substantive freedom leaves previously forbidden behavior unregulated, unless and until the state can reformulate its regulations to give due protection to the offended right.[54] Consequently, substantive freedom rights tend to ratchet down state regulation, and substantive positive rights to benefits ratchet up state regulation. The sphere of freedom or the benefits granted to the population potentially affect everyone. "Potentially," however, is a key qualifier here.

Discrimination claims obviously do not require an interpretation of the scope of any right if the claim relates to unequal treatment in the distribution of resources to which the claimant has no plausible human right, or the imposition of burdens from which the claimant has no plausible human right to claim exemption. But even when a discrimination claim does implicate a human right, it is frequently unnecessary to interpret the scope of a substantive right, because a denial of equal treatment in matters *relating* to substantive rights may qualify as discrimination even if the right itself is not violated. As I observed earlier, an institutional advantage of substantive right claims is that they may help to clarify the meaning and scope of the right in a way that a nondiscrimination claim might not.

For example, suppose a state grants mortgage subsidies to persons of a race *R* who buy homes or rent in area *A*, but not to persons of other races in that area. Article 12(1) of the CCPR provides: "*Everyone* lawfully within the territory of a State shall, within that territory, have the right to liberty of movement and freedom to choose his residence." It would be difficult to argue that a person not of race *R* who wishes to live in area *A* is being denied the freedom to choose his residence by the subsidy; the state itself is imposing no direct obstacle to the claimant.[55] Nor can the claimant argue that he has a human right to the subsidy per se. As the previous discussion explained, the claimant has an article 26 equal protection argument, because that provision has been interpreted not to require a violation of a substantive human right. Nonetheless, a human rights authority would be justified in finding the state in violation of the article 2 nondiscrimination right without the need for interpreting article 12(1) to confer either a right to subsidized housing or an absolute right to choose a place of residence regardless of ability to pay. The state measure may not infringe a substantive human right, but it seriously compromises the ability of the claimant to enjoy that right on equal terms, and so invoking the nondiscrimination

54. *Cf.* Railway Express Agency, Inc. v. New York, 336 U.S. 112 (1949) (Jackson, J., concurring) ("Invalidation of a statute or an ordinance on [substantive liberty right] grounds leaves ungoverned and ungovernable conduct which many people find objectionable. Invocation of the equal protection clause, on the other hand, does not disable any governmental body from dealing with the subject at hand. It merely means that the prohibition or regulation must have a broader impact.").

55. There is, of course, an indirect obstacle, insofar as the subsidy drives up housing prices in area *A*, and thereby makes it more difficult or impossible for persons not of race *R* to buy homes or rent in area *A*.

paradigm allows the claimant to vindicate his interest without the need for a problematically aggressive interpretation of article 12(1).

Another significant consequence of framing a claim in substantive terms is that such claims tend to emphasize the public effect of a state measure on society in general as much as on the claimant or a specific class of persons to which the claimant belongs, because rarely do human rights violations result from state measures that affect an isolated individual only. When a person complains of a substantive right violation, it usually indicates a measure generally not in conformity to the state's IHRL obligations. It is of course possible that a state would suppress the free speech of only one person or fail to investigate one isolated crime in the absence of any more general pattern of misconduct. But problems on an international scale arise only when the state suppresses a whole class of speech or speakers, or engages in a routine practice of neglecting criminal investigations by the police or against certain classes of victims. To assert that the state has violated a substantive human right of one person tends strongly to imply that the state is deficient with respect to society at large, or some significant segment of it. The substantive rights paradigm, then, represents a general indictment of the state's treatment of those under its jurisdiction. A human rights remedy imposed on the state is accordingly intended to benefit society as a whole as a class of actual or potential victims of the nonconforming state measure. Although only a single claimant may recover compensatory damages, once the measure has been found nonconforming by an authoritative decision process, the human rights authority has set a precedent for future claims by others adversely affected by the measure, and a law-abiding state may be expected to amend the impugned practice.

A rising tide lifts all boats, but such remedies do not necessarily affect all right holders equally. The concomitant of this aspect of substantive rights claims is that remedies for substantive violations tend to apply across society and ignore the unequal effects of a state measure. In practice, any given state measure will tend to affect different classes of persons differently. By their nature, state measures of general applicability can never totally avoid inflicting different kinds and amounts of harm and benefit on different groups of society. Even a state measure intended to be universal or neutral in application will generally affect politically and economically powerless groups or other vulnerable segments of society differently. Substantive rights claims do not always vindicate the interests of the groups most harmed by the impugned measure. If a measure's application is *generally* reasonable and nondiscriminatory, then the measure will not normally be considered to violate a substantive right, even though some groups of individuals may suffer disproportionately and indeed unreasonably from the measure.

In the absence of a discrimination claim, then, a certain paradox arises. An unpopular group, the members of whom suffer disproportionate effects on their rights due to a state measure, might have more success in challenging the measure based on the (lesser but significant) harm that the measure inflicts or could inflict on the majority. For example, anti-blasphemy laws discriminate against atheists and members of minority religions by criminalizing the open discussion of the religious precepts accepted by representatives for the majority religion. But such laws also silence religious discussion, investigation, and dissent by believers in that majority religion. Similarly, anti-sodomy laws affect homosexuals more than heterosexuals, but anti-sodomy laws could be challenged for impinging on the private sex lives of heterosexuals as well. A claim on behalf of the dissenting majority in each case will sometimes succeed more readily than a claim on behalf of the minority.

One consequent advantage of focusing attention on substantive rights is that it tends not to disadvantage unpopular groups by triggering the biases and stereotypes of human rights authorities. In many countries, the legal elites that interpret and enforce human rights laws are drawn mainly from a limited pool of candidates. These candidates will tend to share certain characteristics that distinguish them from those most likely to be subjected to discriminatory measures, or those who benefit least or suffer most from neutral measures having differential effects on different groups. National human rights decision-makers such as judges and government officials tend to be wealthy, educated, politically connected, male professionals drawn from the majority race and religion. Sometimes this tendency is overwhelming. The socially and economically independent, and relatively politically powerful, professionals who staff government agencies and courts are susceptible to few sources of social control as potent as the state. Their perspectives about social control are accordingly biased by their personal independence and ability to exert social control in their turn over others. For them, the state—and especially a populist state—is the most effective actor among a relatively small universe of actors who could exercise decisive control over them. Demographically, these elites are maximally unrepresentative of the most vulnerable groups in society. Many accordingly view the state as the sole important threat to human rights based on self-interest, rationalized post hoc, rather than on reasoned analysis based on empirical evidence. Unless they happen to be exceptionally enlightened, insightful, impartial, and self-examining, their willingness and ability to see through the eyes of the underprivileged or socially unpopular, and to understand and counteract their own biases and stereotyping cognition, will be limited. The paradox, then, is that vulnerable and unpopular groups may find more success in appealing to the universal effects of a state measure than its particular effects on the group itself, even though these may be much more severe and burdensome.

2. The Discrimination Claiming Paradigm

In contrast to substantive rights claims, discrimination claims emphasize the social, economic, and political inequalities in the society. Facts demonstrating these inequalities buttress any discrimination claim against groups shown to be harmed unequally by a measure. The stronger the showing of inequalities in power and resources between the group and society in general, the more solicitous an unbiased human rights authority will tend to be toward that group, and the less weight that authority should attribute to the measure's beneficial effects on society in general. This observation follows Rawl's maximin principle,[56] but it does not dictate the outcome of discrimination analysis so much as provide one weighty factor in that analysis. Another factor, mentioned earlier, is the extent to which a measure distinguishes between groups based on identity and involuntary characteristics.

It follows that remedies for discrimination claims will tend to equalize treatment between different segments of society without necessarily improving conditions in society generally. Although the invalidation of a discriminatory state measure may

56. John Rawls, A Theory of Justice 328 (1971) ("The basic structure is just throughout when the advantages of the more fortunate promote the well-being of the least fortunate, that

have the same liberty- or benefit-enhancing effect as the invalidation of a measure on substantive grounds, benefits may be granted in a differential manner. There may be no rising tide, only a leveling of state treatment. Indeed, it is possible for the invalidation of discriminatory measure to deprive some groups of benefits that they would otherwise receive, thus "leveling down" the benefits granted by the state.[57] For example, it would be difficult to invalidate an affirmative action program benefiting a historically disadvantaged group as violating some person's substantive rights, but it is entirely possible to invalidate the same program as discriminating against members of other groups. The invalidation of the program deprives the disadvantaged group of a benefit otherwise available. In consequence, nondiscrimination remedies do not necessarily enhance the benefits of IHRL for society generally in the same way that substantive rights remedies tend to do.

The universal nature of substantive rights claims has led some to endorse the substantive rights paradigm as in some ways superior to a nondiscrimination paradigm. For example, Kenji Yoshino has argued that protecting substantive rights "stresses the interests we have in common as human beings rather than the demographic differences that drive us apart. . . . [I]t is less likely to essentialize identity."[58] Yoshino seems to present a tautology—by definition, a nondiscrimination claim points to the ways in which different groups or classes of conduct are treated differently. But his conclusion misapprehends the logic of discrimination claims. A claimant does not demand equal treatment because of his or her demographic differences from societal majorities. By pointing out a harmful difference in treatment, a nondiscrimination claim effectively insists that the claimant or the claimant's group is *not* relevantly different from others who receive superior treatment. Sometimes, others in society "essentialize" a person's identity for him by stereotyping persons who share certain of his characteristics. In such a case, the victim of discrimination may merely be demanding recognition of an alleged preexisting fact of state or social discrimination or classification. He does not necessarily recognize it, or its relevance, on his own part. For the reasons discussed earlier, the social perception of difference becomes invisible in the course of analyzing a substantive rights claim in a way it would not through the lens of the nondiscrimination paradigm.

In short, the essentialization of identity and consequent group cohesion may be consequences of discrimination as well as causes. They could easily evaporate as the fact of discrimination diminishes. Drawing attention to the discrimination may be functional and constructive. We would fully expect members of a privileged group to resist such claims as divisive. But this would be merely a rhetorical attempt to sublimate a power struggle between more and less privileged groups by denying the status of the latter as a group at all. The more privileged group thus hopes to put the less privileged group into a catch-22. If the discriminatory measure at issue undermines the group interest by disadvantaging the group, then by denying the separateness and difference of the group and treating society as a homogenous entity,

is, when a decrease in their advantages would make the least fortunate even worse off than they are. The basic structure is perfectly just when the prospects of the least fortunate are as great as they can be.").

57. For a discussion of this point in the civil rights context, see Kenji Yoshino, *The New Equal Protection*, 124 Harv. L. Rev. 747, 787 (2011).

58. *Id.* at 793, 795–97.

we merely ignore the fact of discrimination. It does not disappear. The illusion of homogeneity makes discrimination easier.

The illusion is insidious, because homogeneity in state measures is the rule in no society. As noted, even superficially neutral measures will tend to affect different groups differently, and disempowered groups will frequently benefit least from formally neutral beneficial measures and be harmed most by neutral impositions. Flat taxes, for example, benefit disproportionately those with the most disposable income; draconian criminal penalties for street drug crimes tend to fall most heavily on drug users, who are predominantly poor; and advanced educational classes for high-performing students are less likely to benefit students from broken homes or who have uneducated parents. In those societies with serious disparities in wealth and political power between groups based on race, ethnicity, sex, or other identity characteristics, the effects on poorer groups of such seemingly neutral measures exacerbate social divisions. It is usually precisely *because* political and economic elites are unaware of, apathetic about, or the positive beneficiaries of existing social inequalities that human rights authorities cannot afford to ignore group differences in nondiscrimination analysis.

Because most lists of prohibited grounds for discrimination are open, and many international human rights instruments include independent nondiscrimination clauses or equal protection clauses, international human rights authorities face the possibility of diverse challenges to state measures and private acts of distinction based on grounds not specifically included in a treaty list. The result is that, in such societies, a very wide variety of formally neutral state measures become susceptible to characterization as discriminatory. In theory, any credible claim of discrimination could potentially justify human rights authorities in reviewing and evaluating the legitimacy and appropriateness of virtually any state measure, and (except in the United States) nondiscriminatory intent is no defense. In the NBC television series *The Office*, white male sales representative Dwight Shrute tries to convince a representative of his employer to let him participate in an executive training program reserved for minorities:

> GABE: This is Print in All Colors, Sabre's Minority Executive Training Program.
>
> . . .
>
> DWIGHT: How do I apply?
>
> GABE: You have to be a minority.
>
> DWIGHT: Uh, glasses wearers? Cholera survivors? Geniuses? Non-organic family farmers? The list goes on and on, you want me to keep going?
>
> GABE: Those really don't count. We're thinking more, ethnic and racial minorities.[59]

The fictitious exchange illustrates a potential hazard of discrimination analysis that does not arise in the substantive rights context. The nature of human rights analysis theoretically allows the decision authority to substitute its judgment about the legitimacy, wisdom, fairness, and precision of a measure for the state's own judgment. The relativism of the nondiscrimination right, which makes it so valuable as a bulwark against arbitrary state action, could provoke the proliferation of human rights claims based on a minute examination of differences in the social, political,

59. *The Office, Season Six: Body Language* (NBC television broadcast, Apr. 29, 2010).

and economic advantages enjoyed by various groups. The very decision to engage the questions required in discrimination analysis challenges the state's authority and judgment, raising potential separation-of-powers concerns.[60]

Some distinctions will obviously fall at the extremes of necessary (e.g., protecting the environment from serious harms) and proportionate (e.g., offering modest subsidies to prosocial acts), and sail through a human rights law analysis. Others will prove transparently unnecessary (e.g., discouraging harmless nonconformist behavior) and disproportionate (e.g., using severe criminal punishment when a modest fine would suffice), and a successful human rights challenge may be expected. Most public policies fall somewhere between the extremes, and human rights authorities may wade into deep subjectivity when evaluating the necessity or legitimacy of a state measure that falls close to the middle of the range. The subjectivity of, and factual complexity underlying, such judgments assume heightened sensitivity when the state regulates private behavior. Although such judgments may be necessary for substantive rights claims as well, substantive rights are conceptually bounded by their subject matter, whereas a nondiscrimination right, and an equal protection right especially, is not. If abused, an unbounded nondiscrimination right poses significant risks to the stability of the public order.

The fear of such open prohibitions led U.S. Supreme Court Justice Rehnquist to inveigh against a broad nondiscrimination doctrine protecting disadvantaged or vulnerable groups:

> It would hardly take extraordinary ingenuity for a lawyer to find "insular and discrete" minorities at every turn of the road. Yet, unless the Court can precisely define and constitutionally justify both the terms and analysis it uses, these decisions today stand for the proposition that the Court can choose a "minority" it "feels" deserves "solicitude" and thereafter prohibit the States from classifying that "minority" different from the "majority."[61]

Justice Rehnquist's analysis is not especially discerning, however. No state or human rights authority could hope to implement any prohibition on arbitrary distinctions without setting up criteria for more and less persuasive grounds. Applicants before the European Court of Human Rights or the Inter-American Court of Human Rights have usually relied on well-established grounds for challenging the nondiscrimination right; slippery slope arguments pose a challenge to the open right that is no more persuasive than in other contexts. What Justice Rehnquist's invective against the judicial recognition of pervasive state and societal discrimination does illuminate, though, are his commitments as a member of a dominant and privileged race, sex, class, and profession in his country.[62] It illustrates the point

60. *See* Olivier de Schutter, *Le concept de discrimination dans la jurisprudence de la Cour de Justice des Communautés Européennes (égalité de traitement et liberté de circulation)*, *in* Union Européenne et nationalités 11, 14, 29 (Emmanuelle Bribosia et al. eds., 1999).

61. Sugarman v. Dougall, 413 U.S. 634, 657 (1975) (Rehnquist, J., dissenting).

62. The late William Rehnquist, like most U.S. Supreme Court justices, was a white male Protestant professional lawyer from a wealthy family. *See* John A. Jenkins, The Partisan: The Life of William Rehnquist (2012).

made earlier about the difficulty to the average legal or political elite of breaking free from the biases and stereotypes inculcated or motivated by his or her distinct demographic background, and supplies a strong practical reason for favoring the substantive rights paradigm, weak as any conceptual objection may be.

Nonetheless, there is a mote of truth in Rehnquist's analysis: as observed earlier, a broadly framed nondiscrimination right could in theory become a "super-right" that opens the door to a very wide variety of claims of questionable value. The Strasbourg Court furnished an example of the perils of an aggressive construction of the nondiscrimination right in *Thlimmenos v. Greece*, in which the applicant had been denied a license to practice accounting because of a prior criminal conviction.[63] The conviction had resulted from his refusal to contribute military service based on his beliefs as a Jehovah's Witness. The applicant could not claim that he had suffered from discrimination, because all persons convicted of "serious crimes" were denied the right to practice the accounting profession. Nonetheless, the Strasbourg Court considered that the state measure had no relation to the objective of protecting the public from dishonest accountants. "[A] conviction for refusing on religious or philosophical grounds to wear the military uniform," the Court observed, "cannot imply any dishonesty or moral turpitude likely to undermine the offender's ability to exercise this profession."[64]

The step from judging the state measure illogical to finding prohibited discrimination required conceiving of the nondiscrimination right, not merely as a right to equal treatment, but as a right not to be subjected to illogical state measures. This broader right implies the converse of equal treatment—a right to different treatment when equal treatment would be arbitrary: "the right not to be discriminated against in the enjoyment of the rights guaranteed by the Convention is also violated when States without an objective and reasonable justification fail to treat differently persons whose situations are significantly different."[65] Because persons convicted of a crime were barred from the profession of accounting regardless of whether the crime involved dishonesty or moral turpitude, the Court found the measure discriminatory.

In *Thlimmenos*, the Strasbourg Court broadened the concept of discrimination to encompass this super-right. Discrimination means unjustifiably treating like cases differently; the converse—failing to account for differences and distinguish accordingly—is not discrimination, but rather regulation with insufficient nuance. In the Court's conception, an overbroad law designed to regulate persons in Category A would "discriminate" against persons in Category B by lumping them together with persons in Category A rather than treating them equivalently to all other persons (such as unregulated persons in Category C).[66] But it would be

63. Thlimmenos v. Greece, 31 E.H.R.R. 15 (2001).

64. *Id.* para. 47.

65. *Id.* para. 44.

66. The CJEU has endorsed the Strasbourg Court's concept of discrimination as well. *See, e.g.*, Arcelor Atlantique et Lorraine & Others, Case C-127/07, 2008 E.C.R. I-9895, para. 23; Association Belge des Consommateurs Test-Achats ASBL v. Council of Ministers, Case C-236/09, 2011 E.C.R. I-00773, Judgment of Mar. 1, 2011, para. 28.

more accurate to say that the law is arbitrary in not distinguishing between persons in Category A and Category B. When the nondiscrimination right becomes a panacea against all forms of arbitrary state measures, it invites human rights authorities to assume the role of ombudsman for complaints against the rationality and ideal tailoring of municipal laws and measures.

A defender of a broad nondiscrimination right might point out that the proportionality test is well adapted to juridical analysis, because it calls on human rights authorities to examine the logic and evidence of the means chosen by the state to pursue its policy goals. Evaluating logic and evidence is something courts and commissions staffed with lawyers are well adapted to do. But questions about the measure's goal—what kinds of distinctions between classes of persons are "necessary" or "legitimate" in the first place—require nuanced policy analysis and almost always rely on subjective judgment about what strength of evidence should justify distinctions based on the ground at issue and how much overinclusion or underinclusion can be tolerated in a state measure. As discussed at length in Chapter 3, the evidence supporting a necessary or legitimate distinction between different groups will range in its correlation between the groups and the harm identified or benefit sought. There is no natural point at which a distinction always and for all groups goes from being unnecessary to necessary for any given public policy goal. No doubt the necessity of some distinctions is transparently implausible and serves only to mask an attempt to demean or disadvantage an unpopular group, or (as in *Thlimmenos*) has arbitrary effects that in no way serve the purpose of a legitimate measure. For many others, however, evaluating the legitimacy and proportionality of a measure call for some subjective judgment about the desirability of a state's policy goals and the acceptability of the inevitably arbitrary effects of the measure on some members of society.

To be clear, this is not the same as criticizing discrimination doctrine as antidemocratic or somehow subversive of state sovereignty. Some states do horrid things, and most states do some unjustifiable things, in the way of discrimination, and therefore an independent judgment about the legitimacy and wisdom of distinctions made by states cannot be considered uniformly bad if rendered with proper restraint. There is no special virtue in democratically enacted discriminatory legislation. There is virtue, however, in the relativistic nature of the nondiscrimination right, by which it can reach social problems that no substantive right could resolve effectively. To apply a nondiscrimination right, it is necessary to measure the treatment of the right holder against a baseline of the "normal" implementation of the right by the state. By virtue of its reliance on relativistic implementation, the nondiscrimination right can protect the beneficiary against a deprivation that would not otherwise rise to a violation of a substantive human right.

Moreover, as noted earlier, most international human rights authorities have adopted self-limiting techniques to reduce the potentially vast and politically intrusive power of the nondiscrimination right. Three such techniques were discussed. One is a relatively narrow interpretation of "other status" as prohibited grounds of discrimination. Human rights authorities have tended to dismiss claims of discrimination by any except vulnerable or disempowered groups, or when an identity characteristic, and especially an involuntary one, is at stake. One problem with the *Thlimmenos* judgment is that the Court made no effort to justify how "persons convicted of crimes not implicating moral turpitude" could be a status meriting protection from discrimination along these lines.

Another technique is implicit or explicit deference to close questions of state policy. The proportionality doctrine and especially the margin of appreciation used by the Strasbourg Court allow a great deal of deference, sometimes to a fault, in accepting a discriminatory state measure as consistent with the ECHR when no coherent reasons could justify it. However much deference is given, some amount surely will always be necessary to avoid unbounded judicial interference in legislated public policies. The U.S. Supreme Court made an especially strong articulation of this deference in a case in which a company that advertised by truck was found to violate a local law allowing such advertisements only on trucks that delivered the kinds of goods or services that were being advertised on the truck itself.[67] The petitioner's equal protection claim pointed out that, if advertising on trucks was considered to pose a danger of distraction to drivers and pedestrians, then it posed no less a danger on delivery trucks than on trucks devoted solely to advertising. To this, the Court replied by denying an ability to substitute its judgment for that of local regulatory authorities:

> The local authorities may well have concluded that those who advertised their own wares on their trucks do not present the same traffic problem in view of the nature or extent of the advertising which they use. It would take a degree of omniscience which we lack to say that such is not the case.... It is by such practical considerations based on experience rather than by theoretical inconsistencies that the question of equal protection is to be answered.... It is no requirement of equal protection that all evils of the same genus be eradicated or none at all.[68]

The Court's humility is exemplary, although its dismissal of "theoretical inconsistencies" was ill-considered; it would have been possible to reject the petitioner's equal protection claim on logic and common sense alone, combined with the recognition of some latitude for the state's judgments.[69]

A third technique of self-restraint, also used frequently by the Strasbourg Court, is to decide the case based on a substantive rights violation rather than a discrimination claim. Although the analysis of the legitimacy and proportionality of the state measure is formally the same, the focus of substantive rights, being on effects of the measure on society as a whole, dilutes the importance of effects on a group allegedly subjected to discrimination. For example, a prohibition on posting

67. Railway Express Agency v. New York, 336 U.S. 106 (1949).

68. *Id.* at 110.

69. There are a limited number of delivery trucks in any given city operating at any given time, but the number of trucks that could be deployed solely to advertise, further congesting the streets, creating air and noise pollution, and dangerously distracting drivers and pedestrians, is limited only by the economic incentives for such advertisements.

political placards on public streets disadvantages poorly endowed political candidates relative to well-funded candidates, who can afford to lease private space for their publicity. Viewed in terms of discrimination, the social problem may seem very great, as it will tend to preclude some candidates from promoting their political agenda and being elected to office. But viewed in terms of the substantive rights to freedom of speech and participation in government, the focus is not on the difference in treatment but on whether these rights should encompass the crowding of public spaces with advertisements for candidates who can attract little support from moneyed interests. The analysis is not tied to a difference in effect so much as the merits of the claims of the least advantaged persons weighed against other public policy considerations. Thus, in *Thlimmenos*, if the Court wished to find Greece in violation of the ECHR, it could have evaluated the consistency of the measure with the applicant's substantive rights, most obviously the right to freedom of religion or the right to work. By choosing a discrimination paradigm, the Court had to stretch nondiscrimination doctrine to accommodate the applicant's claim. Had it approached the claim with substantive rights in mind, it could have considered the more general questions of, first, the human rights implications for freedom of religion and conscience of the original criminal conviction, and second, the implications for the right to work of the denial of a professional license based on overbroad criteria.

C. COMPLEMENTARITY OF NONDISCRIMINATION AND SUBSTANTIVE RIGHTS CLAIMS

Thus far, I have highlighted the theoretical and practical differences in substantive rights and nondiscrimination rights as alternative paradigms for protecting community values. They operate in different ways, in one case by protecting interests considered universal, and in the other by redressing unequal treatment. But they do not reflect mutually exclusive philosophies about values; in each case, the aim is respect for human dignity and flourishing. Universal rights serve this aim by identifying the minimum legal conditions necessary for a dignified life. Nondiscrimination and equal protection rights serve the same aim by requiring states to respect the equal dignity of all human beings, especially by discouraging unfair measures and measures that reflect or reinforce stereotypes and prejudices that demean other groups because of characteristics that are morally irrelevant. The Inter-American Court of Human Rights has acknowledged this complementarity of substantive and nondiscrimination rights:

> There is an inseparable connection between the obligation to respect and guarantee human rights and the principle of equality and nondiscrimination. States are obliged to respect and guarantee the full and free exercise of rights and freedoms without any discrimination.[70]

70. *Juridical Condition and Rights of Undocumented Migrants*, Inter-Am. Ct. Hum. Rts., Advisory Opinion OC-18/03 of Sept. 17, 2003, at 95, para. 85.

Actually, the relationship between the two paradigms is more complex than the Inter-American Court represents. Because they serve the same basic purpose through very different approaches, they can be combined to extend legal protection synergistically beyond what either kind could accomplish alone. This potential may explain the inclusion of both substantive and nondiscrimination rights relating to the same subject matter in most international human rights instruments. The Universal Declaration and CCPR, for example, both separately protect freedom of religion and prohibit discrimination on the basis of religion.[71] Each paradigm can achieve a kind of social engineering that the other cannot, and so the adoption of both paradigms to serve a community value enhances the options available to human rights authorities for maximally protecting and fulfilling the value.

The manner in which the paradigms might complement each other is easy to illustrate. A state that monitors the telephone communications of all within its territory violates the right to privacy without discrimination. The nondiscrimination right simply does not work in protecting the privacy interest in that case. In contrast, a state that monitors only the telecommunications of persons whom an impartial judge, after reviewing relevant evidence, has determined are with high probability engaged in criminal activity would not seem to impinge on the universal privacy interest unduly, because the state's interest in preventing or punishing crime outweighs the individual's interest in committing crime without detection. If in executing the law, the state primarily monitors the telecommunications of suspected criminals who are members of the political opposition and ignores most of the others, the situation has not changed. The person whose criminal activities are detected because of his political stance has no more right to privacy than a person whose criminal activities are detected because of his clumsy criminal abilities. By definition, all persons have an equal interest in universal substantive rights. As for the state, its interest in detecting crime is no less when the criminal's politics oppose the government's than it does for those whose politics align with the government's. The case for a nondiscrimination claim in such a scenario is clear by the same logic that justifies the government's monitoring of its political opponents. If a person's political stance is irrelevant to the public interest in preventing and punishing crime, then discrimination against political opponents is ipso facto arbitrary. Here, the nondiscrimination right reaches an interest that the substantive right cannot.

This complementarity of nondiscrimination and substantive human rights is also evident in the tendency of different human rights authorities to treat similar human rights claims alternatively as violations of universal, substantive rights and as violations of rights against arbitrary discrimination. An instructive contrast is provided by the Strasbourg Court's decisions relating to the human rights of sexual minorities, which tend to be premised on violations of a substantive right—the ECHR article 8 right to privacy—whereas the U.N. Human Rights Committee has found similar state discrimination to violate articles 2(1) and 26 of the CPPR (relating to discrimination) rather than the article 17 right to privacy.[72] The Court

71. *See* UDHR arts. 2 (discrimination), 18 (freedom of religion); CPPR arts. 2 (discrimination), 18 (freedom of religion).

72. Aaron Xavier Fellmeth, *State Regulation of Sexuality in International Human Rights Law and Theory*, 50 Wm. & Mary L. Rev. 797, 802 n.4 (2008).

and Committee are respectively seeking to protect a sphere of human activity from harmful treatment by the state in each case, but the approaches and consequences differ.

More generally, because human rights claims require analyzing the intricacies of public policies that affect different groups differently, in considering such a claim, the human rights authority necessarily evaluates the role the state should play in regulating, restricting, or rewarding private activity in general and by what means the state may carry out that role. The exercise in each case is not fundamentally different, which may explain why human rights authorities apply the same basic requirements (legitimate aim and proportional means) and tests (necessary to serve a pressing need in a democratic society and both effective at serving and narrowly tailored to serve that need) to both substantive rights claims and discrimination claims. In other words, both substantive rights and nondiscrimination rights call upon the authority interpreting or enforcing the right to evaluate the measure in light of some political theory about the proper role of, requirements of, and limits on government action in a democracy. Nonetheless, nondiscrimination claims rely less on formulating a coherent political theory, because they can frequently be resolved by an analysis of which groups are similarly situated to others in logic or by empirical evidence.

PART THREE

Negative and Positive Human Rights

We have now reached the last set of paradigms. As some of the preceding discussion illustrates, among the most important and controversial questions affecting the scope and content of human rights is their framing in negative or positive terms.[1] The negative or positive framing of a right carries potentially weighty legal, political, ethical, and pragmatic consequences. The distribution of rights as negative or positive also has implications for the effectiveness of the human rights system as a whole. This distinction indeed lies at the crux of a continuing dispute about the proper role of human rights law in the world public order. Although nobody denies the necessity of negative rights, states and scholars disagree acutely on the desirability of extensive positive human rights. Many proponents of positive rights view them as morally necessary, a precondition for legitimate global and national governance.[2] Some view

1. It is important to distinguish the concepts of negative and positive "freedoms" or "liberties" with negative and positive rights. The former concepts, often attributed to Isaiah Berlin, may be described in Hohfeldian terms as a distinction between "privileges" and "immunities" (negative freedoms) on one hand and "claim-rights" (positive freedoms) on the other. *See* Isaiah Berlin, *Two Concepts of Liberty*, *in* ISAIAH BERLIN, FOUR ESSAYS ON LIBERTY (2002); Gerald C. Macallum, Jr., *Negative and Positive Freedom*, 76 PHIL. REV. 312 (1967). *Cf.* Wesley Newcomb Hohfeld, *Fundamental Legal Conceptions as Applied in Judicial Reasoning*, 23 YALE L.J. 16, 39, 47, 60 (1913). Negative and positive freedoms are commonly considered opposing concepts. In contrast, negative and positive rights in Hohfeldian terms are both claim-rights—a point that will be developed later in this Part. Rights and freedoms are interrelated, but for purposes of this discussion the conceptual distinction must be observed. A negative liberty, after all, can give rise to a positive right.

2. The UNESCO Committee on Theoretical Bases of Human Rights originally put special emphasis on the state's obligation to secure "positive liberties." UNESCO, HUMAN

them as flatly inevitable in any meaningful rights discourse. Opponents of positive rights typically view them as impractical at best, and at worst appointing a fox to guard the henhouse.

This Part explores the legal and policy implications of the decision to frame a right as negative or positive. In the course of that exploration, I will clarify some problems with how positive and negative rights are conceived in the dominant legal and philosophical discourses, and will illuminate some of the unnoticed consequences of framing choices. Chapter 5 begins with an overview of the conventional distinction between negative and positive rights, focusing especially on whether the distinction can be justified ontologically. It reveals how the perspective one adopts in ethical analysis colors one's perceptions of the character of negative and positive rights. It then expands on the discussion by analyzing the possibility that some rights are "basic" and therefore must be positive for the human rights system to function meaningfully.

Chapter 6 discusses the doctrinal consequences of alternative framing choices. It begins by analyzing the effects of negative or positive framing on the scope of the right, showing that, despite their names and the demonstration in Chapter 5 that negative and positive rights imply different kinds of duties, negative and positive rights are not opposites in any meaningful sense. I will then expand on this analysis by arguing that negative and positive rights are also non-redundant, and by demonstrating how negative and positive paradigms can be used together to enhance protection of a right. Finally, I will analyze the difficulties of interpreting rights that are ambiguous as to whether they correlate to negative or positive duties. The phrasing of international human rights treaties does not always lend itself to the easy classification of a right as negative or positive. "The right of freedom of expression shall not be abridged" is probably intended as a negative right, whereas "All persons shall enjoy freedom of expression" could be interpreted as establishing either a negative or positive right.

Chapter 7 discusses negative and positive paradigms in the broader context of the world public order. Framing a right as negative or positive affects not only the meaning and operation of the right, but it reflects a more fundamental choice of political theories about the role of the state and its relationship to protected individuals. This chapter is intended to illuminate how the choice of paradigms

RIGHTS: COMMENTS AND INTERPRETATIONS, App. II at 263 (1949). Since then, Amartya Sen has further developed the theme of deprivation as a limit on human capabilities and positive freedoms; *see generally* AMARTYA SEN, DEVELOPMENT AS FREEDOM (1999). However, there is a meaningful conceptual distinction between liberty as an ontological concept and the value that liberty has to a person. *See* JOHN RAWLS, A THEORY OF JUSTICE 204–05 (1971).

not only helps determine the scope and content of specific human rights, but the way that choice influences the effectiveness of the international human rights system as a whole. In the course of this discussion, I will address Thomas Pogge's argument that wealthy states, as beneficiaries of an unjust world public order, have a negative duty to renounce the benefits of that injustice and redistribute resources accordingly. Finally, Chapter 7 will explore the ethical implications of the previous arguments. A coherent definition of these rights demonstrates the poverty of ideological debates about whether and how international human rights law should encompass positive rights. If the goal of international human rights law is the protection and promotion of human dignity, I argue, then any minimally persuasive ethical theory must embrace positive rights. Whether states should be obligated to fulfill, or only to protect, any given right depends on the nature of the right in question as well as the most common source of threats to that right.

5

Are Negative and Positive Distinct and Meaningful Categories?

A. THE CONVENTIONAL DISTINCTION BETWEEN NEGATIVE AND POSITIVE RIGHTS

1. Common Definitions

It was established in Chapter 1 that every legal right entails a correlative legal duty,[1] and the meaning and scope of a right cannot be ascertained without understanding what this duty is and who bears it. A right "to" or "against" something has meaning only if it entitles the right holder to demand action on, or restraint respecting, the right by some identifiable person or persons. In that sense, a right is the basis for claiming action or inaction by another. Rights can be moral or legal, and both will be examined here, because moral human rights play a critical role in justifying legal human rights. The main purposes of this chapter are to analyze whether it is ontologically and pragmatically meaningful to frame a legal right in negative terms, and if so, whether there are certain categories of human rights that for ethical reasons should never be framed in purely negative terms.

Negative rights are usually considered to entail duties of self-restraint. In the context of international human rights law, a negative right is an entitlement not to be subjected to a specific kind of harmful action by the state. Negative rights are sometimes said to entail the state's duty to "respect" the right, meaning that the state and its agents will take no measure in derogation of the right.[2] However, a negative right imposes no duty on the state to prevent others from infringing the

1. This point was developed by Wesley Hohfeld, who organized a typology of concepts that are often referred to as "rights" but that differ significantly in their content. The kind of rights with which this discussion is primarily concerned are called in Hohfeldian terms "claim-rights," which differ from other so-called rights by entitling the right holder to demand the observation or fulfillment of the right by a corresponding duty holder. *See* Wesley Newcomb Hohfeld, *Fundamental Legal Conceptions as Applied in Judicial Reasoning*, 23 Yale L.J. 16, 31 (1913).

2. U.N. Committee on Economic, Social and Cultural Rights, General Comment No. 12: The Right to Adequate Food, para. 15, U.N. Doc. E/C.12/1999/5; *see SERAC v. Nigeria*, African Ct. Hum. & Peoples' Rts., Commun. No. 155/96, para. 45 (2001) [hereinafter *The Ogoniland Case*].

right, as this is commonly said to require "positive" action by the state. *Positive* rights, in contrast, are commonly considered to impose affirmative duties to act for the benefit of the right holder in the face of some exogenous threat. Such rights create a more participatory duty to assist the right holder to enjoy the right in the face of surmountable impediments. However, these simple definitions belie a great deal of confusion about the meaning of positive and negative in the human rights context among both lawyers and philosophers.

International human rights treaties do not explicitly dichotomize rights into negative and positive categories, but the distinction is commonly inferred from the phrasing of most rights. Provisions of treaties and other legal instruments that do no more than prohibit the state from acting in a specific manner epitomize the negative right. Article 9 of the Universal Declaration of Human Rights, for example, provides: "No one shall be subjected to arbitrary arrest, detention or exile."[3] At least superficially, article 9 imposes a mere duty of self-restraint; the state that arrests, detains, or exiles a person must restrain its officials and agents from acting arbitrarily. By itself, article 9 does not clearly require the state to protect anyone from arbitrary or unlawful detention by an individual or organization acting in a private capacity. For example, if private individual *X* kidnaps or falsely imprisons private individual *Y*, article 9 does not unambiguously state that *Y*'s human right to freedom from arbitrary detention has been violated.

Positive rights are conventionally thought to require the state to collect and allocate resources to ensure that the right may be realized throughout society. Article 22 of the Universal Declaration, for example, provides:

> Everyone, as a member of society, has the right to social security and is entitled to realization, through national effort and international co-operation and in accordance with the organization and resources of each State, of the economic, social and cultural rights indispensable for his dignity and the free development of his personality.[4]

Implicit in this constellation of rights is the state's duty to take measures to provide an economic safety net and to make facilities and resources available for the economic, social, and cultural flourishing of the state's citizens, regardless of whether the state government itself, or something else entirely, is the source of "social insecurity" or poses an obstacle to any person's dignity or development. In no conceivable scenario could the state satisfy article 22 by self-restraint; that provision provides for positive rights par excellence.

The U.N. Committee on Economic, Social, and Cultural Rights ("ECOSOC Committee") has further elaborated on the concept of positive rights by dividing the correlative duties into two classes: duties to "protect" and to "fulfill" the right.[5] A *duty to protect* requires the state to adopt measures to ensure that third

3. UDHR art. 9.

4. *Id.* art. 22.

5. U.N. Committee on Economic, Social and Cultural Rights, General Comment No. 12: The Right to Adequate Food, para. 15, U.N. Doc. E/C.12/1999/5. Not all human rights authorities follow the ECOSOC Committee's typology of positive rights. The European Court of Human Rights

parties—including private actors—do not interfere with the right holder's exercise of the right.[6] The state must not only restrain itself and its agents from obstructing the exercise of the right but must devote resources to the protection of the individual from depredations by others, including private individuals or organizations.[7] To execute these duties, the state may be obligated to adopt legislative, judicial, regulatory, or other enforcement and remedial measures to ensure observation of the right by private actors. It is well established that IHRL imposes duties on states to protect their nationals from violations of certain rights by others and to take positive measures to assist in the fulfillment of the basic conditions of subsistence and autonomy.[8] For example, the duty codified in article 4 of the CERD to prohibit and punish the public expression of "ideas based on racial superiority or hatred" by private individuals illustrates a positive duty to protect.[9] In particular, the CERD requires the state to adopt laws prohibiting racist speech, to hire police to investigate and apprehend violators, to set up agencies and courts to prosecute violators, and to implement sanctions to deter and punish violations.

The duty to protect is not usually construed as guaranteeing a specific result, such as absolute freedom from private violence; it is rather a procedural duty to take appropriate measures or to act with reasonable diligence to prevent, investigate, and punish private intrusions on the right.[10] Nonetheless, as the CERD article 4

usually uses the broad term "positive rights" without distinguishing between rights to protection and fulfillment. *See* Jean-François Akandji-Kombe, *Positive Obligations under the European Convention on Human Rights*, Council of Europe, Human Rights Handbook No. 7, at 5 (2007). However, in practice the Strasbourg Court's interpretation of the duties of Council of Europe member states frequently distinguishes, as it must, between the two kinds of positive rights.

6. *See The Ogoniland Case, supra* note 2, para. 46.

7. International human rights instruments sometimes impose direct, positive obligations on the state to take measures to protect human rights by modifying private behavior. Article 5 of the CEDAW furnishes an example:

> States Parties shall take all appropriate measures:
> (a) To modify the social and cultural patterns of conduct of men and women, with a view to achieving the elimination of prejudices and customary and all other practices which are based on the idea of the inferiority or the superiority of either of the sexes or on stereotyped roles for men and women . . . .

Convention on the Elimination of Discrimination against Women art. 5, G.A. Res. 34/180, 34 U.N. GAOR Supp. (No. 46) at 193, U.N. Doc. A/34/46, *entered into force* Sept. 3, 1981 [hereafter CEDAW].

8. *See, e.g.*, Peace Communities of San José de Apartadó v. Colombia, Inter-Am. Ct. Hum. Rts., Order of June 18, 2002, paras. 10–11, *available at* http://www.unhcr.org/refworld/docid/4268c86f4.html (holding that a party to the American Convention on Human Rights "is under the obligation, *erga omnes*, to protect all persons who are under its jurisdiction," including the duty "to adopt such security measures as are required for their protection.").

9. Convention on the Elimination of All Forms of Racial Discrimination art. 4, G.A. Res. 2106 (XX), Annex, 20 U.N. GAOR Supp. (No. 14) at 47, U.N. Doc. A/6014 (1966), 660 U.N.T.S. 195, *entered into force* Jan. 4, 1969 [hereinafter CERD].

10. *See, e.g.*, González v. Mexico ("Cotton Field Case"), Inter-Am. Ct. Hum. Rts., Judgment of Nov. 16, 2009, para. 280, 49 I.L.M. 640, 680 (2010); Velásquez Rodríguez v. Honduras,

example illustrates, the duty to protect may impose on the state significant burdens to gather and distribute resources. It may also interfere with the rights of other private persons (in this case, the right to freedom of speech) that are not generally threatened when the state merely observes a negative right. As will be discussed, this potential to create conflicts in rights provides the basis for one common objection to positive rights.

A step beyond the duty to protect is the *duty to fulfill* the right.[11] "Fulfillment" means not only that the state refrains from interfering, and tries to prevent others from interfering, with the exercise of the right; the state assumes the further duty of expending its resources to ensure meaningful enjoyment of the right regardless of the absence of any direct threat to the right by identifiable private actors.[12] For example, the U.N. General Assembly resolution on access to clean water and sanitation calls upon states and international organizations "to provide financial resources, capacity-building and technology transfer" to ensure the fulfillment of the right.[13] Such a duty would require state governments to take appropriate measures to provide clean water and sanitation to any of its nationals who could not reasonably procure these resources for themselves, even though no specific person or group may be unjustly or illegally impeding those individuals from obtaining water on their own. The resolution, then, would recognize clean water and sanitation as a positive right that the state must not only protect, but fulfill by providing in all reasonable circumstances.

This distinction is not unique to the ECOSOC Committee in modern legal discourse. Other international institutions have adopted the Committee's tripartite distinction in their own positions on human rights issues, such as the World Health Organization and the U.N. Committee on the Rights of the Child.[14]

2. The Basis for the Negative and Positive Distinction

In international human rights instruments, some rights appear to be framed as positive and others as negative, and still others are framed ambiguously. Nonetheless, the plain wording of an instrument rarely dictates its interpretation by human

Inter-Am. Ct. Hum. Rts., Judgment of July 29, 1988, para. 176, Ser. C, No. 4; López-Ostra v. Spain, 20 E.H.R.R. 277, para. 51 (1995); Yakin Erktürk, U.N. Special Rapporteur on Violence against Women, *The Due Diligence Standard as a Tool for the Elimination of Violence against Women* para. 14, UN Doc. E/CN.4/2006/61 (2006).

11. Some courts and commentators refer to the same concept as a duty to "implement" the right. For brevity and clarity, only the term "fulfill" will be used here. "Fulfill" is in any case a more accurate term, because the state may "implement" a negative as well as a positive right.

12. *See The Ogoniland Case, supra* note 2, para. 47. The African Court added a fourth category—positive duties to "promote" the right, which includes the duty to educate citizens about their rights. The Court acknowledged that much of this category overlapped with the duties to protect and fulfill. *Id.*, paras. 46–47.

13. G.A. Res. 64/292 (July 28, 2010). The vote was unanimous, but with forty-one abstentions.

14. *See, e.g.*, World Health Organization, Fact Sheet No. 323: Right to Health (Aug. 2007), at 2; Committee on the Rights of the Child, General Comment No. 16, at 8, U.N. Doc. CRC/C/GC/16 (2013).

rights authorities. The interpretation of IHRL, as of all international law, is colored by community policies as well as traditional doctrines of construction.

Frequently, however, canons of construction fail to resolve the meaning of ambiguous rights, and, even when they do, other—formally extralegal—factors influence the authoritative decision process. The cultural beliefs of decision-makers influence the interpretation of human rights instruments inevitably. These beliefs may be widely shared, creating a basis for intersubjective understandings of the instruments. Among some subsets of legal and political elites in particular, there are cultural predispositions that make framing a right in negative or positive terms seem to follow naturally from the right's content. For many persons, free speech seems to present an example of a prototypically negative right that should primarily, if not exclusively, protect against government impositions such as censorship. Many states do not conceive of the right as requiring the state to prevent private interference with the freedom of expression in ways consistent with law. For example, although some states have laws requiring fair access to alternative views in the mass media, many states would decline to interfere in a private television station's decision to bar an advocate of insurance regulatory reform from airing her views on one of the station's programs even while presenting the views of opponents of reform in full vigor. Even fewer states conceive of the right as requiring them to provide a forum for those whose ideas cannot otherwise attract an audience, beyond allowing speech in traditional public fora such as streets, parks, and the Internet.[15]

Conversely, the interest in subsistence strikes many as the basis of a prototypically positive right. Except in the unusual case where the government directly prevents someone from feeding himself,[16] the right can be vindicated only if some other person—most obviously the state[17]—provides nutritive resources to those in need. Fulfillment of the state's duty may require the state's legislature to adopt laws allocating budgetary funds to the procurement of food and commanding the government to use those funds and distribute the resulting purchases to persons

15. The existence of exceptions to general rules described in this article should be taken as implicit. In this case, some countries, such as the United States, have adopted a view of human rights that positively obligates the state to make existing public spaces available for assemblies and free speech without discrimination as to content. *See, e.g.*, Carey v. Brown, 447 U.S. 455 (1980); Kunz v. New York, 340 U.S. 290, 293 (1951); Schneider v. State, 308 U.S. 147, 163 (1939). The cases have never gone so far, however, as to establish a positive obligation for the state to create *new* public spaces for the exercise of freedom of speech.

16. Communist China's Great Leap Forward, in which command economy policies resulted in food rationing and ultimately the starvation deaths of some 20 million persons, stands as a rare example since the Second World War of a state infringing the negative right to subsistence on a large scale. *See* Jonathan D. Spence, The Search for Modern China 579–83 (1990); Jasper Becker, Hungry Ghosts: Mao's Secret Famine *passim* (1996). More recently, some states have been accused of violating the (again, negative) right by intentionally starving political prisoners. *See, e.g.*, Yang Su, *Mass Killings in the Cultural Revolution: A Study of Three Provinces, in* The Chinese Cultural Revolution as History 96 (Joseph W. Esherick et al. eds., 2006); Lee Jong-Heon, *North Korea's Gulags Hold 200,000 Political Prisoners*, UPI Asia, Jan. 20, 2010, *available at* http://www.upiasia.com/.

17. Most obviously, but not necessarily exclusively. The Committee on Economic, Social and Cultural Rights has controversially interpreted the human right to food to implicate

facing starvation. A right to subsistence that would merely prevent the government from denying individuals access to private food markets, or even prevent private actors from doing so, would not vindicate the fundamental human need for nourishment.

The basis for these intuitions will be explored later. For now, it is important to acknowledge that such preferences exist, even if the reasons for them are not always clearly conceived or articulated. The preferences have influenced the core international human rights treaties a great deal. At its formative stages, IHRL was concerned primarily with protecting individuals against the state's unchecked power.[18] The political origins of modern human rights law can be traced back to perceived oppression by the British Empire (the American Revolution) and the French monarchy (the 1789 Revolution), and more immediately to atrocities committed by Germany and Japan during the Second World War, and the Soviet Union during Stalin's reign. In each case, it was the state's injustice and depravity that inspired the need for legally protected human rights. Private oppression, however widespread, and the more generalized horrors of poverty and deprivation did not generate equivalent momentum for complex reasons. Negative rights thus dominated early international legal instruments, and many of what are considered the core modern treaty-based human rights are accordingly framed as negative.[19]

Nonetheless, the major instruments hardly neglect positive rights. The Universal Declaration, CESCR, CERD, CEDAW, the Convention on the Rights of the Child,[20] the Convention on the Rights of Persons with Disabilities,[21] and others contain extensive positive rights, calling on the state to promote the interests of its population by providing social and economic resources such as food, shelter, basic education, the possibility of gainful employment, and protection from private discrimination. In addition, many other treaties touching on human rights, such as those negotiated under the aegis of the International Labor Organization, provide for extensive positive rights.[22]

The trend of human rights discourse also continues toward promoting positive rights. The movement for enhancing the responsibility of states to assume positive

wide-ranging private "responsibilities." *See* Comm. on Econ., Soc. & Cultural Rts., Gen. Comment No. 12, para. 20, *in* Report of the Committee on Economic, Social, and Cultural Rights, U.N. ESCOR, Supp. No. 2, at 102, 106, U.N. Doc. E/2000/22 (2000).

18. *See* W. Michael Reisman, *Why Regime Change Is (Almost Always) a Bad Idea*, 98 Am. J. Int'l L. 516, 516–17 (2004).

19. *E.g.*, UDHR, arts. 5, 9; CERD, art. 2(1)(a)–(c).

20. G.A. res. 44/25, annex, 44 U.N. GAOR Supp. (No. 49) at 167, U.N. Doc. A/44/49 (1989), *entered into force* Sept. 2, 1990.

21. G.A. res. 61/106, Annex I, U.N. GAOR, 61st Sess., Supp. No. 49, at 65, U.N. Doc. A/61/49 (2006).

22. *E.g.*, Worst Forms of Child Labour Convention, ILO No. 182, June 17, 1999; Discrimination (Employment and Occupation) Convention, ILO No. 111, June 25, 1958; Equal Remuneration Convention, ILO No. 100, June 29, 1951; Right to Organise and Collective Bargaining Convention, ILO No. 98, July 1, 1949; Freedom of Association and Protection of the Right to Organise Convention, ILO No. 87, July 9, 1948.

duties to protect against and punish violations of human rights by private actors, especially multinational enterprises,[23] has been gaining momentum, as discussed in Part I. Similarly, human rights authorities have interpreted ambiguously framed rights, and sometimes rights framed in more or less clearly negative terms, as granting positive rights. Indeed, for many years now, the default position in Europe has been to interpret all human rights as correlating to positive state duties.[24] The European Court of Human Rights in particular has interpreted virtually every right in the European Convention, however framed, as imposing at least some positive duties on member states through the application of the "principle of effectiveness." Under this principle, the Strasbourg Court will interpret listed rights as imposing positive duties on the state to the extent that merely negative duties will not adequately ensure the ability of right holders to enjoy their rights.[25]

B. WHAT MAKES A RIGHT NEGATIVE?

Before we analyze the legal, ethical, and systemic consequences of the choice between negative or positive paradigms, it is necessary to clarify the definition of negative and positive rights in light of how the terms are used in philosophical and legal discourse. Specifically, the previous explanation of the distinction between negative and positive rights finds a loose parallel in the literature on ethics and some jurisprudence. Ethical theorists sometimes distinguish between negative and positive rights based on the kinds of duties they entail. They usually ground this distinction on the character of the duty. For example, the *Stanford Encyclopedia of Philosophy* distinguishes them as follows:

> The holder of a negative right is entitled to non-interference, while the holder of a positive right is entitled to provision of some good or service. A right against assault is a classic example of a negative right, while a right to welfare assistance is a prototypical positive right ....
>
> It is sometimes said that negative rights are easier to satisfy than positive rights. Negative rights can be respected simply by each person refraining from interfering with each other, while it may be difficult or even impossible to fulfill everyone's positive rights if the sum of people's claims outstrips the resources available.[26]

23. *See, e.g.*, U.N. Secretary General, Special Representative's Report on the Issue of Human Rights and Transnational Corporations and Other Business Enterprises (Apr. 22, 2009), U.N. Doc. A/HRC/11/13, paras. 2, 13–14, 48.

24. *See* Samantha Besson, *Les obligations positives de protection des droits fondamentaux—Un essai en dogmatique comparative*, 1 Rev. de Droit Suisse 49, 51 (2003).

25. *See* Airey v. Ireland, 2 E.H.R.R. 305, para. 24 (1979) ("The Convention is intended to guarantee not rights that are theoretical or illusory but rights that are practical and effective.").

26. Leif Wenar, *Rights* 2.1.8, Stan. Encyclopedia of Philosophy (2007), *at* http://plato.stanford.edu/entries/rights/.

A distinction between negative and positive rights based on the entitlement to goods or services from another is also reflected in some case law discussions of rights and liberties. For example, Judge Posner, writing for the U.S. Court of Appeals for the Seventh Circuit, characterized the difference between negative and positive rights as "just the difference . . . between negative liberty—being let alone by the state—and positive liberty—being helped by the state."[27] The conflation of rights and liberties may be harmless in the context of some individual ethical considerations, but a definition of negative rights that turns on the state's duty to refrain from action, versus a positive right that turns on an entitlement to aid or resources, makes little sense in the context of IHRL.

The reason the positivity or negativity of a right cannot turn on a duty to provide goods or services relates to the nature of the duty holder. In the context of individual ethics, a person's main task for fulfilling a negative duty, whether legal or moral, is the exercise of self-restraint. For example, if Adam owes a duty to Betsy not to trespass on Betsy's land, we can speak coherently about Adam observing his duty through self-restraint, that is, by not setting foot on Betsy's property. It is possible to challenge this characterization of Adam's duty by observing that not setting foot on Betsy's property may require Adam to take positive steps, as it were, such as rerouting his path through public property or negotiating an agreement with Betsy allowing him to cross Betsy's property. The distinction between negative and positive duties cannot turn on the duty holder's need to take action alone, because "positive" action will frequently be necessary to fulfill even a negative duty. On the other hand, the action need not include providing a good or service to Betsy. By rerouting, Adam is not rendering a service to Betsy; he is merely depriving himself of a convenience or facility. It is possible, and in practice common, that Adam will be able to respect Betsy's negative right without any expenditure of resources of any kind. By the same token, if Charles is a person of violent proclivities, he need not expend any resources (aside from psychological effort) to refrain from violating Douglas's negative right to personal safety.

However, when the duty holder is not an individual but a corporate entity, the nature of the duty changes. In the context of IHRL, the right holder is always a private person (natural or juristic), and the duty holder is nearly always the state. To observe its duty, the state must *always* use more elaborate techniques for fulfilling its duties than are necessary for individuals. A corporate person cannot act except through individuals, and the greater the number of individuals empowered to act on behalf of that person, the more difficult it is to supervise and discipline its agents to ensure that each of them fulfills a duty of restraint. State duties under IHRL have accordingly been characterized as "second-order duties" in the sense that states are obligated to bind themselves by "first-order duties" through the adoption of a municipal system of human rights law—an observation inapplicable to individual duty holders.[28] Municipal authorities have accordingly been

27. *See, e.g.*, Jackson v. City of Joliet, 715 F.2d 1200, 1204 (7th Cir. 1983), *cert. denied*, 465 U.S. 1049 (1984).

28. Samantha Besson, *The Egalitarian Dimension of Human Rights*, *in* LAW, SCIENCE, TECHNOLOGY: PLENARY LECTURES PRESENTED AT THE 25TH WORLD CONGRESS OF THE

described by Scelle as serving a *dédoublement fonctionnel* that no private individual could have.[29] A state typically employs tens of thousands, in some cases many more,[30] of individuals to act on its behalf. In the corporate context, the duty of restraining the "self" can be meaningful only when the duty translates to restraining the entity's officials and agents. The more agents a corporate entity has, and the more autonomy an agent has to fulfill his or her responsibilities, the more active the state must be in supervising its agents and preventing them from violating the negative rights of others.

In practice, this means adopting laws or regulations to guide official behavior, designing and adopting a system for training the agents to respect the right, monitoring their compliance, and instituting remedies for any infringement. To the extent that legal rights require an expenditure of effort or resources to ensure their effective realization, all rights, including negative rights, call for proactive measures by the state.[31] The question of the negativity of the duty consequently cannot turn on the obligation to take action or expend resources. At least some positive acts and resource expenditures will be necessary for observing all negative rights, and in some cases these resources must be substantial in order to respect the right effectively. The question cannot even turn on whether the state is obligated to provide some goods or services to the right holder. Many negative rights inevitably obligate the state to provide costly services directly to the right holder. For example, the right to a fair criminal trial entails the gathering, organizing, and sharing of information to the defendant, the provision of legal representation to him, and supervision of prosecutorial behavior to restrain abuses.[32] In this sense, states that agree to respect negative rights ipso facto commit to the "positive duty" of expending resources to comply with their duties.[33]

This observation does not reduce the set of all negative international human rights to null, however. The state remains a unitary actor as far as IHRL is concerned.

International Association for Philosophy of Law and Social Philosophy 43 (Ulfrid Neumann et al. eds., 2013).

29. Georges Scelle, *Le phénomène juridique du dédoublement fonctionnel*, *in* Rechtsfragen der Internationalen Organisation: Festschrift für Hans Wehberg 324–42 (Walter Schätzel ed., 1956).

30. The U.S. government employed 4.2 million individuals full-time in 2014. U.S. Office of Personnel Management, Historical Federal Workforce Tables, *at* http://www.opm.gov (last visited Jan. 27, 2016). The same year, Japan had about 640,000 government employees. Japan National Personnel Authority, 2015 Profile of National Public Employees in Japan, at 3 (undated), *available at* http://www.jinji.go.jp/en/infonpa/profile.pdf (last visited Jan. 27, 2016).

31. Allen Buchanan, *Equality and Human Rights*, 4 Politics, Philos. & Econ. 69, 84 (2005).

32. *See* CCPR art. 14. This is a negative right insofar as it requires the state to restrain its agents from convicting any person of a crime without following certain procedures and providing certain guarantees to the accused.

33. *Cf.* Besson, *supra* note 28, at 65 ("*le concept de restriction cesse d'être un critère de distinction valable au fur et à mesure que l'intervention des pouvoirs publics grandit dans tous les domaines de la vie quotidienne.*").

State measures designed solely to restrain the state's own agents are the corporate equivalent of an individual restraining himself (psychologically or otherwise) from violating another person's negative right. In the ECOSOC Committee's schema, a negative duty is one of self-restraint in this sense. The state undertakes to prevent itself, and by extension its officials and agents, from interfering with the right holder's exercise of the right, at any reasonable expenditure of resources. But, as noted, positive duties are divided into two categories: protection and fulfillment. In neither case does the positivity of the duty depend on the necessity of expending resources or providing goods or services to right holders, although in practice the performance of positive duties almost always does require such measures. Instead, the positivity of the state's duty seems to depend on the source and nature of the threat posed to the relevant rights.

Specifically, a right to protection imposes a duty on the state to take measures to prevent third parties from interfering with the right holder's exercise of the right. Such third parties may include private individuals, private organizations, local subdivisions of the municipal government, foreign states, or intergovernmental organizations. The performance of such duties may require extensive action and the expenditure of very substantial resources because, unlike in the case of a negative right, which can be violated only by the state or its agents, the positive right can be violated by virtually anyone. Private individuals and organizations in any society greatly outnumber public officials and employees, and these private persons are not necessarily subject to any natural duty to obey or advance the government's policies beyond complying with the minimum requirements of law. The threat they pose to individual rights is diffuse and beyond the state's immediate control. The defining feature of the right is not the necessity of expending exceptional resources, but rather the necessity of protecting the right against threats posed by the universe of persons other than the state itself and its agents. The greater expenditure of resources normally required to achieve protection is thus a practical consequence, not a definitional element, of a positive right.

The positive duty to "fulfill" a right similarly does not depend on the need to expend resources, although, again, such an expenditure will always be necessary in practice to perform the duty. Instead, a duty of fulfillment can be defined by the irrelevance of the source of the threat to the right. A state performing its duty of fulfillment must not only restrain itself and third parties from violating the right, but must try to counter abstract or impersonal forces that threaten enjoyment of the right. The duty to fulfill a right to clean water, for example, requires the state to provide water despite the fact that neither the state's agents nor any private party is preventing the right holder from obtaining clean water. A dearth of water caused by drought, overpopulation, poverty, or possibly even the right holder's own faulty judgment will suffice to trigger the duty. The positive duty to fulfill is not, however, absolute. A right to fulfillment requires states not to guarantee a result, but rather to make reasonable efforts to vindicate the interest at stake regardless of the source of the impediment to the right holder's enjoyment of the right. For example, a positive right to fulfillment of the security of the person requires the state to take reasonable preventive and remedial measures in the event of a natural disaster such as an earthquake or hurricane. It does not require the state to utterly disaster-proof every building or house in its territory.

Establishing a coherent definition of negative and positive rights, and a useful typology of positive rights, does not in itself settle whether the distinction between negative and positive paradigms is conceptually sound, useful in practice, and ethically defensible. Some scholars have denied the ontological existence of negative rights, and others have denied the possibility that limiting state duties to such rights can be morally permissible. These are analytical questions with weighty implications for the interpretation of state duties under IHRL.

C. CAN THERE BE NEGATIVE RIGHTS?

Rational choice theory is based on the assumption that human beings act logically and in their greatest self-interest. It ignores the possibility of social altruism or communal conceptions of self-interest, reducing human nature to amoral solipsism. If we hypothesize a rational right holder viewing the world through solipsistic lenses, we must conclude that he cares nothing about the origin of a threat to his right. He cares only about the effect of a threat on his enjoyment of the right. Whether that enjoyment is blocked or diminished by the state or a private person matters little to him, if he is rational; the critical fact is the diminution in enjoyment itself.

Although many persons are solipsists some of the time, very few are true solipsists all of the time. Nonetheless, the international system of human rights law, like many modern legal systems, is based on an assumption of solipsism. Legal duties, unlike moral duties, must necessarily be designed so that duty holders may ascertain their duties ex ante with some certainty. A nebulous legal duty multiplies opportunities for costly disputes about whether the duty holder has fulfilled his or her obligations. Ambiguity also tends to impose unfair burdens on both the duty holder and right holders. The duty holder cannot reasonably be held to a standard of behavior that even legal experts cannot ex hypothesi articulate clearly and definitely. The right holder may be led to believe that she has greater rights than legal authorities will in practice recognize when it comes to enforcement. By assuming individuals will act solipsistically—in effect, establishing legal rights and duties at the lowest common denominator of social behavior—the legal system ensures that all individuals have the same basic legal rights and duties.

The solipsistic right holder, if he existed, would have definite views about the desirability of positive rights. Recall that, when performing a positive duty to protect or fulfill, the state must not only restrain itself, but must adopt reasonable measures to restrain others from undermining the right's enjoyment. The need to monitor, deter, and punish a vast multitude of potential violators of the right typically calls for a well-designed legal system funded by a substantial, ongoing outlay of financial and other resources by the state. The solipsistic right holder, however, is not concerned with the cost to the state of ensuring his rights; he concerns himself with whether he is enjoying the right, and, as noted, the source of any interference is immaterial to him.

A solipsistic right holder flush with political and economic power may view the state as the primary threat to that power and oppose positive rights as a mechanism for transferring that power to the less privileged or to the state itself. But to the solipsistic right holder lacking great political or economic power—a set that comprises the great majority of members of any given society—an international human rights system composed of exclusively negative rights would be entirely unsatisfactory. Although the system would relieve the right holder of threats to the right by one extremely powerful actor—the state—the right holder would be left defenseless against myriad private threats that might prove much more damaging. The abused child typically has much less to fear from the state than from its parents or strangers. We may predict, then, that the rational solipsistic right holder with limited socioeconomic power craves positive rights. The threats may come from an oppressive majority;[34] from a disproportionately powerful subset of society, as in the case of male domination over women through skewed political representation, sexist legal regulation, and private religious, economic, and social institutions;[35] or from impersonal environmental or economic forces, such as prolonged famine or general poverty. The solipsist victimized by such forces will rationally seek positive rights from the state in any case in which the state is capable of guaranteeing them.

Because, in any given state, only an insignificant number of citizens possess sufficient power to protect themselves against all serious threats to their human rights without assistance, many human rights will be meaningfully enjoyed only if the state undertakes positive duties. Such considerations have led some observers to conclude that all human rights are necessarily positive or require positive action. Stephen Holmes and Cass Sunstein, for example, contend that a person whose "wrongs" are not "fairly and predictably redressed" by an expenditure of resources by the government has no meaningful legal right.[36] The importance of positive state action becomes most manifest in the case of violation. No legal right worthy of the name could be violated with impunity without sapping the very concept of all vigor. The state is the most likely candidate to enforce the right effectively because of the state's unique combination of power and authority. To Holmes and Sunstein, negative legal rights do not really exist: "No right is simply a right to be left alone by public officials. All rights are claims to an affirmative governmental response."[37] "All rights," they conclude, "are positive rights."[38] Similarly, some philosophers have pointed out that "positive actions" are always required to implement "negative rights," without necessarily concluding that the negative category is meaningless.[39] It follows from such observations, however, that the distinction does not

34. *See, e.g.*, Aaron Xavier Fellmeth, *Choice of Gender Identity in International Human Rights Law, in* Looking to the Future: Essays on International Law in Honor of W. Michael Reisman 499, 508–10 (Mahnoush Arsanjani et al. eds., 2011); Aaron Xavier Fellmeth, *State Regulation of Sexuality in International Human Rights Law and Theory*, 50 Wm. & Mary L. Rev. 797, 800–09 (2008).

35. See, *e.g.*, Karen Knop, *Re/Statements: Feminism and State Sovereignty in International Law*, 3 Transnat'l L. & Contemp. Probs. 293, 296 (1993).

36. Stephen Holmes & Cass R. Sunstein, The Cost of Rights 43 (1999). It was Mill who originally formulated this position, albeit with a nuance: "When we call anything a person's right, we mean that he has a valid claim on society to protect him in the possession of it, either by force of law, or by that of education and opinion." John Stuart Mill, Utilitarianism 54 (1861). This latter qualification Holmes and Sunstein seem not to have adopted.

37. Holmes & Sunstein, *supra* note 36, at 43–44.

38. *Id.* at 48.

39. *See, e.g.*, Buchanan, *supra* note 31, at 83.

carry much conceptual meaning or great moral weight. I will refer to this argument as the Equivalence Position.

The *Stanford Encyclopedia of Philosophy* adopts the Equivalence Position when it asserts that "when it comes to the enforcement of rights, [the] difference [between negative and positive rights] disappears."[40] The Equivalence Position has also influenced the Strasbourg Court's interpretation of facially negative rights in the European Convention. A case in point is the right to private and family life under ECHR article 8:

> 1. Everyone has the right to respect for his private and family life, his home and his correspondence.
> 2. There shall be no interference by a public authority with the exercise of this right except such as is in accordance with the law and is necessary in a democratic society in the interests of national security, public safety or the economic well-being of the country, for the prevention of disorder or crime, for the protection of health or morals, or for the protection of the rights and freedoms of others.

Foreign nationals denied the privilege of immigrating into or residing in Council of Europe member states frequently challenge the state's refusal as a violation of article 8, based on the applicant's desire to live with family members already resident in that state. On the plain language of article 8, this seems a difficult argument to make. The language strongly suggests recognition of a negative right only. The duty to "respect" in paragraph 1 represents the prototypical phrasing of a negative right, and paragraph 2, far from expanding the scope of the right into a positive entitlement, is limited to prohibiting "interference by public authority."

The Court and erstwhile European Commission on Human Rights have sometimes interpreted the state's article 8 duty with respect to the applicant as negative, such as when state officials expel a foreign national seeking to be united with his or her family members in that state. In such cases, however, the state's duty could be characterized alternatively as a negative one—to refrain from denying entry to, or expelling, the alien—or a positive one—to issue a visa or residence permit to the alien. In *Ahmut v. The Netherlands*, for example, the Commission held such a refusal to constitute an "interference" in the applicant's family life.[41] Before the Strasbourg Court, the Netherlands argued that it had no positive duty to grant entry and residence; it had only a negative duty not to withdraw residence. The Court, accepting the Netherlands' premise, characterized the state's duty to grant entry as a "positive duty," and discussed article 8 on that basis:

> [T]he boundaries between the State's positive and negative obligations under this provision do not lend themselves to precise definition. The applicable principles are, nonetheless, similar. In both contexts regard must be had to the fair balance that has to be struck between the competing interests of the individual

40. *See* Leif Wenar, *Rights* 2.1.8, Stan. Encyclopedia of Philosophy (2007), *at* http://plato.stanford.edu/entries/rights/.

41. Ahmut v. The Netherlands, 24 E.H.R.R. 62, para. 45 (1997).

> and of the community as a whole; and in both contexts the State enjoys a certain margin of appreciation. The present case hinges on the question whether the Netherlands Government was under a duty to allow Souffiane to reside with his father in the Netherlands, thus enabling the applicants to maintain and develop family life in its territory.[42]

Relying on this interpretation, the *Ahmut* Court held that the Moroccan minor son of a Netherlands national living with his wife in Rotterdam was not entitled to reside with his father in the Netherlands after his mother died.[43] Instead, the Court suggested that the national should move to Morocco and raise his child there, away from home, new wife, and established employment. The Court's interpretation of the article 8 duties, repeated in later cases,[44] reflects the Equivalence Position, with the result that the Court has consistently asserted that the analysis of a state's compliance with its negative duties is "similar" to the analysis of compliance with positive duties.[45] In later cases, the Court has adhered to the position that not deporting an individual respects a negative right, whereas affording him or her "the opportunity to exercise the [family] rights in question without interference" implements a "positive obligation."[46]

The problem with such analyses is that, as discussed, a human right does not assume a positive character merely because it requires the state to take action and grant benefits to an individual. The state is not being asked to "fulfill" the applicant's right to a family life or protect it from a private interference; the state itself is being asked to exercise self-restraint by not interfering with the applicant's attempts to reunite with his or her family. As the Court implied in *Ahmut*, the state does not create the family, the individuals do: "a child born of a marital union is *ipso iure* part of that relationship; hence, from the moment of the child's birth and by the very fact of it, there exists between him and his parents a bond amounting to 'family life.'"[47] If so, a state denying a minor child the right to reunite with his only parent, who is a national of that state, violates a negative, not a positive, duty. It remains unclear whether the Strasbourg Court's interpretation of article 8 as imposing a positive duty persuaded the Court to interpret the Netherlands' duties as less strict than if the state were violating a negative duty to refrain from interfering in the applicant's family life. However, given the result, it does seem likely that the misapprehension of negative and positive paradigms influenced the outcome.

At bottom, the fundamental flaw in the Equivalence Position lies in its uncritical adoption of the solipsistic right holder's perspective, tempered only by recognition of the state's limited power and resources but without further analysis of

42. *Id.* para. 63.

43. *Id.* para. 73.

44. *E.g.*, Sen v. The Netherlands, 36 E.H.R.R. 7, paras. 28, 31.

45. *See, e.g.*, Sanchez v. Spain, 54 E.H.R.R. 24, para. 62 (2011); Draon v. France, 42 E.H.R.R. 40, para. 105 (2005); Kutzner v. Germany, 35 E.H.R.R. 25, para. 62 (2002); Stjerna v. Finland, 24 E.H.R.R. 195, 195–96 (1994).

46. Sisojeva v. Latvia, 43 E.H.R.R. 33, para. 104 (2005).

47. *Ahmut*, 24 E.H.R.R. 62, para. 60.

the consequences of these resource limitations. The solipsist has reason to demand assistance from the state whenever any of his rights are impaired, regardless of who or what is interfering with the enjoyment. As long as the state acts to rectify the impairment, the solipsistic right holder is satisfied. But the solipsistic right holder's viewpoint is not the only one worthy of consideration. The state as duty holder has its own interests. The solipsistic duty holder's perspective is the diametrical opposite of the solipsistic right holder's. To a duty holder, the enjoyment *vel non* of the right is beside the point; the critical information is whether the duty holder himself has acted appropriately. If so, his duty is fulfilled regardless of whether the right holder reaps any actual benefit. If solipsist Amy has a duty to compensate Barney for Barney's services, Amy fulfills her duty by paying Barney, even though on the following day hyperinflation drains the payment of all value to Barney.

The state is not a solipsistic duty holder in its own right, but it will tend toward a solipsistic position because resources for the promotion of human rights are always and everywhere limited. Any resource allocated to any specific right holder necessarily detracts to some degree from the demands of other right holders.[48] A state therefore could never be held to the standard demanded by any given solipsistic duty holder unless, by doing so, it made no sacrifices of other, equally important interests.

As noted, a (negative) duty of self-restraint does typically require active measures by the state, at a minimum because the state is a corporate actor. The characterization of negative rights as imperfect or nugatory is based on the described definitions used by some philosophers, who define a positive right as a right "to other persons' positive actions," and a negative right as a right "to other persons' omissions or forbearances."[49] This account is oriented toward individual relationships, where it sometimes makes sense. A duty to refrain from harming another person may have ethical implications and consequences quite different from those associated with a duty to provide another person with benefits and services.

The same distinction applies much less readily to public-private legal relationships. If the state, as a corporate actor, must always take "positive measures" to ensure that human rights, whether negative or positive, are observed, then the necessity of such measures cannot form the basis of the distinction between negative and positive rights. The logical conclusion is not that all negative rights are ultimately positive, but rather that the philosophical definition of positive rights is inapplicable in the context of international law. For that definition to have any value at all, it must be confined to the context of ethical duties to other individuals and not to the public sphere, in which duties primarily rest on the state or other public corporate actors. The Equivalence Position defines positive rights in a manner than renders them analytically useless in this latter context. A different definition is called for.

48. I do not deny that maximally fulfilling the human rights of some persons might have positive spillover effects on other individuals. My point is merely that such synergies are not the dominant forces in human rights enforcement, and so they do not alter the basic dynamics of the trade-off when the state makes great expenditures of resources for some while allocating scant resources for others.

49. Joel Feinberg, Social Philosophy 59 (1973).

The ECOSOC definition of positive rights is well-tailored for this purpose and has been adopted widely in international human rights law.[50] A critical analysis of ECOSOC's scheme reveals that what defines a right as negative or positive is not the necessity of action for the right's enforcement. Instead, it is the nature and source of the threat that the state must counteract that determines the type of right. As noted, if the state's duty is limited to restraining itself and its agents, then the duty is negative. But if the duty is to protect the right against exogenous threats, such as private actors or impersonal social or environmental forces, then the duty is positive. On this basis, negative and positive paradigms may be distinguished meaningfully. In the remaining portion of this and subsequent chapters, I will show that such a distinction between negative and positive rights is both legally operative and, in certain limited contexts, ethically defensible.

D. THE CONCEPT OF "BASIC" POSITIVE RIGHTS

1. A Justification for Devoting More Resources to Some Rights than to Others

Can we go beyond these general observations and identify some criteria for which vigorous state efforts at protection, or even fulfillment, are ethically required? One influential attempt to justify the state's positive ethical duties is found in Henry Shue's *Basic Rights*. As the book's title implies, Shue limited his argument to a subset of rights deemed "basic," which he defines as those rights whose fulfillment is a precondition to the enjoyment of every other right. A person dead from starvation or a lethal beating cannot enjoy any other right, so the rights to subsistence and protection from violence are basic. Basic rights, Shue argues, always imply positive ethical duties,[51] because "[i]n any imperfect society enjoyment of a right will depend to some extent upon protection against those who do not choose not to violate it."[52] Consequently, "the whole notion that there is a morally significant dichotomy between negative rights and positive rights is intellectually bankrupt."[53]

It bears repeating that, despite this unqualified indictment of purely negative rights, Shue does not try to justify the rejection of all such rights on moral grounds, because some rights are not "basic" in the sense he uses. Shue adopts something like

50. *See, e.g.*, X & Y v. The Netherlands, 8 E.H.R.R. 235, para. 23 (1986) ("[T]here may be *positive obligations* inherent in an effective respect for private or family life . . . These obligations may involve the adoption of measures designed to secure respect for private life even *in the sphere of the relations of individuals between themselves*.") (emphasis added); Inter-Am. Comm'n on Hum. Rts., Report on Ecuador, 1997, OEA/Ser.L/V/II.96, Doc. 10 rev. 1, ch. X ("The right to equal protection of and before the law may also require the adoption of *positive measures* to protect against discriminatory treatment within the public *and private sectors*. For example, positive measures may be necessary to ensure equality of treatment within the public-private spheres of education and employment.") (emphasis added).

51. Henry Shue, Basic Rights: Subsistence, Affluence, and U.S. Foreign Policy 53 (2d ed. 1996).

52. *Id.* at 39.

53. *Id.* at 51.

the ECOSOC Committee's typology of rights and maximizes the positive duties he would impose on states with respect to basic rights. In other words, his argument would hold states to the highest standard of positive duties with respect to basic rights—not only to respect and protect the right, but to fulfill it.

Because every state's resources and abilities are limited, the set of basic rights must be a relatively small one if states can be expected realistically to fulfill them. We can have little use for a theory of ethics that obligates states to accomplish the impracticable.[54] Even if states were able to fulfill a large set of "basic" rights, however, there are reasons we should hesitate to impose extensive duties of fulfillment on them. There is no empirical basis for assuming that the state is uniformly best positioned to fulfill all fundamental human needs. The right holders themselves, their families, and their communities and social networks should bear, and often are most capable of bearing, the responsibilities for fulfilling many human rights. In many cases, the state is best conceived as a kind of backstop rather than the primary fulfiller of all rights. Moreover, there are costs and dangers associated with the state assuming a very active role in fulfilling human rights generally, which will be discussed in the last chapter. From this, I conclude that there are two criteria for delegating to the state the ethical duty of fulfilling, as opposed to merely protecting, a right: first, the right must be sufficiently important to justify an exceptional commitment of resources for the right holder's benefit, and second, the state must be the duty holder best positioned to fulfill the right on a societal level when the normal sources fail. When these two criteria are satisfied, the foundation has been laid for holding the state to a duty to fulfill.

On the point of importance, Shue's conception of basic rights provides a strong starting point. By definition, all international human rights protect important interests; that all rights depend upon the fulfillment of a "basic" right implies a more fundamental importance of the basic right itself. Yet, Shue's definition of "basic" requires refinement; it is underinclusive in its current state, due to the universality of Shue's principles. Shue tries to identify rights as basic without regard to the context in which the right functions.

An acontextual approach to protecting human rights cannot be complete, because the pursuit of human dignity and flourishing can only be accomplished in an organic social setting that varies between cultures and societies. The list of basic rights Shue identifies is diminutive—subsistence, physical security, and freedom of movement—and therefore seems well adapted to span the wide global variety of cultures and political, economic, and social settings. However, the very variety of these variables also implies that a broad range of human rights may qualify as necessary for the exercise of, if not all other rights, then a very significant portion of them in some places at some times. For example, in a society with rampant governmental abuse of human rights, the right to free speech may be absolutely necessary to draw public attention to abuses that would otherwise result in pervasive denials of other rights. Similarly, wherever private racial or sex discrimination is pervasive, it may be difficult or impossible for members of the disadvantaged group to exercise other rights, such as the right to political participation, the right to own property,

54. *See, e.g.*, Vienna Convention on the Law of Treaties art. 61, May 23, 1969, 1155 U.N.T.S. 331.

or the right to a fair trial. In such a society and for such persons, the right against discrimination becomes necessary for the exercise of many other rights.

Shue recognizes that there may be basic rights other than the three he lists, but he conceives of basic rights as intrinsically basic rather than contextually so. Shue limits "basic rights" to those rights necessary for the exercise of *all* other rights as a basis for an argument for maximal observance of these rights. Yet, his insistence on universality limits the utility of his concept unnecessarily. He offers no complete justification for such a narrow definition. I cannot see any reason that a right upon which the exercise of a wide spectrum of other rights depends should be treated in a categorically different manner from a right upon which the exercise of all other rights depends. Suppose there is a universe of twenty separate human rights. Suppose further that the nineteen others depend on observation of human right number 1, but only eighteen depend on observation of human right number 2. What rationale can justify treating number 1 as fundamentally different from number 2 in requiring the state to take measures to ensure the enjoyment of the right? It seems to me more justifiable, if less precise, to say that basic rights are those rights upon which very many other rights depend in the relevant social context.

2. Is Shue's Definition of Basic Rights Overinclusive?

Shue's definition might also be considered overinclusive when applied to moral rights, because it treats the rights he identifies as "basic" despite the fact that, again depending on the circumstances, all of the rights he identifies will not necessarily satisfy his criteria. It is indisputable that, under no circumstances could the right to life be anything but basic as he defines that term. But Shue treats other abstract rights as inherently coherent and delimited concepts when their significance and meaning varies according to the environment in which they are asserted. A human right, like any abstract concept, is an artificial construction that assumes meaning only in the social context in which it operates. For example, the right to physical security can be threatened in a variety of ways. A threat to physical security only necessarily compromises the victim's enjoyment of other rights when the threats are pervasive or life-threatening. Not all threats to physical security undermine the enjoyment of all (or most) other rights. This point is equally applicable to political participation, the right to freedom of movement, and other rights. The identification of a right as "basic" *in abstracto* tends to boil down to a question of definition, and because rights are intersubjectively determined concepts, the extent to which the enjoyment of any given right is necessary for the enjoyment of other rights will vary according to how the right is interpreted and, again, its social context.

The relevance of the social context plays out in that the conditions for the enjoyment of any given right does not solely depend on whether rights are legally guaranteed. One could argue that a society may be so situated or organized that its members enjoy secure access to the valued freedom or resource, even without a legal right to it.[55] In a society with a liberal democratic government and minimal violent crime rate, the right to life may not require much legal protection. In a society with abundant food, there may be no need for a right to subsistence. In such a

55. *See* THOMAS W. POGGE, WORLD POVERTY AND HUMAN RIGHTS 45 (2d ed. 2008).

society, the enjoyment of a non-basic right—say, the right to freedom of religion—could nonetheless be hampered by widespread discrimination or state measures. The right to freedom of religion is necessary in such a society at such a time, but in what sense, then, is a "right" to life or subsistence a precondition to the enjoyment of the right to freedom of religion?

There are both theoretical and practical rejoinders to this argument, however. The theoretical response is that, if human rights are intended to elevate important individual interests to a position of priority in the balancing of individual and societal interests generally, then the fact that an interest or value is not threatened should carry no weight in the decision whether to assign a right to the interest.

The practical response is that the overinclusiveness argument erroneously treats social systems as static. Access to food is likely to vary in any given state between social classes and over time. Indeed, in the United States, where food is plentiful and inexpensive, millions of low-income households suffer from food insecurity and malnutrition.[56] Similarly, droughts, natural disasters, or armed conflicts can close off a previously secure source of food. Social and political conditions could change, and then a right to life would then become necessary in that society. Human rights are framed in general terms in the major treaties precisely to accommodate both temporal and social variability in access to the interests protected by the right.

Shue further responds that, in situations where an interest is unlikely to benefit from state protection, such as political interests in a nondemocratic state, the interests can never qualify as *rights* at all because they cannot be enforced.[57] But here, Shue seems to have transitioned from an argument about moral rights into an observation about legal rights. It is entirely possible to have a meaningful moral right that is never enforced, whereas a consistently ignored legal right ceases to be a right in the juridical sense. In the context of IHRL, then, Shue's observation holds true.

A right should be treated as "basic" from a legal standpoint, then, if, *in its relevant social context*, its fulfillment is a theoretical precondition for the exercise of a *broad spectrum of* other rights. It follows from my revised definition that, although some rights will be basic universally, other rights may be "basic" in some societies (and, indeed, in some segments of a single society) at some periods of time, but not in other societies (or segments) at other times. This is different from Shue's definition, but I consider it slightly more useful for analyzing the consequences of classifying human rights in a legal context. When a right fulfills these criteria, the case for treating it as "basic" in the sense of imposing a positive duty of fulfillment on the state is at its apogee.

Accepting *arguendo* my adjustments to the definition of basic rights, the next question becomes whether imposing a uniform duty of fulfillment on states for such rights is justified. The fact that attaching an ethical duty of fulfillment to basic rights is desirable does not lead inexorably to the conclusion that basic rights automatically imply a sufficiently forceful moral duty of fulfillment to justify a concomitant legal duty. Basic rights clearly imply some significant duty on the part of the

56. Nancy S. Weinfield et al., Hunger in America 2014: National Report 2 (2014).

57. Shue, *supra* note 51, at 82.

state, but the extent of that duty depends on many factors. Consider two scenarios using the basic right to subsistence, held by individual *P*, a national of Patria:

{1a} Patrian government officials declare *P* to be *caput lupis* and impede *P*'s right to subsistence by forbidding anyone to employ *P* or to provide *P* with food or funds necessary to purchase food. *P* faces starvation because of Patria's actions.

{1b} *Q* is *P*'s employer. *Q* is the only employer providing a job for which *P* is qualified. *Q* terminates *P*'s employment for economic reasons. Patria does not provide *P* with a job or economic relief; *P* now faces starvation.

Scenario {1a} describes a classic violation of a negative right by Patria, which committed the violation by actively interfering in *P*'s attempts to achieve subsistence. In {1b}, Patria has failed in its duty to protect or to fulfill, and thereby committed a violation of *P*'s right to subsistence by refraining from taking positive action. Although there is no doubt that Patria has an ethical duty to *P*, Shue's dismissal of the distinction between {1a} and {1b} as intellectually bankrupt overlooks important ethical factors. From the limited perspective of the solipsistic right holder, perhaps the violation of {1b} is no better than the violation of {1a}. Both intrusions on *P*'s rights are harmful to *P*, who (as a rational solipsist) cares only about the harm and not about its source. However, the state is a morally relevant actor as well, and its interests cannot be ignored or entirely sublimated to the interests of right holders.

If the state were a solipsistic duty holder, the distinction between the state as right violator and as right neglecter or, in psychological terms, between malevolent and indifferent, would be a critical one. In scenario {1b}, Patria (unless it has a command economy) does not claim a monopoly over jobs or food; it is not the only possible source of these for *P*. There are excellent arguments that both malevolence and indifference are morally reprehensible in the context of IHRL, but there are also strong arguments against equating these two attitudes. In terms of individual ethics, apathy is less worthy of condemnation than malevolence both because of its likely relative consequences for other persons and its implications for the moral character of the actor himself. The distinction between indifference and malevolence is less compelling when the actor has a specific duty to protect the right holder or to secure the enjoyment of the right, but this is precisely the point. The argument that scenario {1a} and {1b} are equivalent assumes the state has such a duty. In other words, Shue's insistence that purely negative human rights are morally unacceptable relies on a premise that not everyone will be prepared to accept. It adopts the rational solipsistic right holder's perspective and ignores the state's.

This is not to say Shue's premise is wrong. Indeed, there is a strong argument for accepting Shue's premise with respect to basic rights, especially as I have amended the definition. The state exists in a special moral relationship to persons under its jurisdiction. One of the reasons justifying Patria's political authority over *P* is its mission (indeed, its *raison d'être*) to promote the interests of its nationals. *Q* has no such mission, and his duty to *P* is accordingly far more attenuated and disputable.[58]

58. Shue also argues that Q has a moral duty to *P*. This claim is debatable, but for our purposes, we may safely ignore Q as jurally insignificant. As discussed in Chapter 2, Section A, IHRL

One need not accept the fiction of a social contract[59] to realize that, unless the state protects those under its authority from systematic and preventable threats to their acknowledged rights, there can be no moral justification for the state's authority in the first place.

This observation justifies the state's moral duty to *protect* human rights, but it does not necessarily justify a duty to *fulfill* human rights. That justification requires accepting the premise that we cannot assume a priori that there is a morally significant distinction between a threat to human rights originating in private persons and a threat originating in more diffuse social or environmental forces. There are reasons there might be such a moral distinction. One is that the state has limited resources, and these resources should be allocated in such a way as to maximize the enjoyment of rights for the greatest public benefit. If protecting a certain right from private intrusion confers a greater benefit on society than attempting to fulfill the right, considering the costs and externalities of attempting to fulfill and the alternative uses of its resources, then the state should prioritize its allocation of resources in favor of protection rather than fulfillment. Conversely, if fulfilling a right confers a greater benefit than merely protecting the right, again weighing as well the costs and externalities, then the state should undertake to fulfill rather than merely to protect the right.

Nonetheless, given the critical importance of basic rights, it seems natural to favor a moral duty to fulfill basic rights over a mere duty of protection in general. Because basic rights are those whose enjoyment carries the greatest consequences for the enjoyment of other rights, the state should allocate more resources to the enjoyment of basic rights than to other rights, to the point at which basic rights are widely and meaningfully enjoyed. Again, the rational solipsistic right holder knows that the enjoyment of a right has no relation to the source of a threat to the right. Therefore, the same reasons justify binding the state equally to fulfill and to protect basic rights, regardless of whether private actors or more diffuse sources threaten the right's enjoyment.

Of course, one might raise the prior question of why the state should be morally bound to allocate its resources to the enjoyment of internationally recognized human rights in the first place.[60] The simple answer is that, because human rights represent those interests considered the most fundamental in the international community at any given time, there is no better candidate for the allocation of state resources. The only other logical option is for the state either to allocate resources

can impose no duty on *Q* under these circumstances even if we agree that *Q* has a moral duty toward *P*.

59. The social contractarian theories of Thomas Hobbes, John Locke, and Jean-Jacques Rousseau would all support, at a minimum, imposing such a duty on the state. Immanuel Kant's justification for state authority relies on the state's role in the preservation of rights as well. *See* IMMANUEL KANT, THE METAPHYSICS OF MORALS (1797), *in* IMMANUEL KANT, PRACTICAL PHILOSOPHY 365, 455–56 (Mary J. Gregor trans., 1999). John Rawls's social contractarian thought experiment justifies the state's role as protector of rights primarily on Kantian grounds. *See* JOHN RAWLS, A THEORY OF JUSTICE (1971).

60. Michael Payne questions Shue's argument on this ground. *See* Michael Payne, *Henry Shue on Basic Rights*, 9(2)(5) ESSAYS IN PHILOSOPHY 3–4 (2008).

to less important interests—a position not worth considering—or to collect and allocate no resources at all, which, if accepted, would return us to the question of why state authority should be respected in the first place. This does not mean that states necessarily violate an ethical duty by allocating resources to uses other than the direct enjoyment of individual human rights, such as improving infrastructure, increasing total national wealth, or protecting the natural environment. It does suggest that states violate an ethical duty by allocating such resources before all human rights are widely and meaningfully enjoyed. And, because the enjoyment of basic rights is a precondition to the enjoyment of many rights in any given society, states are morally bound to allocate resources for the enjoyment of basic rights with appropriate priority.

3. Does International Human Rights Law Recognize Some Rights as More "Basic" than Others?

Another possible objection to the priority of basic rights is based on a theory that human rights are of equal value either by definition or at law. Martin Scheinin, for example, has argued in the *Oxford Handbook of International Human Rights* that Shue's typology does not reflect positive human rights law, because the latter "highly favours the universality, indivisibility, and equal value of all human rights."[61] Specifically, he argues that, because human rights treaties do not hierarchize rights, Shue's position differs from international human rights law.

Granted that Shue's specific choice of rights to be designated as basic may not reflect a formal hierarchy of IHRL, the more general argument that all human rights are equal reflects a recently propagated myth rather than consistent international practice. It is based specifically on two related misconceptions. The first is that the absence of any mention of a general hierarchy in human rights treaties means that no such hierarchy exists. The second and related misconception is the conflation of the preambles and texts of treaties, together with their commentaries by their monitoring committees, with international law, in which all rights are implicitly or explicitly treated as equally important.

On the first point, it suffices to observe that no treaty text contains a complete statement of all law relating to the subject it covers, nor does it include a self-validating exegesis. Nor do the canons of treaty interpretation dictate how human rights authorities are to resolve cases of multiple conflicting rights or a conflict between a human right and an important public policy. To answer such questions, human rights authorities must balance values and interests against each other, and inevitably some will appear more weighty or pressing than others. It is impossible to imagine a scenario, for example, in which the right to freedom of religion would outweigh the right to life precisely because the latter is more important or "basic" in the sense used here than the former. True, a human rights authority would find relatively little assistance in making this judgment in the text of the CCPR. Although the nonderogation provision of article 4(2) provides some help, as Scheinin points out, that provision reflects a judgment that the suspension of the listed rights would

61. Martin Scheinin, *Core Rights and Obligations*, *in* Oxford Handbook of International Human Rights Law 527, 528 (Dinah Shelton ed., 2013).

not conceivably be necessary in any public emergency rather than a judgment on the "basicness" of the rights listed.[62] But the fact that human rights authorities draw on values and reasoning exogenous to the treaty texts does not detract from the legal force of their judgments.

Moreover, in addition to treaty texts, public international law encompasses customary international law, which is traditionally defined as the widespread, longstanding, and consistent practice of states arising from a sense of legal obligation, or *opinio iuris sive necessitatis*. Here, too, we find in practice a clear hierarchy in human rights. Almost all states almost always much more categorically forbid, protect their nationals from, protest violations by others of, and deny accusations of their own violation of, some rights than others. Generally, such rights include those falling within the category of *ius cogens*—such as the prohibitions on slavery, torture, and arbitrary execution—that coincide with many of Shue's basic rights. They also include other rights that states evidently consider to have the most legitimacy and urgency. Judging by the statements and actions of states in both domestic and international arenas, they evidently consider violations of voting rights less urgent than violations of the freedom of movement or the deprivation of nationality. They take stronger measures to prevent and remedy violations of the right to a fair trial than the right to privacy. Such rankings are not only common, they are inevitable. Shue's division of rights into basic and non-basic categories may not reflect the exact hierarchy that human rights authorities tend to adopt in their authoritative decision processes, but at a minimum, they do treat the rights Shue identifies as basic with a definite priority.

4. Basic Rights and the Duty of Fulfillment

That states and international human rights authorities recognize some priority of some human rights over other does not suggest the universal acceptance that basic rights entail duties of fulfillment. A duty of fulfillment poses certain risks not present in the same degree in duties of protection. Most prominently, in trying to fulfill a right, it is possible that the state will pose a greater threat to that right (or other rights) than the original threat poses to the right the state is trying to fulfill.[63] Protection tends to be reactive; the state's duty comes into play only when identifiable private actors present an identifiable threat to the right. The state may take preventive measures before that occurs, but these measures do not actually protect the right unless they are well tailored to prevent a realistic threat to the enjoyment of the right. In contrast, the threats to a right to fulfillment tends toward greater diffusion and abstraction, and so the necessity and extent of prophylactic measures required generally calls for highly subjective judgments. The duty to fulfill a subsistence right can be reasonably narrowly defined, but what about a duty to redress systematic social discrimination, or one to ensure physical security by providing

62. *Id.* at 529.

63. An argument of this kind is made in the U.S. constitutional context by Frank B. Cross, *The Error of Positive Rights*, 48 U.C.L.A. L. Rev. 857 (2001).

preventive healthcare? How far must the state go, and to what extent may it limit the rights of others in order to fulfill the rights?

It is possible for the state to "overfulfill" basic rights to the detriment of other rights. Overfulfillment can be seen in operation in Cuba and the People's Republic of China, for example. In justifying a high standard of protection of physical security from crime, of bodily and mental soundness through free healthcare, and of subsistence through subsidized food and clean water, these governments have systematically repressed political rights. Overfulfillment may carry risks even in liberal democratic states, however. As states undertake greater commitments of fulfillment, they must aggregate wealth and power to themselves for that purpose. As states grow in size and power, they become more difficult for the population to supervise and control due to a variety of factors. These include the large state's superior organization and disproportionate power, the relative anonymity of officials in large bureaucratic organizations, and the large number of candidates to whom an official may "pass the buck" to avoid accountability and liability. The more active the state becomes in trying to advance the enjoyment of human rights, the more intrusive and less directly controllable it tends to become, and the more likely it is to exercise an odious influence on the enjoyment of all human rights.

The answer to these objections is that, by my definition, basic rights include only those rights for which the state is the duty holder best positioned to fulfill the right on a societal level. In most societies at most times, the nature of the state, as the principal municipal institution having the authority to regulate the entire spectrum of private behavior and holding a monopoly on the use of force for enforcement purposes, will be best positioned to fulfill the most fundamental human rights, such as the right to subsistence, physical security, health, and freedom from discrimination. Private individuals and organizations will at almost all times and places simply lack the moral authority, coercive power, wealth, incentives, and will to rectify society-wide threats to these rights.

Not only is the state often in the best position to fulfill basic rights, it may also bear responsibility for the existence of social injustices that offend or undermine those rights. Diffuse social or environmental threats to the enjoyment of basic rights have at least part of their origin in state action or inaction, or the reverberations of such action or inaction. In other words, the state may frequently be expected to bear direct or indirect moral responsibility for creating the conditions that led to a threat to the basic right through pathological public policies. Some impersonal threats to the exercise of basic human rights, such as global warming or new disease pandemics, originate in forces beyond the control of any one state, but most such threats can be traced at least in part to government policies of one or more states. Throughout the world, most discrimination based on race, sex, religion, ethnicity, sexual orientation, and similar grounds has historically been caused or exacerbated by state policies reflecting or encouraging such discrimination. For example, in states with formal segregationist regimes, such as the United States from the end of slavery until 1964, and South Africa from 1948 until 1994, much social inequality was mandated by law. The abolition of the laws did nothing to redress the entrenched racial imbalances in wealth, education, healthcare, and other preconditions to the enjoyment of human rights. Similarly, widespread poverty in many states may be traced to government policies as well, from regressive tax policy to corruption to economic mismanagement.

Even environmental threats to the exercise of human rights, such as droughts, hurricanes, and earthquakes, may be exacerbated by government policies. States with laws or policies encouraging wasteful or shortsighted farming or water usage magnify the effects of droughts that threaten subsistence rights. States with ill-considered or poorly enforced building codes suffer more casualties from earthquakes and cyclones. States that fail to inspect and maintain dams, levees, and breakwaters exacerbate the damage caused by hurricanes and floods. If the purpose of the state is to protect human dignity and encourage its flourishing, the state can rarely disclaim all responsibility for threats to basic human rights such as subsistence, physical security, and freedom from debilitating discrimination. As a direct or indirect contributor to these threats, the state bears moral responsibility for taking practical and effective measures to assist its population to enjoy their human rights.

The most obvious solution to overfulfillment of basic rights is to rein in abuses of power and restrict the state's ability to intrude on one human right in the service of another, through improvements to such already well-established doctrines as proportionality. The fact that some states abuse duties of fulfillment or that such duties carry risks of aggrandizing state power cannot justify exonerating the state of fulfillment duties unless such abuses and risks fulfill two conditions: they must not be reasonably avoidable, and the costs and risks of such duties must outweigh their benefits. Admittedly, the ability and suitability of the state to fulfill basic positive rights is an empirical question, but that merely supports the argument against rejecting extensive positive duties by a priori assumption. To the extent that the state in fact meets the criteria of ability and democratic responsiveness, it must be admitted to have a moral mandate to fulfill basic rights as long as we conceive of the state's fundamental purpose as promoting the enjoyment of rights among its nationals.

The case for holding the state to a duty to fulfill all non-basic rights is much weaker; the resource commitment and potential dangers of delegating the state to fulfill such rights as freedom of expression or the right to own property in most contexts are sufficiently obvious to require no explanation. A more difficult question is the extent to which the state has a positive ethical "duty to protect" non-basic rights from private intrusion. Scenario {1b} above provided a convenient example in the state's duty to secure for its nationals the right of employment (ignoring the subsistence point for the moment).[64] In most states at most times, employment would not qualify as a basic right. Although *P*'s loss of employment is unfortunate, the state's failure to procure employment for *P* does not carry the same moral consequence as its failure to prevent *P* from starving to death. The right to employment being a positive right, clearly the state must take some measure to benefit *P*. But there is no strong basis for attributing to the state the duty to "fulfill" *P*'s right to work by employing *P* itself or forcing a private employer to do so. Protecting *P* against the consequences of a severe economic downturn, its own economic mismanagement, unjustified employment discrimination, and similar threats without actually ensuring employment would satisfy Patria's duty. As noted earlier, protection is not a unitary concept. Although all human rights require the possibility of

64. *See* UDHR art. 23.1; CESCR art. 6; Banjul Charter art. 15.

at least some state positive protective measures to ensure their meaningful enjoyment, the precise measures required will vary according to circumstances. These circumstances include the extent of the state's resources, the nature and severity of threat to the right, and the ability of morally relevant others, including the right holder himself or herself, to defuse a threat to the right. The extent of the resources and efforts needed to satisfy the state's moral duty cannot be defined a priori, unless one assumes counterfactually that the state is always and everywhere uniformly best placed to prevent or redress all threats to everyone's human rights.[65]

5. The Enforceability of Positive Rights

Another argument against positive rights, advanced by Cass Sunstein in a related context, is that such rights cannot be effectively enforced by courts (more broadly, we might say human rights authorities, including international treaty bodies), because these entities lack the expertise and legitimacy to craft a political or legal regime that would guarantee the observation of such rights.[66] Underlying this objection is the observation that positive rights frequently require elaborate institutions for their protection, and it is only the legislative and executive authorities of states who have the expertise and ability to establish, fund, maintain, and monitor such institutions. Although a court may possess the technical authority to declare state duties to fulfill such positive rights as a right to sustenance, healthcare, or a reasonable opportunity for employment, courts cannot themselves design and implement food banks, hospitals, public health insurance systems, or macroeconomic measures for economic growth and job creation.

No doubt courts lack the resources and expertise to design and manipulate social institutions to solve shortcomings in the enforcement of positive human rights. The same is not true, at least to the same degree, with regard to intergovernmental organizations. These do indeed sometimes establish complex enforcement institutions, including criminal tribunals, compensation commissions, monitoring bodies such as the U.N. Human Rights Council and U.N. Human Rights Committee, and executive agencies such as the Offices of the High Commissioners for Human Rights and Refugees (two separate organs of the United Nations). As for municipal courts, Sunstein's conclusion that positive rights are unenforceable by judicial channels for reasons of resources and competence is a *non sequitur.* Judicial authorities need not construct a compliant regime; their role is merely to determine whether the state is in compliance with its duties. This is the normal mode of judicial decision-making. Courts bear no general responsibility for erecting institutions to solve social problems; their role is to adjudicate whether the legislative and executive organs of the state have failed to perform their duties according to such general standards as "reasonable best efforts" and "due diligence." If found noncompliant, the responsibility lies on the political branches of government to adopt measures of compliance. To call a positive human right to sustenance unenforceable because judges cannot personally compel the government purchase of food and

65. *See, e.g.*, SANDRA FREDMAN, HUMAN RIGHTS TRANSFORMED 23, 189 (2008).

66. *See* Cass Sunstein, *Against Positive Rights*, E. EUR. CONST. REV., Winter 1993, at 35, 37.

its distribution to starving persons makes no more sense than to call constitutional voting rights unenforceable because judges cannot organize and conduct elections, or rights to free speech unenforceable because courts have no power to compel the government to halt the practice of censorship.

Summary

In this chapter, I argued that, in international human rights law, the distinction between negative and positive rights cannot rest on the common philosophical definitions, which distinguish between rights requiring positive action or an allocation of resources by the state and those that do not. Such a definition may arguably be useful on the context of individual ethics, but the corporate nature of the state renders it incoherent in the human rights law context. Instead, the definition of positive rights rests much more coherently on the source and nature of the harm that the state is obligated to prevent or remedy. A duty to redress harms originating most directly from the state itself—including its officials and agents—is a negative duty. A duty to redress harms originating most directly from sources other than the state itself is a positive duty.

The argument in this chapter also defends the concept of negative rights as conceptually meaningful. To explain why, I introduced the potentially competing understandings of negative rights from the perspectives of a rational solipsistic right holder and rational solipsistic duty holder. The former conceives of his right as imposing a duty on the state to ensure the right holder's enjoyment of the right regardless of the source of the threat. The latter (the state, in this context) conceives of its correlative duty as satisfied if its action conforms to the standard of behavior legally required of it, regardless of its effect on the right holder's enjoyment of the right. This distinction illuminates the assumption among some theorists that only the right holder's perspective matters.

I also argued that it is necessary for the state to fulfill, or ensure the enjoyment of, certain "basic rights." Slightly modifying Henry Shue's well-known definition, I identify these such rights to include the subset of rights whose enjoyment, in the context of the state in which they are operative, is necessary for the enjoyment of a broad spectrum of other human rights, and whose enjoyment the state is best positioned to guarantee on a societal level as a backstop. Regardless of whether states have yet accepted positive duties to fulfill such rights as a matter of international law, they are morally obligated to do so. Recognizing only negative duties to respect basic rights, or even positive duties to protect right holders against private actors threatening their enjoyment, inexorably falls short of the state's minimum moral duties.

6

The Legal Consequences of Negative and Positive Paradigms

The previous chapter dealt with some of the ethical dimensions of negative and positive rights; this chapter analyzes some of their legal characteristics and consequences. As always in legal analysis, language matters, because it intermediates the subjective understandings of participants in the system. In terms of the negative and positive paradigms, the phrasing of the right or correlative duty are highly consequential, because some ostensibly negative rights may be converted into positive rights, and vice versa, by subtle lexical changes. Before we explore how this might work, it is important to establish how the terminology relating to negative and positive rights may be deceptive ab initio.

A. THE SCOPE OF NEGATIVE AND POSITIVE RIGHTS

1. Negative and Positive as Non-opposites

Although negative and positive rights are coherent categories if properly defined, it is easy to misapprehend their significance. As applied in international human rights theory, the terms seem to be misnomers. In chemistry, "negative" and "positive" characterize ionic charges of opposite value. The negative charge of an electron neutralizes a positively charged ion, and vice versa. In an electric battery, the mingling of negative and positive energy flows may have explosive consequences. Even in common parlance, negative and positive are considered antonyms, connoting mutual exclusivity or opposition.[1] But negative and positive human rights share none of these characteristics. These are not polar opposites but rather cognate concepts. Both impose duties on the state with respect to the right holder; they differ primarily in the scope of the duty implied. Negative and positive rights are not opposed and do not cancel each other out in the legal realm. The misnomers with which they are labeled lead to their differences being frequently exaggerated.

The non-opposition can be seen most obviously from the fact that positive rights nearly always encompass negative rights. Nobody has a positive right to protection from torture by private individuals alone; as the primary holder of human rights

1. *See* Oxford Dictionary of English (2d ed. 2010).

duties, the state is always obligated to respect the right as well.[2] Positive rights consequently impose more expansive duties than do negative rights, and in ways that cause them to overlap negative rights, in all but a few exceptional cases. By augmenting the duty of self-restraint with a duty to protect, the state generally assumes responsibility, not just to monitor the behavior of its own agents, but to take appropriate measures to monitor and counteract a broader set of private threats to the right. There is no inconsistency or even tension in the two classes of rights.

2. Nonuniformity in the Strength and Scope of Rights within Categories

"More expansive" does not mean more burdensome or definite, however. Because the distinction between positive and negative paradigms relates to the source of threat to the right and not to the extent or kind of state action required to defend the right, the choice of positive or negative framing has no effect on the specificity of the right and its parameters. A negative right can impose duties quite as definite and detailed as those correlative to a positive right and vice versa. The phrasing, rather than the choice of paradigm, of the right expresses the scope of protected activity and the strength of the protection in terms of prohibited or required acts.

Nondiscrimination rights illustrate this point well. The effect of a nondiscrimination right depends on the social context in which the right applies and the framing and phrasing of the right itself. An equal right to employment opportunities framed as a negative right simply prohibits the state from interfering in a discriminatory manner with a person seeking employment. Application of the right may well leave persons in class *A* with a higher unemployment rate than persons in class *B* for entirely arbitrary reasons. When framed as a positive right, however, the state may be interpreted to have a duty to expend resources in order to help provide employment opportunities to class *A* in order to achieve parity with the employment rate of class *B*.[3] Reframed in positive terms, the right tends toward egalitarian

2. Of course, the state maintains certain privileges to encroach on broadly defined human rights in a way typically forbidden to private individuals. For example, a state may deprive a person of freedom of movement through imprisonment upon conviction following a fair trial, yet the state would violate the same person's human right by tolerating a similar deprivation by private persons. The scope of the negative right is nonetheless the same for the state with respect to its own officials and agents and private persons. The fact that the state is privileged to engage in some behaviors impermissible to private persons is a function of the state's role as public authority, and it is accordingly bound by restrictions on such behavior (such as the requirement of affording the detained person due process of law, a timely trial, and punishment proportionate to the crime) that do not apply to private persons. It would thus be inaccurate to say that the state's positive duty with respect to the right of freedom of movement is broader than its negative duty. The duties have different characters.

3. For example, the International Covenant on Economic, Social, and Cultural Rights in article 6 imposes a positive obligation on states to "take appropriate steps to safeguard" the right to work and lists some of the steps this obligation includes. G.A. Res. 2200A (XXI), 21 UNGAOR Supp. (No. 16) at 49, U.N. Doc. A/6316 (1966), 993 U.N.T.S. 3, *entered into force* Jan. 3, 1976 [hereinafter, CESCR].

distributional consequences. The state must elaborate a nondiscrimination policy with greater nuance and to greater social effect for the positive right. Yet, this is not a uniform effect of positive framing. As Joseph Raz has observed, nondiscrimination rights do not necessarily have an egalitarian character, precisely because the effect of a rule depends on the social context in which the rule applies.[4]

The organic flexibility of language makes generalizing about the consequences of framing rights and duties within broad categories hazardous. It is even possible for a positive right to offer less protection when put into practice than a negative right covering the same subject matter. The phrasing of a right and the social context in which it operates frequently matter more than the negative or positive framing when it comes to the concrete effects of the right. The appropriateness and real-world effect of an abstract right depends on the nature and source of the threats to the right and to the character and resources of the state government charged with its protection. The phrasing of the right may also narrow or broaden the scope of the protection. A negative "right to privacy" described as a right against unnecessary government interference in one's life is much more expansive than a positive right to privacy described as a right against unauthorized access to personal data. Framing affects the scope and content of the right; it does not determine all aspects of it.

3. Pseudo-Positive Rights

One consequence of the confusion wrought by the common philosophical definitions of negative and positive rights is that many negative rights in the corpus of IHRL give a deceptive appearance of imposing positive duties. Phrasing the state's duty in terms of taking affirmative measures may create a phantom of a positive right, resulting in what might be called a "pseudo-positive" right. A pseudo-positive right is a negative right that is phrased in such a manner that it emphasizes the state action involved in respecting the right without appearing to impose a duty to protect or fulfill the right.

For example, consider a negative right, and then consider a semantic variation of the right that emphasizes the positive action associated with it:

{2a} States are prohibited to subject any person to torture or inhumane or degrading treatment or punishment.[5]

{2b} States are obligated to treat persons under the state's power humanely and with due recognition of and respect for their inherent dignity.

These two statements, although not equivalent, overlap a good deal in the scope and content of protection. Under {2a}, the state may exercise its discretion to punish, subject to the stated limitation. When {2a} is rephrased as {2b}, the duty does not seem to change much, unless one were to interpret "humane" treatment to

4. *See* Joseph Raz, The Morality of Freedom 225–26 (1986).

5. *See* European Convention on Human Rights art. 3, 213 U.N.T.S. 222, *entered into force* Sept. 3, 1953 [hereinafter ECHR].

differ from treatment that is "not inhumane."[6] Torture is inhumane by its nature. Importantly, in both {2a} and {2b}, the state alone is obligated to treat persons in a prescribed manner; in neither case has the state assumed a duty to "protect" or to "fulfill" the right to humane treatment, even though {2b} appears to be framed in positive terms. This is precisely why, as discussed in the previous chapter, the positive character of a right cannot turn on the duty holder's obligation to take action. Both {2a} and {2b} express negative rights; statement {2b} merely appears superficially to establish a positive right. It actually remains a negative right.

A slight change in wording will, however, turn {2b} into a true positive right in the legal sense:

> {2c} States are obligated to ensure that persons under the state's power are treated humanely and with due recognition of their inherent dignity.

In {2c}, the positive right imposes a correlative duty on the state to protect as well as to respect. Although {2b} and {2c} may seem superficially comparable, their scopes are in fact quite different. In {2c}, the state has assumed a responsibility not only to prevent its officials from engaging in torture or inhumane treatment, but to "ensure" that individuals under the state's power are treated humanely. The contrast between {2a} and {2b} illustrates how not all changes in phrasing necessarily reframe the right under a different paradigm. Statement {2c} shows how an ostensibly minor change in wording can reframe the right. In {2c}, a change in the scope of the state's duties was effectuated by changing the operative verb in negative duty {2b} from "to treat" to the clause "to ensure . . . are treated." Any addition of a verb suggesting the concept of state protection such as "ensure" or "protect" (or, equivalent verbs, such as "guarantee," "secure," or "implement") may reframe a negative duty as a positive one. The substitution of the verb "to treat," which relates to action by the state directly regarding the right holder, in {2b} with the verb "to ensure . . . are treated" in {2c} alters the meaning to denote a guarantee respecting the right holder's treatment. The guarantee being nowhere limited to the state's own treatment of the right holder, it follows syntactically that {2c} obligates the state to guarantee the right holder's humane treatment without reference to the source of that treatment. The focus of right {2c} is not specific conduct by the state but rather a more general duty to protect individuals subject to the state's power. Version {2c} establishes a genuinely positive right.

One reason confusion between these versions might arise is that the state is generally thought to pose the primary threat to persons detained by the state itself or its agents. In that case, all three variants seem to protect the same interest to the same extent. But persons in the state's power may be vulnerable to threats other than those originating from the state's officials and agents. Duties {2a} and {2b} do not explicitly require the state to protect imprisoned convicts from abuse by other prisoners, for example. Duty {2c}, in contrast, engages the state's duty to protect a person whose capacity for self-protection the state itself has substantially impaired.

6. It could be argued that the change in framing makes it semantically more difficult to exploit the gray area between humane and inhumane treatment. For example, the argument that waterboarding is humane treatment is even less credible than the claim that it is not "torture" or "inhumane or degrading treatment."

The mistaken opposition of negative rights to pseudo-positive rights can have pathological consequences for human rights doctrine, as can sometimes be seen from U.S. civil rights practice. For example, some U.S. politicians and judges have an ideological commitment to protecting negative constitutional rights to the exclusion of positive rights. In denying legal relief to those who have suffered or died from government inaction, U.S. courts are fond of announcing that the Constitution is an enumeration of negative rather than positive civil rights.[7] This opposition, coupled with the incoherent definition of positive rights discussed in Chapter 5, has sometimes led the U.S. Supreme Court to mischaracterize negative rights as positive in order to achieve an ideological goal of exonerating the state from duties imposed by the Constitution.

In *Bowers v. Hardwick*, for example, the Court characterized privacy and sexual freedoms as pseudo-positive rights—calling on the federal government to protect homosexuals from state interference with "a fundamental right to engage in homosexual sodomy"—in order to justify federal abstinence when states criminalized private sexual activity between consenting adults.[8] To some degree, the Court merely engaged in the lawyer's trick of defining the right to privacy with such specificity that it seems trivial on superficial examination. Any human right can be redefined ad absurdum in this manner. By the same logic, one could posit there is no fundamental right to engage in heterosexual intercourse. Any *specific* behavior is only one of an infinite number of potential manifestations of a more general right, in this case the right to privacy. To draw attention to the specific aspects of behavior and deny it manifests a right because of its specificity is to deny any rights at all. Several years later, the Court corrected this error,[9] but the fundamental misunderstanding of negative and positive rights remains common in U.S. jurisprudence.

The Supreme Court was also making a mistake more important for the purpose of this discussion. By mischaracterizing the rights at stake in the case as a "right to engage in" private acts rather than a "right to freedom from arbitrary government interference in private acts," the Court rhetorically converted a negative right to respect to a pseudo-positive right to government protection in private decisions "to act." This misapprehension is especially troubling because, when applied at the individual level, all negative rights can be described in these terms. To the extent that rights entitle the right holder *to do things*, then all rights might be interpreted as pseudo-positive. The description of an act as manifesting a right is an artifact of the natural rights mythology from which IHRL was born,[10] and it may serve the purposes of advocates of extensive claims on state resources for ideological reasons.

7. *See* David P. Currie, *Positive and Negative Constitutional Rights*, 53 U. Chi. L. Rev. 864 (1986).

8. 478 U.S. 186, 192–94 (1986).

9. Lawrence v. Texas, 539 U.S. 558 (2003).

10. *See* Paul Gordon Lauren, The Evolution of International Human Rights: Visions Seen 13–14 (2d ed. 2003); *see, e.g.*, Jacques Maritain, Les droits de l'homme et la loi naturelle (Maison Française 1942). John Locke influentially grounded his political theory in natural rights. *See* John Locke, Two Treatises on Government 124, 128, 163 (Peter Laslett ed., 1947) (1690).

The right to freedom of expression and the right to work impose duties on the state to provide public speaking and publishing forums and to ensure full employment. The state becomes the omnipresent patron of all valued human activity.

Those who reject this conception of the state's role are handed the tools to deny not just positive rights but negative rights as well, because the logical consequence of conflating negative and positive rights is that the limitation of (pseudo-)positive rights leads to the limitation or rejection of quintessentially negative rights. If the right to freedom of movement is the same as the right to move, then rejecting the argument that the state must assist persons in moving (for example, to locations closer to their families or where jobs are available) becomes identical to rejecting the freedom of movement itself, including the negative right to change addresses without the state's consent or to leave the country. Maintaining the distinction between negative rights as rights to freedom from government interference, and positive rights as rights to government assistance through protection and fulfillment, also maintains a conceptual core of rights that are difficult to attack ideologically and that, at a minimum, protect right holders against the state harming the protected interest using its own considerable power.

B. COMPLEMENTARY FRAMING

Because positive duties to protect or fulfill a right generally encompass a concomitant duty to respect the right, it may be thought that framing a right in positive terms renders superfluous a negative right relating to the same subject matter, unless for some reason the correlative positive duty is strictly limited to protecting the right against threats posed by third parties. As mentioned earlier, the government is usually the most potent single actor in the state. There are few human rights that can be adequately guarded by requiring state protection from private intrusion without limiting the prerogative of the Leviathan itself to intrude freely on the right.

Nonetheless, the effect of framing choices is not so simple. Language, pithy legal language especially, is finite in its capacity to define methods of social control, while the varieties of seriously morally unacceptable individual and social behavior approach the infinite. A person's dignitary interests are by nature susceptible to abuse or neglect in unforeseeable variability. Therefore, multiple approaches to the same policy outcome, which in law frequently means multiple rules converging on the same value or interest, can augment the legal system's ability to address different kinds of threats to that value or interest. Appearances notwithstanding, framing the same right in both negative and positive terms—what I will call "dual framing"—may not result in much redundancy at all.

Dual framing can, in fact, enhance the right's scope considerably. Consider the right to life. As a negative right, its protections are nearly absolute with respect to state acts; the state may not kill an individual except under exceptional circumstances.[11] As a positive right of protection, the protection afforded is much broader, but the state's correlative duty is more limited; the state must adopt all reasonable and appropriate measures to protect the lives of its nationals against arbitrary

11. *See* CPPR, arts. 6(2), (4), (5); McCann v. United Kingdom, 21 E.H.R.R. 97 (1996).

deprivation by others.[12] The negative and positive duties together protect the same interest from different kinds of threats and in different ways.

Even negative and pseudo-positive rights can work together effectively. Several international human rights instruments frame the same general right in both negative and pseudo-positive terms.[13] Article 9(1) of the CCPR illustrates this point well:

> 1. Everyone has the right to liberty and security of person. No one shall be subjected to arbitrary arrest or detention. No one shall be deprived of his liberty except on such grounds and in accordance with such procedure as are established by law.

The Universal Declaration also uses dual framing of negative and pseudo-positive rights. Article 15 of the Universal Declaration provides:

> (1) Everyone has the right to a nationality.
> (2) No one shall be arbitrarily deprived of his nationality nor denied the right to change his nationality.

In both examples, a pseudo-positive right, phrased at a high level of abstraction in the first sentence, is joined to one or more specific negative rights. Despite their overlapping coverage, the rights are not identical in their protections. In CPPR article 9(1), the first sentence establishes a right of sufficient generality that, on a plain reading, it would encompass a duty to protect individual liberty and security of person against private threats. However, the rights are sufficiently general that their meaning is subject to a good deal of interpretation. The second and third sentences establish negative rights that superficially fall within the scope of the first sentence and might be considered redundant. However, because of their relative specificity, they open the door to an interpretation of the right sufficiently expansive to encompass certain duties that might otherwise have been interpreted out of article 9, such

12. *See, e.g.*, Osman v. United Kingdom, 29 E.H.R.R. 245, para. 115 (2000); Sawhoyamaxa Indigenous Community v. Paraguay, Inter-Am. Ct. Hum. Rts., Judgment of Mar. 29, 2006 (merits), para. 152. At least as the positive right is currently interpreted, it is a duty to protect and does not include a duty of fulfillment. For example, a state is not obligated to invest in medical technologies to artificially prolong the lives of its nationals at the expense of other policy priorities. Such an interpretation of the positive right would be sufficiently expansive to be self-invalidating. However, a few human rights authorities have interpreted the right to include a positive duty to fulfill by adopting measures that would ensure the availability of medical treatment for life-threatening diseases. For example, a joint report of the Office of the U.N. High Commissioner for Human Rights and the Joint U.N. Programme on HIV/AIDS intimidated, albeit without justifying or explaining, that "right to life" obligations were "relevant" to HIV/AIDS. International Guidelines on HIV/AIDS and Human Rights ¶ 102 (2006 Consolidated Version). According to one author, the Colombia Constitutional Court has held more explicitly that a denial of HIV/AIDS treatment violates the right to life. *See* Alicia Ely Yamin, *Not Just a Tragedy: Access to Medications as a Right under International Law*, 21 Bos. U. Int'l L.J. 325, 335–36 (2003).

13. *E.g.*, UDHR, arts. 13, 17; CPPR, art. 23(1)–(2).

as arrest without reasonable ground for suspicion or detention at the discretion of public officials with minimal guidelines to prevent abuse.

Article 15 of the Declaration provides even greater diversity of coverage between the two paragraphs. Because only the state itself can grant nationality, positing a human right to a nationality necessarily implies that every person's right to a nationality has to be granted by some state or other. Thus, the first paragraph establishes a duty to fulfill the individual's interest in a nationality, which can be accomplished only by states providing procedures for the grant of nationality and ensuring that persons under their jurisdiction are not deprived of a nationality.[14] The first paragraph covers the case in which *R* is born in Patria to Smalldonian nationals resident in Patria. Patria grants nationality based on *ius sanguinis*, whereas Smalldonia grants nationality based exclusively on *ius soli*. Under article 15(1), Patria and Smalldonia must arrive at an accommodation that ensures *Q* has an appropriate nationality. Paragraph 1 does not dictate how Patria and Smalldonia will settle the question, but it does require that the outcome involve *R* having a Patrian or Smalldonian nationality.

Article 15(2) requires no such thing. Instead, the second paragraph covers the case in which the Patrian government seeks to deprive *R* of an established Patrian nationality, perhaps as punishment for a serious crime or in retaliation for political dissent. With a view to complying with article 15(1), Patria negotiates with Smalldonia for the expatriation of *R*, with the proviso that Smalldonia will grant *R* nationality. Article 15(2) prohibits Patria from depriving *R* of his nationality under these circumstances, even though Patria has ostensibly complied with article 15(1) by ensuring that *R* has a nationality.

The example shows how it would be mistaken to conclude that positive human rights invariably afford greater scope and stronger protection to individuals than do negative rights. To the extent that positive rights impose duties of protection from threats exogenous to the state government, they will provide broader protection to individual interests. However, the scope of protection afforded by any right depends on whether it is phrased expansively or narrowly—a consideration independent from its negative or positive framing. A negative right can be phrased to impose expansive duties on the state. Indeed, one could imagine a maximally broad negative right that expresses an ultraminimalist vision of state government. A right to liberty unimpeded by state interference except insofar as necessary to protect the same right of others, for example, would be a very broad negative right indeed. A positive right can conversely be phrased to impose narrow duties; for example, the right to the bare minimum quantum of sanitary water necessary to sustain a healthy life.[15]

In short, complementary framing of the same right in positive and negative paradigms can be used to increase the scope of protection and to specify duties with greater precision than would be easily accomplished by an exclusively positive right. In *Evans v. United Kingdom*,[16] the European Court of Human Rights

14. *See, e.g.*, Yean & Bosico Children v. Dominican Rep., Inter-Am. Ct. Hum. Rts., Judgment of Sept. 8, 2005, paras. 140–42, 156–58, Ser. C, No. 130.

15. For an extended discussion of the right to water, *see* INGA T. WINKLER, THE HUMAN RIGHT TO WATER: SIGNIFICANCE, LEGAL STATUS AND IMPLICATIONS FOR WATER ALLOCATION (2012).

16. Eur. Ct. Hum. Rts., App. No. 6339/05, Judgment of Apr. 10, 2007, *available at* http://www.echr.coe.int.

implicitly recognized the complementary roles of negative and positive rights in the context of privacy. The Court conceived the right (ECHR article 8) as imposing both kinds of duties. The negative right was expressed as a state duty to refrain from unnecessary interference with an individual's private life. The positive right included the right to protection of one's privacy from unnecessary interference by others through balancing the individual's interest in privacy with the interests of other individuals and the public in general. The Court has held such duties to be "inherent in" various other rights as well, including the rights to family life and freedom from degrading treatment or punishment.[17] It has accordingly interpreted rights framed in seemingly negative terms as if they implied positive duties to ensure adequate enjoyment of the right.[18]

The UN Human Rights Committee has also interpreted article 2(1) of the International Covenant on Civil and Political Rights, which generally obligates parties to "ensure" all rights provided in the Covenant, as imposing a general positive duty despite the negative framing of many rights:

> The article 2, paragraph 1, obligations are binding on States [Parties] and do not, as such, have direct horizontal effect as a matter of international law. The Covenant cannot be viewed as a substitute for domestic criminal or civil law. However the positive obligations on States Parties to ensure Covenant rights will only be fully discharged if individuals are protected by the State, not just against violations of Covenant rights by its agents, but also against acts committed by private persons or entities that would impair the enjoyment of Covenant rights in so far as they are amenable to application between private persons or entities.[19]

Although the case for state duties to take appropriate measures to protect persons within its jurisdiction from private violations of their human rights is strong, the Committee's comment reads perhaps too aggressively on the positive law. Read literally, it would convert a general commitment to taking seriously the norms embodied in the Covenant into a modification of the clear terms of certain plainly negative rights codified in the treaty. Whatever the ethical merits of the Committee's position, it rests on a legally questionable interpretation of the Covenant's provisions that seems to reflect neither the intent of the parties nor subsequent international practice.[20] As for rights framed ambiguously so that they could be interpreted alternatively as positive or negative, the analysis becomes more complicated.

17. *E.g.*, M.C. v. Bulgaria, 40 E.H.R.R. 20, para. 150 (2005); X & Y v. Netherlands, 8 E.H.R.R. 235, para. 23 (1986).

18. *See, e.g.*, Siliadin v. France, ECHR App. No. 73316/01, Judgment of 26 July 2005, 45 I.L.M. 962, paras. 77–89 (finding a positive obligation to protect vulnerable persons against private forced labor).

19. Hum. Rts. Comm., General Comment No. 31, para. 8, U.N. Doc. CCPR/C/21/Rev.1/Add.13 (2004).

20. *Cf.* Diane F. Orentlicher, *Settling Accounts: The Duty to Prosecute Human Rights Violations of a Prior Regime*, 100 Yale L.J. 2537, 2569–70 (1991) (noting the absence of evidence in the *travaux préparatoires* of any intent to impose universal positive rights in the Covenant); Monica Hakimi, *State Bystander Responsibility*, 21 Eur. J. Int'l L. 341, 352–53 (2010) (observing that

C. AMBIGUOUSLY FRAMED RIGHTS

Although the distinction between negative and positive rights is clear in the abstract, some international human rights instruments contain provisions that so straddle the line between positive and negative rights that it is difficult or impossible to tell which was intended. As noted, equal protection clauses such as article 24 of the ACHR may be read either as negative or positive nondiscrimination rights (although they are usually interpreted as the latter). At least in theory, two tribunals confronting the same language could interpret it to confer on the state duties of entirely differing scopes. Substantive rights are frequently ambiguous in this regard as well. Consider a typically ambiguous right from article 20 of the Universal Declaration:

> {3} All persons have the right to peaceful assembly and association.[21]

This provision might be read to recognize a negative right to freedom from government interference in assembly and association. However, the language of the Declaration may also be construed to imply a positive right in stating that persons "have the right to . . .," as opposed to saying that the state shall not abridge or deny the right. The language itself is sufficiently vague to leave room for doubt.[22] Does the state fully satisfy its duty if it refrains from interfering with the privilege of assembly and association? Must it protect those seeking to assemble or associate from private threats, as when a group of thugs attack a rally advocating an unpopular cause? Should example {3} indeed be read to create a state duty to facilitate private association, such as allowing the creation of nonprofit limited liability corporations or making public facilities such as schools or public parks available for meetings of civic groups? Each reading is facially credible.

Just as using a duties paradigm helps to clarify the scope of the correlative right (Chapter 2, Section C), explicitly positive framing of rights makes it possible to clarify the scope of the intended duties by specifying the community's expectations of which threats the state should counter and what kinds of resources it should allocate to facilitate the enjoyment of the right. Ambiguity in the right's framing as positive or negative, in contrast, opens the door to divergent interpretations of the correlative duty. And the interpretive choice will have important ethical

human rights treaty bodies do not in practice interpret the conventions to obligate states to protect individuals from third-party violations of every protected right).

The same is true, albeit to a lesser degree, of the national implementation of human rights law. The constitutions of most countries, including Canada, the United States, and most of Europe and Africa, primarily focus on negative rights. However, the constitutions of some, especially in Latin America and Asia, give significant attention to positive rights. *See, e.g.*, CONST. OF BRAZIL arts. 5–7 (1988); CONST. OF INDIA arts. 21A, 38–47 (2007); CONST. OF INDONESIA ch. X (1949); CONST. OF MEXICO arts. 3–4 (2005).

21. UDHR art. 20(1).

22. The corresponding provisions of the CPPR are framed ambiguously as well, but they include specific negative obligations, which might be read to suggest that the drafters of the UDHR had a primarily negative right in mind. *See* CPPR arts. 21–22.

consequences. States frequently tend to understand their duties as the minimum, negative ones, whereas beneficiaries of the right, human rights advocates, or independent interpretive authorities predictably construe the duty more expansively.

The *Belgian Linguistics* case furnishes an instructive example of the unpredictability that may result from ambiguous framing. That case concerned a provision of Protocol I of 1952 to the European Convention, which provides in the first sentence of article 2: "No person shall be denied the right to education."[23] Semantically, the provision seems to belong to the negative rights paradigm, because the "denial" of *the right to* education it forbids demands restraint from interference in education. The second sentence of Protocol I seems to confirm this interpretation. It provides:

> In the exercise of any functions which it assumes in relation to education and to teaching, the State shall respect the right of parents to ensure such education and teaching in conformity with their own religious and philosophical convictions.

The use of the "any functions which it assumes" language strongly suggests the state is *not* obligated to assume any specific functions, such as positively providing public education. The official French text uses parallel language: "*Nul ne peut se voir refuser le droit à l'instruction.*" Had the Protocol proclaimed a right to education, forbidden the denial of education as opposed to merely the right to education, a positive right would be clearly indicated. Even had the second sentence used the word "its" instead of "any" to qualify the state's education functions, it would at least imply that the state *has* an educational function, as opposed to having the option to assume such functions.

Here, the French text is more ambiguous: "*L'État, dans l'exercice des fonctions qu'il assumera dans le domaine de l'éducation . . . .*" "*L'exercice des fonctions*" could mean either "exercise of *the* functions" of "exercise of *any* functions," and "*qu'il assumera*" translates literally to the predictive "that it will assume," but colloquially could mean "that it assumes." To say less ambiguously that the adoption of a mission of public education was optional, the text could have read: "*qu'il pourrait assumer*" ("that it might assume") or "*qu'il aurait assumer*" ("that it will have assume"), or more definitely still, "*qu'il choisit d'assumer*" ("that it chooses to assume"). Nonetheless, read in combination with the English text, the intention to impose a negative right alone seems manifest. This was the Belgian government's proposed interpretation—that the sentence should be read to create nothing more than a duty not to "prevent persons within its jurisdiction from obtaining education." Due to its negative framing, Belgium concluded, article 2 does not require the state to provide an education to all within its jurisdiction.[24]

A semantic objection to this reading is that article 2 contains a double negative and is written in the passive voice in both languages, which means that it omits a grammatical subject. It does not explicitly forbid *the state to deny* an education to

23. Protocol I to the ECHR, Mar. 20, 1952, E.T.S. No. 9, art. 2.

24. *Belgian Linguistics Case*, Eur. Ct. Hum. Rts. Judgment of July 23, 1968 (merits), 1 E.H.R.R. 252 (1968).

any person; on a plain reading, it forbids any person from being denied an education by anyone. Because article 2 does not limit the duty to any specific source of denial, another possible construction is that the state must protect individuals from being denied education by others (e.g., parents who wish to deprive their own children of an education). If so, article 2 creates a positive right, as the Strasbourg Court concluded in the case, although more precise phrasing could have eliminated the doubt. But does it impose on the state just the duty to protect, or also an obligation to fulfill the right? Had the language been identical to the corresponding right in the Economic, Social, and Cultural Rights Covenant ("Every person has a right to a free primary education."[25]), there would be no doubt that the state had a duty to fulfill the right and thus to provide universal education. But nothing about a prohibition on "denying" all persons an education necessarily obligates the state to create institutions to provide that education.

Because Belgium, like all Council of Europe member states, already had in place a system of general public education, the Strasbourg Court was able to avoid resolving whether article 2 imposed a "duty to fulfill" by creating new public institutions. However, the Court interpreted article 2 to include at least the right to benefit from the educational institutions then existing. Stressing the words "right to education," the Court held that such a right "by its very nature calls for regulation by the State.... It goes without saying that such regulation must never injure the substance of the right to education nor conflict with other rights enshrined in the Convention."[26] The Court seemed therefore to side with the applicant on that point.

The Strasbourg Court's conclusion might be defensible, but its reasoning is somewhat opaque. It may be deduced that, if article 2 did *not* impose a duty to fulfill but were instead limited to a duty to protect, the only basis for concluding that no person should be denied access to *existing* educational institutions would be a right against discriminatory denial of education (article 14 of the European Convention), in this case based on native language. But the Court made no reference to article 14 in its discussion of article 2. It seems that the Court interpreted the words "right to education" as carrying within them a duty to fulfill in the sense of providing effective education with whatever resources the state had allocated to that purpose. Yet, if Belgium had chosen not to assist the impecunious to obtain an education in any manner, would the Court have concluded that Belgium had met its duties under article 2 by not interfering with those persons who could afford a private education?[27] It seems unlikely. In effect, the Court's logic may be read to turn the phrase "right to education" into a positive right to fulfillment, regardless

25. CESCR art. 13(2). Admittedly, statement {3} does not specify who holds the correlative obligation, but, given that the statement appears in a treaty, clearly it is the state parties to the treaty that have undertaken the obligation.

26. *Id.*

27. A positive right to free public primary or elementary education is guaranteed by the UDHR, the CESCR, the European Social Charter, and several other widely adopted international legal instruments. *See, e.g.*, UDHR art. 26; CESCR art. 13; European Social Charter (Revised) art. 17(2), ETS No. 163, May 3, 1996. It is theoretically possible, but unlikely, that the Strasbourg Court would have interpreted the European Convention in a manner less protective of the right than the Universal Declaration or CESCR.

of the surrounding words. If there had been no independent authority to resolve the dispute and no parallel but more precisely worded duties in other human rights treaties, the state would maintain its discretion to interpret its own duties expansively or conservatively, according to its inclination.

As noted previously, the Strasbourg Court has recently taken to reading each operative article of the Convention in light of article 1 to apply the principle of effectiveness. Article 1 provides that the Council of Europe member states are obligated to "secure to everyone within their jurisdiction the rights and freedoms defined" in the Convention.[28] The Court interprets the term "secure" as suggesting a duty to protect. Under this interpretation, the ECHR could be read to require states to protect from private infringement even rights framed in unambiguously negative terms. The Court has done precisely that with increasing frequency,[29] to the point where some publicists now consider article 1 of the ECHR "the cornerstone of the Convention system," itself providing an independent source of positive duties for Council member states.[30] In a few cases, the Court has even inferred positive duties from the very concept of the "rule of law." For example, in *Matheus c. France*, the Court interpreted the clearly negative right against arbitrary deprivation of property in article 1 of Protocol I to the ECHR to encompass a positive right to protection of the property from private intrusion.[31] The "real and effective exercise of the right," asserted the Court, "must not depend solely on the State's duty to refrain from all interference and must involve positive measures of protection . . . ."[32] The Court's theory was that, if a state does not protect human rights from private intrusion, vigilante or private justice-seeking contrary to the rule of law might result.[33] Such decisions implicitly reflect a more general political theory about the central place of positive rights in the moral justification for and effective functioning of the state.

Of course, a semantic approach to the duty to "secure" in ECHR article 1, much less to the term "right" in article 2, stretches the meaning of the European Convention precisely as much as the Human Rights Committee stretched the meaning of article 2(1) of the CPPR. If use of the term "right" in a human rights instrument automatically imposed a duty of fulfillment on the state, then by the same logic any provision not framed explicitly as a prohibition could be interpreted as imposing maximal positive duties. By definition, positive rights extend the state's duty beyond self-restraint; positive rights are, therefore, most appropriate when either third parties or impersonal forces constitute any serious threat to a right. Poverty is one of the primary threats to the right to education, and, with respect to remedies, the strong position of the state as a provider of free public education

28. ECHR, art. 1.

29. *See, e.g.*, Broniowski v. Poland, 43 E.H.R.R. 1 (2006) (right to property); Vgt Verein gegen Tierfabriken v. Switzerland, 34 E.H.R.R. 4 (2002) (freedom of expression).

30. Jean-François Akandji-Kombe, *Positive Obligations under the European Convention on Human Rights*, Council of Europe, Human Rights Handbook No. 7, at 9 (2007).

31. ECtHR App. No. 62740/00, Judgment of Mar. 3, 2005.

32. *Id.* para. 69 (my translation).

33. *Id.* para. 71.

is evident from the fact that the great majority of state constitutions guarantee it to their nationals.[34] Moreover, the integral nature of education to the enjoyment of other human rights, such as political and cultural participation, freedom of expression, and health, justify an expansive interpretation of the right. It is not its label that gives the right its character, but the nature of the human interest in education, the predominant source of threats to that right, and the role of the state relative to other potential sources of fulfillment.

At the same time, using article 1 of the European Convention to color the interpretation of every other article potentially expands the commitments of the parties to the Convention beyond what they originally intended. For example, in the *Fadayeva* case, the Strasbourg Court interpreted the article 8 right to respect for private and family life to require the state to protect the natural environment against the depredations of private industry that may affect a person's health and well-being.[35] Similarly, in the *Ogoniland* case, the African Court of Human and People's Rights interpreted the Banjul Charter's guarantees of the right to health and to a "general satisfactory environment favourable to their development" to entail a state duty to "take reasonable and other measures to prevent pollution and ecological degradation, to promote conservation, and to secure an ecologically sustainable development and use of natural resources."[36] Such interpretations are justified given the specific language of the treaties and their purpose of protecting and promoting human dignity, but they necessarily entail the exercise of great judicial discretion in evaluating the extent to which the state's environmental regulations are satisfactory, unless restrained by other doctrines and judicial sensitivity to the prerogatives of state sovereignty and to the principle of the separation of powers.

The ambiguity so common in international human rights instruments may arise from a desire to build in flexibility so that the instrument can evolve with changing social conditions. Or it may represent a decision to paper over entrenched disagreement among treaty negotiators about the scope of the right. In some cases, the ambiguity merely reflects poor drafting. Whatever the reason, ambiguous framing delegates the politically delicate function of defining the scope of the right and its correlative duties to institutional human rights authorities that may (as in the case of certain municipal or international tribunals) or may not (as in the case of most convention-based committees) have enforcement powers to back up their interpretations.

The delegation of such discretion puts human rights authorities between two fires. Aggressive interpretation of rights as implying expansive positive duties undermines the legitimacy of the authority when its interpretation is ignored. Even when respected by states, such an interpretation may create the impression of a judicial or international bureaucratic seizure of the policymaking role from state governments. Demagogues eager to distract popular attention from state misdeeds might enflame public opinion against international interference to divert criticism to alleged human rights "imperialism," "neocolonialism," or subversion of

34. *See* Katharine Tomasevski, *UNESCO Manual on Rights-Based Education* 15 (2004).

35. Fadeyeva v. Russia, 45 E.H.R.R. 10, para. 89 (2007).

36. SERAC v. Nigeria, African Ct. Hum. & Peoples' Rts., Commun. No. 155/96, para. 52 (2002).

democracy. Yet, a conservative interpretation of state duties will frequently validate unethical state practices and set an inertia-inducing precedent requiring states and human rights advocates to activate the ponderous and uncertain international law-making process to rectify it.

Human rights authorities have dealt with these problems in practice by developing tests for the recognition of legitimate state interests that would justify derogation from the general right as well as a test for evaluating the appropriate balance between the state interest and the human rights.[37] Such tests require fact-intensive judgments and inevitably some discretion. They cannot, therefore, totally deflect all attacks on expansive interpretations of state duties. This leaves positive constructions of international human rights law that are far in advance of popular opinion or state consensus, a practice fraught with peril. Yet, as we have seen, international human rights authorities nonetheless frequently interpret ambiguously phrased international human rights to impose positive duties beyond what might have been the preferences of states. The practice continues. Recently, for example, the U.N. Special Rapporteur on Freedom of Speech interpreted the CCPR to impose on states a

> positive obligation to promote or to facilitate the enjoyment of the right to freedom of expression and the means necessary to exercise this right, including the Internet. Hence, States should adopt effective and concrete policies and strategies—developed in consultation with individuals from all segments of society, including the private sector as well as relevant Government ministries—to make the Internet widely available, accessible and affordable to all.[38]

At first blush, this interpretation is aggressive far beyond what would be justified by examining the intent of the treaty parties. Freedom of expression is usually conceived as a prototypically negative right, implicating no duty to protect individuals from private interference with their speech (for example, a crowd booing down a soapbox speaker). Much less has it been interpreted to provide every person with a platform and resources to be heard or expensive technological means to receive communications from others,[39] such as free hearing aids for the elderly or Internet access. Even the Strasbourg Court has not clearly recognized a state duty to *fulfill* the right to freedom of speech. In making this claim, the Special Rapporteur did very little to advance the human right to freedom of speech, and much to undermine his own credibility. Nonetheless, the intuition underlying the Rapporteur's argument will in some cases justify characterizing freedom of expression as a positive right. For example, in many countries, concentration of media ownership in

37. *See, e.g.*, U.N. Hum. Rts. Comm., General Comment No. 18: Non-discrimination, para. 13 (Nov. 10, 1989); Toonen v. Australia, U.N. GAOR, Hum. Rts. Comm., 50th Sess., Communication No. 48/1992 at 226, paras. 8.3–8.4, U.N. Doc. A/49/40 (Sept. 21, 1994); Karner v. Austria, 38 E.H.R.R. 24, para. 41 (2004).

38. Report of the U.N. Special Rapporteur on the Promotion and Protection of the Right to Freedom of Opinion and Expression, U.N. Doc. A/HRC/17/27, para. 66 (2011).

39. *See, e.g.*, Richard B. Brandt, Ethical Theory 450–51 (1959).

the hands of a private monopolist or oligopolists has resulted in the systematic exclusion of certain views—most obviously, those critical of the media itself or the government that supports it—from public discourse. In such cases, the argument in favor of requiring the state to vindicate a positive right to freedom of expression becomes compelling, either through industry regulation or by dissipating market concentration through competition measures, mainly because of deficiencies in the state's regulation of economic and social practices (in this case, failure to preserve speech markets from anticompetitive behavior). The treatment of this right as a positive one as a *general* rule, however, would be difficult to justify.

Although ambiguity complicates the task of interpreting a right and may create contention over the meaning of the right, I do not mean to paint ambiguity in this context as an evil to be uniformly shunned. Given the context-dependence of human rights law in a system of global or regional application, ambiguity about negative or positive paradigms will be functional in some circumstances. It allows the same apparent rule or principle of human rights law to apply to states in highly disparate situations without forcing those states in which a strong positive right is less feasible to unequivocally breach its international legal obligations. At the same time, when a negative human right is the maximum commitment that can attract consensus in the international community, ambiguous framing leaves the door open for an evolutionary interpretation of the right that expands its scope and protections in synchronicity with state capabilities. Ambiguity, in short, preserves the role of political negotiation in a legal framework that keeps international human rights law both vital and acceptable to states having diverse economic, cultural, and political regimes.

7

Structural Implications of Negative and Positive Paradigms

The use of negative or positive right paradigms may affect more than the scope or meaning of a human right itself. Human rights laws express a specific cultural understanding of the role of the state and its agents in the world public order in relation to private individuals. In every universal or regional rule of human rights law, there is an implicit assumption regarding the social and political context in which the rule will operate. Specifically, the promulgation of a legal rule characteristically assumes that the rule is capable of obedience, and that it represents an appropriate and generally effective means to serve the policy purposes for which it is designed.[1] Decisions about IHRL paradigms generally both communicate the beliefs of the international community about the role of law in the world public order and recursively shape the order itself.

The subtext or connotation that might accompany a choice of framing fundamental values places certain responsibilities on the drafters of international human rights instruments. Framing choices can affect the interpretation of a right by state governments and international authorities to the benefit or detriment of many persons. Seemingly trivial semantic variations might undermine or reinforce the value in unforeseen ways. Although the elevation of an interest to the status of a human right implies a certain consensus on the definition and parameters of the right, rights—like all principles of law—require interpretation and construction by legal authorities acting through an authoritative decision process. The absence of a single, easily ascertained meaning for most human rights gives them an even more dynamic character than most other laws. No verbal formula can precisely embody the balance of interests that reflects the world community's values on the subject of the right, to the extent consensus exists. But conventional rules can provide varying

1. As with most generalizations, this one admits exceptions. Some rules are in fact "made to be broken," in the sense that violation serves the (usually covert) policy goals of the enacting authority, most commonly for exemplary purposes, to stigmatize disfavored groups, or for fundraising. Legal rules may also be adopted by irresponsible authorities with no concern for their place in the social order. However, IHRL serves more prosocial policy purposes, specifically (as I have said throughout) the protection and promotion of human dignity and flourishing.

degrees of specificity regarding the actors and situations implicated.[2] How well specificity in a conventional human right serves the value or interest underlying that right depends partly on how accurately the language of the law encompasses the range of actions or situations that could threaten, undermine, or negate that value or interest.

If we focus exclusively on the legal and abstract ethical consequences of framing decisions, we might overlook the systemic effects of the right in its operative social context. Universal human rights as public international law indicate a commitment to an achievable world public order in which the rights express consensus values. In practice, state commitments to these values, and capabilities of enforcing the rights adequately, vary significantly. As noted, positive rights tend to demand a greater resource commitment—not by definition or necessity, but because self-restraint is usually less burdensome than policing an entire society to protect tens or hundreds of millions of individuals from threats from diverse and diffuse sources. Whatever one's view of positive rights on pragmatic, ideological, or ethical grounds, the widespread imposition of resource-intensive rights dependent on protection by state governments, in a world of limited resources and some variation in the conception of human dignity, suggests a system designed to respond sensitively to political pressures.

A. POSITIVE RIGHTS AND ECONOMIC DEVELOPMENT

A resulting paradox is that relying on a positive rights paradigm has sometimes proved useful to those governments with the fewest resources to devote to social and economic programs for the protection and fulfillment of positive human rights. The explanation lies in two complicating facts. First, the more resources IHRL requires states to expend, the more aspirational they appear.[3] Impecunious governments may excuse themselves from costly measures to protect or fulfill rights through the maxim that every modern legal system recognizes in some form: *ad impossibilia nemo tenetur*. A state incapable of mustering the resources to fulfill extensive positive human rights duties to provide universal healthcare, education, employment, or sustenance and sanitary water cannot be held to have violated its duties under international law, and by necessary extension the human rights of its nationals. For this reason, the Universal Declaration qualifies positive economic, social, and cultural rights as binding "in accordance with the organization and resources of each State."[4] Similarly, the extensive positive rights in the CESCR include the qualification that the state parties only undertake the duty in the Covenant "to take steps . . . to the maximum of [the state's] available resources, with a view to achieving

2. *See* Frederick Schauer, *Prescriptions in Three Dimensions*, 82 Iowa L. Rev. 911, 912–15 (1997).

3. *Cf.* Samantha Besson, *Les obligations positives de protection des droits fondamentaux—Un essai en dogmatique comparative*, 1 Rev. de Droit Suisse 49, 66, 75–76 (2003).

4. UDHR art. 22. *Cf.* Cyrus Vance, U.S. Sec'y of State, Law Day Address at the Univ. of Ga., Human Rights and Foreign Policy, Apr. 30, 1977, 76 Dep't of State Bull. 505 (1978) ("We recognize that the fulfillment of [economic and social rights] will depend, in part, upon the stage of a nation's economic development.").

progressively the full realization of the rights."[5] The ECOSOC Committee, the Human Rights Council, and international tribunals have accordingly accounted for practical limitations on the state's power when assessing their compliance with their duties under human rights law.[6] The positive right correlates not to an absolute duty, then, but to an obligation to employ "reasonable best efforts" or to take "all appropriate measures" to implement the right.[7]

From either a legal or ethical standpoint, the state's lack of resources for implementing positive rights does not excuse its duty to prioritize working actively toward the realization of the rights. The Committee on Economic, Social, and Cultural Rights accordingly interprets the "available resources" language of article 2 to require not absolute and immediate, universal realization of the rights, but rather "steps towards" the realization of the rights "within a reasonably short time after" the Covenant enters into force. The Committee considers "resource constraints applying within the country concerned" to be relevant to the question of compliance, meaning that the full realization of the rights "will generally not be able to be achieved in a short period of time."[8] For reasons too complex to discuss here, the international community has not consistently pressed developing countries to take radical political and economic steps to fulfill all conventional positive human rights. In the developing world, resource constraints act as a potent policy counterweight to the positive right holder's solipsism.

Extensive positive rights may also play a role in some states insidiously subversive of human dignity. The professed inability of the state to guarantee widespread positive rights may become a pretext for failing to implement modest improvements in positive rights well within the resources of the state, or still more disturbingly for respecting negative rights. The very strength of the guarantees inherent in the more aggressive positive rights might make fully fulfilling them appear so unrealistic that it relieves pressure on the governments to take direct and immediate action. With positive rights thus discredited, all human rights—including eminently fulfillable negative political rights, such as freedom of speech and the right to participate in governance—become vulnerable to intimations of utopianism by association or, in the developmentalist argument, subservience to more fundamental but unfulfilled rights such as subsistence and public order.[9] Statements in human

5. CESCR art. 2(1).

6. *See, e.g.*, Ilaşcu v. Moldova, App. No. 48787/99, Judgment of July 8, 2004, paras. 330–33, 40 E.H.R.R. 46 (2005) (finding that, where the respondent state lacked control and authority over its own territory, it could not be expected to fulfill the ordinary obligation to protect).

7. *See* Human Rights Committee, General Comment No. 31 (May 26, 2004), CCPR/C/21/Rev.1/Add.13, para. 8; Committee against Torture, General Comment No. 2 (Jan. 24, 2008), CAT/C/GC/2, paras. 17–18.

8. U.N. Committee on Economic, Social, and Cultural Rights, General Comment No. 3: The Nature of State Parties' Obligations, paras. 2, 9–10, U.N. Doc. E/1991/23, Annex III, at 86 (1990).

9. *See* Kenneth Christie & Denny Roy, The Politics of Human Rights in East Asia 6 (2001); Eva Brems, Human Rights: Universality and Diversity 346–49 (2001); U.S. Dep't of State, Press Release, Speech by Ass't Sec'y Michael H. Posner, *The Four Freedoms Turn 70* (Mar. 24, 2011), *available at* http://www.state.gov/g/drl/rls/rm/2011/159195.htm ("For decades,

rights instruments and claims by international political elites that human rights are inherently indivisible and interdependent,[10] although intended to refute arguments that states can pick and choose which human rights to observe and which to de-emphasize or ignore, may, in a further irony, have been used by states with insufficient resources and control to fulfill expansive positive duties to justify a failure to implement negative eminently feasible rights, especially political and civil rights.[11]

At the same time, the multiplication of expansive positive rights has potentially prosocial implications. Recognizing positive rights opens the door to arguments that economically developed states, or the international community as a collectivity, share responsibility to assist in the realization of positive rights for resource-poor members of the international community. This proposition finds support in article 22 of the Universal Declaration, which implies a duty to structure the world

the Soviet states and the Non-Aligned Movement critiqued the United States for a perceived failure to embrace economic and social rights. They used the rhetoric of economic, social and cultural rights to distract from their human rights abuses. They claimed economic rights trumped political rights, while in fact failing to provide either."); *see, e.g., The Compass Fails*, The Economist, Sept. 17, 2011, at 61 (the Ethiopian prime minister's response to international criticism for the state's violations of civil and political human rights is that such rights are subservient to the economic needs of the people, which are served by "stability"); Fareed Zakaria, *Culture Is Destiny: A Conversation with Lee Kuan Yew*, For. Affairs, Mar.–Apr. 1994, at 109, 111 ("The expansion of the right of the individual to behave or misbehave as he pleases has come at the expense of orderly society."); Jahangir Amuzegar, *Rights, and Wrongs*, N.Y. Times, Jan. 29, 1978, at E17 ("[C]are must be taken not to paper over certain harsh economic realities in the developing countries with a mere magnificent façade—that is, not to crucify their basic human needs on the altar of abstract "human rights.").

The U.N. Committee on Economic, Social, and Cultural Rights asserted in 1993 at the Vienna World Conference that the "shocking reality" is that states and the international community tolerate breaches of economic and social rights that "if they occurred in relation to civil and political rights, would provoke expressions of horror and outrage and would lead to concerted calls for immediate remedial action." UN Doc. E/1993/22, Annex III, para. 5. Whether this statement reflects "reality" is doubtful. It is not immediately clear that negative political human rights are enforced more vigorously by the international community than positive economic, social, and cultural rights. Violations of both kinds of rights are and have always been extremely common, as even a cursory glance at the docket of the European Court of Human Rights or Inter-American Court of Human Rights, or the annual Human Rights Watch *World Report*, attests. Indeed, the states most staunchly advocating positive economic rights—the Soviet Union and its satellite states—were also among those least observant of negative political rights. *See* Paul Gordon Lauren, The Evolution of International Human Rights 245 (2d ed. 2003).

10. *E.g.*, Optional Protocol to the International Covenant on Economic, Social and Cultural Rights pmbl., G.A. Res. 63/117, U.N. Doc. A/RES/117 Annex (2009); G.A. Res. 60/251 pmbl., U.N. Doc. A/RES/60/251 (2006); Proclamation of Teheran, International Conference on Human Rights para. 13, U.N. Doc. A/CONF.32/41 (1968), *available at* http://www.unhchr.ch/html/menu3/b/b_tehern.htm; Vienna Declaration and Programme of Action, U.N. GAOR, World Conf. on Hum. Rts., 48th Sess., 22d plen. mtg., part I, para. 5, U.N. Doc. A/CONF.157/24 (1993), *reprinted in* 32 I.L.M. 1661 (1993); United Nations Population Fund, Human Rights Principles 2005, *available at* http://www.unfpa.org/resources/human-rights-principles.

11. For a nuanced evaluation of the claim of indivisibility, *see* James W. Nickel, *Rethinking Indivisibility: Towards a Theory of Supporting Relations between Human Rights*, 30 Hum. Rts. Q. 984 (2008).

public order in a manner conducive to the meaningful implementation of positive human rights:

> Everyone, as a member of society, has the right to social security and is entitled to realization, through national effort and international co-operation . . . of the economic, social and cultural rights indispensable for his dignity and the free development of his personality.[12]

UDHR article 28 provides more generally that all persons are "entitled to a social and international order in which the rights and freedoms set forth in this Declaration can be fully realized."[13] The CESCR similarly establishes a duty of international cooperation, "especially economic and technical," to assist other countries in the realization of the guaranteed rights.[14]

Developing countries have sometimes proposed planting just such a legal duty in firmer ground,[15] but the wealthier and better organized states have so far resisted the codification of a general duty of assistance and cooperation in legal terms[16] to maintain the discretion and flexibility of using economic policy and international cooperation for the promotion of foreign policy goals. Yet, states have sometimes agreed in "soft law" instruments to a moral duty to assist poor countries to develop economically through technical and financial assistance. Most notably, in 1975, the U.N. General Assembly adopted the Charter of Economic Rights and Duties of States, which provides that states "have the responsibility to co-operate" economically and technologically "for the promotion of economic and social progress throughout the world, especially that of developing countries."[17] It further establishes that each state "has the duty to co-operate in promoting a steady and increasing expansion and liberalization of world trade and an improvement in the welfare and living standards of all peoples, in particular those of developing countries."[18] This includes "extending active assistance" to developing countries to accelerate their economic and social development, and providing economic and technical assistance.[19] These are quintessentially positive duties that would facilitate the realization of human rights globally.

12. UDHR art. 22 (emphasis added).

13. *Id.* art. 28.

14. CESCR art. 2(1).

15. *See, e.g.*, Commission on Hum. Rts., Rep. of the Open-Ended Working Group to Consider Options regarding the Elaboration of an Optional Protocol to the International Covenant on Economic, Social and Cultural Rights on Its Third Session, Mar. 14, 2006, E/CN.4/2006/47, paras. 77–86 (statements of Angola, Egypt, Ghana, Indonesia, Iran, and Morocco).

16. See Fons Coomans, *The Extraterritorial Scope of the International Covenant on Economic, Social and Cultural Rights in the Work of the United Nations Committee on Economic, Social and Cultural Rights*, 11 Hum. Rts. L. Rev. 1, 17, 34–35 (2011).

17. U.N. G.A. Res. 3281 (XXIX), art. 9 (Jan. 15, 1975).

18. *Id.* art. 14.

19. *Id.* arts. 17, 22.3.

These instruments provide the basis for arguments in favor of a legal duty of cooperation and material assistance in development. The ECOSOC Committee now interprets the Covenant more specifically to impose special obligations on developed states to aid developing countries through economic and technical assistance.[20] Similarly, the Committee has interpreted the right to adequate food as including a state duty not only to avoid denying food to countries facing starvation, but to protect and facilitate access to food in other countries "and to provide the necessary aid when required."[21] Members of the Organization for Economic Cooperation and Development did in fact increase their direct foreign development aid between 1975 and 2010 significantly.[22]

These commitments do not require any specific level of aid from any specific country, but they do require sufficient assistance to make the global enjoyment of basic rights possible. Given the inequalities in wealth and technology between states, positive rights will not be realized in most of the world without quite substantial international cooperation. Charles Beitz has taken this argument one step farther and suggested that, to the extent that international regimes or actors have adopted policies, such as trade treaties or intellectual property rules, that impose heavy costs on states struggling to fulfill their positive duties, changes in such regimes might be considered a component of the enforcement of human rights.[23] The strength of his argument rests on the nature of human rights as claims that normally prevail over lesser considerations of public policy. Unless one wishes to argue, for example, that free trade or the expansion of intellectual property rights rises to a level of urgency and importance equivalent to conventional human rights, such as the rights to subsistence or basic medical care,[24] then international cooperation must be considered a core component of the enforcement of positive human rights as a project of public international law.

Again, however, recognizing this facet of positive rights does not dictate that any *specific* act or policy beyond cooperation and assistance is necessary for the fulfillment of state duties. Rather, it opens the door to a range of demands on economically privileged states, and former colonizers especially, by the international

20. *See* U.N, Committee on Economic, Social, and Cultural Rights, General Comment No. 3, paras. 13–14. The Covenant itself is more ambiguous; it obligates each party to "take steps, individually and through international assistance and co-operation, especially economic and technical," to fulfill the rights enumerated in the Covenant. CESCR art. 2(1).

21. U.N. Committee on Economic, Social, and Cultural Rights, General Comment No. 12, para. 36.

22. Specifically, OECD development aid rose from $34 billion to $91 billion in 2010 dollars. Calculated using the OECD International Development Statistics database, StatExtracts DAC7b (Total Net Official Development Assistance), *available at* http://stats.oecd.org/Index.aspx?DatasetCode=REF_TOTAL_ODF.

23. *See* Charles R. Beitz, The Idea of Human Rights 40 (2009).

24. Although intellectual property bears indirectly on several well-established human rights, the general position that intellectual property ownership qualifies as a broad human right has been considered and rejected by several thoughtful commentators. *See, e.g.*, Robert L. Ostergard, *Intellectual Property: A Universal Human Right?*, 21 Hum. Rts. Q. 156 (1999); Laurence R. Helfer, *Human Rights and Intellectual Property: Conflict or Coexistence?*, 5 Minn. Intell. Prop. Rev. 47 (2003).

community as a whole. On the less extreme end of the spectrum, for example, sits the claim that states refusing to cooperate in creating a world public order fulfilling the conditions necessary for development in the poorest countries—especially those states that prioritize economic self-aggrandizement without regard to the costs it imposes on others—have failed in their duties just as surely as if they had denied their own citizens these same rights. Closer to the other end of the spectrum would be claims by a state incapable of guaranteeing a right to work of its own nationals that wealthier states have the duty to allow its migrant workers admission to seek employment in their territory, or to allow admission of "economic refugees."[25] Characterizing positive rights as dependent upon international cooperation for their fulfillment may not validate any specific policy claim, but it does legitimate claims to cooperation and assistance as a genus.

B. IS THERE A NEGATIVE DUTY TO RENOUNCE BENEFITS FROM INJUSTICE?

The context-dependence of ethical duties suggests that duties may vary according to the relative situations of the duty holder and right holder. Human rights and their correlative duties do not exist in a void as eternal truths; they are premised on preexisting relationships colored by political and cultural constructs that condition the expected behavior of the dramatis personae. History furnishes part of that context. International human rights law exists in a world public order arising from centuries of global politics in which a reasoned moral conscience rarely played a more than subordinate role. The present world order is a product of exploitation of the weak by the strong, the entrenched consequences of which the forces of modern political idealism are only beginning to redress.

In a world where resources are distributed unequally due to the victimization of some groups by others, the heirs of the victimizers may be thought to carry the proportionate ethical duty of compensating the heirs of the victims to better balance the prospects of universal enjoyment of human rights. From this, Thomas Pogge has concluded that a negative duty can require the same kind of resource allocation as a positive duty when the right holder has suffered a severe disadvantage from acts of the duty holder.[26]

Pogge's premise is that powerful states have colluded to structure the world public order in such a manner as to impose all but inescapable poverty on billions of persons.[27] This structure results from policy choices rather than impersonal and inexorable historical forces. For example, international intellectual property rules could impede access by developing countries to life-saving pharmaceuticals, or they could be restructured to make drugs more widely available at some reduced profit to the inventors and manufacturers of these pharmaceuticals. The first choice

25. *Cf.* Michelle Foster, International Refugee Law and Socio-Economic Rights: Refuge from Deprivation 344–45 (2007) (arguing that economic deprivation should be considered as a factor in refugee analysis).

26. I wish to thank Jim Nickel for drawing my attention to the implications of Pogge's argument for my own.

27. Thomas Pogge, World Poverty and Human Rights 15, 26, 139 (2d ed. 2009).

creates a systemic harm to the world's poorest and most vulnerable persons while preserving the benefits to wealthy pharmaceutical companies and the governments that tax them. The second choice avoids that consequence at some cost to inventive industries and their governments. Pogge claims that states that have historically played a role in structuring an unjust world public order have a moral duty, not just to take positive measures to rectify the consequences of historical wrongs, but to take measures not to benefit from that order. He accordingly considers the "duty to ensure that others are not unduly harmed (or wronged) through one's own conduct" to be a negative rather than a positive duty.[28]

Several aspects of Pogge's argument are interesting and controversial,[29] but the one bearing on the present discussion is his characterization of an ethical duty not to benefit from an existing world public order as a negative duty. Because a negative duty correlates to a negative right, if Pogge is correct, then the right to subsistence, traditionally conceived as a prototypical positive right, is really a negative right correlative to a duty held by those states that have cooperated in imposing the conditions for the denial of that subsistence right. Pogge's argument implies that every person has, not just a positive right to subsistence, but a *negative* right to freedom from an unjust world order that denies them the possibility of subsistence. Pogge would accept that a negative duty is one of self-restraint, but he claims that refusing to benefit from one's own cooperation in imposing an unjust world public order on others qualifies as such rather than as a positive duty of fulfillment.

There are both semantic and analytical objections to Pogge's characterization of negative rights. Semantically, Pogge has redefined the concept of restraint by turning it on its head in a limited set of circumstances. His definition is idiosyncratic and does not reflect the normal understanding of negative and positive duties. An idiosyncratic definition would not be objectionable per se; the problem is that it appears to reflect atemporal reasoning. Pogge claims he is concerned solely with how states behave in the "present" world public order,[30] but implicit in his argument is a condemnation of the decision of powerful states to structure the world public order unfairly in the past. In other words, in previously structuring the world public order in a manner that harms the prospects of those living in developing countries, Pogge considers states to have violated a negative duty *at that time* not to interfere with the rights to subsistence and development. To that extent, his argument is unobjectionable. But the conventional understanding of negative and positive duties[31] takes the environment as a given and proposes ethical and legal duties based on the preferable choice of conduct under the present circumstances.

28. *Id.* at 15, 130.

29. For example, Pogge shares Peter Singer's maximalist belief that all persons are bound to prevent morally important harm to others anywhere in the world to the extent that such assistance does not inflict a comparable moral harm on the duty holder. *See* Peter Singer, *Famine, Affluence, and Morality*, 1 PHIL. & PUB. AFFAIRS 29 (1972).

30. Thomas Pogge, *Severe Poverty as a Violation of Negative Duties*, 19 ETHICS & INT'L AFF. 55, 55 (2005).

31. Pogge distinguishes between duties and obligations. Obligations, to Pogge, are specific reasons for action derivative of general and morally fundamental duties. *Id.* at 68. For our purposes, we may treat the concepts as comparable.

It follows that the state's *present* moral (and legal) duties depend on its *past* observation of its moral (and legal) duties. Present respect for human rights duties does not excuse past violations, although it may mitigate their effects. Pogge considers the duty to redress a past injustice as a positive duty,[32] because to change the world public order requires not that states restrain themselves from depriving persons of basic rights, but rather that the responsible states take positive action to allocate resources away from their current uses and toward redressing the injustice.[33] In conventional terms, the state's violation of a negative right to subsistence in the past through policies that deprive the affected population of the means of subsistence gives rise to a present positive duty to redress the violation. Pogge justifies his approach on grounds of expediency; the injustice suffered by the global poor due to the violation of a present negative duty becomes a matter of moral priority, whereas a positive duty to help others can be shrugged off as less morally pressing.[34] At least, this is how I understand the argument.

One problem with Pogge's contention is that the distinction between negative and positive rights is not premised on any assumption that negative rights are inherently more justifiable than positive rights. As the next part of this chapter will demonstrate, the case for states having positive moral duties is quite as persuasive as the case for states having negative duties. Even were that not the case, however, Pogge's artifice is unnecessary. A weighty and present moral duty can follow from one's past conduct as well as one's current conduct. It is just as convincing to say that a state's past violations of negative moral duties not to deprive any person of the right to subsistence or health justify an urgent moral demand for positive action to redress the continuing consequences of those past violations. Moral duties do not depend on accepting the present distribution of resources completely out of context.

Pogge's characterization of negative rights also translates rather poorly from ethical theory[35] into international human rights law. In the realm of ethics, atemporal reasoning may present theoretical problems, but it is at least possible to craft an internally consistent theory justifying an ethical duty on the haves to share inherited wealth with the have-nots. In international law, however, atemporal reasoning undermines the sequential logic of cause and effect on which all legal systems are based. Legal conclusions can be drawn only from evidence of a causative

32. *Id.* at 68–69.

33. Rowan Cruft has characterized both (1) the moral duty to cease an ongoing or forthcoming violation of another's human rights, and (2) the moral duty to remedy a past human rights violation, as positive duties. *See* Rowan Cruft, *Human Rights and Positive Duties*, 19 Ethics & Int'l Aff. 29, 30–31 (2005). The first characterization confuses positive obligation with positive action. As suggested earlier in this chapter, the duty to cease violation is encompassed by the duty not to violate. It is a duty of restraint and, therefore, a negative duty par excellence. The second may be a positive obligation in an ethical sense, but in a legal sense, it is not a human rights obligation; it is an obligation arising under the general rules of state responsibility for wrongful acts. *See* Draft Articles on Responsibility of States for Internationally Wrongful Acts arts. 1, 12, 31, G.A. Res. 56/83 (Dec. 12, 2001), Annex, UN Doc. A/56/49(Vol. I)/Corr.4.

34. Pogge, *supra* note 27, at 139.

35. *Id.* at 130.

relationship, because effect always follows cause by some lapse of time, however brief. Atemporal reasoning overlooks the need for evidence to sustain claims of a human rights violation. Specifically, legal claims require sufficient evidence of the blameworthy acts and the causation of harm by means of those acts. To advance a credible legal claim for redress under IHRL, it is not enough simply to assume that, because Patria is politically powerful and the world public order is unjust, Patria has violated a legal duty to all states that fail to prosper in that unjust order. The claimant must carry the burden of showing the specific past acts of Patria that justify the judgment that Patria has acted wrongfully toward specific developing countries and caused the alleged harm.[36] In so doing, the claimant could be identifying violations of a past negative duty even while alleging that Patria can remedy this violation by undertaking positive action or by refraining from future violations (continued negative action). Logical evidentiary requirements reinforce the analytical rigor of IHRL and moral theory alike, but in the former case they are, as it were, positively necessary.

Evidentiary requirements also allow the possibility of falsifiability. Whatever the role that Patria played in harming any specific developing country does not justify holding Patria to a duty to help all developing countries. Pogge's argument depends inter alia on the assumption that all developed countries contributed to and benefit from a world public order that imposes or historically imposed great disadvantages on all developing countries. Such generalizations are in reality empirical assertions that can only be evaluated on a country-by-country basis. It simply cannot be assumed that Norway or Poland or Liechtenstein directly contributed to forming a world order that created or sustains poverty in developing countries. Poverty in developing countries can be traced to many empirical causes, of which such factors as oppressive intellectual property law treaties might contribute only trivially.[37]

C. ARE POSITIVE RIGHTS GENERALLY DESIRABLE?

1. Ethics and Positive Rights

To some, positive rights represent a malevolent government intrusion on individual freedom, or a quixotic promise that ends by diluting all rights. To others, a state that promises little more than to refrain from actively harming persons within its jurisdiction, while leaving them exposed to the slings and arrows of outrageous fortune, fails in its fundamental purpose. This radical disagreement might reflect

36. It is important to the argument that under customary international law, states as corporate entities continue to maintain liability for past harmful acts, regardless of whether the government responsible for those acts remains in power. *Cf.* Articles on the Responsibility of States for Internationally Wrongful Acts arts. 4, 10, G.A. Res. 56/83 (2001), Annex, U.N. Dox. A/56/49 (Vol. I)/Corr.4; PATRICK DUMBERRY, STATE SUCCESSION TO INTERNATIONAL RESPONSIBILITY 233 (2007).

37. For example, the average annual income in India was about $1,500 according to the World Bank, but instead of investing in poverty relief and economic development, the Indian government has chosen to develop nuclear weapons and a space program to put its own satellite into orbit around Mars.

nothing more than a clash of insipid political dogmas, but it might also follow from differing opinions about the capability of an organized government to improve the lives of its nationals. Let us assume *arguendo* that the state is at least sometimes the actor best positioned as a practical matter to repel an assault on, or ameliorate a private interference with, at least some human rights. That assumption will frequently be factually accurate. The question then arises whether the state fulfills its ethical duties by limiting its human rights-related activities to observing negative rights. In other words, beyond basic human rights discussed in the last chapter, does the state have an ethical duty to accept positive *legal* duties toward those under its jurisdiction, on condition that it can fulfill those duties adequately? If so, what is the extent of this ethical duty and its concomitant legal duty?

One aspect of negative rights that has attracted criticism is that they offer little or no benefit to powerless right holders threatened by forces other than the state itself. In any given state, threats to the right can originate from a multiplicity of sources. Rational persons can have no interest in a system that attributes to them rights they cannot realistically expect to enjoy. It follows that meaningful protection of human rights requires imposing at least some positive duties of protection on the state to the extent the enjoyment of those rights is considered a policy priority. If the state's only duty was one of self-restraint, it is free to stand by while its population is attacked, oppressed, and starved, so long as state agents themselves bear no direct responsibility. Complete indifference to the suffering of the state's population is not a morally viable position in any minimally defensible political theory. It is a *legally* viable position in the sense that a regime could be structured with such a limited purpose in mind, and the regime might well achieve its purpose; a right protected from the state, but not from private society, correlates to a definite duty on the state's part. Yet, the effects on human enjoyment of the right will be predictably diminished, if not nugatory.

As discussed previously, in Part I, if the international system framed its mandates in terms of duties instead of rights, the duties could be formulated to avoid the implication that the state must take measures to ensure the population's enjoyment at any level of the subject of the duty. Although we may distinguish conceptually between having a right and the worth of a right, they are in practice and in law intimately connected by the principle of effectiveness, explicit in the Strasbourg Court's jurisprudence but implicit in the IHRL system generally. The right holder may not be entitled to enjoy the right under every circumstance, regardless of the cost to the state or other right holders, but at a minimum, the principle of effectiveness suggests that, by framing the interest as a right, the state acknowledges that meaningful enjoyment should be an important goal of the system. This makes the basic case for the necessity of positive rights in the IHRL system; if accepted, states should be held to a general duty to take reasonable measures to protect all human rights of their nationals from at least the most serious, foreseeable, and preventable forms of private intrusion and deprivation.

When it comes to specifying what forms of protection the ethical duty requires, generalizations become problematic. IHRL establishes a broad array of entitlements and relies for its functioning on balancing of public and private interests. Any interpretation of state duties under IHRL depends on an understanding of the social context in which the rights function. Although this is especially true of nondiscrimination rights, as I emphasized in Part II, it applies to some extent to all human rights. A negative human right to form a family with another consenting, mentally competent adult forbids the state from interfering in the decision of such persons to wed. As a positive right to protection, it would require the state to take measures to ensure that private persons cannot prevent the couple from exercising their matrimonial right meaningfully. For example, the right might be interpreted to oblige the state to take measures to prevent and punish employers who dismiss married employees, landlords who refuse to rent to married couples, or dating services that admit only unmarried persons. Whether the right to marriage is meaningful without such protection depends on the social context in which the right operates as well as one's subjective opinions about the proper role of the state in ordering private relationships. However, at a minimum, by recognizing an interest as a human right, the state commits to doing more than respecting the right itself; it further commits to giving each right holder a fair chance at enjoying the right in some meaningful manner. This is not the same as an unqualified guarantee of protection against private interference, but it does follow that a purely negative human right will rarely be fully adequate from the standpoint of world public order.

It follows that the claim that positive rights are generally undesirable for ideological reasons cannot reflect a compelling theory of political ethics. Such opposition to positive rights can usually be traced back to libertarian and social contractarian premises that grounded Mill's political theory: "the sole end for which mankind are warranted, individually or collectively, in interfering with the liberty of action of any of their number is self-protection."[38] Minimalist dogmas usually begin from a Natural Rights Theory that assumes that liberty (usually very narrowly defined) is the highest human value, and any imposition on an individual's liberty is presumptively immoral.[39] Starting from this premise, many authors have opposed positive rights as proceeding from the need to curb the state as the primary threat to those rights worth having,[40] or to a related faith that "that government is best which governs least."[41] This is of course to misconstrue Mill, but in any case, the popular theory is that a regime characterized exclusively by negative rights, except in most cases for rights to government protection from physical violence and property theft, is designed to neutralize the state while leaving private arrangements to deal with supposedly lesser (private) threats to individual freedom and development. The state, then, is assumed to be the primary, if not the sole, important threat to individual liberty. From this perspective, positive human rights other than the

38. John Stuart Mill, On Liberty 9 (Hackett Pub. ed. 1978) (1859); *see* H.L.A. Hart, *Are There Any Natural Rights?*, *in* Society, Law and Morality 173 (Federick A. Olafson ed., 1961); John Rawls, A Theory of Justice 303 (1971).

39. *See, e.g.*, David D. Boaz, *Rights, Responsibilities, and Community: A Libertarian View*, *in* International Rights and Responsibilities for the Future 43, 44 (Kenneth W. Hunter & Timothy Mack eds., 1996).

40. *See, e.g.*, Richard Epstein, Takings (1985); Loren Lomasky, Persons, Rights, and the Moral Community (1987); Robert Nozick, Anarchy, State, and Utopia (1974); Friedrick Hayek, The Constitution of Liberty (1960); Charles Murray, What It Means to Be a Libertarian 36–44 (1997); *see also* Libertarian Party Platform, June 2014, *available at* http://www.lp.org/platform.

41. Henry David Thoreau, Civil Disobedience 1 (1849).

aforementioned one to protection from violence or theft not only distract attention from the chief menace to individual freedom and development, but actually aggravate that menace by empowering the state to impinge on the interests of individuals in the service of promoting the expansive rights of other individuals and of society.

The assumptions on which this view is based are deeply problematical. They are: (1) that individual liberty is the highest value the state should pursue; (2) that liberty should be defined as freedom from state interference as opposed to the ability to flourish physically, emotionally, and intellectually; and (3) that the main threat to liberty (and the ability to flourish) is everywhere and always the state itself.[42] The rejection of any one of these assumptions seriously undermines the case against positive rights having redistributive consequences. For example, anyone who does not accept the elevation of liberty over the universal human interest in sustenance, education, healthcare, or employment is unlikely to be persuaded by the minimalist argument ab initio. Most philosophers and, more important, the international community as a whole, rank among those who reject it.[43] Although the protection of liberty undergirds many of the internationally recognized human rights, there is no human right to liberty as such; it is instead a central value that influences many, though not all, human rights.[44] The implementation of the full panoply of international human rights requires significant redistributions of wealth to guarantee the positive rights, and many minimalists consider any redistribution of wealth an illegitimate use of coercion against sacred freedom.[45]

A generalized right to freedom may not trump other rights, but it is true that, notwithstanding the popular assertions that all human rights are "indivisible" and therefore equally important,[46] some rights take clear precedence over others in most conceivable situations. The rights to life and against torture, for example, nearly always and everywhere take precedence over the rights to freedom of

42. Some such theories, such as Hayek's, are also based on a fourth, straightforwardly counterfactual assumption: (4) Individuals would be or can be free and autonomous apart from a society, and so the dependency fostered by government transfer programs (another contentious claim) undermines their responsible citizenship.

43. *See* Allen Buchanan, Ethics, Efficiency, and the Market 64–86 (1985); Allen Buchanan, Justice, Legitimacy, and Self-Determination: Moral Foundations for International Law 88–93 (2007).

44. The closest international human rights law comes to recognizing liberty per se is in the rights to privacy, family life, and freedom of movement. These rights, the right to privacy especially, have sometimes been interpreted to carve out a sphere of personal life presumptively free from irrational or unjustifiable state interference. *See, e.g.*, Dudgeon v. United Kingdom, 4 E.H.R.R. 149, para. 60 (1982) ("The Convention right affected by the impugned legislation protects an essentially private manifestation of the human personality."). Privacy is one of many rights that necessitate limitations on the freedom of members of society for the benefit of the underprivileged. For an instructive beginning to the analysis of privacy doctrine from a U.S. constitutional perspective that is in my opinion susceptible to application in IHRL, *see* Jed Rubenfeld, *The Right of Privacy*, 102 Harv. L. Rev. 737 (1989).

45. *See, e.g.*, Nozick, *supra* note 40, at 167–74; Libertarian Party Platform, *supra* note 40.

46. *See* sources cited in note 10, *supra*.

expression and education. I can imagine few scenarios in which a person, or even a hundred persons, could legitimately claim the right to speak even though it will certainly cause the death of another person. Nor could a person or a hundred persons demand the right to education if it requires the torture of another (other than the student, naturally). Liberty is not one such elevated value in the human rights law canon.

Franklin Delano Roosevelt once observed: "Necessitous men are not freemen."[47] The second assumption denies Roosevelt's observation by defining freedom narrowly to mean nothing more than the absence of a specific kind of restraint; specifically, measures of control by state governments. That view has been challenged by Amartya Sen among others, who consider substantive freedom to encompass the conditions of living with dignity and empowerment for the flourishing of all persons.[48] More fundamentally, although it is possible to separate conceptually liberty and the worth of liberty,[49] it is the instrumental worth of liberty that justifies it as a desirable value. Because different kinds of liberty are valuable to individuals in different positions, it is incoherent to insist that one kind of liberty—freedom from government interference—should be considered more important than other kinds of liberty to everyone regardless of their position. The minimalist's viewpoint merely represents that of the rare solipsistic right holder whose power and wealth immunize him from any threat but the state's.[50] Even for one rejecting the view that assisting members of society to realize their greatest potential is a key justification for any political organization, the value of state intervention should be judged by its ethical and practical consequences rather than its conformity to a rigid dogma.

On the third point, the rejection of positive rights as appointing the fox to guard the coop follows from the long-outdated perception of the state as the sole threat to basic human values. As one author opined:

> [G]overnment leaders themselves historically have been the greatest violators of human rights, and none could survive a test of either consistency or untarnished achievement.... They are the ones, as we have seen, who traditionally have used the great power of the state at their disposal to abuse rights, to retain privilege, to keep international norms and institutions weak, and to hide behind the claims of national sovereignty.[51]

47. Franklin D. Roosevelt, State of the Union Message to Congress (Jan. 11, 1944).

48. *See* Amartya Sen, Development as Freedom (1999). *See also* Jeremy Waldron, Liberal Rights: Collected Papers 1981–1991, at 13 (1993) ("Humans live as embodied and needy beings in a material world also populated by others.").

49. On this point, see Rawls, *supra* note 38, at 204.

50. Sen has applied the same to the distribution of primary social goods—goods that every person would need or want in some minimum amount. In this view, because individuals have different capabilities for using such goods, an egalitarian system may entail differential distributions to account for these differing capabilities. *See* Amartya Sen, Inequality Reeexamined (1992).

51. Paul Gordon Lauren, The Evolution of International Human Rights 291 (2d ed. 2003).

As noted earlier, this view is an artifact of the political history of the eighteenth and nineteenth centuries. The municipal concept of human rights developed in the form of civil rights with the foremost concern being restraint of the government. Much early IHRL, like so much of public international law in the late nineteenth and early twentieth centuries, extrapolated from municipal legal concepts.[52] The constitutional orders of the states that most influenced early IHRL were designed primarily for restraining the government rather than unleashing the state's power to benefit the population. First things first.

No doubt the most violent and oppressive forms of control were exercised by the state over individuals in preindustrial and post-Communist Revolution societies. That observation no longer reflects a uniformly valid empirical fact, however. No objective observer could conclude that the state is the universal bête noire to be feared above all other threats to fundamental human interests.[53] In most countries, governmental power does greatly overshadow private power. But the power of the state is not overwhelming everywhere, and even where the state dominates, it will not be the only serious threat to private liberty and rights. As B.F. Skinner pointed out:

> A permissive government is a government that leaves control to other sources.... The fundamental mistake made by all those who choose weak methods of [state] control is to assume that the balance of control is left to the individual, when in fact it is left to other conditions.[54]

By "conditions," Skinner meant other sources of control. Some states have weak governments whose power is contested or sapped by private armed groups, criminal organizations, influential multinational corporations, religious figures, and other private actors. In capitalist strongholds, the power of multinational corporations, industry groups, unions, and even well-organized civil society groups can seriously threaten private rights. Radical political individualism ignores, as one scholar put it, "the need to protect individual rights and liberties against encroaching and powerful bureaucracies other than the state."[55]

Such "conditions" also include differentials in the power of individuals who exert control over others, limiting their freedoms or inflicting harm on them in a private capacity. Social control flows from many sources, and these sources are not egalitarian in their constraints on the lives of their citizens. Today, business organizations and individuals, supported by a social structure conducive to private influence and control over other individuals, pose at least as great a threat in some places and at some times to individual liberty. A human rights doctrine blind to immense private power and wealth disparities within contemporary societies fails to give

52. *See generally* Hersch Lauterpacht, Private Law Sources and Analogies of International Law (1927).

53. On this point, *see, e.g.*, Audrey R. Chapman, *Reintegrating Rights and Responsibilities*, *in* International Rights and Responsibilities for the Future 3, 9 (Kenneth W. Hunter & Timothy Mack eds., 1996).

54. B.F. Skinner, Beyond Freedom and Dignity 92, 94 (rev. ed. 1990).

55. Meir Dan-Cohen, Rights, Persons, and Organizations 165 (1986).

equal protection to those disempowered by prevalent social forms, such as at-will unskilled employees, women, children, animals, and various kinds of nonconformists in most of the world's societies. The unequal effects of equal treatment is one of the most valuable contributions of Feminist thought to modern legal theory,[56] and the insight applies beyond women's experiences to all radical inequalities in power relationships. Parents may abuse their children, husbands may abuse their wives and wives their husbands, employers may abuse employees, cliques of schoolchildren may bully outsiders, all within the cherished sphere of private liberty exempt from state intrusion.

Uniform opposition to positive rights also ignores the fact that at least some organized societies have a proven role in promoting human development. Human development inexorably requires an opportunity to pursue fundamental interests besides freedom, such as comfort, enlightenment, affection, and physical and mental health. These interests can only be pursued effectively in a community supportive of individual growth and identity formation. Ideally, the state represents one such community. Obviously, individuals do not form societies and states pursuant to a new social contract every generation to serve their liberty interests. Individuals and their interests are formed both physically and psychologically by the societies in which they are born and raised, and they accept their society and its restrictions on their freedoms, to the extent they do, for the benefits their society offers, and because at least some of the restrictions are integral to their individual and cultural identities.

Many arguments have been made that the state has an ethical duty to take positive action to assist its nationals to achieve subsistence[57] or, ultimately, an optimal life.[58] There is no need to rehearse these often elaborate arguments here. However, the character of positive and negative rights as non-opposites, discussed in Chapter 6, bears repetition here. Positive and negative duties are merely related and alternative means of social control. Each is a tool useful in some circumstances and counterproductive in others. If we accept that the best justification for state government is to create the conditions for protecting its citizens from harm and encouraging their flourishing, then we ought to be initially neutral in our preference for the state to assume negative or positive duties. Autonomy means not just freedom from restraint (negative freedom), but ability to exercise one's powers

56. For example, some have argued that, due to the predominance of private over public violence against women, the state-centric structure of international law leaves women vulnerable to the most vicious and ubiquitous forms of oppression. *See, e.g.*, Karen Knop, *Re/Statements: Feminism and State Sovereignty in International Law*, 3 TRANSNAT'L L. & CONTEMP. PROBS. 293, 296 (1993); Hilary Charlesworth & Christine Chinkin, *The Gender of* Jus Cogens, 15 HUM. RTS. Q. 63, 72–73 (1993). From this perspective, the de-emphasis on positive human rights to protection embodies a fundamental gender bias in favor of men, who use the limitation of state authority in private relationships to perpetuate sexism and the disempowerment and abuse of women.

57. *See, e.g.*, POGGE, *supra* note 27, at 55–57, 82–96; SANDRA FREDMAN, HUMAN RIGHTS TRANSFORMED *passim* (2008); HENRY SHUE, BASIC RIGHTS *passim* (2d ed. 1996).

58. *See, e.g.*, JOSEPH RAZ, THE MORALITY OF FREEDOM 409–16 (1986); LOUIS HENKIN, THE AGE OF RIGHTS 9–10 (1990).

through meaningful life choices (positive freedom).[59] Under many circumstances a reduction of negative rights can prove much less significant to that end than an increase in positive rights. Freedom from molestation in the ownership of property means little to the landless poor and much to the wealthy; the right to subsistence affects the groups contrarily. In pursuing a mandate of maximizing shared values among all members of society, the state must necessarily assume both negative and positive duties.

2. Positive Rights as a Practical Concept

To be clear, I am not arguing that positive rights to fulfillment are always justified for non-basic rights, for precisely the same reason that positive rights are frequently justified. No state is unfailingly beneficent and effective under all circumstances. Here, it may be helpful to separate the question of how much responsibility the state is morally obligated to assume in implementing positive duties from the question of whether widespread positive duties are a practical and desirable development in IHRL. The latter question requires us to recognize an important and sometimes underappreciated facet of positive rights. Using a positive rights paradigm in preference to a negative rights paradigm recasts the state from the role of chief peril to human rights into the seemingly opposite role of protector, power broker, or source of personal empowerment. The conception of the state evolves from a subject of public distrust to the role of parens patriae simply by varying the framing of the rights. These are weighty consequences for what may superficially seem like a pedestrian expansion in the scope of the state's duties from "respect" to "protect" or "fulfill."

This metamorphosis reflects the great paradox of IHRL observed by Paul Gordon Lauren: "[T]he evolution of international human rights lies in the fact that states have been both the most significant abusers and the most significant protectors of rights—both the cause and the cure."[60] But the same state is not always both the cause and the cure for all rights. The role the state plays with respect to the realization of human rights depends on the nature of the state and the problems faced by persons under its jurisdiction.

Like all law, IHRL does not achieve desirable results by merely existing as a self-consistent system on paper. The expansion of human rights by formal law cannot guarantee practical results in itself. Positive framing may in most circumstances elevate the protection afforded by the right under international law, but it does not ipso facto improve anyone's condition. The desirability of imposing positive duties on states from an ethical standpoint does not mean that IHRL may be optimized by uniformly promoting positive duties as necessary correlatives of all human rights. Whether a moral duty should translate into a legal duty depends on the relationship between the form of the state government, its legal institutions, and the society that they govern. Whether the right actually creates the intended benefit depends

59. On this point, I find Raz's argument compelling. *See* RAZ, *supra* note 58, at 415–16.

60. LAUREN, *supra* note 51, at 292; *see also* DAN-COHEN, *supra* note 53, at 178 (observing that there is "no inconsistency in the state being at the same time a major protector of and a major threat to individual liberties.").

on the environment in the implementing state and the world public order generally. In some states, the exalted role of protector and facilitator of fulfilled human potential has become more or less institutionalized in the governmental structure and culture, and incorporated into its governing ethos. In such states, extensive positive rights will tend to maximize the benefits of state activity.

But not every state shares these characteristics. Within those states in which the government itself remains a primary threat to human rights, framing those rights in aggressively positive terms accentuates the disjunction between the role the state should play in public life and the role it plays in fact. Such states face an incentive to seek positive framing of rights for reasons additional to buttressing their claims to assistance from wealthier countries in fulfilling the rights for their nationals. As noted, the very idealism of many positive rights also dooms them to aspirational status not only in many developing countries, but sometimes in the most economically advanced. A practice of interpreting international human rights treaties in a manner uniformly expansive of the duties that such treaties impose[61] would be insufficiently nuanced in light of state intentions and ultimately counterproductive.[62] The acceptance of the imperfect realization of positive rights reflects neither ideal theory nor future expectations about the development of more protective human rights doctrines in the course of the development of the world public order, but merely a concession to present realities. The ideal balance would appear to be an ambitious interpretation of rights that maintains pressure on states to increasingly conform their practices to a minimum standard of protection and fulfillment of human rights.

The converse of this point is that states eminently capable of protecting and fulfilling important positive human rights—and especially wealthy and well-organized states with long traditions of respect for the dignity of the individual—are poorly equipped to rely on an ideology of skepticism toward the state itself to justify implementing exclusively negative rights. A blanket relegation of fulfillable human rights commitments to negative duties in such cases can be justified on neither ethical nor practical grounds. Consistent with the jurisprudence and positions of the Strasbourg Court, Human Rights Committee, and Committee on Economic, Social, and Cultural Rights,[63] most enlightened states accept the duty to protect and fulfill many human rights, even if they do not formally characterize

61. One commentator has characterized the jurisprudence of the Inter-American Court of Human Rights in this manner. *See* Lucas Lixinski, *Treaty Interpretation by the Inter-American Court of Human Rights: Expansion at the Service of the Unity of International Law*, 21 Eur. J. Int'l L. 585, 588 (2010).

62. Unregulated expansion of *new* human rights has long been criticized on precisely these grounds. *See, e.g.*, Philip Alston, *Conjuring Up New Human Rights: A Proposal for Quality Control*, 78 Am. J. Int'l L. 607 (1984). The same concerns support caution in reframing negative rights in positive terms.

63. The Strasbourg Court tends to interpret the rights listed in the European Convention to impose positive duties. *See, e.g.*, *Rantsev v. Cyprus & Russia*, 51 E.H.R.R. 1 (2010) (treating the right to life as a positive right); *Belgian Linguistics Case*, Eur. Ct. Hum. Rts. Judgment of July 23, 1968 (merits), 1 E.H.R.R. 252 (1968) (treating the right to education as a positive right). *See generally* A.R. Mowbray, The Development of Positive Obligations under the European Convention on Human Rights by the European Court of Human Rights (2004); Dimitris Xenos, The Positive Obligations of the State under the European Convention of

such duties as positive.[64] Yet, some of the most tragic illustrations of human rights abuses have occurred precisely when a state, well-positioned to take positive measures to protect an individual's human rights from private infringement, has shirked its responsibility based on simplistic dogmas.

The United States, though sometimes touting itself complacently as a leader in human rights or global moral authority,[65] furnishes disturbing examples of the consequences of renouncing positive human rights. The U.S. Supreme Court has hewed increasingly closely to an exclusively negative interpretation of civil constitutional rights,[66] exalting "the right to be let alone—the most comprehensive of rights and the right most valued by civilized men."[67] The choice of words, "civilized men," is fortuitous insofar as, globally, men benefit from overwhelming advantages over women and children in exercising political, social, and economic power. As the discussion of the solipsistic right holder made clear, negative rights appeal to the rationally self-interested powerful actors alone. The downtrodden frequently have reason to distinctly prefer *not* to be let alone. It is no accident that the Supreme Court is and has always been composed overwhelmingly of persons with privileged demographic and economic backgrounds,[68] and much of its jurisprudence

HUMAN RIGHTS (2011); Frédéric Sudre, *Les obligations positives dans la jurisprudence européenne des droits de l'homme*, 1995 REV. TRIMESTRIELLE DES DROITS DE L'HOMME 363.

64. Germany, for example, has implemented positive obligations on a constitutional interpretive level. *See* Roza Pati, *Rights and Their Limits: The Constitution for Europe in International and Comparative Legal Perspective*, 23 BERK. J. INT'L L. 223, 235–36 (2005); Besson, *supra* note 3, at 62–63. In an unusually advanced opinion recognizing the state's duty to protect foreign nationals in foreign lands under the state's military aegis, the Court of Appeal at the Hague held the Netherlands liable for failing to act reasonably to preserve the lives of Bosnian refugees in a U.N. compound occupied by Dutch peacekeepers. *Srberenica Case*, Case No. BR0132 (Ct. App. The Hague, July 5, 2011), *available at* http://www.rechtspraak.nl/ljn.asp?ljn=BR0132; *see* Cees van Dam, *The Netherlands Found Liable for Srebrenica Deaths*, ASIL INSIGHTS, Sept. 19, 2011, *available at* http://www.asil.org.

65. *E.g.*, Remarks at Town Hall Meeting, Dean Acheson Auditorium, Washington, D.C. (Jan. 31, 2005), *available at* http://merln.ndu.edu/archivepdf/nss/state/41414.pdf (statement of U.S. secretary of state Condoleeza Rice); *State Department Legal Adviser Describes U.S. Approach to International Law*, 104 AM. J. INT'L L. 271, 273 (2010) (statement of Harold Koh, U.S. Department of State Legal Adviser); *see also, e.g., Women's Rights Are Human Rights: U.S. Ratification of the Convention on the Elimination of All Forms of Discrimination against Women (CEDAW)*, Hearing Before the Senate Judiciary Comm., Subcomm. on Hum. Rts. & the Law, Nov. 18, 2010, *available at* http://judiciary.senate.gov/hearings/hearing.cfm?id=4861 ("Throughout our history, the United States has done more to advance human rights than any other country in the world.") (statement of Senator Dick Durbin, Subcomm. Chair); *id.* ("[T]he moral leadership of our country on human rights matters.") (statement of Melanne Verveer, Ambassador-at-Large for Global Women's Issues, U.S. Dep't of State). *See generally* Aaron Xavier Fellmeth, *Leading from (a Bit) Behind: The United States and International Human Rights Law*, 40 N.C. J. INT'L L. & COMM. REG. 977 (2015).

66. *See generally* David P. Currie, *Positive and Negative Constitutional Rights*, 53 U. CHI. L. REV. 864 (1986).

67. Olmstead v. United States, 277 U.S. 438, 478 (1928).

68. That all but a handful of Supreme Court justices have been Christian white males is well known. Less known, but probably not surprising, is that with few exceptions they come from

has, probably not coincidentally, reflected the narrow interests and perspectives of the privileged classes who are overrepresented on it.

The tragic consequences of a systemic fixation on the rights valued by powerful elites in society may be observed daily in the condition of underprivileged persons in the United States, as elsewhere, but were illustrated grimly in *DeShaney v. Winnebago County Department of Social Services*.[69] There, the U.S. Supreme Court considered whether the state has a duty to protect a child from foreseeable and preventable domestic violence. The child's human right to freedom from physical abuse and deprivation of life could not be in doubt. At issue was the whether the state, which had been alerted to the father's severe violence against the child numerous times, had failed in its duty to protect the child after taking no preventive action. Eventually, the father beat his child into a coma and incurable mental retardation. The Court found nothing in the U.S. Constitution that obligates the state to act with reasonable diligence to protect its citizens, including children, from private violence. The purpose of the Constitution, concluded the Court, is "to protect the people from the State, not to ensure that the State protect[s] them from each other."[70] The state is not constitutionally obligated to protect its citizens even "when where such aid may be necessary to secure life, liberty or property interests of which the government itself may not deprive the individual."[71]

The Supreme Court has more recently reaffirmed that the U.S. government and its subdivisions have no duty to try to protect individuals from private violations of their fundamental human rights. In a 2005 case, the Court held that the police had no duty to enforce a judicial restraining order against a woman's estranged, abusive husband. The husband had kidnapped the couple's three children and, despite state law requiring police to enforce the order, and the woman's repeated requests for enforcement, the police did nothing. Eventually, the husband murdered the three children.[72] The Court exonerated the state, finding that the police had discretion to ignore the mandatory court order, and the aggrieved mother had no constitutional right that the order be enforced for the protection of herself or her children. Consonant with these decisions, the U.S. Constitution is now routinely interpreted by courts as "a charter of negative rather than positive liberties."[73] This

upper class socioeconomic backgrounds, whereas those seeking redress of their grievances are frequently drawn from the underprivileged classes. *See* Peter Irons, A People's History of the Supreme Court xiii–xiv (2006). For example, a recent survey of the justices indicated that seven out of nine were millionaires or multimillionaires, and the other two were close. *See* Bill Mears, *Justices Are Well-Off, Well-Traveled,* CNN, June 4, 2008, *available at* http://www.cnn.com.

69. 489 U.S. 189 (1989).

70. *Id.* at 196.

71. *Id.; accord* Jackson v. City of Joliet, 715 F.2d 1200 (7th Cir. 1983), *cert. denied*, 465 U.S. 1049 (1984) (holding that a police officer violates no constitutional right of persons trapped and burning to death in an overturned automobile when he made no effort to discover whether the car was occupied).

72. Town of Castle Rock, Colo. v. Gonzales, 545 U.S. 748 (2005).

73. *Jackson*, 715 F.2d at 1203.

interpretation excuses the United States from taking reasonable measures to protect its citizens using the very institutions set up for that purpose, funded by the very persons who may legally be denied the protections for which their taxes pay.

The facts that the state may have had the best knowledge, position, and power to protect the children from their father in each case, that the state's creation of the legal parent-child relationship empowered the father to commit the violence privately, and that private attempts to rescue the child from the father could have exposed the rescuers to legally justified private violence from the father or criminal prosecution by the very state that failed in its moral duty to protect the children, made no apparent impression on the Court majority in either case.[74] The Court's decisions recognized that any legal obligation of the United States and its political subdivisions is limited to a negative duty not to impair the life or liberty of American children through the harmful direct action of its own agents.

The needs of children for protection from adults, and adults for protection from more powerful and better organized adults, explains why no positive human right is better established in international law than the right to reasonable protection from private violence. The European human rights system accordingly comes to a very different conclusion under analogous circumstances.[75] By exonerating the U.S. government from any legal obligation to protect its citizens from private harm, the Court put the United States at odds with some of the most fundamental guarantees of IHRL. Although many states encode positive rights in their constitutions, a

74. Justice Brennan, writing in dissent in *DeShaney*, was influenced by these considerations, however. *See* DeShaney v. Winnebago Cty. Dep't of Soc. Servs., 489 U.S. 189, 210 (1989) (Brennan, J., dissenting) ("Through its child-welfare program, in other words, the State of Wisconsin has relieved ordinary citizens and governmental bodies other than the Department of any sense of obligation to do anything more than report their suspicions of child abuse to DSS. If DSS ignores or dismisses these suspicions, no one will step in to fill the gap. Wisconsin's child-protection program thus effectively confined Joshua DeShaney within the walls of Randy DeShaney's violent home until such time as DSS took action to remove him. Conceivably, then, children like Joshua are made worse off by the existence of this program when the persons and entities charged with carrying it out fail to do their jobs.").

75. *See, e.g.*, Opuz v. Turkey, 50 E.H.R.R. 28, para. 128 (2010) ("The Court reiterates that the first sentence of art. 2(1) enjoins the state not only to refrain from the intentional and unlawful taking of life, but also to take appropriate steps to safeguard the lives of those within its jurisdiction. This involves a primary duty on the state to secure the right to life by putting in place effective criminal law provisions to deter the commission of offences against the person backed up by law-enforcement machinery for the prevention, suppression and punishment of breaches of such provisions. It also extends in appropriate circumstances to a positive obligation on the authorities to take preventive operational measures to protect an individual whose life is at risk from the criminal acts of another individual."). A more ambiguous case is Osman v. United Kingdom, 29 E.H.R.R. 245, paras. 115–22 (2000), in which an obviously unbalanced teacher who had become obsessed with a student attacked him and his father with a shotgun, injuring one and murdering the other. The Strasbourg Court affirmed a positive state obligation to establish "effective criminal law provisions to deter the commission of offences against the person backed up by law-enforcement machinery for the prevention, suppression and sanctioning of breaches of such provisions." *Id.* para. 115. However, the Court exonerated the accused government on the ground that the police knew of no unequivocal evidence that the teacher employed violence against the specific student with whom he was obsessed. *Id.* para. 120–22.

state could just as well comply with its human rights obligations through legislative or administrative measures.[76] Yet, the United States has not adopted on the federal or state level a comprehensive program for complying with the positive duties set forth in the international treaties and other instruments it has approved or adopted.

It bears emphasizing that a political entity cannot justify its existence by the purely negative act of restraining itself from harming its nationals.[77] Even extreme Libertarians acknowledge the minimal justification for the state requires it to protect all citizens and their property from private violence. Every coherent modern political philosophy, in Asia at least from Meng Zi forward,[78] and in Europe from at least Plato's *Republic* forward,[79] recognizes the fundamentally protective purpose of the sovereign state. The logical corollary, of holding the state to legal duties to promote the fulfillment of important human needs and ambitions, has proven part of the evolution of human rights precisely because, once basic human rights are

76. Mary Ann Glendon has noted that there may have been some negative repercussions and compensation arising from Wisconsin's failure to protect DeShaney's life. *See* GLENDON, *supra* note 26, at 96. However, her apologia for *DeShaney* overlooks two important points. First, the consequences she recites (meager statutory damages, disciplinary action against the negligent social worker, and post hoc criminal punishment of the father), even if they actually occurred, do not vindicate the child's human right. The state's obligation under international law is to take reasonable measures to *protect* the lives of those within its jurisdiction and to offer full compensation for any failure to do so, not merely to take belated and ineffectual action after failing in its primary obligation. Second, because these are local remedies that may vary from state to state, there is no guarantee at the national level that *any* attempt will be made to deter, punish, and compensate private human rights violations, and the Supreme Court's opinion categorically excludes imposing any constitutional obligation on the states or municipalities.

77. *Cf.* WALDRON, *supra* note 48, at 24–25. Waldron asks rhetorically what would be the point of setting up a government for the purpose of not violating one's rights.

78. Meng Zi, or Mencius, laid great emphasis on the importance of respect for human beings, and on governmental benevolence and sensitivity to the moral and material needs of the people, such as taking positive measures to prevent or remedy the effects of famine. *See* 2 THE CHINESE CLASSICS: THE WORKS OF MENCIUS bk. 1, pt. 1 (James Legge trans., 1895) (circa 300 B.C.E.); *see also* Irene Bloom, *Confucian Perspectives on the Individual and the Collectivity, in* RELIGIOUS DIVERSITY AND HUMAN RIGHTS 129 (Irene Bloom et al. eds., 1996).

Mencius's predecessor, Confucius, implied in several places in the *Analects* that government is for the benefit of the people, although he generally justified the benefit as serving the ruler's self-interest. Most specifically, his advice to a ruler is: "Let him preside over [the people] with gravity; then they will reverence him. Let him be final and kind to all; then they will be faithful to him. Let him advance the good and teach the incompetent; then they will eagerly seek to be virtuous." CONFUCIUS, ANALECTS 1:2 (circa 500 B.C.E.). His emphasis was on the ruler and ministers setting a virtuous example for the people and being "laborious in their affairs." *Id.* 3:13. For example, "Good government obtains when those who are near are made happy, and those who are far off are attracted." *Id.*

79. *See* PLATO, THE REPUBLIC 19, 44 (A.D. Lindsay trans., 1992) (ca. 386 B.C.E.). Plato, although certainly limited in his view of most human rights, *see, e.g.*, Plato, *Crito*, *in* FIVE DIALOGUES 51, 53 (G.M.A. Grube trans., 1981) (ca. 360 B.C.E.); PLATO, THE LAWS 447, 451–52, 500 (Trevor J. Saunders trans., 1986) (ca. 341 B.C.E.), considered the purpose of the state as being to secure "justice," or balance in society while doing evil to no one; to advance the common individual interests of the state's members; and to make the society "as happy as possible." THE REPUBLIC, *supra*, at 98. Plato further developed these ideas in *The Laws*: "[A] state ought to be free and

recognized as desirable, the source of the threat is irrelevant so long as it is beyond the control of the right holder and within the reasonable control of the state. We are accordingly justified in adopting a neutral stance regarding the source of the threat to human rights under these circumstances. The direst threats to human dignity and freedom do not always come in the crude form of unjust force by the state itself or even specific, identifiable persons within it. Aside from minimalist social contract fantasies, there are no morally coherent reasons for expecting the state to protect individuals against other individuals but not, say, accidental injury, random serious illness, or a cataclysmic asteroid strike, much less forces such as famine, unemployment, or illiteracy, to which the state may have contributed through ill-considered public policies.

The conception of the state as a facilitator of human development has gained increasing recognition in the international community. The U.N. General Assembly declared back in 1986 that:

> States have the right and the duty to formulate appropriate national development policies that aim at the constant improvement of the well-being of the entire population and of all individuals, on the basis of their active, free and meaningful participation in development and in the fair distribution of the benefits resulting therefrom.[80]

The Obama administration in a press release publicly accepted the binding nature of positive economic rights.[81] The release does not seem to represent a change of policy, however, inasmuch as the U.S. legal framework broadly rejecting most positive rights continues in force. At the time the Obama administration released this announcement, for example, the United States was continuing to insist before the Inter-American Commission on Human Rights that IHRL imposes no positive duty on the state to act diligently to protect its nationals from private violence[82]—a position predictably rejected by the Commission.[83]

wise and enjoy internal harmony, and that this is what the lawgiver should concentrate on in his legislation. . . . [A] lawgiver should frame his code with an eye on three things: the freedom, unity and wisdom of the city for which he legislates." The Laws, *supra*, 142, 155.

80. U.N. Declaration on the Right to Development art. 2(3), G.A. Res. 41/128, Annex, U.N. GAOR, 41st Sess., Supp. No. 53, U.N. Doc. A/41/53 (1986).

81. *See* U.S. Dep't of State, Press Release, Speech by Ass't Sec'y Michael H. Posner, The Four Freedoms Turn 70 (Mar. 24, 2011), *available at* http://www.state.gov/g/drl/rls/rm/2011/159195.htm.

82. *See* Gonzales v. United States, Inter-Am. Comm'n on Hum Rts., Rep. No. 80/11 (July 21, 2011), para. 55. Instead, the United States characterized the duty to protect as a "moral and political" duty. *Id.* para. 57.

83. *Id.* para. 111. Meanwhile, the Legal Adviser to the State Department asserted that Muammar Qaddafi had "forfeited the responsibility to protect his own [*sic*] citizens" in Libya by using armed force against civilians. U.S. Dep't of State, Press Release, Remarks by Harold Hongju Koh, Statement regarding Use of Force in Libya (Mar. 26, 2011), *available at* http://www.state.gov/s/l/releases/remarks/159201.htm. Given the consistent U.S. position on the subject and the context in which Koh's remarks were made, it seems likely that Koh interpreted "responsibility to protect" idiosyncratically as a negative rather than a positive duty.

Again, it bears emphasis that this discussion does not lead to an unqualified endorsement of positive rights as a panacea for the ills plaguing human dignity. The pathologies potentially attendant upon the misuse of positive rights themselves counsel prudence in their deployment. The appropriate circumstances for the use of a positive right in one country or region may be predicted to differ from those in another. It should not be surprising, then, that there is considerable variation in the content of human rights law and human rights enforcement in regional human rights systems, although the variation is perhaps not as extreme as circumstances would suggest. Expansive positive human rights are much more likely to be realized in wealthier states with an established domestic tradition of civil, political, and socioeconomic rights than in other states. The world public order remains regionally fragmented in the operational codes of its human rights systems.

Formally, of course, the international bill of rights applies its code of duties to parties without distinction as to wealth, form of government, or otherwise, and it includes expansive positive rights without the sensitivity to context that a network of regional human rights systems could have. The dissonance between the desirable myth system of universally binding positive rights and the exigent operational code of variation among regions in the implementation of even negative rights imposes a tension in the system of IHRL that will continue for the foreseeable future. The problem is not that a high degree of regional variation in respect for human dignity is desirable for cultural reasons, although sensitivity to the possibility that other cultures have valuable insights as to the nature of human dignity and the best manner of promoting it should no doubt be a permanent aspect of the interpretive project of the IHRL system. The problem is that, even though, as I have argued, positive rights are a morally mandated component of the world public order, including duties of fulfillment of basic human rights, negative rights must remain *structurally prior* to positive rights in the sense that the first project of the world public order must be to implement negative rights. Again, my reason is not that negative rights are more morally justifiable than positive rights; it is that governments in practice have radically varying resources, capabilities, and attitudes toward human dignity. A state that will not realistically renounce the role of oppressor of its population cannot be expected to adopt the role of protector of the population and promoter of its dignity without exacerbating the threat posed by the state. The goal of implementing an optimal world public order demands the eventual recognition of positive duties by all states on the terms discussed here, even if, in the short term, the international community rationally focuses its attention on securing compliance with negative rights among those states least committed to the advancement of human dignity in pursuit of the project of converting them from the role of chief oppressor to that of chief protector.

Epilogue

The response to human rights skepticism implied in my analysis is that, by virtue of the role of human rights in protecting fundamental community values against the state's polymorphous need for regulating private conduct—and, equally important, against the needs of most states *not* to assume unlimited responsibility for regulating private conduct—human rights concepts demand multiple and flexible choices for framing the value at stake. It may seem paradoxical that IHRL, as a body of rules protecting the most fundamental community values, is framed in terms that are especially vague and susceptible to subjective judgment. The vagueness creates special problems when it impedes states and individuals from understanding their rights and duties, and when it stands in the way of predictable enforcement by the international community. But some flexibility in the rules is not merely salutary; it is essential to the function of human rights law as a guardian of fundamental interests and values. The possibility of alternative paradigms does not necessarily obstruct either the definition or enforcement of human rights. It can, if used properly, facilitate both. Multifaceted rules, invoking rights and duties, positive and negative, substantive and relative, all protecting the same values can capture different aspects of these values more effectively to close off more of the infinite paths to their degradation. The structure of the IHRL system reflects these multiple and converging avenues toward human dignity, even if the possibilities of such structural features of the system have not yet been fully appreciated.

One of my goals in writing this book has been to promote this understanding by demonstrating that not everything about the current structure of the international system of human rights law is inevitable or desirable. It is far from certain that the choice of human rights itself as the primary paradigm of fundamental interest protection dictated the relative neglect of a duties paradigm, as I discussed in Part I. A fundamental duties paradigm can promote some important interests with greater facility than a fundamental rights paradigm. In some cases, fundamental duties capture community values in a way for which a rights paradigm is manifestly ill-suited. This is not to denigrate the preference for human rights over institutional duties as the primary paradigm of the world public order, but I do argue that the neglect of a fundamental duties paradigm sacrifices some critical public policy goals.

In Part II, I argued that the nondiscrimination paradigm *is* essential, but that nondiscrimination doctrine in IHRL suffers from conceptual vagueness and inconsistencies on some important points. I also argued that the implications of and interaction between substantive rights and nondiscrimination rights have been undertheorized. In the course of trying to rectify that deficiency, I suggested some avenues for reforming nondiscrimination doctrine better to advance the goals of protecting and promoting equal human dignity. Most notably, a careful analysis of nondiscrimination doctrine suggests that open lists of grounds for prohibiting discrimination have many advantages over closed lists, but some grounds for discrimination can justify greater skepticism than others. I have also tried to show how nondiscrimination rights can reach some kinds of interests, in some kinds of ways, that substantive rights cannot, and vice versa. The two paradigms work best when used in a complementary manner, which is in practice how human rights treaties use them to some degree. Unfortunately, authoritative interpretations of IHRL have not always displayed a full appreciation of the subtleties of the two paradigms and their interaction, with the result that one is sometimes misused when the other would have advanced the value in question more effectively.

Finally, I argued in Part III that the division of rights into negative and positive paradigms, if defined properly, offers a good deal of conceptual traction, but that international human rights instruments and their authoritative interpreters do not always approach the distinction with a coherent theory of public welfare. Many decision-makers and scholars alike have succumbed to the lure of oversimplification, advocating the negative or positive paradigm as the exclusive ideal, when a more nuanced approach that uses sometimes one, sometimes the other, sometimes the two of them complementarily, can most effectively advance the goals of the human rights system. Henry Shue's work has been justifiably influential on this score, and I have both defended and proposed a minor modification of his argument, as well as offering some observations about the doctrinal implications of his development of the concept of "basic rights."

It is important to emphasize that my analysis does not suggest a pervasive dysfunction in the system of IHRL. On the contrary, the approach that authoritative decision-makers have taken at the international and regional level to the challenges posed by the complexities of the three paradigms discussed here have been well considered on the whole, even if my argument concludes that some important innovations should be adopted. In Part I, I argued that individual legal duties under IHRL are unworkable unless extremely limited, and this is precisely the system adopted in international criminal law. I have also argued that it is both morally justifiable and practically feasible to apply duties directly under IHRL to multinational enterprises under some conditions, and that too is gradually being done. As for fundamental state duties independent of but comparably positioned to individual human rights, that does remain a project for the future.

In Part II, I proposed that nondiscrimination doctrine could be rationalized through a more structured analytical approach, especially to the concepts of prohibited grounds and interests protected. Although human rights decision-makers continue the practice of ad hoc and sometimes contradictory techniques of analysis, their major trends conform to this approach, albeit inconsistently. There is much room for greater consistency in nondiscrimination doctrine, and in how and when human rights authorities use substantive and nondiscrimination rights when either or both are raised in the same case.

Part III proposed a hierarchy of positive duties, with all basic rights correlative to duties of fulfillment, and other rights generally presumed positive rights to protection except when moral or practical reasons would justify a duty of fulfillment or make a positive interpretation counterproductive. International human rights authorities have not exactly adopted this approach, but they have tended to prefer positive to negative duties. A uniform preference for positive duties is problematic for reasons I have discussed, but much less objectionable than a uniform rejection of positive duties. Although the system is reasonably coherent and functions fairly well doctrinally, there are practical reasons for prioritizing the negative rights paradigm that do not comport with the theoretical priorities of positive and negative rights.

Another of my goals has been to encourage the cross-fertilization of human rights jurisprudence with philosophical theory, especially ethics. To date, philosophers have dominated the metaphysical discussions about human rights because they are adept at analyzing first principles. Lawyers are trained as social engineers, and much of this book has examined the practical consequences not only of paradigm choices, but of framing and phrasing choices. Nonetheless, law does not exist in a vacuum. It is a relationship formed in the minds of a society's members for the purpose of social and institutional control. All competent jurists recognize the importance of understanding the reasons behind the law's policy goals, because the relationship between the promulgator of the law (the treaty negotiators, the legislature, and so on) and the authoritative interpreter of the law (the international human rights tribunal, the monitoring committee, the municipal court charged with enforcing human rights legislation) tends to subordinate the intentions and expectations of the latter to the former.

The policy goal behind IHRL is commonly understood to be the promotion and protection of equal human dignity. Yet, defining dignity is a metaphysical exercise par excellence, the kind of exercise at which philosophers excel. It is also a concept frequently invoked but woefully undertheorized in the law. The definition most often used references the inherent value of human life, but surely the entire corpus of IHRL cannot be dedicated to so simple a task as preserving human life. There is not much dignity in a life of ignorance and chronic suffering. Those theorists who represent dignity as encompassing not just the inherent value of life, but the value of exercising one's powers and potential in an ethically justifiable manner, of what I have called human flourishing, capture the concept better. Of course, flourishing is itself a compound concept comprising fundamental values and interests such as happiness, liberty, comfort, enlightenment, and freedom. I have not tried to justify my choices about which values should be considered integral to human dignity, but I do believe jurists would benefit from the insights of philosophers and political theorists in contemplating that question. The formation and interpretation of IHRL, if it really is to protect and promote human dignity, should begin from a reasoned theory, rather than vague intuitions, about what we mean when we speak of dignity.

It is also important to consider other values and how they interact with and weigh relative to human dignity. The paradigm choices of the founders of the modern IHRL systems were vague on this point. They do not specify when the nondiscrimination right should take precedence over a conflicting substantive right, how to balance substantive rights in conflict with each other, and exactly when general social welfare interests such as national security, public health, animal dignity, environmental integrity, or public order justify derogating from human rights.

Nor are they always clear about how far the state must extend itself in the service of such human interests as employment, leisure time, association, or privacy. That leaves the task of reconciling conflicting norms to the authoritative human rights decision-makers. In the preceding pages, I have tried to elucidate some of the analytical options available, as well as some of the important ethical and practical consequences of the options. My hope is that a thorough analysis of the three paradigms and their philosophical underpinnings might help us better to understand the nature of the current IHRL system and suggest ways in which we could refine it to achieve the aspirations that originally motivated the Universal Declaration of Human Rights and that continue to motivate international lawyers today.

Index

Affirmative action 123, 151–55
African Charter on Human and Peoples' Rights 18–19, 41, 155, 172, 256
  African Court on Human and People's Rights 172–73, 256
Alexander, Larry 40, 149–51, 177
American Convention on Human Rights 17, 122, 127–28, 145, 154–57, 252
  Protocol of San Salvador 58
American Declaration of the Rights and Duties of Man 16–18, 22–23
Amnesty International 68–69
Animal rights 51–54, 92–95
Apartheid, *see under* South Africa
Arab Charter on Human Rights 122
Arbitrary arrest, detention or exile, human right to freedom from 216
Aristotle 9, 105, 113
Association and assembly, human right to freedom of 157, 172–74, 189, 252
Association of Southeast Asian Nations (ASEAN)
  Human Rights Declaration 21–22, 29–30, 69

Banjul Charter, *see* African Charter on Human and Peoples' Rights
Basic human rights 230–41
  See also Shue, Henry
Bayefsky, Anne 138, 140
Beitz, Charles 264
Bentham, Jeremy 7, 10
Besson, Samantha 104
Buchanan, Allen 4, 7, 13, 92, 103–04
Bulgaria
  Constitution 26
Business organizations, *see under* Duties
Butler, Samuel 54–55

Canada 130
  Constitution of 252
Categorical imperative, *see* Kant, Immanuel
Child rights 41, 53, 120, 127, 196, 278–79
  Convention on the Rights of the Child 41, 79–80, 141, 220
    Committee on the Rights of the Child 218
  Insulting or demeaning names 142
China, People's Republic of 238
  Constitution of 26
  Great Leap Forward 219
Christian morality 10
Collective action problems 42, 98
Committee on Economic, Social and Cultural Rights, *see under* International Covenant on Economic, Social, and Cultural Rights
Committee on the Elimination of Racial Discrimination, *see under* International Covenant on the Elimination of All Forms of Racial Discrimination
Common heritage of humankind 48
Communitarianism 147
Condorcet, Marquis de 83
Confucius 9–10, 280
Consequentialism 8–9, 12, 52, 55, 148–50
  See also Utilitarianism

Convention on the Elimination of All Forms of Discrimination against Women 45, 107, 141, 149–52, 155, 161, 177, 220
  Committee on the Elimination of Discrimination against Women 152
Convention on the Prevention and Punishment of the Crime of Genocide 27–28
Convention on the Rights of the Child, *see under* Child rights
Convention on the Rights of Persons with Disabilities 107–08, 220
Corporate social responsibility 31–35
Council of Europe 142, 165
  European Commission on Human Rights 50, 118, 127–28, 227
  European Court of Human Rights 4, 15, 50, 85, 89–90, 112–13, 115–20, 127–29, 136, 138, 141–43, 148, 152, 161–65, 170, 173–76, 182–83, 186–89, 192–93, 204–10, 221, 227–28, 250–51, 253–56, 269, 276, 279
  European Convention for the Protection of Human Rights and Fundamental Freedoms 20, 123, 127, 141–43, 155–56, 162, 176, 180, 182–83, 186, 188–89, 192–93, 221, 227–28, 251, 256
    Protocol No. 1: 31, 173, 253–55
    Protocol No. 12: 127, 143–44
  Framework Convention for the Protection of National Minorities 19–21, 121–22, 193, 197
Crimes against humanity, *see* International criminal law
Cruft, Rowan 267
Cuba 238
Cultural relativism 164–65, 261–62
Culture, human right to participation in 184, 196–97

Dédoublement fonctionnel 222–23
Difference principle, *see under* Rawls, John
Dignity, definition 38, 49–55, 80, 285
Discrimination, *passim*
  Age 134–35, 137
  Disability 134–35, 137, 168
  Identity characteristics 166–69, 173–74, 193, 202
    Defined 166
  Involuntary characteristics 168–69, 171
  Legitimacy of birth 129–33, 135–36
  Marital Status 136
  Physical appearance and attractiveness 170–72
  Political opinion 137, 172–73
  Pregnancy 134–35
  Property ownership 173–74
  Race, color, ethnicity and national origin 126, 129–33, 136, 149, 168, 175, 184–85, 192–94, 217
  Religion 120, 122–23, 129–35, 137, 139, 188–89, 200
  Sex and gender 126–27, 129–32, 135–36, 138–39, 143, 145, 148–49, 161, 165, 185
  Sexual orientation 128–29, 133–37, 139, 143, 150, 164, 170, 183, 185, 200, 209–10, 247
  Tattoos 169
  Wealth 137, 147
Douglas, William 57
Draft Declaration on Human Social, *see under* InterAction Council
Due process of law and fair trial, human right to 146
Duties, fundamental, *passim*
  toward animals 51–54, 82, 92–95
  of business organizations 23, 31–36, 77–79, 135
  ecological 51–59, 71–72, 92, 98–101
  toward future generations 47–48, 92, 95–96
  of individuals 11, 15–31, 67–77
  negative, defined 221–25, 266–68
  toward oneself 48–49
  positive, defined 216–18, 221–25, 266–68
  relational 40–45
Dwarf-tossing 49–50
Dworkin, Ronald 86

Earth Charter 59
Ecological duties, *see* Duties, fundamental: ecological

Education, human right to 181–82, 184, 196, 253–54
Effectiveness, principle of 221, 251, 255, 269
Environment, right to a safe and healthy 21, 57–59, 238–39, 256
  World Summit on Sustainable Development 96
  see also Stockholm Declaration on the Human Environment
  United Nations: Rio Declaration on Environment and Development
Environmental duties, *see* Duties, fundamental: ecological
Equal protection of the laws, human right to 122, 124, 130–38, 145–46, 160, 165–66, 169, 175, 184–86, 199
European Union 33, 136, 152, 161
  Charter of Fundamental Rights of the European Union 19, 114, 122, 128
  Court of Justice of the European Union 114, 161
  European Social Charter 254
European Convention for the Protection of Human Rights and Fundamental Freedoms, *see under* Council of Europe
European Court of Human Rights, *see under* Council of Europe
Expression, human right to freedom of 20, 184–85, 219, 257–58
  see also United Nations: Special Rapporteur on Freedom of Speech

Family life, human right to, *see* Privacy and family life, human right to
Feinberg, Joel 13, 54, 94
Feminist legal theory 274
Food, human right to, *see* Subsistence, human right to
Framework Convention for the Protection of National Minorities, *see under* Council of Europe
France, Anatole 190
Freedom, putative human right to 270–72
French Declaration of the Rights of Man and of the Citizen 10

Gandhi, Mohandas 7
Geneva Conventions of 1949: 28
Germany 277
Glendon, Mary Ann 75–76, 85, 280
Government, human right to participation in 159–60, 172
Group rights and duties 19–21, 41–45, 121–22, 191–97

Hague Declaration on the Environment 59
Halo effect 170
Hart, H.L.A. 61
Health, human right to highest standard of 256
Henkin, Louis 7
Hiskes, Richard 71–72
History of human rights 10
Hobbes, Thomas 235
Hohfeld, Wesley 12, 215
Holmes, Stephen 68, 226
Human Rights Committee, *see under* International Covenant on Civil and Political Rights

Identity characteristics, *see under* Discrimination
India
  Bhopal disaster 35–36
  Constitution of 26–27
  Economic situation of 268
  High Court of Kerala 52
Indigenous peoples 22, 44, 195
Inhuman or degrading treatment, human right to freedom from 182, 245–46
Intellectual property, human right to 8, 264
InterAction Council 24
  Universal Declaration on Human Social Responsibilities 24–25, 67–70, 73
Inter-American Commission on Human Rights 4, 108, 116, 157, 164, 281
Inter-American Court of Human Rights 89–90, 108, 119–21, 127–28, 145, 157, 163–64, 191, 204, 208
International Commission of Jurists 70
International Convention on the Elimination of All Forms of Racial Discrimination 23, 107, 121–22, 141, 149, 151, 155, 161, 177, 217, 220
  Committee on the Elimination of Racial Discrimination 4, 23–24, 88

International Court of Justice, *see under* United Nations
International Covenant on Civil and Political Rights 16, 64, 99, 125, 138–41, 144–46, 152, 156, 161, 169, 176, 187, 192, 196–200, 236–37, 249, 251, 255, 257
  Human Rights Committee 4, 49, 99, 115–16, 118–20, 125–26, 138, 144–45, 152, 156–57, 161, 164, 169–70, 176–77, 209, 240, 251, 255, 276
  Optional Protocol No. 1: 126
International Covenant on Economic, Social, and Cultural Rights 16, 23–24, 88, 90–91, 125–26, 141, 152, 157, 169, 192, 196–97, 220, 254, 260–63
  Committee on Economic, Social and Cultural Rights 4, 23–24, 35, 88, 119, 125–27, 152, 157, 216–18, 230, 261–62, 264, 276
International Criminal Court 4, 27–28, 46
  Rome Statute of 28, 46
International criminal law 27–28, 46–47, 84, 88
International Criminal Tribunal for Rwanda 88
International environmental law, *see* Duties, fundamental: ecological
International humanitarian law 28, 46
International Labor Organization 33, 220
Internet, human right to 8
Involuntary characteristics, *see under* Discrimination
Ius cogens 108, 190–91, 237
Ius standi 194

Jefferson, Thomas 10, 83

Kant, Immanuel 10, 37–38, 49, 51, 235
King Jr., Martin Luther 48

Lauren, Paul Gordon 275
Libertarianism 250, 270–72, 274, 280–81
Life, human right to 231–35
Locke, John 10, 49, 89, 235
Malta 96
Margin of appreciation doctrine 116, 129, 163–65, 170, 174, 207
Maximalism 89
Mencius (Meng Zi) 280
Midgley, Mary 100
Mill, John Stuart 226, 270
Minority groups, *see* Group rights and duties
Movement, human right to freedom of 231–35
Multinational enterprises, *see* Duties: Business organizations

Nationality 41
Natural Rights Theory 10–11, 270
Negative rights, defined 221–25, 266–68
Netherlands 277
Nickel, James W. 63, 86–88, 262
Nuremberg Charter and trials 46, 84

O'Neill, Onora 52–53, 64–66, 80–81, 87
Nussbaum, Martha 93–94
Organization of American States 58
Organization for Economic Cooperation and Development 33, 264

Paine, Thomas 7, 83
Participation in government, human right to, *see* Government, human right to participation in
Peaceful assembly, human right to 187–88
Persons with green hair 192
Physical security, right to, *see* Life, human right to
Plant rights 54–56
Plato 9, 280
Pogge, Thomas 62, 81–82, 265–68
Poland, Constitution of 122
Positive rights, defined 216–18, 221–25, 266–68
Privacy and family life, human right to 20, 143, 157, 182–84, 192–94, 200, 227–28, 250–51, 256, 270
Property, human right to 173–74, 176–77, 255
Pseudo-positive rights 245–49

Rational choice theory 225–29
Rawls, John 172, 201, 235
  Difference Principle 172
  Maximin Principle 201
Raz, Joseph 12, 63–65, 87, 168, 194–96, 245, 275
Reisman, Michael 197
Religion, human right to freedom of 182, 184, 188–89, 196
Rights *passim*
  Specific rights are alphabetized according to subject matter
Roosevelt, Franklin Delano 272
Rousseau, Jean-Jacques 10, 235
Ruggie, John 34–35

Sadomasochism 50, 183
Saul, Ben 72–73
Scelle, Georges 222–23
Schauer, Frederick 137
Scheinin, Martin 236–37
Schrute, Dwight 203
Schutter, Olivier de 162–63
Schwarzenberger, Georg 112
Science, human right to share in benefits of 8
Self-determination, right of a people to 191–97
Sen, Amartya 212, 272
Shelton, Dinah 115–16, 178
Shue, Henry 88–89, 230–41, 284
Skinner, B.F. 273
Social contract theory 235, 270, 274
Social security, human right to 216
Solipsistic actors, *see* Rational choice theory
South Africa
  Apartheid 46, 132–33, 238
Soviet Union 84
Stanford Encyclopedia of Philosophy 221–22, 227
Stockholm Declaration on the Human Environment 21, 57, 59
Stone, Christopher 56, 100
Subsistence, human right to 89, 92, 219–20, 231–35, 264, 266, 274
Substantive due process, *see under* United States: Constitution and Bill of Rights
Sunstein, Cass 68, 226, 240

Ten Commandments, *see* Christian morality: Decalogue

Union Carbide disaster, *see* India: Bhopal disaster
United Nations
  Charter 83–84, 107, 192
  Economic, Social and Cultural Organization (UNESCO) 25
  General Assembly 2, 25, 84, 281
    Charter of Economic Rights and Duties of States 263
    Declaration on the Elimination of All Forms of Intolerance and of Discrimination Based on Religion or Belief 161, 166
    Declaration on the Right to Development 281
    Declaration on the Rights of Indigenous Peoples 22, 195
    Declaration on the Rights of Persons Belonging to National or Ethnic, Religious and Linguistic Minorities 195
    Resolution on the Human Right to Water and Sanitation 2, 218
    Universal Declaration of Human Rights 15–16, 24–25, 84, 106–07, 119, 140, 146, 216, 220, 249–50, 252, 254, 260, 262–63
  High Commissioner, *see* Office of the High Commissioner
  Human Rights Commission 25, 33, 58 (*see also* United Nations: Human Rights Council)
  Human Rights Committee, *see under* International Covenant on Civil and Political Rights
  Human Rights Council 4, 29, 34, 69, 240, 261
    Guiding Principles on Business and Human Rights 34

United Nations (*Cont.*)
International Court of Justice 4, 79, 89–90, 97
Office of the High Commissioner for Human Rights 29, 69–70, 240, 249
Office of the High Commissioner for Refugees 240
Rio Declaration on Environment and Development 58
Secretary General 34
Security Council 3, 28
Special Rapporteur on Freedom of Speech 257
United States 279–281
Civil Rights Act of 1964, as amended 134–35
Constitution and Bill of Rights of 10, 122, 130–34, 137–38, 184–85, 247, 252, 276
Equal Protection Clause 122, 130, 185–86
Substantive due process 137–38, 184–86
Defense of Marriage Act 134
Department of State 29
Obama administration 281
Racial segregation 238
Supreme Court 31, 130–38, 160, 165–66, 178, 184–86, 195–96, 204, 207, 247, 276–79
Universal Declaration of Human Rights, *see under* United Nations: General Assembly
Utilitarianism, *see* Consequentialism

Vattel, Emerich de 50
Virtues 45–46
Vlastos, Gregory 153

War crimes, *see* International criminal law
Water, human right to 2, 218
Waldron, Jeremy 280
Wertheimer, Alan 149
World Court, *see* United Nations: International Court of Justice
World cultural heritage, *see* Common heritage of humankind
World Health Organization 218

Yoshino, Kenji 202